# Indigenous Philosophies of Education Around the World

This volume explores conceptualizations of indigeneity and the ways that indigenous philosophies can and should inform educational policy and practice. Beginning with questions and philosophies of indigeneity itself, the volume then covers the indigenous philosophies and practices of a range of communities—including Sami, Maori, Warlpiri, Navajo, and Kokama peoples. Chapter authors examine how these different ideals can inform and create meaningful educational experiences for communities that reflect indigenous ways of life. By applying them in informing a philosophy of education that is particular and relevant to a given indigenous community, this study aims to help policy makers and educational practitioners create meaningful educational experiences.

**John E. Petrovic** is Professor of Educational Philosophy and Policy Studies at University of Alabama.

**Roxanne M. Mitchell** is Associate Professor of Educational Administration at University of Alabama.

# Routledge International Studies in the Philosophy of Education

For more titles in the series, please visit www.routledge.com/Routledge-International-Studies-in-the-Philosophy-of-Education/book-series/SE0237

**The Educational Prophecies of Aldous Huxley**
The Visionary Legacy of Brave New World, Ape and Essence, and Island
*Ronald Lee Zigler*

**Parallels and Responses to Curricular Innovation**
The Possibilities of Posthumanistic Education
*Brad Petitfils*

**Posthumanism and Educational Research**
*Edited by Nathan Snaza and John A. Weaver*

**Education Reform and the Concept of Good Teaching**
*Derek Gottlieb*

**Education, Justice and the Human Good**
Fairness and Equality in the Education System
*Kirsten Meyer*

**Systems of Reason and the Politics of Schooling**
School Reform and Sciences of Education in the Tradition of Thomas S. Popkewitz
*Edited by Miguel A. Pereyra and Barry M. Franklin*

**K-12 Education as a Hermeneutic Adventurous Endeavor**
Education as a Sovereign Agent for Humanity
*Doron Yosef-Hassidim*

**Indigenous Philosophies of Education Around the World**
*Edited by John E. Petrovic and Roxanne M. Mitchell*

# Indigenous Philosophies of Education Around the World

Edited by John E. Petrovic
and Roxanne M. Mitchell

NEW YORK AND LONDON

First published 2018
by Routledge
711 Third Avenue, New York, NY 10017

and by Routledge
2 Park Square, Milton Park, Abingdon, Oxon, OX14 4RN

*Routledge is an imprint of the Taylor & Francis Group, an informa business*

© 2018 Taylor & Francis

The right of John E. Petrovic and Roxanne M. Mitchell to be
identified as editor of this work has been asserted by them in
accordance with sections 77 and 78 of the Copyright, Designs and
Patents Act 1988.

All rights reserved. No part of this book may be reprinted or
reproduced or utilized in any form or by any electronic, mechanical,
or other means, now known or hereafter invented, including
photocopying and recording, or in any information storage or
retrieval system, without permission in writing from the publishers.

*Trademark notice*: Product or corporate names may be trademarks
or registered trademarks, and are used only for identification and
explanation without intent to infringe.

*Library of Congress Cataloguing-in-Publication Data*
A catalog record for this book has been requested

ISBN: 978-1-138-04248-3 (hbk)
ISBN: 978-1-315-17360-3 (ebk)

Typeset in Sabon
by Apex CoVantage, LLC

# Contents

1 Introduction: Philosophizing about Indigenous Philosophies
of Education     1
JOHN E. PETROVIC AND ROXANNE M. MITCHELL

### PART 1
## Philosophical Approaches toward Indigeneity     15

2 Re-imagining "Indigeneity": From Dichotomous toward
Intrinsic Based Understanding of Indigenous Philosophy
and Pedagogy     17
PAUL L. LANDRY

3 The Notion of Ubuntu and the (Post)Humanist Condition     40
LESLEY LE GRANGE

4 Indigeneity and African Education: Cultivating
Decolonized University Teaching and Learning     61
NURAAN DAVIDS AND YUSEF WAGHID

5 The Deaf as an Indigenous Community: Philosophical
Considerations     82
TIMOTHY REAGAN

6 Transformational Leadership in Chinese Schools: An Analysis
from the Perspective of the Confucian Idea of Transformation     105
JING PING SUN, XINPING ZHANG, AND XUEJUN CHEN

### PART 2
## Understanding Indigenous Cultures and Education     127

7 Indigenous Education Reform: A Decolonizing Approach     129
JOHN P. HOPKINS

vi *Contents*

8 Untamed Education: The Philosophical Principles Behind the Kokama School 148
EDISON HÜTTNER AND ALEXANDRE GUILHERME

9 Home Within: Locating a Warlpiri Approach to Developing and Applying an Indigenous Educational Philosophy in Australian Contexts 168
AARON CORN WITH WANTARRI JAMPIJINPA PATRICK

10 Connecting Sami Education to the Land and Lived Experience 195
YLVA JANNOK NUTTI

11 Ainu Puri: Content and Praxis of an Indigenous Philosophy of a Northern People 211
JEFF GAYMAN

12 Everyday Hope: Indigenous Aims of Education in Settler-Colonial Societies 228
JOANNA KIDMAN, ADREANNE ORMOND, AND LIANA MACDONALD

PART 3
Coda 247

13 Comparative Reflections on Philosophies of Indigenous Education around the World 249
JOHN E. PETROVIC AND ROXANNE M. MITCHELL

*Contributors* 265
*Index* 272

# 1 Introduction

## Philosophizing about Indigenous Philosophies of Education

*John E. Petrovic and Roxanne M. Mitchell*

### What Is Philosophy of Indigenous Education?

Drawing upon the techniques devised within the discipline, philosophers engage in the conceptual project of working out a general, systematic, coherent, and consistent picture of all that we know and think. The work of philosophers occurs, broadly speaking, within three traditions: the metaphysical, the analytic, and the normative. Philosophers of education have applied their skill in analyzing arguments, assessing the status of knowledge claims, exposing assumptions, and making syntheses of ideas from disparate fields, to throw light on all manner of educational challenges and on the validity of the very things they themselves are trying to argue as philosophers. In education, this includes dealing with questions of how and why children should be educated and toward what personal and societal ends. Of course, any number of philosophical questions can be raised: What should we teach in schools? How should we teach it? Why should we teach it? To whom should we teach it? In other words, philosophers of education connect the discipline of philosophy and its intellectual tools to questions of education, the first step in the process of developing a philosophy of education. As such questions reveal, philosophers of education explore and inform through philosophic analyses central concepts in educational policies, pedagogic methods, curricula, and specific practices of schooling. In short, drawing upon the techniques devised within the discipline, philosophers of education engage in the conceptual project of working out a general, systematic, coherent, and consistent picture of what education should be and for whom. Thus, our working assumption is that there is some relationship between the fields of philosophy *and* education, philosophy *of* education being a form of applied philosophy.

Turning attention back to the three general branches of philosophy mentioned, metaphysics addresses the many questions that arise about what lies beyond the physical world of sensory experience. What is the essence of beauty? Was there a prime mover of the universe? What are the features of human nature? Questions of human nature and other questions of ontology hold great importance for the philosopher of education. For if society

## 2 John E. Petrovic and Roxanne M. Mitchell

is, as Plato suggested, the individual writ large, the education of people for that society must take on specific characteristics. Such questions are, of course, related to the question of how and why we can or cannot "know" such things and, even more basically, what it means to "know" something. These questions of truth and knowledge—questions of epistemology—are important to philosophers of education as they consider curricular questions such as what to teach and why and how different ways of knowing should inform such questions. For example, van Wyk[1] shares the Khoisan people's philosophy toward land: "the land is not ours, we belong to the land." This way of knowing the land and one's relationship to it, has myriad effects on societal organization and education. From a Western understanding, land is a mere commodity from which to profit; whereas, for the Khoisan "it is inseparable from the process of living" (van Wyk also adds "education" here). It enhances an understanding of life as community and cooperation, as opposed to individuality and competition.

What we now term "analytic philosophy" surfaced in great part from Aristotle's work on ethics. Indeed, the *Nicomachean Ethics*, in which Aristotle was trying to analyze or explain the use of certain moral terms that occur in everyday speech in a more clear and consistent way than the layperson could do, might appropriately be identified as one of the earliest essays in this field. In education, analytic philosophy has made substantial contributions in providing conceptual analyses and clarity to basic notions, and seemingly self-evident terms, such as "teaching," "learning," "education," and "indoctrination." As Burbules has pointed out, this method specialized in offering fine-grained distinctions and typologies; diagnosing hidden equivocations or blurriness in the ordinary concepts found within educational slogans or clichés.[2] In this vein, an important concept to be addressed in this introduction and in several chapters throughout the volume is that of indigeneity. Who can and cannot rightly be referred to as "indigenous" and why? Who should have the authority to make such a determination? What, then, counts as an indigenous philosophy and why? Subsequently, we seek to provide a tentative definition of indigenous, even as we deny our right to define any group as such or, in the process of naming "indigenous," excluding any group from such definition.

Within the normative tradition of philosophy, the philosopher, having reached some conclusions in her or his metaphysical investigations and having come to a common understanding of the terms through the application of analytic philosophy, might attempt to establish norms, standards, or guidelines for the conduct of human affairs and human institutions. Philosophers of education carry out this same project in their examination of the aims, goals, or standards for schooling. What should we teach in schools and from whose perspective? How should we teach it? Why should we teach it? To whom should we teach it? As regards this volume, should what we teach be "indigenous" knowledge from an "indigenous" perspective?

To these descriptions, a couple of disclaimers must be added. First, having demarcated these three traditions, it must now be said that it is most

*Introduction* 3

inappropriate to do so. When engaging in any philosophical activity, these three traditions necessarily merge with and cross over each other in myriad ways. (Plato's *Republic* is the quintessential example of this.) Second, often what is considered "'philosophy' of education" is not philosophical in a technical sense. It is what might properly be described as deep, cultured reflection. In fact, some of the most influential "'philosophers of education" have provided us invaluable non-philosophical philosophies of education including John Locke (*Some Thoughts Concerning Education*), A. S. Neill (*Summerhill*), and Paolo Freire (*Pedagogy of the Oppressed*). This tells us simply that "What is philosophy of education?" is a complex, deeply philosophical question itself. This volume is, in many ways, quite reflective of this ambiguity. Some chapters are clearly "technically philosophical" while others, most in fact, provide deep, cultured reflection on what education *should* be for *indigenous* students, providing contributions from around the globe.

There is any number of related questions for such an endeavor: Should said education reflect indigenous cultures and languages? To what extent? Why? Would such reflection constitute a philosophy of indigenous education? Or, would such a philosophy delve more deeply? Taking aboriginal ways of being and knowing in the Australian context, for example, to what extent should these ways of being and knowing drive curriculum and pedagogy? Why? Who should decide that? Can the answers to such questions drive a general philosophy of education vis-a-vis indigenous students that can inform all cases? Such questions are illustrative of the philosophical method engaged toward the goal of a philosophy of education for indigenous populations, toward the end of making normative claims about the shape or direction of educational policies vis-a-vis indigenous peoples or pedagogical concerns in teaching indigenous students, for example. But this names *philosophy of indigenous education*, that is, a philosophy that discusses how one should approach the education of indigenous students. This is not the same as a uniquely *indigenous philosophy of education*. The former is more a sort of metaphilosophy, concerning the boundaries and types of questions relevant to philosophizing about indigenous education. An important caution here, especially in a project like this, is that the philosopher must seek to avoid the trap of presenting a philosophy that is everywhere, while pretending to come from nowhere. Addressing this concern is also a metaphilosophy, a philosophy of philosophy that seeks to understand the limits of our analyses to the extent that they begin in some tradition. Our point here is a parallel one to Connell's important work on the extent to which sociology, as a discipline, is built on northern notions of how it is and should be applied.[3]

A philosophy of indigenous education is more than the deployment of the philosophical method to address the educational needs of indigenous students; it is also the defense of that indigeneity which becomes the driving ethos behind normative claims about indigenous education. Notice that the normative claim that such should be the case is prerequisitely a

4   *John E. Petrovic and Roxanne M. Mitchell*

normative claim deriving from a *philosophy of indigenous education*. In other words, a philosophy of indigenous education would justify the pursuit of an indigenous philosophy of education that, to be such, embraces the culture, practices, ways of being, and ways of knowing, among other things, of the indigenous community to inform and enact educational policy, pedagogy, and curricula. For example, in South Africa, we might consider the indigenous philosophy of *ubuntu* or, synonymously, *hunhu* in Zimbabwe[4] to drive an indigenous philosophy of education. In the U.S., "the first hallmark of American Indian philosophy is the commitment to the belief that all things are related—and this belief is not simply an ontological claim, but rather an intellectual and ethical maxim."[5] What might this mean for or developed as a Native American philosophy of education? What are the implications for curriculum, policy, pedagogy, and/or leadership models? In considering the implications for such questions as they are informed by Native American maxims, it becomes clearer why the study of the specific branches of philosophy, such as epistemology, must be pursued. As importantly, however, it should be noted explicitly that much of the groundwork toward the development of indigenous philosophies of education cannot be engaged through the discipline of philosophy alone. As deep, cultured, reflection, philosophizing about indigenous education requires deep sociological and/or anthropological study, among study from many other disciplines. For without a deep understanding of the culture, its norms, practices, and taken for granted understandings, to what does *indigenous* philosophy refer?

Clearly, it is important for any volume that discusses philosophies of indigenous education to define what is meant by indigenous and what is meant by indigenous education. This is no easy task given that the term indigenous has been used to represent a multitude of different meanings across a multiplicity of contexts, and at times has been regarded as having a derogatory connotation. Along with the term indigenous other terms have been used interchangeably such as "First Peoples", "First Nations", "tribesmen", "aboriginals", and "ethnic groups" to name a few. Rather than give a universal definition of indigenous, the United Nations (UNESCO) chose to identify a number of factors that this term encompasses. Self-identification was considered the primary factor that would distinguish a group of people as indigenous. Other factors included their existence prior to colonial subjugation; strong ties to specific territories, regions, or lands; a distinct social, economic, and political system; a unique language, culture, and beliefs; existence as a non-dominant group; and a strong motivation to maintain and reproduce their ancestral ways of living and knowing as a community of people.

In keeping with this conceptualization, Jacob, Cheng, and Porter stated that indigeneity refers to

> "a sense of distinctiveness and cultural coherence for those who live in remote or distinct locations (or pursue a lifestyle inconsistent with

modern national boundaries), who speak some remnant of a distinct language, who struggle with /against concurrent claims for government authority, and who self-identify as belonging to a place prior to its annexation or colonization.[6]

This definition points out that identification as indigenous is also indicative of identification as an agent of change. Inherent then in this term is the sense that those who identify as indigenous are wrestling against Western hegemonic conceptualizations. They are striving to assert their own identity, seeking to gain respect and dignity for their precise ways of knowing and being, and asserting their own experiential reality. This would further suggest that indigenous identification and knowledge is birthed out of struggle and resistance against Western ideologies.[7] It is routed in the unique experiences of a particular group or community as they fought to survive and preserve their knowledge, customs, communication, traditions, beliefs, values, and systems of government over time, all of which have been passed down from generation to generation.[8]

We would like to point out that while indigeneity is often associated with connection to a particular land and region that this may not always be the case. For instance, Timothy Reagan (in this volume) argues that the deaf community sees themselves outside of the boundaries ascribed to the dominant cultural group. They have a shared distinctive culture and language, a shared awareness and group identity, and they share a unique worldview. They have been oppressed by the dominant hearing group and as such have struggled to assert their identity and to garner respect as do other indigenous communities. Here, again, we see the importance of the philosophical method, analytic philosophy in this instance.

Understanding indigeneity in these tentative ways, it is also incumbent upon us to similarly operationalize "indigenous education" if we are to consider a philosophy thereof. For the most part, the chapters in this volume seek a philosophy of indigenous education applicable to the formal institution of schools. Even as education occurs through the community, interaction with others, and varied experiences beyond the walls of the school for all students, this is probably even more important for indigenous education. Thus, we understand the limiting nature of focusing on education as it occurs within the limited and limiting confines of the institution of school. It may even be contrary to indigeneity itself which is organic, natural, communitarian, and omnipresent. In this way, formal education easily becomes—or, perhaps more accurately, always already is—a case of cultural imperialism. Historically, one need but recall the cultural, linguistic, epistemic, and physical violence effected by missions and mission schools across the globe.[9] Nevertheless, we believe we can and should identify the characteristics of indigenous education within schools, for we, too, believe "It is possible to accomplish something important in the institutional space of a school or college in order to help

# 6 John E. Petrovic and Roxanne M. Mitchell

the transformation of society."[10] Such transformation may begin with the revaluing of indigenous ways of knowing—releasing them from their subjugation—against and alongside Western ethnocentric and colonial understandings.[11] In this vein, indigenous education, especially philosophy thereof, draws on framings from a variety of related starting points: critical theory, post-colonial theory, critical race theory, and anti-racist scholarship, among others.

As Jacob, Cheng, and Porter (2015) explain it, indigenous education provides

> the path and process whereby individuals gain knowledge and meaning from their indigenous heritages. Indigenous education involves knowledge that is generated, obtained, and adapted to fit the historical contexts and needs of indigenous peoples and is then transmitted through educative means to others.
>
> (p. 3)[12]

Indigenous education, then, seeks out the particular ties that bind—language and/or ways of expression, culture, ways of knowing—and teaches about and through them, while deconstructing dominant material conditions. A prime example of this is described by Teresa McCarty in her already classic, "*A Place to be Navajo*," which describes the development of the first American-Indian controlled school in the US.[13] The school was both bilingual and bicultural and the curriculum represented literature by and about the Navajo people. Through such practices, indigenous education works to decenter dominant and hegemonic understandings of what counts as knowledge, how societies (should) function, and ideals of "the good life." As Sefa Dei so rightly puts it, "When reclaimed and affirmed, Indigeneity and Indigenous knowings provide intellectual agency to marginalized, colonized peoples who then become subjects of their own histories, stories, and experiences."[14] Such reclamation occurs not only through community but also, as we have claimed, through the formal institutions of schooling. But this is just not about becoming a subject in one's own story but critically juxtaposing it to dominant narratives in counter-hegemonic fashion. This is the "Precious Knowledge" revealed in the story of the Mexican-American Studies program in Tucson School District (Arizona, U.S.).[15] The program employed critical pedagogy to teach students not only about and from their own story but also to engage them in social justice work, peace, and respect. In the dominant narrative, a disgusting exemplar of modern-day colonialization, the program, teachers, and students were cast as anti-American and seditious. The program was closed through a law specifically written to make it illegal, even as an independent audit found no evidence of illegality.[16] Thus, we turn to our own intellectual resistance to such facile explanations (e.g., anti-American) and imperialist outcomes.

*Introduction* 7

## Chapter Summaries

2. Drawing on discussions with members of the Yakama Nation (U.S.), the purpose of this chapter is to re-examine the concept of "indigeneity" and its sociopolitical implications. The goal is to rethink a concept and term that has produced much debate but far less productive momentum for those seeking alignment with an indigenous people's identity or for the more global society and environs. Paul Landry proposes an approach that reconceptualizes indigeneity as an intrinsic or internal emanating perspective rather than as an externalized vestment [identity] or claim of right. In so doing, a conception of *indigeneity* can be derived that speaks to intrinsic qualities and values which can be affected, positively or negatively by political and social actions. If such distinguishing qualities are of value, then such a conception has merit and the degree to which such values are respected can be considered without devolving into particularized debates over who may legitimately claim or speak in support.

3. Lesley Le Grange explains that we find ourselves at a historical moment where the human has become a geological force capable of affecting all life on the planet, an epoch posited as the Anthropocene distinguished by human destruction of the planet as evidenced by mass annihilation of plant and animal species, polluted oceans and atmospheric change. Against this background of a crisis of humanism, the author invokes the indigenous notion of Ubuntu and argues for its potential as a critical response to Enlightenment humanism (and its notion of education as the cultivation of autonomous rational beings) and the post-human predicament that is concerned with the potential that non-human entities (created by human beings) could have to destroy all life. Ubuntu means humanness and concerns relatedness not only to other humans but also to everything in the cosmos. The author argues that an education informed by Ubuntu shifts the unit of reference from the atomized/arrogant "I" to the ecological/humble "I" and that education should involve learning to care for others and the environment.

4. Indigenous knowledge in South Africa is commonly understood to encompass local, traditional, non-Western beliefs and practices, as well as alternative, informal forms of knowledge. But, while knowledge is necessary to the formation of education, knowledge is not synonymous with education. Certainly, education is and should be used to initiate children into particular traditions and existing ways of being. However, it is equally true that education ought not only to be about that which is traditional, already known, and familiar. Nuraan Davids and Yusef Waghid explore this tension between knowledge and education, between indigenous (natural) and Western (unnatural), asking whether the education of South Africa's incredibly diverse and disparate student population might be addressed through a propagation of an indigenous

8  *John E. Petrovic and Roxanne M. Mitchell*

education. Toward this end, the authors address three interrelated questions: What is an indigenous student? Why would there be a need for an education that speaks specifically to indigenous students? If there is an education that ought to be geared at indigenous students, then should one be speaking about an indigenous education?

5. In this chapter, Timothy Reagan argues that Deaf people see themselves as a distinctive cultural and linguistic community which has been, and continues to be, dominated and oppressed by the far larger, surrounding hearing community. The author asks, if the Deaf-world is a distinctive cultural and linguistic community, is it not also an "indigenous" community? Often associated with "native", "tribal" or "aboriginal" populations, the term "indigenous" does not seem to include deaf culture. However, Deaf people do possess a distinctive culture, characterized by all of the features that are normally associated with indigeneity: an in-group vernacular language, a shared awareness of group identity and members, distinctive behavioral norms, endogamous marital patterns, cultural artifacts, a shared historical awareness, a network of voluntary social organizations, and a distinctive worldview. In this chapter, the case for conceptualizing Deaf people as an indigenous community will be made, and the implications of this case for the education of hearing impaired children will be explored.

6. This chapter provides an interesting shift from indigenous philosophy of education writ large to a more specific consideration of philosophies of educational leadership. It also requires that we understand indigeneity, as a concept, as a way to examine the effects of globalization. Jingping Sun, Xinping Zhang, and Xuejun Chen note that empirical studies of school leadership models began to appear in Chinese academic journals in about 2001 and remain an emergent field of study in China. Among the most studied leadership models is transformational leadership. In this chapter, the authors examine the status of the empirical inquiry into transformational school leadership in China. They trace the root of Chinese transformational leadership to Confucianism. "The Four Books," the classic texts for understanding Confucianism, are examined to understand Confucius's idea of transformation.

7. Recent educational legislation in western states in the U.S., such as Montana and Washington, has required mainstream educators to work cooperatively with Indigenous peoples in the design and implementation of an inclusive curriculum that reflects the cultures and histories of indigenous groups. Against this backdrop, John P. Hopkins analyzes the meaning of "inclusion" that pervades these reform strategies. Their emphasis on inclusion promotes what the author calls an *inclusive conversation* between tribal communities and mainstream educators. However, the author questions whether or not inclusion can reform indigenous education sufficiently, arguing that the inclusion strategies of these reforms miss a critical philosophical problem. An inclusive

conversation fails to account for how mainstream educators, policy makers, and tribal groups already stand in unequal relations within public education. What is required instead is a *decolonizing conversation* recognizing the need for these groups to engage in conversations that directly and explicitly confront colonizing history and its enduring effects in public schools.

8. This chapter begins with a brief history of the Kokama people of Brazil as a "hidden ethnic group" which has only recently begun to assert its identity and rights through the Brazilian Indian Foundation. Seeing the benefit of differentiated, indigenous schools, the Kokama constructed their own Cultural Center and began the revitalization of their rituals, dances, and festivals. The elders praised this as a form of *untamed education*, keeping and encouraging their traditions, which was something that had suffered a great deal under the previous *civilisatory paradigm of education*. As Edison Hüttner and Alexandre Guilherme point out in this chapter, *untamed education* is not savage or wild education, but an education that opposes the previous *civilisatory education* that tried to normalize individuals, forcing indigenous communities to fit into the white man's society. Since little is known about the Kokama, their recent experience provides an interesting philosophical case study and it is the aim of the authors to characterize *untamed education*, identify the philosophical principles behind it, and critically analyze its components.

9. In this chapter, Aaron Corn argues that, in Australia, opportunities for students to learn through Indigenous epistemologies within the formal curricula of schools and universities remain rare and fleeting. Even remote Indigenous communities must constantly fight public education policies to maintain within their local schools any instruction in their own languages or inclusion of their own intellectual traditions beyond the diversionary. This center—periphery dynamic between the enduring Anglocentrism of Australian educational institutions and the traditional holders of Australia's rich Indigenous knowledges perpetuates an Anglocentric colonizing construct. This chapter explores the anti-colonialist work of the Warlpiri educator, artist, and academic, Steven Wantarri Jampijinpa Pawu-Kurlpurlurnu Patrick, through his efforts to extend the transference of classical Warlpiri knowledge from old to young in a remote desert in Australia, and from Warlpiri to others further afield. It follows two initiatives through which this work has been undertaken: the Milpirri Festival at Lajamanu, produced by Tracks Dance Company, and collaborative teaching in the Australian university context.

10. The Sámi people have gone through long period of civilization driven by church, and nationalistic assimilation aspirations in all the countries they live in—through hidden or more conscious processes. The ideas behind these pursuits are based on white supremacy that the Sámi should have been civilized and put under national state societal

organization. History has produced Sámi generations who have lost at least partly their cultural and linguistic special features. This has weakened also their identity in some cases. Given this, Ylva Jannok Nutti argues that the purpose of Sámi education must be to resolve a severe phenomenon in Sámi society whereby structural power has challenged everyday practices. Sámi Education searches for ways to base institutional education on Indigenous knowledge, traditions, and cultural context. Sámi Education is a means to resolve the legacy of assimilation and, in particular, language shift. Sámi Education that is based on a mediating role plays an important part in efforts to revive Indigenous languages and cultures and aims to gain wide access to education, health, economics, wellness, political representation, and other factors that are essential to leading a good life.

11. The Ainu people of northern Japan and the surrounding islands are animists who believe that all material objects, living or not, possess spirits which must be revered and treated with gratitude. Understanding the Ainu philosophy and its cultural transmission requires directing one's examination inward to the core belief system framing the Ainu knowledge system, as reflected in the Ainu oral tradition, as well as outward, to the normative elements of Ainu social life. While the material circumstances surrounding the Ainu people have been greatly altered via the assimilative policies of colonization and the influences of urbanization and globalization, the cultural and knowledge systems of Ainu *puri* (Ainu style of doing things) remain vital in the hearts, minds, and actions of the Ainu people. In this chapter, Jeffry Gayman provides examples of how the Ainu value and belief system is being enacted in different loci of Ainu cultural practice in the contemporary world. Even within constraining and assimilative processes, the Ainu worldview importantly informs education as a societal process at the family and community level.

12. In the twenty-first century, the call of educational policy makers and practitioners in New Zealand is for Māori students to "enjoy educational achievement as Māori." Nevertheless, even with this historical change away from assimilationist policies, little has improved in the material conditions of these indigenous children's lives. In this chapter, Joanna Kidman and Adreanne Ormond argue that education policy and practice need to incorporate an ethical framework that takes indigenous students beyond a preoccupation with the economic and political demands of the state and unveils opportunities for hope and also for anger. Through an affective analysis, the authors explore how a Māori ethos of land and place might inform educational thinking. They argue that indigenous young people need educational spaces that allow them to imagine alternative, hopeful, and even utopic futures in terms of their everyday lives and the ethical challenges and complexities of "growing up indigenous."

13. In the concluding chapter, we seek to find common themes among the chapters and bring them into some conversation that both clarifies and problematizes the project of philosophizing about indigenous education.

## Notes

1. Berte Van Wyk, "The Khoisan Indigenous Educational System and the Construction of Modern Khoisan Identities," in *Indigenous Concepts of Education: Toward Elevating Humanity for All Learners*, ed. Berte Van Wyk and Dolapo Adeniji-Neill (New York: Palgrave Macmillan, 2014), 23.
2. Nicholas C. Burbules, "Philosophy of Education," in *Routledge International Companion to Education*, ed. Bob Moon, Miriam Ben-Peretz, and Sally Brown. (New York: Routledge, 2000), 9.
3. Raewyn Connell, *Southern Theory: The Global Dynamics of Knowledge in Social Science* (Malden, MA: The Polity Press, 2007).
4. For South Africa see Yusef Waghid and Nuraan Davids, "On Hospitality, Responsibility, and Ubuntu: Some Philosophical Remarks on Teaching and Learning in South Africa," in *Citizenship Education Around the World: Local Contexts and Global Possibilities*, ed. John E. Petrovic and Aaron M. Kuntz (New York: Routledge, 2014), 165–179. For Zimbabwe, see Oswell Hapanyengwi-Chemhuru and Ngoni Makuvaza, "Hunhu: In Search of An Indigenous Philosophy for the Zimbabwean Education System," *Journal of Indigenous Social Development* 3 no. 1 (2014): 1–15.
5. Adam Arola, "Native American Philosophy," in *The Oxford Handbook of World Philosophy*, ed. William Edelglass and Jay L. Garfield (New York: Oxford University Press, 2011), 562–573.
6. James Jacob, Yao Cheng Sheng, and Maureen K. Porter, *Indigenous Education: Language, Culture and Identity* (Dordrecht: Springer, 2015), 5.
7. Cf. Courtney Lee Weida, "Containing Interwoven Histories: Indigenous Basket Weaving in Art Education," in *Indigenous Concepts*, ed. B. Van Wyk and D. Adeniji-Nei (New York: Palgrave Macmillan, 2014), 185–196.
8. Jun Xing and Ng Pak-sheung, eds., *Indigenous Culture, Education and Globalization: Critical Perspectives from Asia* (Heidelberg: Springer, 2016), accessed January 10, 2017, http://search.ebscohost.com/login.aspx?direct=true&scope=site&db=nlebk&db=nlabk&AN=1085780.
9. Contemporarily, Petrovic and Kuntz cast the effects of neoliberalism on schools as a form of cultural invasion for all students. John E. Petrovic and Aaron M. Kuntz, "Invasion, Alienation, and Imperialist Nostalgia: Overcoming the Necrophilous Nature of Neoliberal Schools," *Educational Philosophy and Theory* (2016): 1–13. doi: 10.1080/00131857.2016.1198249.
10. Ira Shor and Paulo Freire, *A Pedagogy for Liberation: Dialogues on Transforming Education* (South Hadley, MA: Bergin & Garvey Publishers, 1987), 130.
11. Cf. Marjorie O'Loughlin's call for such an interface. Also, this is not to suggest that only indigenous knowledge, depending on how one defines indigenous, has been subjugated. Here we remind the reader of Patricia Hill Collins's work. See, respectively, Marjorie O'Loughlin, "Being at Home in the World: Philosophical Reflections with Aboriginal Teachers," in *Indigenous Concepts*, ed. B. Van Wyk and D. Adeniji-Neill (New York: Palgrave Macmillan, 2014), 73–86; Patricia Collins, *Black Feminist thought: Knowledge, Consciousness, and the Politics of Empowerment* (New York: Routledge, 2008).
12. Jacob et al., *Indigenous Education*.

12  *John E. Petrovic and Roxanne M. Mitchell*

13. Teresa L. McCarty and Fred Bia, *A Place to Be Navajo: Rough Rock and the Struggle for Self-Determination in Indigenous Schooling* (New York: Routledge, 2002).
14. George Sefa Dei, "Introduction," *Counterpoints* 379 (2011): 4.
15. *Precious Knowledge*, directed by Ari Luis Palos, Eren McGinnis, Sally Jo Fifer, Jacob Bricca, and Naïm Amor (Tucson, Arizona: Dos Vatos Productions, Service Independent Television, Broadcasting Latino Public, Media Arizona Public, and Broadcasting Corporation for Public, 2011), DVD.
16. Cambium Learning, Inc., *Curriculum Audit of the Mexican American Studies Department Tucson Unified School District* (Miami Lakes, FL: Author, 2011). Not only does this report find no evidence of the program breaking the new law (even as the law was written specifically for that purpose), but also found that students participating in the program graduated at much higher rates.

## Bibliography

Arola, Adam. "Native American Philosophy." In *The Oxford Handbook of World Philosophy*, edited by William Edelglass and Jay L. Garfield, 562–573. New York: Oxford University Press, 2011.

Burbules, Nicholas C. "Philosophy of Education." In *Routledge International Companion to Education*, edited by Bob Moon, Miriam Ben-Peretz, and Sally A. Brown, 3–18. New York: Routledge, 2000.

Cambium Learning, Inc. *Curriculum Audit of the Mexican American Studies Department Tucson Unified School District*. Miami Lakes, FL: Author, 2011.

Collins, Patricia Hill. *Black Feminist Thought: Knowledge, Consciousness, and the Politics of Empowerment*. New York: Routledge, 2008.

Connell, Raewyn. *Southern Theory: The Global Dynamics of Knowledge in Social Science*. Malden, MA: The Polity Press, 2007.

Hapanyengwi-Chemhuru, Oswell and Ngoni Makuvaza. "Hunhu: In Search of an Indigenous Philosophy for the Zimbabwean Education System." *Journal of Indigenous Social Development* 3 (2014): 1–15.

Jacob, W. James, Sheng Yao Cheng, and Maureen K. Porter. *Indigenous Education: Language, Culture and Identity*. Dordrecht: Springer, 2015.

McCarty, Teresa L. and Bia Fred. *A Place to Be Navajo: Rough Rock and the Struggle for Self-Determination in Indigenous Schooling*. New York: Routledge, 2002.

O'Loughlin, Marjorie. "Being at Home in the World: Philosophical Reflections with Aboriginal Teachers." In *Indigenous Concepts of Education: Toward Elevating Humanity for All Learners*, edited by Berte Van Wyk and Dolapo Adeniji-Neill, 73–85. New York: Palgrave Macmillan, 2014.

Petrovic, John E. and Aaron M. Kuntz. "Invasion, Alienation, and Imperialist Nostalgia: Overcoming the Necrophilous Nature of Neoliberal Schools." *Educational Philosophy and Theory* (2016): 1–13. doi:10.1080/00131857.2016.1198249.

*Precious Knowledge*. Directed by Ari Luis Palos, Eren McGinnis, Sally Jo Fifer, Jacob Bricca, and Naïm Amor. Tucson, Arizona: Dos Vatos Productions, Service Independent Television, Broadcasting Latino Public, Media Arizona Public, and Broadcasting Corporation for Public, 2011.

Shor, Ira and Paulo Freire. *A Pedagogy for Liberation: Dialogues on Transforming Education*. South Hadley, MA: Bergin & Garvey Publishers, 1987.

Van Wyk, Berte. "The Khoisan Indigenous Educational System and the Construction of Modern Khoisan Identities." In *Indigenous Concepts of Education: Toward Elevating Humanity for All Learners*, edited by Berte Van Wyk and Dolapo Adeniji-Neill, 17–30. New York: Palgrave Macmillan, 2014.

Waghid, Yusef and Nuraan Davids. "On Hospitality, Responsibility, and Ubuntu: Some Philosophical Remarks on Teaching and Learning in South Africa." In *Citizenship Education Around the World: Local Contexts and Global Possibilities*, edited by John E. Petrovic and Aaron M. Kuntz, 165–179. New York: Routledge, 2014.

Weida, Courtney Lee. "Containing Interwoven Histories: Indigenous Basket Weaving in Art Education." In *Indigenous Concepts of Education: Toward Elevating Humanity for All Learners*, edited by Berte Van Wyk and Dolapo Adeniji-Neill, 185–196. New York: Palgrave Macmillan, 2014.

Xing, Jun and Pak-sheung Ng. *Indigenous Culture, Education and Globalization: Critical Perspectives from Asia*. Heidelberg: Springer, 2016.

# Part 1

# Philosophical Approaches toward Indigeneity

# 2 Re-imagining "Indigeneity"

## From Dichotomous toward Intrinsic Based Understanding of Indigenous Philosophy and Pedagogy

*Paul L. Landry*

If I am to define myself as "not you," then neither you nor I truly understand who I am. Only by exploring my own "being" and "becoming" may either come upon the truth.

> The next important step is 'understanding' Indianness. This requires comprehending how Native people think, feel, and make decisions. . . . How do Indians think? Do they think about Indian history in a different way? The answer is a confirmed 'yes.'[1]

### Opening Reflections: Removing Blinders

This chapter discussion suggests re-envisioning indigenous philosophy and its relation to education, seeking alternative ways of experiencing and understanding ways of knowing[2] and ways of being through an indigenous lens. Rejecting an "either/or" dichotomy, it suggests complementary rather than oppositional or antithetical approaches to knowing. Indigenous philosophies ironically predate many notions within orthodox Eurocentric philosophy. Yet the colonizing filter of "Western-Enlightenment thought" leaves current school curriculum largely devoid of ways of knowing and knowledge construction derived from the indigenous.[3] Re-imagining looks anew to "see" relevance in unacknowledged philosophies. Past rejection of indigenous philosophies often eschewed indigenous knowledge as "local" or "primitive" and thus irrelevant. Such dichotomous bias embedded in traditional academic discourse may have led to an opacity or "blindness" regarding the beneficial importance of indigenous ways of knowing, obscuring recognition even from well-intentioned inquiry.

> Can any philosophy transcend its cultural barriers and speak to the larger question of how we perceive and interact with the world around us? What is the potential for a philosophy to help us make sense of our lives? The West has certainly not solved that problem; it has only used its tremendous political and economic power to render the question moot.[4]

## 18   *Paul L. Landry*

Discussion surrounding the "indigenous," such as indigenous peoples, indigenous cultures, indigenous rights, indigenous practices and indigenous philosophies, has generated increasing heat and light, but yielded little in broader substantive understanding. Controversy in academia, perhaps owing to dichotomous bias or parochialism, centers on indigenous knowledge as a serious and discreet episteme. Traditional academia allows for examination of the indigenous as a curiosity or as "folk" wisdom, but until recently serious inquiry tended to be marginalized, despite a nagging persistence of the inexplicable "other."

Eurocentric philosophy has many examples of dichotomous bias. Once a particular philosophical approach gained acceptance, usually involving alignment with elite political and economic power, alternative or potentially contradictory philosophies were rejected as perceived threats. From the death of Socrates for corruption of youth for challenging accepted knowledge, to the Copernican "Heliocentric" revolution, to Einstein's revolutionary "theory of relativity" challenging Newtonian universal gravitational precepts, alternative lenses for viewing and making sense of the world have collided with a protective orthodoxy. The reaction to novelty has been to regard it as antithetical rather than simply alternative or divergent. Radical voices from within the Eurocentric milieu have challenged such dichotomous bias and called for more open, tolerant and holistic approaches to empiricism and evolution of knowledge. Examples include Hume (Skepticism), James (Pragmatism), Popper (Fallibilism), Kuhn (Incommensurability) and Rorty (Anti-representationalism). Each of these philosophers challenged epistemological orthodoxy; and each was viewed to some extent as unorthodox interloper. Asked to challenge Schlick's treatise on "realism," Einstein's response was an apt critique of this philosophical dichotomous bias:

> I am supposed to explain to you my doubts? By laying stress on these it will appear that I want to pick holes in you everywhere. But things are not so bad, because I do not feel comfortable and at home in any of the "isms." It always seems to me as though such an ism were strong only so long as it nourishes itself on the weakness of its counter-ism; but if the latter is struck dead, and it is alone on an open field, then it also turns out to be unsteady on its feet. So, away we go![5]

This exclusionary bias obstructs consideration and incorporation of indigenous ways of knowing in public school curriculum. The bias is philosophical and sociocultural. Traditional schooling rejects alternative ways of knowing derived from cultures prejudged by dominant discourse as primitive, savage or the "other."[6] Such labels are tools and myths of dominant Eurocentric orthodoxy to justify rejection, obstacles consistently raised against new or alternative epistemologies arising from the subaltern.[7] How can we understand the "indigenous" or indigenous ways of being or knowing, or the very fact of "*indigeneity*" when they are preempted from serious discussion?

These doubts are erected as discursive entry barriers by normative educational philosophy. To break through, we must re-imagine and recreate.

An axiom of post-enlightenment Western thought and philosophy has been a belief that "existence" is defined by the bending and shaping of the forces of nature and the universe to the will of man. Despite implied hubris involved and numerous negative examples, this belief has been remarkably persistent. Yet with every setback or failure of colonial, post-colonial and modern societal practices, more attention shifts toward persistent and long-standing ethics and ways of knowing that might offer insights to more sustainable society and ecology. Even the concept of "modernity" may need to be challenged, to the extent that its use signifies inferiority or obsolescence in differing ways of knowing that predate colonial intercession.[8]

One pathway beyond the opacity may be to seek perspective *through* indigenous eyes and voices, rather than continued reliance upon externally based definition, i.e., talking *about* and *around* indigeneity.[9] Access to indigeneity begins with listening to and honoring indigenous voices, both inside and outside of academia, voices largely dismissed, suppressed or deflected.

The author's positionality is inescapable and relevant. Born in the Midwestern United States at the inception of the Civil Rights Movement, my subjection to discrimination, segregation and marginalization have yielded a subaltern influence and perspective. African American and Native American ancestry provide no presumptive claim to *indigeneity*, but also yield no proclivity to reject indigenous knowledge. Native American ancestors, as history was related to me, were abducted and enslaved along with Africans on a plantation in the South. An American ethno-societal rule of "one drop" regarded my family as Negro or Black. Yet stories and lessons of my great-grandmother, I now realize, were a marvelous mixture of history, knowledge and lore passing down from her Seminole mother and African father. My earliest experiences were imbued with stories of truth, history, wisdom and fancy, all indistinguishable to my young but impressionable mind.

My current faculty position as Teacher Educator is with a private university primarily serving students of Mexican descent and those of Native American heritage. It is the only such private university (not tribal college) situated on American Indian (Yakama Nation) land. My heritage, life experiences, education and exposure to different cultures around the world may contribute perspectives which dominant U.S. society and academia may have overlooked.

## Entry Points and Pathways: Seeing Through an Indigenous Lens

The views and experiences of the indigenous have been vocalized, but largely unheard in quarters where most education policy decisions emanate. Mainstream beliefs about Native Americans tend to be stereotypical presumptions originating from dominant cultural frames of reference. The path

## 20   Paul L. Landry

toward understanding must acknowledge that most of what we think we know, and how we interpret information about the indigenous, is filtered through embedded preconceptions or doubts of the *possible* that may not align with what simply *is* within indigenous experience.[10]

Expanding awareness of alternative possibilities could foster appreciation of indigeneity, not just who claims to be indigenous, but what *being* and *knowing through* indigeneity may be. The journey must begin with shedding notions of indigenous philosophy as alien, exotic, tribal, savage or primitive. These and a host of other discursive labels or "code" are often affixed to devalue indigenous knowledge.[11] In addition, understanding indigeneity also requires awareness and respect for the indigenous experience. Begun during the brutal colonial subjugation, suppression of indigenous ways of knowing through assimilation or extermination of indigenous peoples was deliberate and strategic. Indigenous peoples were separated not only from their homes and familiar surroundings, but from their sense of place. With greater understanding of indigeneity, as experienced by indigenous people, the magnitude of that violence, beyond mere "relocation," becomes apparent.

Indigeneity in the North American context extends beyond the history and experience of Native tribes and peoples within politically ascribed United States borders and contexts. Erasure and suppression was applied to recorded knowledge of a great Mayan civilization, which flourished for thousands of years and dissipated about 400 years prior to the arrival of the Spanish.[12] Indigenous knowledge of Mayan and Aztec Empire accomplishments was suppressed by Spanish invaders as artifacts were destroyed. Critical exploration of highly developed civilizations is lacking in most schools in the United States and many in Meso-America. Similar erasure occurred regarding Mississippian culture in North America over 1000 years ago. It is not clearly known why the Mississippians disappeared or dissipated (approx. 1450 CE) not long before arrival of Europeans.[13] Recent archaeology has explored mounds and sacred places, seeking an understanding of Mississippian culture. But precolonial Native American history is not widely taught in U. S. schools.

Narrative histories told through indigenous experience are available for exploration by those open to it, but such narratives are not to be found in standard U.S. public school curriculum or on most higher education campuses.[14] However, more institutions of higher education have begun developing American Indian and Indigenous Studies programs over the past two decades.[15] Many of these programs still reflect dichotomized orientations. They either focus upon history and anthropology (talking *about* the indigenous—objectification) or they are designed primarily *for* Native American students (the indigenous as specialized or exotic—marginalization). Few are directed toward appreciation of indigenous philosophy and knowledge within curriculum, pedagogy and educational philosophy generally.

Another obstacle of dominant cultural discourse to envisioning indigenous philosophy manifests in the material effects of colonial and post-colonial hegemonic oppression. Decades of hegemonic pressures for assimilation or extinction have challenged indigenous identity. The genocide and suppression of Indian languages and culture raise barriers to accessing indigenous thought. These effects have obscured indigenous peoples' connection with traditional ways of being, and created wariness about sharing with dominant culture. The resurgence and revitalization of expressions of indigenous thought, particularly over the past two decades, appears in writings and storytelling by Native Americans. They present an opportunity to glimpse indigeneity through eyes and voices of Native Americans.

It is important to note that characterizing indigeneity may be too broad a task, in the sense that it seeks to unify or essentialize epistemologies of peoples from vastly different places and experiences and their differing indigenous philosophies. Widely varying life worlds of peoples across two continents have been lumped together under the label of "Indian." Even limiting focus to the indigenous in North America is challenging. However, philosophies arising from different cultures and regions of the world may share some common characteristics which can provide insight and coherence to the concept of indigenous philosophy.

> First of all, some people might say that there is no one Indian perspective. It is true that at present there are 562 federally recognized tribes, and all of these nations have a different view about Indian history. . . . The complexity becomes greater when adding in the First Nations of Canada and Indigenous groups of Mexico and South America. Yet Indian people, and individuals who know Indians very well, would agree that there is an Indian perspective.[16]

The aim here is to explore common characteristics of indigenous philosophies, and to consider factors contributing to their exclusion from Western academic and general discourse. We employ the eyes, ears and voices of indigenous scholars and authors which present significant alternative ways of knowing and ways of being. If we can be open to alternative ways of knowing and being through indigenous voices, we may discover insights potentially beneficial to all life on the planet.

## Other Voices "In the Winds": Indigenous Scholars

As noted previously, voices and perspectives of indigenous scholars come from varied circumstances and disciplines, in part because their voices often have not been recognized within academic spaces reserved to philosophy.[17] Historical and biographical works can also provide insight, given the paucity of philosophical texts.[18] Indigenous philosophy tends to be best illustrated through descriptive and holistically oriented iterations, parables,

## 22 Paul L. Landry

allegories and oral history lessons. Indigeneity may be manifest in literature or storytelling,[19] or discussion of ethno-science and sustaining the natural environment,[20] yet not presented as formal philosophical essay or treatise. In addition, socio-historical necessity has, in too many instances, aligned ways of *being* with ways of *survival*, which positions the indigenous in a context that is resistant and oppositional rather than as generative agency.

Cajete observes, as do others, that a "quality of informality" characterizes indigenous teaching and learning because transmission of knowledge is often contextualized and communal.[21] It is embedded and reflected in practical daily living, but with a foundational premise that recognizes reciprocity between human actions and nature; there is always deeper learning and levels of meaning in all teachings. Luther Standing Bear noted: "knowledge was inherent in all things. The world was a library, its books were the stones, leaves, grass, brooks, and the birds and animals that shared, alike with us, the storms and blessings of the earth."[22] Characteristics of indigenous knowledge can also be deciphered from concrete practices, past and present, such as the cosmology of Mayans manifest in architecture, or the ecology manifest in land and water management rituals and practices among the Yakama Nation.

Cajete also indicates that there is no literal translation for epistemology in American Indian languages, but there are many understandings that reflect knowledge and ways of being.[23] He and American Indian scholars, including Deloria, Wildcat, Marker and others describe the holistic cultural ethic which honors natural interdependence among humans, their social and cultural worlds and the natural world.[24] Often expressed through symbolic representations which occur in various forms in all American Indian languages, these "mythic metaphors are the philosophical infrastructures and fields of knowledge" that underlie American Indian ways of knowing.[25] The Tree of Life, Earth Mother, Great Turtle, Corn (or Game), Holy Wind and Sacred Directions are among these common symbolic constructs. The symbols are interwoven in relation to creation myths and the Great Mystery within which identity is both individual and composite as it is formed and matures in a quest for wholeness among self, community and natural world.

It is striking that such mythic symbols appear in many other indigenous philosophical constructs (cf. Corn, this volume). The Corn (Maize) deity and the Sacred Directions, as examples, are also central to Mayan Civilization and are depicted in their artifacts. The appearance of many of these symbols in indigenous life-worlds of the Aztecs, Incas, Maori and African civilizations in different forms points to their centrality to philosophical orientation of place in the Universe. Two Mayan orientations or beliefs align with Native American belief systems: the idea that the "gods" are not discreet, but rather are interconnected and part of a unified or holistic system; and the belief in reality as continual regeneration and cycles, rather than permanence.[26]

# Re-imagining "Indigeneity" 23

These holistic, cyclical, ecological and regenerative themes are characteristic of indigenous thought. The roles of the Earth Mother and Great Turtle "embody the understanding of the Whole Earth as a living, breathing and knowing entity who nourishes and provides for every living thing," an appreciation of connectedness that is transcendent through a sustained process of living.[27] Symbolic references to maize are more complex than superficial concepts of food and agriculture or geography, reflecting a cycle of sustenance to be actively respected.

The Sacred Directions and the Holy Winds also represent more complex constructs in multiple indigenous communities. The symbology of American Indian tribes includes natural phenomena beyond flora and fauna.[28] Atmospheric characteristics, weather patterns and cosmic elements are part of a whole. "By perceiving themselves in the middle of these directions, they oriented themselves to multidimensional fields of knowledge and phenomena of their physical and spiritual worlds."[29] The Holy Winds carry metaphysical symbolism representing spirituality in kinds of thought or impending change tied to and integrated with the natural lifeworld. It is, thus, not surprising when indigenous peoples are harbingers of potentially irreversible environmental damage and outspoken on climate change.

In his work, *God is Red*, Deloria explicates two fundamental philosophical differences between Western European thought and American Indian knowing and teaching. One difference is divergent understanding of, and reliance upon, time and space. The lands of American Indians hold the high levels of importance. Thought, statements and actions are made in reference to a relationship with the natural world.[30] A sense of place or spatial orientation is central to life and being. For European immigrants, time or history is at a more superficial level, viewing place as subordinate or transitory. The distinction is profound. For the European immigrant, a place entails assumptions of exploitation and maximum value yielded in the least amount of time, or at least marked by time. Indeed, the amount of time spent in a place may depend upon a calculation of time as invested or wasted. Time and history are linear and the focus is upon what happened when, with the more recent deemed presumptively better (i.e., modernism).

In contrast, indigenous peoples have viewed context and place as highly important to their relations with the natural environment and with each other. "Places where revelations were experienced were remembered and set aside as locations where, through rituals and ceremonials, the people could once again communicate with the spirits."[31] This affinity to place is based upon a deep sense of connection and responsibility to conserve, protect and live in harmony with the land. Wildcat defines the "indigenous" as "peoples or nations who take their tribal identities as members of the human species from the landscapes and seascapes that gave them their unique tribal cultures."[32]

The revelatory nature of a sacred place is also considered spatial and processual, rather than fixed in time (historical) as in Eurocentric perception.

## 24   Paul L. Landry

Past, present and future coalesce in the moment, and the metaphysical interconnects with the physical in a wholeness of being. Distinctions in Eurocentric philosophy separating the existential from the phenomenological may not translate to indigeneity; outer and inner lived experiences are inseparable. We are not *in* the environment; we collectively *comprise* the environment, along with all living things. Sacred spaces, for American Indians, hold continuing significance, both spatial and spiritual.

Understanding the significance of this connectedness and sense of continuing relationship and responsibility may lead to better appreciation of the violence of forced removal of Native Americans, as in the Trail of Tears in 1830. There were many other similar forced relocations. That violence has manifested in higher infant mortality rates and continues to affect Native peoples.[33] Similarly, the abduction and removal of American Indian youth to boarding schools, in many instances hundreds of miles from their families, native lands and community connections, was a hideously brutal physical and psychological insult. Children were separated by force from their parents and family, and because of that separation were severed from all cultural, spatial and spiritual bases for orienting the child in the world.[34] For many, the process of reconnection and reorientation is painful and continuing.[35]

Another important distinguishing characteristic serving as a backdrop for re-envisioning indigeneity is the concept of spirituality or "religion." Eurocentric Judeo-Christian notions of religion differ from most American Indian spiritualistic beliefs in several important ways.[36] One major distinction is Eurocentric reliance upon an anthropomorphic deity, which American Indian spiritualism does not.[37] While there is belief in creation, and there is discussion of grandfathers and grandmothers as spiritual guides, indigenous spirituality does not rest on a single all-powerful deity. Indeed, Indigenous peoples tend to see creation as a complex and harmonious interaction of all living things positioned within the universe, and may view Eurocentric notions of man being made in the "image of God" as confusing, if not a bit arrogant.

Another religious distinction is the belief that separates humans from the Earth, and views humans as corrupted and in need of redemption. While some Indigenous people may have adopted Western Eurocentric religions due to missionary and other hegemonic social influences, separation of the people from the earth and from each other is not an inherent tenet of Indigenous spirituality. This distinction may manifest in attitudes in Western dominant culture, also reflecting a space versus time distinction, that one's present actions are less important or accountable because there is opportunity for redemption at some later point in time.

In contrast, indigenous spirituality requires one to walk upright upon the earth at all times, *in a good way*, and to be cognizant of a relationship to others and to respect all living things and the natural environment.[38] What one does here and now is important and reflects not only upon self and community, but also reflects upon ancestors (past) and grandchildren (the future). This holistic perspective recognizes interrelated cycles within cycles.

The belief in separation of living beings as apart from the Earth would deny continuing responsibility that is part of a sacred indigenous belief system.[39] Deloria recounts the actions of Young Chief, who refused to sign the Treaty of Walla Walla because of his obligation to give voice to the lands, which were appointed by the Great Spirit to sustain life and the Indian people.[40] Signing the treaty would have dishonored the voices and trust. To act intentionally to despoil the natural environment and its sustaining relationship with Indian people would shame and dishonor self and ancestors for failing to steward resources passed down. Doing so would also be a dereliction of responsibility toward the grandchildren for whose benefit the lands are entrusted. The ethic of personal choice is shaped and guided by an inseparable connection to the family and community and sustaining the natural environment.[41]

Another major philosophical disconnect lies in the conception of sovereignty. Eurocentric beliefs in sovereignty relate to power and authority, typically consolidated, to govern, control or dominate territory or people.[42] This differs from Native American conceptions. As in the case of Young Chief, Euro-Americans have appointed an individual Indian to sign a treaty, with an assumption that the person they have designated as "leader" has authority to speak for or control all other tribal members. They failed to comprehend that such power, or sovereignty, is both distributed and collective among Native peoples.

## The Yakama Nation and "Sovereignty"

Accepting a faculty position at Heritage University, a unique institution of higher education situated upon tribal lands of the Yakama Nation, was both an honor and a challenge. As a newcomer, and as a trained practitioner of critical race theory, I was immediately struck by concern for potential conflict arising from a post-colonial institution within a Native American space. Yes, I was conditioned to dichotomous thinking. I wondered as well, since I teach in the College of Education, whether and how Teacher Preparation Programs, controlled in many ways by Washington State and Federal rules and standards, would align with indigenous ways of teaching, learning and knowing. After all, the programs involve preparing educators, Native American and others, for teaching in Washington's Central Valley with substantial indigenous populations. I wondered whether the relationship between the University and the Yakama Nation would be characterized by resistance or symbiosis. The answer is not definitive, but appears to reflect the latter. However, my journey is a continuing process of shedding dichotomous thinking and discursive labels, an ongoing effort to understand through listening to indigenous voices.

## 26  Paul L. Landry

The Yakama and the tribes now constituting the Yakama Nation, have been related to these lands for hundreds of generations. It would be a mistake, perhaps, to say that they are inhabitants on this land because they are instead *a part* of the land, as much as the salmon, the game, the berries and the corn the land yields. They are a part of the cycles in which Pahto (*Standing high, or She who greets the Sun;* Mt. Adams to non-Indians) collects the snows and awaits the call of Mother Earth to release the waters so the land can sustain and fulfill the regenerative cycles that support the salmon, game, agriculture and the people. As the Yakama say, this is truth *from time immemorial.*

An early "lesson" involved a University gathering in November of 2015 for indigenous people, but open to all University and faculty. No one "briefed" me on what to expect or gave me any text to study. I would learn through experience, as would any Yakama child. I listened carefully to Tribal Elders' invocations and ritual songs. I watched and participated as the water was served as the opening step, followed by the salmon and other parts of the ritual. Everything seemed natural and I was treated as though I belonged there. When I looked confused, the significance of each step was gently explained. After the meal, I learned the significance of the feather. Each person could hold the feather and speak to all in thanksgiving and to offer thoughts and comments, until everyone who wished to had spoken. Everyone listened to the feather-holder respectfully. The Elder closed the gathering and thanked all for participating, stating that the act of coming together would help assure a good school year.

Other lessons would follow. The public schools with high numbers of Native American students could expect absentees during the first couple of weeks of the school year. Children and their families participate in long-standing rituals, and some youths were participating in coming-of-age rituals related to hunting game, salmon or gathering berries. These events are cultural education and are not in defiance of school district rules and procedures. They are natural steps in a *way of being* that is Yakama. I was also reminded of challenges many Native American children and their families face in meeting demands of daily life, including poverty and family health issues.

My education moved to a different level as I sought to understand "sovereignty" from the perspective of the Yakama people. I knew from some experience and reading that sovereignty is something more and different from the legalistic notions typically ascribed by non-Indians.[43] Many of those external interpretations derive from dichotomous thinking of contestation and Euro-American perceptions of "what the Indians want from the whites." But it was very important to set aside preconceptions for this opportunity to listen and learn.

From an indigenous perspective, sovereignty is an affirmation of being the *subject* with agency. It is a status and a way of being that respects connection with place, community, family, self and the natural world. Sovereignty also entails being respected as such. It is an affirmation and conscious decision to be in the world as a member of a group or tribe. Melanie Benjamin addressed the State of the Mille Lacs Band of Ojibway in 2015 characterizing sovereignty as:

> Cultural Sovereignty is ancient, and predates the arrival of non-Indians. It is a kind of sovereignty that we can only lose if we choose to give it up. . . . Cultural Sovereignty is our inherent right to use our values, traditions, and spirituality to protect our future. It goes much deeper than legal sovereignty, because it's a decision to be Anishinaabe, to not just protect a way of life, but to practice living Anishinaabe, every day. Cultural sovereignty is practiced through ceremonies, through relationships, and especially through language. It is what unites us, inspires us, and gives us hope for the future.[44]

Sovereignty is a right of individual and communal integrity to advance self-development and community well-being, consistent with indigenous holistic beliefs, and to honor ancestors and generations yet to come by respecting the lands and traditions that give and sustain life.

One basic non-Indian misconception is that indigenous sovereignty is something that can be taken away by force or legality. Neither can sovereignty be granted by legal device. This is a fundamental, and in some respects incommensurable, misunderstanding of indigeneity. The Euro-American narrative is that, having dispossessed Native peoples of their lands and claimed those lands as "territory," limited sovereignty could be redefined and granted to Native peoples over land designated as "reservations."[45] Based on Eurocentric notions of sovereignty as objectification, domination and control, the narrative makes sense. At the core of indigenous beliefs, however, any dominion over lands is at most a stewardship, a cooperative relationship with the land as part of a holistic system.[46] That a people can be subjugated, however, does not necessarily alter their sense of being. Subjugation or domination is not sovereignty.

When Euro-Americans and their military forces encountered the Yakama, the Yakama Nation, including associated tribes, ranged over eleven million acres in the Central Valley of what is now Washington State. To resolve conflict, a Treaty was signed in 1855 by which the Yakama agreed to confine themselves primarily to approximately 1.4 million acres of those lands. While the "control" of lands was ceded, there was no abandonment of cultural sovereignty by the Yakama. Neither was there any grant of sovereignty by the United States to the Yakama, in the sense the term is understood by Native peoples. Yakama sovereignty and their relationship to the lands existed long before the United States was an idea, and is more mature and enduring.

The agreement also provided for Native peoples to be free of interference with rights to practice their beliefs and customs throughout the Columbia River Basin and usual places. As such, the Yakama would preserve and

## 28  *Paul L. Landry*

continue their way of life, their customs and rituals in what was intended by the Yakama to be a peaceful co-existence with the Euro-Americans. The Yakama would settle on the reserved lands, but would be able to follow the salmon and honor certain harvest practices and rituals according to their customs.[47] Repeated interference by Euro-Americans with Native American fishing, hunting and other rights led to the *United States v. Winans* case (198 US 371, 25 S. Ct. 662, 49 L. Ed. 1089, 1905), decided by the Supreme Court in 1905, affirming Yakama rights.

## Indigeneity as Cultural Sovereignty, and Influence of External Corrupting Influences

Tribal governments in many parts of the U.S., ostensibly established to provide for self-determination and rule on Indian lands, too often became corrupted by Euro-American customs and ethics. Their establishment presumed that indigenous people needed Eurocentric devices for self-governance. This corruption of the traditional concept of sovereignty cannot be viewed in a vacuum. External hegemonic pressures, including virulent discrimination, left little "freedom" in a so-called free market environment. In some cases, Tribal resources and land have been sold off without primary regard for the entire tribe or for the future generations. Such transactions may have been for near-sighted gains, sometimes benefitting tribal leaders more than the tribe as a collective. Deloria laments that some Indian leaders and tribal governments throw around words like "sovereignty" without understanding the meaning, while doing little for generations to come.[48]

In addition, hegemonic influences severely restricted Native American ability to exercise individual and collective sovereignty and to maintain traditional beliefs and practices. Adoption of external or non-Indian behaviors and ethics occurred, even when antithetical and corrosive to traditional indigenous ways of living. The U.S. Bureau of Indian Affairs adopted rules imposing external definitions of tribal membership, including blood percentage restrictions, even though tribal governments ostensibly had the right to define membership under the Indian Reorganization Act. Some tribal councils adopted an exclusionary Eurocentric view of "sovereignty" and exploited it to exclude individuals, based upon percentage of blood relation.[49] This could reflect a form of neocolonialism, a form of racialized violence in which external capitalist and market pressures, as well as political pressures, have been used to maintain control over tribal affairs.

Yet Deloria cautions against oversimplification that yields misunderstanding. His critique of governmental tendencies to racialize and essentialize on the basis of skin color led to policies that classified Indians at times as both white and Black, but most often treated Indians in a collectivized grouping of the "other."[50] Such actions ignored and contravened Indian values and ways of knowing. He observed: "All groups must come to understand themselves as their situation defines them and not as other groups see them. By accepting ourselves and defining the values within which we can be most comfortable we can find peace."[51]

Cultural sovereignty is an articulation and implementation of beliefs, practices and responsibilities embodied in indigeneity. Put another way, indigeneity is the state of being and becoming that is faithful spatially, socially and spiritually to the indigenous group's past, present and future. In this formulation, actions would not be true exercise of sovereignty unless the actions served to support, protect, preserve and carry forward the group's way of life, including relationships with the natural world.

Indigeneity is related to, but not entirely defined by degree of blood relation. One can assimilate into a tribal group of an Indian nation over time, perhaps generations. Indigeneity is related to space, but being in or living in a space does not alone yield indigeneity. The distinction relates to choice, fidelity and commitment. In South Africa, Boers lived and controlled lands for many decades and generations, but imposition and maintenance of apartheid suggested colonialist mentality and non-indigenous status regardless of their length of stay in that space. That cultural and philosophical distance can be cavernous between peoples occupying the same geographical space.

Current disputes continue regarding the Standing Rock Nation and installation of a pipeline using Eurocentric governmental tactics of intimidation and coercion. Despite concerns that the pipeline may permanently despoil sacred land and pollute the drinking water, affecting generations to come, the non-Indian view is that pipeline installation is economically desirable and *urgent*. Courts, police powers and governmental coercion are employed to achieve results driven by Eurocentric philosophy. The dispute reflects how very different ways of understanding human relationships and our relationship to the natural environment can be. Euro-American corporate urgency for transitory access to lands for construction of a pipeline seeks to generate profit while oil can be sold at a premium (time). Indigenous objections and concerns are that sacred space and lands may be irretrievably damaged, and that allowing the pipeline construction is a dereliction of responsibility to the present environment and to the future generations whose life-sustaining water is likely to be fouled (space). Indians even asked Euro-Americans to make the effort to carefully examine environmental risks using U.S. governmental criteria.

Returning to the Yakama Nation, collaboration with Heritage University is in keeping with tribal sovereignty and indigeneity to the extent that it supports broader socioeconomic and societal goals while not undermining Yakama beliefs and values. An important interest of the Yakama people is educating and training their youth for roles that can benefit and sustain the group while supporting their potential independence within larger society. Special Heritage programs in fisheries and wildlife management are well suited to train young tribal members in technological advances. These skills and knowledge bases can build upon cultural knowledge and help restore salmon habitats and populations damaged by years of environmental abuse,

## 30    Paul L. Landry

pollution and mismanagement by non-indigenous people. This restoration can provide future employment and also fulfill a commitment to protect and preserve the natural environment for future generations. Other disciplines such as the development of teachers, physician assistants, nurses, business managers and biologists all provide potential beneficial resources for sustaining the Yakama Nation. In addition, the Yakama can promote better understanding and teach non-Indians alternative ways of understanding the world through relationships developed with the university.

## Implications for Indigenous Philosophy of Education

The key to cultural sovereignty and the vitality of indigeneity, of course, is in the education of youth. As Indian author and speaker Gyasi Ross put it:

> Education is ground zero in the fight for tribal sovereignty. Always has been and still is. Why? Because if you cannot teach your children the values of the local community, those children are not going to be able to help or *fit in* with the local community. You build a community of strangers.[52]

In this regard, we find some similarities between Native American indigenous philosophy and the pedagogical views of John Dewey. Central to Dewey's philosophy is the concept that democracy and maintenance of a society are inseparable from the strategic education of the young and inculcation of socio-historical knowledge, practical experience to apply knowledge and understanding the beliefs and values that hold the fabric of a society together.[53] Dewey envisioned the teacher as a guide who could encourage students to explore their learning experiences more deeply, a trait common to Native American teaching. Much of current U.S. public school curriculum and practice, especially reliance upon standardized testing, has diverged from Dewey's experiential and integrated learning principles.

An example of limited dominant cultural vision is reflected in a story concerning Yakama Nation children in school, as much of Native American wisdom is carried and shared in storytelling. A white student teacher working in a classroom with a large proportion of Native American students could not understand the difficulty getting the students to stay engaged in lessons. Students would quickly get off task and disrupt other students. The student teacher was faithfully following prescribed curriculum and "methods" training received, by breaking down the lesson into small steps. The lesson was based upon the standard English Language Arts curriculum and a novel about the coming of age for a privileged white teen and his friends.

Two important items were revealed when discussing with colleagues, including a Yakama Nation faculty member, how best to support this

Re-imagining "Indigeneity" 31

student teacher with instruction and learning for these Native American students. First, the novel referenced a teen going to a "boarding school" as part of the character description. It never occurred to the student teacher that the concept of a "boarding school" in these students' life-world was an extremely sensitive and traumatic topic. The students only knew of such institutions, Indian Boarding Schools, through painful stories told to them by grandparents who had suffered such experiences. Little wonder the lesson may not have engaged the students.

A second revelation from the Native American colleague was that Indian children are taught holistically from infancy, and indigenous philosophy is grounded in connectedness. As a result, Native American students are more likely to engage if the lesson begins with a discussion of how the learning target fits into a larger picture or frame of reference. She suggested that with a frame of reference, it is easier for the students to engage in the more particularized steps in constructivist teaching because they relate each step to a larger whole. This approach makes perfect sense when viewed from an indigenous perspective, but was not even considered within the traditional pedagogy of dominant culture schooling.

A further caution in exploring indigenous education is to shed discursive biases embedded in educational systems. Persistent notions of deficit cultural model bias against Native Americans must be confronted, as must cultural superiority and privilege dispositions regarding dominant cultures in schooling. Daniel Wildcat suggests, instead of Americanization of indigenous students to educate them, what is needed is an "indigenization" of American education for the benefit of all children's education.[54] One need not be indigenous to employ indigenous philosophies to advance student learning. This transformation also needs awareness and change of traditional mindsets of teachers, policy makers and the public.

Linda Tuhiwai Smith suggests that alteration of education research agendas will be required.[55] At present, research is oriented toward submersion of indigenous children in dominant processes. Their success is measured by the extent they adopt dominant ways of learning and knowing, a dichotomous bias. Examples of schools grounded in indigenous philosophy exist, but their numbers are relatively small and results have tended to be regarded as boutique or marginal social experiments.[56] In the Ethnic Studies Program in Tucson, Arizona, where students participating in classes which embraced indigenous history, cultural practices and knowledge, student engagement and academic performance increased remarkably.[57] That program was shut down by the local school board because of pressure from the state, and similar programs were banned by the Arizona State Board of Education.

Yet another caveat lies in respect for language. As with almost every intersection of cultures, there is a liminal space across which language transports meaning and understanding. Language is more than a mechanical tool for transmitting and receiving data.[58] Language embodies lived-experience

# 32   *Paul L. Landry*

(culture) and identity. Educators engaged in language acquisition and instruction know well the pitfalls of reliance upon grammar and vocabulary (literal translation) as the sole basis for communicative interaction across languages and cultures. While it would be impracticable to expect all teachers of Native American children to be fluent in the native tongue of the student's tribe, an awareness of linguistic difference and the patience and curiosity to explore is warranted when the meaning and context of phrases and concepts used in the dominant language of instruction may not match those of indigenous students. This is basic culturally responsive pedagogy, but many teachers and many school systems do not deem indigenous culture worthy of response.

## Concluding Reflections

Indigenous peoples have been trying to counsel, to "educate," dominant society that there are forces and relationships vital to sustaining the planet and life. This counsel has been largely unheeded. It is not that evidence and indicators upon which this counsel is predicated do not exist; the problem is that they are either unseen or ignored. There is a proclivity for dichotomous thinking, the notion that things Euro-Americans label as *normal* are presumptively best. Anything associated with the "other" is rejected as presumptively suspect and inferior. This bias can obscure alternative ways of knowing that may well provide crucial guidance for survival. Opening minds and ears to alternative ways of knowing, to inform alternative ways of being, may be more important than we generally think. Current discussion of climate change reflects an awakening, as if recently discovering a message indigenous wisdom has long tried to convey.

Gregory Cajete sets forth a model for philosophically grounded[59] indigenous education in the American Indian context which is comprised of seven components. At least three of these aspects merit consideration for incorporation into curricular and instructional practices generally. *Environmental Foundation* refers to indigenous bodies of knowledge and practices observed and derived through interaction with the natural world. "To say American Indians were America's first practical ecologists is a gross understatement."[60] *Artistic Foundation* encourages Native peoples to symbolize and express knowledge, understandings, relationships and feelings through various media and in concrete ways. Expression of these feelings and meanings through art can transcend time and serve as a way of teaching through examination of works wrought by others as reference, as guides in the present, and through active expression by creating art. *Communal Foundation* reflects that the life of the community is a primary context for learning. Through the social context, learning is applied and integrated to support an understanding that all humans are related and that their survival depends upon mutuality. These constructs exemplify ways

*Re-imagining "Indigeneity"* 33

that indigenous philosophy can be complementary and incorporated into current schooling practices.

Daniel Wildcat notes that an awakening and indigenization of our thinking may even be crucial to survival, and far more urgent than simply sustaining life on the planet under optimal conditions.[61] He references indigenous philosophy that embodies the concept of interconnectedness of all living things, and points to the number of species that become extinct each year through ignorance, arrogance, greed and ineptitude. Some of those species may be crucial to our survival. The discovery of plants with great medicinal or nutritional value in unspoiled regions, and the targeting of the same regions for destruction are indicators of the probity and value of his observation. Perhaps what is called for, in terms accessible to non-indigenous philosophy, is a reference to the admonition of Kuhn who contended that a potentially more beneficial advance toward truth lies in a shifting of paradigms. Rather than seeing indigenous knowledge and philosophy as an incremental and reluctant accretion to "accepted" knowledge, perhaps indigenous knowledge can help us reassess what we believe about reality and our existence in the world.

In the arena of educating youth, the first step forward would be to dispel the notion that the value of indigenous education is primarily to address marginal "deficits" of Native American children in the context of public education systems. Certainly, the goal of culturally responsive pedagogy would require addressing ways in which public education has failed Native American peoples.[62] The challenge, however, may be much greater. The current view is that indigenous education involves provision of specialized bodies of knowledge and teaching to a discrete and marginalized group of students to enable them to make up "deficits" in knowledge compared to dominant group (standard) academic performance.

Thinking alternatively, and thinking in a communal and complementary way that indigenous philosophy would inform, the challenge may really be to infuse and integrate indigenous knowledge into public education curricula for all students. There is little risk in teaching children to think holistically and critically. There would be little problem in teaching them to consider implications of what they learn for the entire ecosystem and for social relations among all people. Equally beneficial would be instructing a philosophical orientation for responsibility and accountability for choices and actions. The challenge is the tectonic shift that would be required in teaching methods and transforming the mindsets of traditional educators. To meet this challenge would require opening debate on philosophy and education to indigenous voices, to learn from and through their ways of knowing. And if indigenous philosophy is correct, it could be the difference between continuing on a path toward self-destruction or a course of saving our collective lives and sustaining life on the planet. It is a basic difference between thinking dichotomously, "us versus the other," or thinking communally and complementarily, "we together."

# Notes

1. Donald L. Fixico, "American Indian History and Writing from Home: Constructing an Indian Perspective," *American Indian Quarterly* 33 no. 4 (2009): 555.
2. Akwasi Asabere-Ameyaw, "Foreword," in *Indigenous Philosophies and Critical Education: A Reader*, ed. George Sefa Dei (New York: Peter Lang, 2011), xii.
3. George Sefa Dei, "Introduction" in *Indigenous Philosophies and Critical Education: A Reader*, ed. George Sefa Dei (New York: Peter Lang, 2011), 1–13.
4. Vine Deloria, Jr. et al., *Spirit and Reason: The Vine Deloria Jr. Reader* (New York: Fulcrum Publishing, 2011), 3.
5. Don A. Howard, "Einstein's Philosophy of Science," in *Stanford Encyclopedia of Philosophy*, ed. Edward N. Zalta, Winter 2015, https://plato.stanford.edu/archives/win2015/entries/einstein-philscience/.
6. Arturo Aldama, *Disrupting Savagism: Intersecting Chicana/O, Mexican Immigrant, and Native American Struggles for Self-Representation* (Durham, NC: Duke University Press, 2001); Helen Carr, *Inventing the American Primitive: Politics, Gender, and the Representation of Native American Literary Traditions, 1789–1936* (Cork, Ireland: Cork University Press, 1996).
7. Spivak troubles cultural study that is, itself, filtered through unacknowledged assumptions which presume transparency but silence the subaltern. Gayatri Chakravorty Spivak, "Culture Alive," *Theory, Culture & Society* 23 nos. 2–3 (March 2006): 359–360. Consider also Spivak's critique of the work of Forbes and Said, an approach that requires neither adoption nor antagonism to Eurocentric humanism, but rather a non-alignment. Gayatri Chakravorty Spivak, "Race before Racism: The Disappearance of the American," *Boundary 2* 25 no. 2 (1998): 35–53.
8. Michael Marker, "Sacred Mountains and Ivory Towers," in *Indigenous Philosophies and Critical Education: A Reader*, ed. George Sefa Dei (New York: Peter Lang, 2011), 197; Gregory Cajete, "It Is Time for Indian People to Define Indigenous Education on Our Own Terms," *Tribal College Journal* 18 no. 2 (2006): 56.
9. Cajete, "It Is Time for Indian People to Define Indigenous Education on Our Own Terms," 56.
10. Gregory Cajete, "American Indian Epistemologies," *New Directions for Student Services* no. 109 (2005): 69; Deloria Jr. et al., *Spirit and Reason*, 73–75.
11. Aldama, *Disrupting Savagism*.
12. Joshua Mark, "Maya Civilization," in *Ancient History Encyclopedia*, July 6, 2012, accessed March 3, 2017, www.ancient.eu/Maya_Civilization/. The acoustic marvels of the Pyramid of Kukulcán and the Court of Games at Chichén Itzá, unmatched in many "modern" concert halls, are a present-day testament to the advanced architectural design in the Mayan civilization.
13. Robert Hall, "Cahokia Identity and Interaction Models of Cahokia Mississippian," in *Cahokia and the Hinterlands: Middle Mississippian Cultures of the Midwest*, ed. Thomas Emerson and R. Barry Lewis (Urbana-Champaign, IL: University of Illinois Press, 2000), 44.
14. Roxanne Dunbar-Ortiz, *An Indigenous Peoples' History of the United States* (Boston: Beacon Press, 2014); Aldama, *Disrupting Savagism*.
15. Programs exist in universities ranging from elite private institutions to state universities, e.g., Stanford, Dartmouth, Arizona, UCLA, Washington, Minnesota. See http://colleges.startclass.com/d/o/American-Indian_-_Native-American-Studies.
16. Fixico, "American Indian History and Writing from Home," 554.
17. Katy Brown, "Access in Theory and Practice: American Indians in Philosophy History," *American Indian Quarterly* 27 no. 1 (2003): 113–120.

*Re-imagining "Indigeneity"* 35

18. John Neihardt, *Black Elk Speaks: Being the Life Story of a Holy Man of the Oglala Sioux* (New York: William Morrow & Co, 1932); Kae Cheatham, *Dennis Banks: Native American Activist* (Springfield, NJ: Enslow Publishers, 1997).
19. Robin Kimmerer, *Braiding Sweetgrass: Indigenous Wisdom, Scientific Knowledge and the Teachings of Plants* (Minneapolis, MN: Milkweed Editions, 2014); Peter Cole, "Coyote and Raven Talk about Indigenizing Environmental Education: Or Reconfiguring the Shenanigans of Otis O'Dewey Esquire," *Canadian Journal of Environmental Education* 17 (2012): 15.
20. Cole, "Coyote and Raven Talk about Indigenizing Environmental Education."
21. Cajete, "American Indian Epistemologies," 72.
22. Luther Standing Bear, "My People the Sioux," www.wisdompills.com/2015/01/22/10-quotes-sioux-indian-chief-will-make-question-everything-modern-culture/; www.firstpeople.us/FP-Html-Wisdom/ChiefLutherStandingBear.html.
23. Ibid., 69.
24. Ibid.
25. Ibid., 73.
26. New World Encyclopedia Contributors, "Mayan Civilization, Religion," *New World Encyclopedia*, accessed March 1, 2017, www.newworldencyclopedia.org/p/index.php?title=Mayan_Civilization&oldid=994995.
27. Cajete, "American Indian Epistemologies," 73. A contemporary movement to assert "Earth Rights," to seek a universal declaration protecting the rights of Mother Earth, would seem a reasonable effort from the perspective of indigenous philosophy which views the natural environment as a living part of our reality, is perceived as somewhat progressive. Yet this movement and such recognition by non-Indians would have been unthinkable only a few decades ago. http://therightsofnature.org/universal-declaration/.
28. Melissa Nelson, ed., *Original Instructions: Indigenous Teachings for a Sustainable Future* (Rochester, VT: Bear & Company, 2008).
29. Cajete, "American Indian Epistemologies," 69.
30. Vine Deloria, Jr., *God Is Red: A Native View of Religion*, 30th anniversary ed. (Golden, CO: Fulcrum Publishing, 2003), 61–62.
31. Ibid., 55–56.
32. Daniel Wildcat, *Red Alert! Saving the Planet with Indigenous Knowledge* (Golden, CO: Fulcrum Publishing, 2009), 32.
33. J. David Hacker and Michael Haines, "American Indian Mortality in the Late Nineteenth Century: The Impact of Federal Assimilation Policies on a Vulnerable Population," *NBER Working Paper Series* 12572 (2006), accessed March 3, 2017, doi:10.3386/w12572.
34. Terry Cross, "Child Welfare in Indian Country: A Story of Painful Removals," *Health Affairs* 33 no. 12 (2014): 2256–2259, accessed March 3, 2017, doi:10.1377/hlthaff.2014.1158.
35. An iconic interview with the late Tribal Elder Albert White Hat helps explain why that experience is not an historical event, but a continuing struggle. www.youtube.com/watch?v=8L3MLFtjm5g.
36. This distinction is not intended as dichotomous, because many other religions and philosophies are not based upon an anthropomorphic deity, but space limitations preclude elaboration on such other world religions.
37. Deloria, Jr. et al., *God Is Red*, Chapter 5.
38. Cajete, "American Indian Epistemologies," 73.
39. Deloria, Jr. et al., *God Is Red*.
40. Ibid.
41. Cajete, "American Indian Epistemologies."
42. Oxford *Dictionary*, 7th ed., s.v. "Sovereignty."

36    Paul L. Landry

43. As a former practicing attorney and working in the area of civil rights for decades, I am familiar with many legal issues and interpretations relating to Indian Rights and sovereignty claims.
44. Melanie Benjamin, "2015 State of the Band Address: Protecting the Gift," *Mille Lacs Band of Ojibway*, February 2, 2015, accessed March 3, 2017, http://doczz.net/doc/173333/issue-mille-lacs-band-of-ojibwe.
45. Dunbar-Ortiz, *Indigenous Peoples' History*. Indeed, that narrative has been hegemonically imposed upon American Indian tribes. See Deloria's discussion of "self-government." Vine Deloria, Jr., *The Nations within: The Past and Future of American Indian Sovereignty*, ed. Clifford M. Lytle (Austin, TX: University of Texas Press, 1998).
46. There is a philosophical distinction between control and ownership. If indigenous identity is integrally connected with the lands, then expropriation of the lands has two possible meanings. Either one who takes control of the lands "owns" the indigenous person who is interconnected with the lands, or that which has been appropriated does not include "ownership" of the land insofar as it is bound up with indigenous identity. This is a fundamentally different way of understanding the reality of the relationship with the natural world.
47. Dunbar-Ortiz, *Indigenous Peoples' History*.
48. Ibid.
49. The Mdewakanton Dakota tribe in Minnesota had disputed elections for Tribal Council leadership based, in part, upon how membership was determined. Tribal casino revenues were distributed based upon membership. Some felt that fewer members meant more annual distribution per enrolled member. Others wanted to invest tribal resources in more diversified businesses to provide employment and benefits to a more inclusive membership.
50. Deloria observed that: "people fool themselves when they visualize a great coalition of the minority groups to pressure Congress for additional programs and rights. Indians will not work within an ideological basis which is foreign to them. Any cooperative movement must come to terms with tribalism in the Indian context before it will gain Indian support." Deloria, *Custer Died for your Sins*, p. 195.
51. Ibid.
52. Gyasi Ross, "A Lesson from the Miccosukee Tribe: Importance of Putting the 'Native' Back Into Native Education," *Indian County Media Network*, June 11, 2015, accessed March 3, 2017, https://indiancountrymedianetwork.com/culture/thing-about-skins/a-lesson-from-the-miccosukee-tribe-importance-of-putting-the-native-back-into-native-education/.
53. John Dewey, *Democracy and Education* (Teddington, Middlesex, UK: Echo Library, 2007).
54. Wildcat, *Red Alert!*, 32.
55. Linda Tuhiwai Smith, "Building a Research Agenda for Indigenous Epistemologies and Education," *Anthropology and Education Quarterly* 36 no. 1 (2005): 93–95.
56. The Star School in Flagstaff, Arizona (Navajo), the Little Red School House in Minneapolis, Minnesota (Lakota) and the Kura Kaupapa Maori in New Zealand (Maori) are but a few examples where student engagement was demonstrated in the context of indigenous philosophy based instruction.
57. The Ethnic Studies Program took Tucson High School from a 48% drop-out rate for Mexican American students to a 100% graduation rate, with 85% going on to higher education. *Precious Knowledge*, directed by Ari Luis Palos, et al. (San Francisco, CA: Kanopy Streaming, 2015), e Video.
58. Wayne Thomas and Virginia Collier, "School Effectiveness for Language Minority Students," *NCBE Resource Collection Series of National Clearinghouse for Bilingual Education* 9 (1997).

59. This reference to "grounded" is intentional, because in this view all knowledge emanates and is connected to the natural world, the Earth and all related living and spiritual ecology. Cajete, "American Indian Epistemologies," 69.
60. Cajete, "American Indian Epistemologies," 69.
61. Wildcat, *Red Alert!*, 32.
62. Kelsey Sheehy, "Graduation Rates Dropping among Native American Students," *U.S. News & World Report*, June 6, 2013, accessed March 3, 2017, www.usnews.com/education/high-schools/articles/2013/06/06/graduation-rates-dropping-among-native-american-students; U.S. Department of Education, Institute of Education Sciences, National Center for Education Statistics. National Assessment of Educational Progress, National Indian Education Study 2011.

## Bibliography

Aldama, Arturo J. *Disrupting Savagism: Chicana/O, Mexican Immigrant, and Native American Struggles for Self-Representation*. Durham, NC: Duke University Press, 2001.

Asabere-Ameyaw, Akwasi. *Foreword to Indigenous Philosophies and Critical Education: A Reader*, edited by George Sefa Dei. New York: Peter Lang, 2011.

Benjamin, Melanie. "2015 State of the Band Address: Protecting the Gift." *Mille Lacs Band of Ojibway*, February 2, 2015. Accessed March 3, 2017. http://doczz.net/doc/173333/issue-mille-lacs-band-of-ojibwe.

Brown, Katy Gray. "Access in Theory and Practice: American Indians in Philosophy History." *American Indian Quarterly* 27 no. 1 (2003): 113–120.

Cajete, Gregory. "American Indian Epistemologies." *New Directions for Student Services* no. 109 (2005): 69–78.

———. "It Is Time for Indian People to Define Indigenous Education on Our Own Terms." *Tribal College Journal* 18 no. 2 (2006).

Carr, Helen. *Inventing the American Primitive: Politics, Gender, and the Representation of Native American Literary Traditions, 1789–1936*. Cork, Ireland: Cork University Press, 1996.

Cheatham, Kae. *Dennis Banks: Native American Activist*. Springfield, NJ: Enslow Publishers, 1997.

Chief Luther Standing Bear. "My People the Sioux." www.firstpeople.us/FP-Html-Wisdom/ChiefLutherStandingBear.html.

Cole, Peter. "Coyote and Raven Talk about Indigenizing Environmental Education: Or Reconfiguring the Shenanigans of Otis O'Dewey Esquire." *Canadian Journal of Environmental Education* 17 (2012): 15–29.

Cross, Terry. "Child Welfare in Indian Country: A Story of Painful Removals." *Health Affairs* 33 no. 12 (2014): 2256–2259. Accessed March 3, 2017. doi:10.1377/hlthaff.2014.1158.

Deloria, Vine, Jr. *Custer Died for Your Sins*. Norman: University of Oklahoma Press; Reprint edition, 1988.

———. *The Nations within: The Past and Future of American Indian Sovereignty*, edited by Clifford M. Lytle. Austin, TX: University of Texas Press, 1998.

———. *Spirit and Reason: The Vine Deloria Jr. Reader*, edited by Barbara Deloria, Kristen Foehner, and Samuel Scinta. Golden, CO: Fulcrum Publishing, 1999.

———. *God Is Red: A Native View of Religion* (30th anniversary ed.). Golden, CO: Fulcrum Publishing, 2003.

Dewey, John. *Democracy and Education*. Teddington, Middlesex, UK: Echo Library, 2007.

Dunbar-Ortiz, Roxanne. *An Indigenous Peoples' History of the United States*. Boston: Beacon Press, 2014.

38    *Paul L. Landry*

Fixico, Donald L. "American Indian History and Writing from Home: Constructing an Indian Perspective." *American Indian Quarterly* 33 no. 4 (2009): 553–560.

Hacker, J. David and Michael Haines. "American Indian Mortality in the Late Nineteenth Century: The Impact of Federal Assimilation Policies on a Vulnerable Population." *NBER Working Paper Series* 12572 (2006). Accessed March 3, 2017. doi:10.3386/w12572.

Hall, Robert. "Cahokia Identity and Interaction Models of Cahokia Mississippian." In *Cahokia and the Hinterlands: Middle Mississippian Cultures of the Midwest*, edited by Thomas Emerson and R. Barry Lewis, 3–34. Urbana-Champaign, IL: University of Illinois Press, 2000.

Howard, Don A. "Einstein's Philosophy of Science." In *Stanford Encyclopedia of Philosophy*, edited by Edward N. Zalta, Winter 2015. https://plato.stanford.edu/archives/win2015/entries/einstein-philscience/.

Kimmerer, Robin Wall. *Braiding Sweetgrass: Indigenous Wisdom, Scientific Knowledge and the Teachings of Plants*. Minneapolis, MN: Milkweed Editions, 2014.

Mark, Joshua. "Maya Civilization." In *Ancient History Encyclopedia*, July 6, 2012. Accessed March 3, 2017. www.ancient.eu/Maya_Civilization/.

Marker, Michael. "Sacred Mountains and Ivory Towers." In *Indigenous Philosophies and Critical Education: A Reader*, edited by George Sefa Dei. New York: Peter Lang, 2011.

Miles, Tiya and Ebrary, Inc. *Ties That Bind -the Story of an Afro-Cherokee Family in Slavery and Freedom*. American Crossroads, 14. Berkeley: University of California Press, 2005.

Naylor, Celie E. *African Cherokees in Indian Territory: From Chattel to Citizens*. The John Hope Franklin Series in African American History and Culture. Chapel Hill: University of North Carolina Press, 2008.

Neihardt, John. *Black Elk Speaks: Being the Life Story of a Holy Man of the Oglala Sioux*. New York: William Morrow & Co, 1932.

Nelson, Melissa K., ed. *Original Instructions: Indigenous Teachings for a Sustainable Future*. Rochester, VT: Bear & Company, 2008.

New World Encyclopedia Contributors. "Mayan Civilization." In *New World Encyclopedia*. Accessed March 1, 2017. www.newworldencyclopedia.org/p/index.php?title=Mayan_Civilization&oldid=994995.

*Oxford Dictionary* (7th ed.). s.v. "Sovereignty."

*Precious Knowledge*. Directed by Ari Luis Palos, Eren McGinnis, Sally Jo Fifer, Jacob Bricca, and Naïm Amor. San Francisco, CA: Kanopy Streaming, 2015, e Video.

Ross, Gyasi. "A Lesson from the Miccosukee Tribe: Importance of Putting the 'Native' Back Into Native Education." *Indian County Media Network*, June 11, 2015. Accessed March 3, 2017. https://indiancountrymedianetwork.com/culture/thing-about-skins/a-lesson-from-the-miccosukee-tribe-importance-of-putting-the-native-back-into-native-education/.

Sheehy, Kelsey. "Graduation Rates Dropping among Native American Students." *U.S. News & World Report*, June 6, 2013. Accessed March 3, 2017. www.usnews.com/education/high-schools/articles/2013/06/06/graduation-rates-dropping-among-native-american-students.

Smith, Linda Tuhiwai. "Building a Research Agenda for Indigenous Epistemologies and Education." *Anthropology and Education Quarterly* 36 no. 1 (2005): 93–95.

Spivak, Gayatri. "Scattered Speculations on the Subaltern and the Popular." *Postcolonial Studies* 8 no. 4 (November 2005): 475–486. doi:10.1080/13688790500375132.

———. "Can the Subaltern Speak?" In *Can the Subaltern Speak: Reflections on the History of an Idea*, edited by Rosalind Morris. New York: Columbia University, 2010.

Tedlock, Dennis. *2000 Years of Mayan Literature*. Berkeley: University of California Press, 2010.

Thomas, Wayne and Virginia Collier. "School Effectiveness for Language Minority Students." *NCBE Resource Collection Series of National Clearinghouse for Bilingual Education* 9 (1997): 1–96.

U.S. Department of Education, Institute of Education Sciences, National Center for Education Statistics, National Assessment of Educational Progress. National Indian Education Study, 2011.

Vann, David. Accessed February 28, 2017. www.cherokeebyblood.com/Cherokee_by_blood/Black_Indians.html.

Wildcat, Daniel R. *Red Alert! Saving the Planet with Indigenous Knowledge.* Speaker's Corner. Golden, CO: Fulcrum, 2009.

# 3 The Notion of Ubuntu and the (Post)Humanist Condition

*Lesley le Grange*

## Introduction

In recent decades, the interests of Indigenous peoples have gained prominence. This is evidenced by the General Assembly of the United Nations declaring two consecutive decades (1995–2004 and 2005–14) as that of the World's Indigenous peoples. But, the prominence gained is also demonstrated by a burgeoning body of literature produced by Indigenous scholars and those who work alongside them.[1] These developments serve to reinforce the rights of Indigenous peoples to self-determination, their rights to land, that their ways of knowing and being[2] are respected. It also serves to give dignity to the world's colonised people and articulate ways in which the world might be decolonised. The project of decolonisation is of course, an ongoing one.

An upshot of developments of the past two decades is that the term "Indigenous" has been rethought, denoted by the replacement of the "small I" with the "capital I" in the word. Indigenous (with "capital I") is the process of reclaiming the term by Indigenous peoples. The reclaimed term marks a shift from that which occurs simply in certain isolated places where people live close to the land, as indigenous with a "small I" might suggest. Indigenous has reference to people and peoples who share common experiences of colonialism and therefore a word that holds political implications. As Wilson[3] writes:

> The first peoples of the world have gained greater understanding of the similarities that we share. Terms such as Indian, Metis, Aborigine or Torres Strait Islander do nothing to reflect either the distinctiveness of our cultures or the commonalities of our underlying worldviews. Indigenous is inclusive of all first peoples—unique in our own cultures—but common in our experiences of colonialism and our understanding of the world.

Wilson suggests that the invocation of "Indigenous" is a political move that affirms the common experiences of the world's colonised peoples and signifies a resistance to all forms of colonisation including globalisation.[4] My interest in this chapter is to explore how we might think/imagine an Indigenous education that takes seriously Wilson's notion of Indigenous but relates to a contemporary condition that Braidotti[5] refers to as the (post) human predicament. The (post)human predicament relates on the one hand to a historical moment in which global society finds itself, where the human has become a geological force capable of affecting all life on Planet Earth, giving rise to a new geological epoch, the Anthropocene. But the Anthropocene is as Morton[6] suggests "a strange term" because in this new epoch "non-humans make decisive contact with humans", and so on the other hand the predicament relates to the fact that advanced technologies produced by humans might have capabilities of destroying all life on the planet. In other words, the predicament relates to how one adopts the positive dimension of the (post)human condition by embracing all of life and its interconnectedness, and at the same time how one resists the potential negative effects of advanced technologies (robotics, drones, artificial intelligence, biological warfare, commodification of the human body, ecophages[7]) without being technophobic. The interconnectedness of humans and technology raises the important question of how we now ought to define what "human" is—what the unit of reference for the human now is.

I shall argue that in order to respond to the (post)human predicament, the idea of human as an atomised and autonomous individual (given to us by the European Enlightenment) should be jettisoned and that the unit of reference for human should be imagined differently—as embedded, embodied, extended and enacted—inextricably bound up in the connectedness of the cosmos. It is here, I shall argue that Ubuntu comes into its own because it signifies the interconnectedness of all life whilst affirming the importance of human-to-human relationships as a microcosm of relatedness of all things in the cosmos.

But, before continuing with the discussion, some clarifications are warranted. Firstly, I go along with Dei[8] that indigenous knowledge does not reside in "pristine fashion" outside of the influences of other knowledges because bodies of knowledges continually influence each other, demonstrating the dynamism of all knowledge systems. Therefore, rendering a false dichotomy or "moral evaluation between good [Indigenous] and bad [conventional/Western] knowledges"[9] is therefore not useful. However, Dei[10] importantly points out the need to challenge imperial ideologies and colonial relations of production, which continually characterise and shape academic practices. Moreover, the exclusion of indigenous knowledges from the academy leaves unchallenged space for the (re)colonisation of knowledges and cultures in local environments and contexts[11]. It is in this context that I invoke Ubuntu to provide inspiration for responding to the (post)human impasse so as to imagine a different education to the one that produces rational autonomous beings. Secondly, I accept that the contemporary world is different from when the planet was less densely populated,

## 42  *Lesley le Grange*

kinship networks were stronger and technology was less advanced. Against this background, I shall attempt to theorise an indigenous education that is responsive to challenges of a contemporary world. I divide the chapter into the following sections: Humanism, anti-humanism and the (post) human condition; the notion of Ubuntu; the (post)human[12] condition and Ubuntu; education as the cultivation of (post)human sensibilities; some parting thoughts.

## Humanism, Anti-Humanism and the (Post)Human Condition

Any discussion on (post)humanism inevitably requires some discussion on Humanism.[13] I therefore start with a brief discussion of Humanism. Humanism espouses a particular view of the human. I refer here to humanism that European Enlightenment gave us, first formulated by Protogaros as "man the measure of all things", later renewed during the Italian Renaissance as a universal model, which is depicted in Leonardo da Vinci's Vitruvian Man.[14] The latter became the symbolic image of bodily perfection, expanded to the embodiment of a set of universal mental, discursive and spiritual values. Braidotti[15] elaborates:

> That iconic image [Vitruvian Man] is the emblem of Humanism as a doctrine that combines the biological, discursive and moral expansion of human capabilities into an idea of teleologically ordained, rational progress. Faith in the unique, self-regulating and intrinsically moral powers of human reason forms an integral part of this high-humanistic creed.

The subject of Humanism is the "autonomous rational being" captured in Descartes's[16] *cogito*, "I am thinking therefore I exist." According to Braidotti,[17] in the ninetieth and twentieth centuries Europe announced itself as the origin and site of critical reason and self-reflexivity based on the Humanistic norm. Moreover, resting on this norm was the belief that Europe was not only the seat of universal consciousness but that this consciousness transcended its locatedness—that humanistic universalism was Europe's particularity. Humanism became the impetus for European imperialism and colonialism that was aided and abetted by the use of military power. But it also produced what Braidotti[18] terms, the "dialectics of self and other" where difference has a pejorative connotation. In other words, European identity (embodying consciousness, universal rationality and autonomy) becomes the mirror against which others were declared different and therefore inferior. The dialectics of self and other became the justification for sexism, racism and the separation of human and nature (the more-than-human world). Put differently, "human" came to be defined in a particular way that declares others as less human, sub-human or non-human.

In relation to education, Biesta[19] avers that education which has always been concerned with the cultivation of the human person or the individual's humanity became distorted during the European enlightenment period. He

The Notion of Ubuntu   43

argues that the idea that education is about cultivating the human person could be traced back to the tradition of *Bildung*—[20] an educational ideal that emerged in Greek society, and through its adoption in Roman culture, humanism, neohumanism and the Enlightenment, became one of the central notions of the modern Western educational tradition (see Biesta 2006 for a more detailed discussion). The upshot of these developments was that the term "human being" became configured in a particular way. For example, when *Bildung* became intertwined with the Enlightenment and the particular influence of Emmanuel Kant, *human being* came to mean "rational autonomous being"—consequently the purpose of education was to develop rational autonomous beings. Critical pedagogy and its derivatives followed from this understanding of education—that emancipation was a rational process—a process of conscientization in the case of Freireian pedagogy.

However, events of the twentieth century suggest that Humanism is in crisis. The holocaust, apartheid, genocides in Bosnia, Rwanda and Cambodia forcefully remind us of the effects of Humanism.[21] Levinas[22] goes as far as to argue that the crisis of Humanism began with the inhuman events of recent history:

> The 1914 War, the Russian Revolution refuting itself in Stalinism, fascism, Hitlerism, the 1939–45 War, atomic bombings, genocide and uninterrupted war . . . a science that calculates the real without thinking it, a liberal politics and administration that suppresses neither exploitation nor war . . . socialism that gets entangled in bureaucracy.

Furthermore, the global socio-ecological (environmental) crisis is a manifestation of the crisis of Humanism because its dialectics of self and other resulted in the belief that humans are able to transcend nature, able to manipulate and control it. It was as recent as the middle twentieth century that it first dawned on (Western) humans that we inhabit (or inhabits us[23]) a planet with finite resources and that some human actions have negative impacts on the more-than-human-world. As mentioned, environmental problems and risks have reached unprecedented levels so much so that environmentalists and geologists have postulated a new geological epoch marked by human dominance, called the Anthropocene.

The perennial education crisis is also a crisis of humanism. Education in the Western(ised) world of the twentieth century (and continues to be the case in the twenty-first century) had been characterised by evident instrumentalist approaches to teaching whereby outcomes or aims are predetermined and often derived from existing disciplines. Students are tracked by standardized tests and kept on track by subject disciplines.[24] [25] The effects of instrumental rationality in education are colonising, homogenising, dehumanising, domesticating and so forth.[26] [27] As Le Grange[28] elaborates:

> Curriculum becomes moribund and pedagogy banal. Pedagogy becomes cold and heartless and the earth becomes a stage on which pedagogy is

## 44   *Lesley le Grange*

performed. Furthermore, multiple pathways (that exist prior to human thought) for transforming the world and for creating alternative futures are reduced to a single way of knowing, being and becoming.

The humanist assumptions of critical pedagogy have also been challenged by some scholars, for example, Ellsworth[29] and Deever.[30] Both Ellsworth and Deever argue that the literature on critical pedagogy is highly abstract and utopian and that it is not relevant to the daily workings of teachers and learners. Bowers[31] criticizes the binary logic of critical pedagogy, arguing that its proponents frame capitalism and socialism in a dualistic logic of right/wrong, truth/illusion and salvation/damnation. All these authors point to the construction of an ideal notion of the human being that is disconnected from the realities experience by humans in their daily lives.

The latter half of the twentieth century witnessed the decline of Humanism as a consequence of responses to manifestations of it being in crisis. Anti-humanism took on different forms. In the 1960s and 1970s we witnessed what Braidotti[32] terms an "activist brand of anti-humanism". We witnessed the rise of social movements and protests against sexism, racism, war and colonisation. The most significant intellectual challenge to humanism was that of the radical thinkers of the post-1968 generation. This brand of anti-humanism was radical because it challenged both classical and socialist versions of humanism. The critique of Humanism by French poststructuralists of the post-1968 period is typified in Foucault's[33] seminal work, *The Order of Things* and his announcement of the "death of Man". About the critique of Humanism by these radical thinkers Braidotti[34] writes: "The Vitruvian ideal of Man as the standard of both perfection and perfectibility was literally pulled down from his pedestal and deconstructed".

A more recent critique of Humanism and the anti-humanism of linguistic post-structuralism comes from interdisciplinary fields with an interest in (re)turning to some form of realism, most notably speculative realism and new materialism. As Bryant, Srnicek and Harman,[35] writing from a speculative realist perspective note:

> In the face of the ecological crisis, the forward march of neuroscience, the increasingly splintered interpretations of basic physics, and the ongoing breach of the divide between human and machine, there is a growing sense that previous philosophies are incapable of confronting these events.

A (re)turn to speculative realism and new materialisms (matter-realism) is a response to the perceived limits of linguistic (post)structuralisms and other anthropocentric philosophies. All the realisms mentioned are opposed to what is referred to as naïve realism/materialism—the idea that an external observer is the locus from which the entire world can be grasped. Speculative realism denotes a range of thought but put simply, it is a philosophy that signifies a return to speculating the nature of reality independently of human

The Notion of Ubuntu   45

thought and holds that continental philosophy (phenomenology, structuralism, post-structuralism, deconstruction and postmodernism) has descended into an anti-realist stance in the form of what Meillassoux[36] terms "correlationism". New materialisms represent an interdisciplinary field of inquiry produced by a community of feminist scholars. It short, these scholars share the view that humans are not only socially, discursively and linguistically constructed, but also materially constructed. By material it is meant that human beings and the non-human (more-than-human) world are made of matter and that all human systems (including systems of thought) are underpinned by material flows. Coole and Frost[37] point out that whenever we think about matter, "we seem to distance ourselves from it, and within that space that opens up, a host of immaterial things seem to emerge: language, consciousness, subjectivity, agency, mind, soul; also imagination, emotions, values, meaning and so on". However, all of these seemingly "immaterial" things are as material as the computer that captures these words or the desk on which the computer is placed. Moreover, new materialisms question the privileging of the human subject in the human/non-human binary and hold that all matter (including inorganic matter) has agential capacities. All things, even physical objects such as desks and computers are in-becoming— rocks, human beings as well as systems of thought and language do not have fixity but are always changing. Given their post-anthropocentric stance, both speculative realists and new materialists argue that their philosophies are the basis for more adequate responses to the (post)human condition. These new realisms/materialisms place the human on an immanent plane, thereby stripping it of its ontological privilege.

However, stripping the human from its ontological privilege does not deny its ethico-normative distinctiveness. Deleuze[38] argues that what makes the human animal distinctive is not based on its form, its organs or functions but on the number of affects which it is capable of. We cannot know of what affects we are capable in advance but can engage in a life of experimentation and also to engage in an active life, one that enhances rather than thwarts life. The impetus for living an active life does not lay outside of life itself—it does not transcend life—but is a power within, the power that connects all things in the cosmos, produced by the materials flows and intensities of life. I shall argue that producing affects and being affected by others (both human and non-human) has strong resonance with the African concept of Ubuntu. Further, I posit that affirming human life is not antagonistic to affirming the more-than-human. Before discussing Ubuntu in relation to the (post)human condition, I first turn to a discussion on Ubuntu to clarify its meaning.

## The Notion of Ubuntu

*Ubuntu/Botho*[39] is a concept that is derived from proverbial expressions (aphorisms) found in several languages in Africa south of the Sahara. However, it is not only a linguistic concept but a normative connotation

46   *Lesley le Grange*

embodying how we ought to relate to the other—what our moral obligation is towards the other. Battle[40] avers that the concept *Ubuntu* originated from the Xhosa[41] expression: *Umuntu ngumuntu ngabanye Bantu*, "Not an easily translatable Xhosa concept, generally, this proverbial expression means that each individual's humanity is ideally expressed in relationship with others and, in turn, individuality is truly expressed".

Metz and Gaie[42] argue that there are two ways in which sub-Saharan African morality (as embodied in *Ubuntu*) is distinct from Western approaches to morality. Firstly, they argue that sub-Saharan morality is essentially relational in the sense that the only way to develop one's humanness is to relate to others in a positive way. In other words, one becomes a person solely through other persons—"one cannot realize one's true self in opposition to others or even in isolation from them"[43]. They point out that *Ubuntu* means that our deepest moral obligation is to become more fully human and to achieve this requires one to enter more deeply into community with others. One therefore cannot become more fully human or realize one's true self by exploiting, deceiving or acting in unjust ways towards others. Metz and Gaie[44] argue that the second way in which African morality differs from an Aristotelian or other Western moral philosophy is that it defines positive relationship with others in strictly communal terms. They write:

> One is not to positively relate to others fundamentally by giving them what they deserve, respecting individual human rights grounded on consent, participating in a political sphere or maximizing the general welfare, common themes in Western moral philosophy. Instead the proper way to relate to others, for one large part of sub-Saharan thinking, is to seek out community or to live in harmony with them.

Following from this is that moral obligation concerns: doing things for the good of others; to think of oneself as bound up with others; and to value family (in a broad sense of the term) for its own sake and not for its efficacy.

When reference is made to the other by Metz and Gaie,[45] then they are evidently referring to the human other—that relatedness means connectedness with other human beings. It is because of this understanding that Enslin and Hortsthemke[46] have argued that *Ubuntu* is by definition speciesist and therefore cannot contribute positively towards addressing environmental problems. Through a categorical lens of environmental ethics, we would say that *Ubuntu* is anthropocentric. However, I wish to argue that this is not the case and that *Ubuntu* has very strong ecocentric leanings (if the categorical lens of environmental ethics is used) or that it transcends the binary of anthropocentric and ecocentric. To appreciate the ecocentric leanings of the concept *Ubuntu* a broader/similar concept, *Ukama*, of which it forms part, should be understood.

In the Shona[47] language there is a broader concept *Ukama* which means relatedness—relatedness to the entire cosmos. Murove[48] argues that *Ubuntu*

## The Notion of Ubuntu 47

(humanness) is the concrete form of *Ukama* (relatedness) in the sense that "human interrelationship within society is a microcosm of the relationality within the universe". It is against this backdrop that Murove's[49] assertion that, "ukama provides the ethical anchorage for human social, spiritual and ecological togetherness", might be understood. This idea of ecological togetherness is supported by others such as Bujo[50] who writes: "The African is convinced that all things in the cosmos are interconnected". Also by Tangwa[51] (2004), who avers: "The precolonial traditional African metaphysical, outlook . . . impl[ies] recognition and acceptance of interdependence and peaceful coexistence between earth, plants, animals and humans". And Opuka[52] who notes: "There is community with nature since man [sic] is part of nature and is expected to cooperate with it; and this sense of community with nature is often expressed in terms of identity and kinship, friendliness and respect".

Moreover, humanness is not humanism and is in fact antithetical to it. As Ramose[53] writes:

> Humanness suggests both a condition of being and the state of becoming, of openness or ceaseless unfolding. It is thus opposed to any, '-ism', including humanism, for this tends to suggest a condition of finality, a closedness or a kind of absolute either incapable of, or resistant to, any further movement.

Humanness is therefore inextricably bound up in the human being's connectedness with other human beings and with an ever changing and complex (biophysical) world. The sense of wholeness and interconnectedness of self with the social and natural by implication means that caring for others also involves a duty to care for nature (the more-than-human-world). If *Ubuntu* means that our deepest moral obligation is to become more fully human, then this means not only fostering a closer and deeper relationship with human communities but also with biotic communities and the entire ecosphere. In other words, the realization of one's true self cannot be achieved if other human beings and the more-than-human-world are exploited or harmed.

Understanding *Ubuntu* as a concrete expression of *Ukama* also problematises the categories of anthropocentrism and ecocentrism (and those in between) which have come to characterise debates in environmental ethics/ philosophy and on those who wish to impose such categories on African values such as *Ubuntu*. Nurturing the self or caring for other human beings is not antagonistic towards caring for the-more-than-human world—*Ubuntu* cannot simply be reduced to a category of anthropocentric or ecocentric. The self, community and nature are inextricably bound up with one another—healing/development in one results in healing in all dimensions and so suffering too is transversally witnessed in all three dimensions. Put simply, African spirituality cannot be reduced to a category of anthropocentric.[54]

## 48  Lesley le Grange

## The (Post)Human Condition and Ubuntu

Braidotti[55] argues that (post)humanism is the historical moment that marks the end of the opposition between Humanism and anti-humanism and affirmatively charts new alternatives. She identifies three major strands in contemporary (post)human thought; the first derives from moral philosophy and develops a reactive form of the (post)human; the second derives from science and technology studies and takes an analytic form of the (post)human; and the third derives from anti-humanist philosophies and proposes a critical (post)humanism.

The reactive form of post-humanism is defended by contemporary liberal thinkers such as Martha Nussbaum.[56] Braidotti[57] points out that although Nussbaum acknowledges the challenges presented by contemporary technology-driven global economies, she "responds to them by reasserting humanist ideals and progressive liberal politics." For Nussbaum the only remedy for challenges of the contemporary world such as environmental destruction, fragmentation caused by globalisation, nationalism, ethnocentrism and so forth, is through (re)inscribing universal humanist values. Nussbaum's neo-humanist ethics is based on the view that challenges that afflict contemporary society can only be remedied through a solid foundation of moral values such as compassion and respect for others. Although Nussbaum stresses the importance of subjectivity, she frames it in a universalistic belief in individualism and fixed identities that she pits over feminist and post-colonial insights (for a more detailed discussion see Braidotti[58]).

A second significant strand of (post)human thought comes from science and technology studies. Developments in this interdisciplinary field have raised critical conceptual and ethical questions about the status of the human because it extends moral or agential capacities to non-human machines. However, Braidotti[59] argues that thinkers in this field do not explore fully the implications of developments in their field for a theory of subjectivity. She points out that the influence of Bruno Latour's anti-epistemology and anti-subjectivity stance accounts partly for this reluctance. The works of scholars in the field is of course nuanced. For example, Franklin, Lury and Stacey refer to the technologically mediated world as "panhumanity",[60] suggesting a global sense of interconnection between all humans and between humans and the non-human environment (in all its forms), creating a web of intricate inter-dependencies (Braidotti[61]). Braidotti[62] raises two issues with this new panhumanity: the first is that many of these interconnections are negative and based on a shared sense of vulnerability and fear of imminent catastrophes and, secondly, because this new global proximity does not always lead to peaceful co-existence as instances of xenophobia across the globe forcefully remind us. Another example of analytic (post)human thought drawn from science and technology studies is the work of sociologist of science, Nikolas Rose.[63] Rose provides a solidly grounded analysis of the dilemmas of the (post)human that defends the idea that the subject

*The Notion of Ubuntu* 49

is relational. He proposes new forms of "bio-sociality" and bio-citizenship that draws on Foucault's work on biopolitics. However, Braidotti[64] argues that Rose advocates a particular Foucauldian brand of neo-Kantian normativity that re-instates the centrality of the individual and is incompatible with the process ontology of Foucault that is key to developing a (post) human approach.

Another instance of analytic post-humanism that Braidotti identifies is exemplified in the work of Peter-Paul Verbeek.[65] Verbeek's work suggests the need for a post-anthropological turn that links humans to non-humans. He recognises the productive association between humans and non-humans and the theoretical impossibility of keeping them apart. Verbeek, however, superimposes a revised form of human ethics on post-human technologies by emphasising the moral nature of technological tools as agents that he argues actively contribute to how humans do ethics. In other words, Verbeek shifts the location of traditional moral intentionality from the autonomous transcendental consciousness of the human being to the technological artefacts themselves, be they computers, robots, drones and so forth. Braidotti[66] points out that for Verbeek it is only when we take seriously the morality of things that we can chart a posthuman brand of Humanism in the twenty-first century.

Braidotti[67] takes issue with the analytic (post)humanism of science and technology studies that constitutes one of the important elements of the contemporary (post)human landscape. In short, she raises the following concerns about analytic (post)humanism:

- It introduces selected elements of humanistic values without addressing the contradictions produced in performing such an exercise;[68]
- It expresses a high degree of political neutrality about the (post)human predicament;[69]
- It does not provide an adequate theory of subjectivity;[70]
- Moralizing technology engenders over-confidence in the moral intentionality of technology itself;[71]
- It neglects the current state of autonomy[72] reached by machines (smart-technologies) that can by-pass human decision making at both operational and moral levels.[73]

This brings me to a third strand of contemporary (post)human thought, Braidotti's[74] critical (post)humanism that provides the basis of her critique of the two other strands discussed. Braidotti's critical (post)humanism is informed by her anti-humanist roots and aims to develop affirmative perspectives on the (post)human subject, that is, to affirm the productive potential of the (post)human predicament. Genealogically Braidotti's critical post-humanism can be traced back to poststructuralists, the anti-universalism of feminism and the anti-colonial phenomenology of Frantz Fanon[75] and his teacher Aimé Césaire.[76] Braidotti[77] argues that what all

## 50 Lesley le Grange

these intellectual endeavours have in common is a sustained commitment to work out the implications of (post)humanism for mutual understandings of the human subject and humanity as a whole. Importantly, she points out that the situated cosmopolitan (post)humanism produced by these intellectual endeavours is supported by both the European tradition and by "non-Western" sources of moral and intellectual inspiration. Critical (post)humanism embraces efforts that fight for the rights of subaltern secular spaces, for those with no or little voice, those in exile and those who are unhoused. The latter concerns the fact that homelessness is not a natural state of being but people become unhoused through policies and practices that are socially constructed. It also incorporates the planetary cosmopolitanism espoused by scholars such as Gilroy.[78] Gilroy views colonialism and fascism as a betrayal of the European ideal of the Enlightenment. He takes a strong stand against racism and against fundamentalist appeals to nationalism (micro-fascism), be they in the U.S., Africa or Asia.

Braidotti[79] points out that another powerful source of inspiration for present-day re-configurations of critical (post)humanism is ecological and environmentalism. This relates to the larger sense of the interconnections between self and others, including the more-than-human-world. She points out that environmental theory highlights the link between the Protagorian idea of Man as the measure of all things and the domination as well as exploitation of nature (more-than-human-world). Moreover, that inspiration could be found in a life-sustaining spirituality that concerns a reverence for the sacredness of life based on a deep-seated respect for all that lives.[80]

But, how does Ubuntu align with the different strands of (post)humanism and can Ubuntu provide inspiration for the "cultivation" of (post)human sensibilities? Ubuntu is certainly incompatible with the reactive form of (post)humanism espoused by Martha Nussbaum. The communalism that is central to Ubuntu is at odds with Nussbaum's framing of subjectivity in terms of universalistic individualism. Moreover, Nussbaum's framing of subjectivity in terms of fixed identities and steady locations is antagonistic to the notion of Ubuntu as "a condition of being and the state of becoming, of openness or ceaseless unfolding".[81]

There are some points of convergence between Ubuntu and the strand of (post)humanism that comes from science and technology studies, but there are also points of divergence. Although the "panhumanity" defended by thinkers such as Franklin, Lury and Stacey[82] arose within the context of a contemporary and technologically mediated world, and different to the rural and "pre-modern" context from which Ubuntu emerged, the two ideas share the view that all humans are interconnected and that humans and the more-than-human-world are interconnected, to form an interconnected web of life. Furthermore, the notion of Ubuntu has been subjected to similar criticism to the one that Braidotti levels against Franklin et al.'s "panhumanity"; that global proximity does not always lead to peaceful co-existence. Instances of xenophobia by South African citizens against foreign nationals from the rest of Africa are a case in point. However, these instances of xenophobia might be due to vestiges of colonialism that resulted in erosion of Ubuntu rather than due to Ubuntu being flawed.[83] Ubuntu is also incompatible with Rose's[84] Foucauldian brand of neo-Kantian normativity because contrary to the communalism of Ubuntu, it re-inscribes the centrality of the individual. Furthermore, Ubuntu also might not sit comfortably with Verbeek's[85] notion of moralizing technology because it recognises the ethico-normative distinctiveness of the human being. Ubuntu means humanness and concerns the unfolding of the human being through producing affects in interaction with other human beings and the more-than-human world. Although we do not know in advance what affects the human is capable of,[86] the affects are distinctively human ones. In other words, the affects of humans cannot be superimposed on technologies because this would be tantamount to anthropomorphizing technology. However, Ubuntu can inform an education that is concerned with cultivating (post)sensibilities because it proposes that education involves the unfolding of the human being through producing affects positively disposed to other humans and the more-than-human-world (the natural world and artefacts such as technology) and through the human, being affected by the more-than-human-world. The unit of reference of education is not the atomised individual human being but an assemblage of human-environment-technology. An education informed by Ubuntu is one that opens up pathways for students to take actions that are caring but not brought about by a transcended idea(l)s imposed on them, but through releasing the power (potentia) that is within (and within all of life).[87]

Ubuntu most comfortably aligns with the critical (post)humanism for which Braidotti[88] argues. Both Ubuntu and Braidotti's critical (post)humanism recognise the ethico-normative distinctiveness of the human. In other words, even though the human holds no ontological privilege in the cosmos, it does have a distinct ethical/moral obligation to care for others, to act against injustice and so forth. Its ethical obligation is to enhance life both human life and the more-than-human-world. This ethical obligation is actualised in relation with other humans and the more-than-human-world, and it is not found as a set of abstract universal values that transcend life itself. Central to both Ubuntu and critical (post)humanism is the recognition of the interconnectedness of life, that is, that the unfolding (the affects that it produces) of the human being is dependent on the more-than-human world—forming the basis for rethinking environmental ethics, away from predetermined things to do, to simply and joyfully doing.

Now that I have explored points of convergence and divergence between the different strands of (post)human thought, I shall explore what the implications of this discussion are for education and how (post)human sensibilities might be "cultivated"[89] through education.

## 52  *Lesley le Grange*

### Education as the "Cultivation" of (Post)Human Sensibilities

The historic moment in which we find ourselves sees Planet Earth on the brink of ecological disaster, and where new technologies are affecting our lives to the extent that it is becoming increasingly difficult to know what the unit of reference for the human now is. The destruction of the Earth is a manifestation of the broader crisis of Humanism, brought about by the ontological privileging of humans by Enlightenment Humanism. In the twenty-first century human lives have become so intertwined with advanced technologies that it might require of us to rethink what "human" is. Humans' interconnectedness with technology could open up new and productive pathways for the becoming of the (post)human. Some of these technologies, given the autonomy they possess, also threaten to destroy all of life. Therefore, to respond productively to present-day challenges, (post) human sensibilities need to be "cultivated". In other words, the "cultivation" of sensibilities that are attuned to the oneness of all life (the interconnectedness of humans and the more-than-human-world), that will alert us to the dangers of new technologies without being technophobic—that advances in technology should be embraced, if it enhances life. In times such as these, education needs to be concerned with "cultivating" (post) human sensibilities.

I have shown in the previous section that there are commonalities between Ubuntu and contemporary (post)human thought, and in particular one strand of this thought, critical (post)humanism. Ubuntu might have emerged as a construct at a time when the world was less densely populated, when kinship networks were stronger and when people lived close to the land, but it can now also play a new role in a technology mediated world and inform thought that needs to be responsive to the Earth's rapid destruction, and in so doing, imagine a different "indigenous education".

As noted, the interconnectedness of all life and the fact that humans hold no privileged ontological position in the cosmos is consistent with both Ubuntu and Braidotti's (post)humanism. In line with this, cultivating (post) human sensibilities would mean that education's focus should not only/ chiefly promote the interest of human beings but an interest in enhancing all of life. It is an education that should open up multiple pathways (which cannot be predetermined) for learners to expand their powers of enhancing life and knowledge becomes concerned with the development of capabilities that expand the powers of enhancing life. As Ansell-Pearson[90] so cogently puts it:

> We do not know what affects we are capable of in advance, and this suggests that there is an empirical education' in life, involving a 'long affair of experimentation, a lasting prudence' and a wisdom that implies constructing a plane of immanence. In terms of our becoming-ethical

The Notion of Ubuntu   53

we can say that we do not know what a body can do: it is a mode of practical living and experimenting, as well as, of course, a furthering the active life, the life of affirmativity, for example, cultivating the active affects of generosity and joyfulness, as opposed to the passive and sad affects of hatred, fear and cruelty.

In other words, education should involve experimentation with the real, whereby educational encounters (pedagogical episodes) are moments in a lifelong affair of experimentation. If learning is to occur through experimentation, then educational outcomes cannot be predetermined as is the case with dominant approaches to curriculum, where learners are kept on track through subject disciplines and predetermined outcomes, and tracked through instruments such as standardised tests. If education is to play a role in developing (post)human sensibilities, then mainstream education requires radical rethinking.

Education concerned with the cultivation of (post)human sensibilities requires a reimagined subject—that subjectivity needs to be reconceptualised. An education informed by *Ubuntu* and critical (post)human thought marks a shift from what Doll[91] (2015) calls the arrogant "I" (of Western individualism) to the humble "I"—to the "I" that is embedded, embodied, extended and enacted. This would suggest that teaching and learning not be viewed as distinctive activities and that teachers and students come to work alongside one another. Moreover, that learning activities not be narrowly focused on the individual but that students learn with one another, that learning happens in communities and in the natural environment—that the students' and teachers' becoming is relational. This reconfigured notion of subjectivity is captured neatly by Le Grange:[92]

> The subject of sustainability education that is post-anthropocentric is not an atomised individual but is ecological; embedded in the material flows of the earth/cosmos, constitutive of these flows, making the subject imperceptible. Pedagogies that are produced in the classroom are not performed on the earth but bent by the earth—teacher and student/learner become imperceptible and represent a microcosm of the living wholeness of the earth/cosmos. . . . [I]mprovisation could also be expanded to not only be concerned with the human that reverberates from within and is animated, but to include the vibrations of the earth, its flows, rhythms and creative intensities.

It is the ethico-normative distinctiveness of the human, which is consistent with Ubuntu and critical (post)humanism that makes education possible, and in this instance an education in the interest of "cultivating" (post) human sensibilities. Education therefore must be concerned with promoting active lives—lives that will take actions in the interest of social justice, in the

## 54  *Lesley le Grange*

interest of conserving the earth's resources, and that will resist technologies that do not enhance life—and embrace those that do.

## Some Parting Thoughts

The (post)human condition presents particular challenges for society in the twenty-first century, how to reverse the unsustainable course of humanity and how we might think differently about what it is to be human in a technology mediated world. Many of the problems and risks faced by contemporary society such as environmental destruction, wars, xenophobia and genocides are all manifestations of the crisis of Humanism. This crisis gave rise to several critiques of Humanism, collectively called anti-humanism. Anti-humanist strands include the critique of Humanism by anti-colonial phenomenologists, feminist movements, poststructuralists and so forth. More recently we have witnessed a return to realisms such as speculative realism and matter-realism (new materialists) that question the anthropomorphizing of the more-than-human-world and recognise that the human is not only socially and discursively, but also materially constructed. A (re)turn to the mentioned realisms marks a shift from anti-humanism to what might be termed (post)humanism. In this chapter three strands of (post)humanism were reviewed and I argue that one of these, critical (post)humanism, has particular resonances with Ubuntu.

Earlier in the article I noted that there is an emerging new Indigenous paradigm, indicated by the replacement of the small "I" with a capital "I" in the word Indigenous. Scholars such as Wilson[93] argue that to reclaim "Indigenous" is a political move that unites all colonialized peoples, and that recognises the common beliefs, experiences and interests. The move is important because it opens up new ways of thinking about Indigenous education, not as something that is only home grown and occurring in distant rural places. It potentially opens up ways of thinking about Indigenous education in relation to challenges of a contemporary world. The latter is important because we can't turn back the clock, we can't reverse the advancement of new technologies and therefore contemporary challenges need to be viewed as bearers of alternative possibilities. It was with this in mind that resonances between emerging (post)human thought and Ubuntu were explored, as a basis for "cultivating" (post)human sensibilities through education.

In Kappelar's[94] words:

> I do not really wish to conclude and sum up, rounding off the arguments so as to dump it in a nutshell for the reader. A lot more could be said about any of the topics I have touched upon. . . . I have meant to ask questions, to break out of the frame. . . . The point is not a set of answers, but making possible a different practice.

—a different way of viewing Indigenous education.

# Notes

1. See, for example, Linda Tuhiwai Smith, *Decolonising Methodologies: Research and Indigenous Peoples* (London: Zed Books, 1999); Marie Battiste, ed., *Reclaiming Indigenous Voice and Vision* (Vancouver: University of British Columbia Press, 2000); Marie Battiste, *Decolonising Education: Nourishing the Learning Spirit* (Vancouver: University of British Columbia Press, 2013); Catherine A. Odora Hoppers, ed., *Indigenous Knowledge and the Integration of Knowledge Systems: Towards a Philosophy of Articulation* (Claremont: New Africa Books, 2002); Raewyn Cornell, *Southern Theory* (Cambridge: Polity Press, 2007); Shawn Wilson, *Research Is Ceremony: Indigenous Research Methods* (Halifax & Winnipeg: Fernwood Publishing, 2008); Margaret Kovach, *Indigenous Methodologies: Characteristics, Conversations, and Contexts* (Toronto: University of Toronto Press, 2009); Bagele Chilisa, *Indigenous Research Methodologies* (Los Angeles: Sage Publications, 2012); Jean Comaroff and John Comaroff, *Theory from the South: Or, How Euro-America Is Evolving toward Africa* (Boulder: Paradigm Publishers, 2012).
2. Although I have separated it here, for Indigenous peoples knowing and being are not separated. Epistemology is always onto-epistemology.
3. Wilson, *Research Is Ceremony*, 15–16.
4. I distinguish between globalisation (a process that has homogenising effects) and internationalisation that involves cooperation or the building of solidarities as is the case with the internationalisation of Indigenous.
5. Rosi Braidotti, *The Posthuman* (Malden, MA: The Polity Press, 2013).
6. Timothy Morton, *Hyperobjects: Philosophy and Ecology after the End of the World* (Minneapolis, MN: The University of Minnesota Press, 2013), 5.
7. Ecophages are self-reproducing molecular substances that nanotechnology can potentially produce, which will have the capability of gobbling up things.
8. George Sefa Dei, "Rethinking the Role of Indigenous Knowledges in the Academy," *International Journal of Inclusive Education* 4 no. 2 (2000): 113.
9. Ibid.
10. Ibid.
11. Ibid.
12. I use the parenthesis in (post)human because of the ontological oneness of all modes of nature, and because placing the human on a plane of immanence does not deprive the human of its ethico-normative distinctiveness.
13. I refer here to humanism that European Enlightenment gave us.
14. Braidotti, *The Posthuman*, 13.
15. Ibid.
16. René Descartes, *A Discourse on the Method*, trans. Ian Maclean (Oxford: Oxford University Press, 2006), 28.
17. Braidotti, *The Posthuman*, 15.
18. Ibid.
19. Gert Biesta, *Beyond Learning: Democratic Education for a Human Future* (London: Paradigm Publishers, 2006).
20. Bildung is an educational ideal that emerged in Greek society and through its adoption in Roman culture, humanism, neohumanism and the Enlightenment became the central idea of the modern Western educational tradition. It concerns what constitutes an educated or cultivated human being. See Biesta, *Beyond Learning*, 2–3.
21. Ibid.
22. Ibid., 5.
23. According to Hroch, "Human Beings Are Nested Entities, They Are Constituted by Their Habitats." See Petra Hroch, "Deleuze, Guatarri, and Environmental

## 56   Lesley le Grange

Pedagogy and Politics," in *Deleuze & Guattari, Politics and Education*, ed. Matthew Carlin and Jason Wallin (New York: Bloomsbury, 2014), 61.

24. Lesley Le Grange, "Curriculum Research in South Africa," in *International Handbook of Curriculum Research*, 2nd ed., ed. William Pinar (New York: Taylor & Francis, 2014), 272.

25. Lesley Le Grange, "*Currere's* Active Force and the Concept of Ubuntu," in *Understanding the Tasks of Curriculum Theorists: A Global Manifesto*, ed. Nicholas Ng-A-Fook, Awad Ibrahim, William F. Pinar, Bryan Smith, and Christyne Herbert (New York: Palgrave MacMillan, 2017a). Forthcoming.

26. Lesley Le Grange, "Decolonising the University Curriculum," *South African Journal of Higher Education* 30 no. 2 (2016a).

27. Lesley Le Grange, "Sustainability Education and (Curriculum) Improvisation," *Southern African Journal of Environmental Education* 32 (2016b): 33.

28. Ibid., 33.

29. Elizabeth Ellsworth, "Why Doesn't This Feel Empowering? Working through the Repressive Myths of Critical Pedagogy," *Harvard Education Review* 59 no. 3 (1989): 297–324.

30. Brian Deever, "If Not Now, When? Radical Theory and Systematic Curriculum Reform," *Journal of Curriculum Studies* 28 (1996): 171–191.

31. Chet Bowers, "Curriculum as Cultural Reproduction: An Examination of the Metaphor as Carrier of Ideology," *Teachers College Record* 82 no. 2 (1980): 282.

32. Braidotti, *The Posthuman*, 16.

33. Michel Foucault, *The Order of Things* (London: Tavistock Publications, 1970).

34. Braidotti, *The Posthuman*, 23.

35. Levi Byrant, Nick Srnicek, and Graham Harman, "Towards a Speculative Philosophy," in *The Speculative Turn: Continental Materialism and Realism*, ed. Graham Harman, Levi Byrant, and Nick Srnicek (Melbourne: Re Press, 2011), 3.

36. Quentin Meillassoux, *After Finitude: An Essay on the Necessity of Contingency*, trans. Ray Brassier (New York: Continuum, 2008), 5.

37. Diana Coole and Samantha Frost, "Introducing the New Materialisms," in *New Materialisms: Ontology, Agency and Politics*, ed. Diana Coole and Samantha Frost (Durham: Duke University Press), 1–2.

38. Giles Deleuze, *Spinoza: Practical Philosophy*, trans. Robert Hurley (San Francisco: City Light Books, 1988), 124.

39. In this chapter I shall use the term *Ubuntu* which derives from the aphorism '*Umuntu ngumuntu ngabantu*' found in the Nguni languages of Zulu, Xhosa or Ndebele. However, I wish to point out that a similar concept Botho exists in Sotho-Tswana languages derived from the proverbial expression, '*Motho ke motho ka batho babang*'.

40. Michael Battle, "The Ubuntu Theology of Desmond Tutu," in *Archbishop Tutu: Prophetic Witness in South Africa*, ed. Leonard Hulley and Louise Kretzschmar (Cape Town: Human & Rousseau, 1996), 99.

41. The Xhosa people are Bantu language speakers living in the southeast of South Africa. The main tribes of the Xhosa are: Mpondo; Mpondomise; Bonvana; Xesibe; and Thembu. isiXhosa is one of the 11 official languages of South Africa.

42. Thaddeus Metz and Joseph B. R. Gaie, "The African Ethic of Ubuntu/Botho: Implications for Research on Morality," *Journal of Moral Education* 39 no. 3 (2010): 275.

43. Ibid.

44. Ibid.

45. Ibid., 273–290.

46. Penny Enslin and Kai Horsthemke, "Can Ubuntu Provide a Model for Citizenship Education in African Democracies?" (paper presented at the 9th Biennial

The Notion of Ubuntu  57

Conference of the International Network of Philosophers of Education, Madrid: Universidad Complutense, 2004).

47. Shona is the collective name for several groups of people in the east of Zimbabwe and southern Mozambique. The Shona-speaking people are categorised into five main ethnic groups: Zezuru; Manyika; Karanga and Kalanga; Korekore; and Ndau. There are substantial numbers of Shona-speaking people in South Africa and Botswana.

48. Munyardzi F. Murove, "An African Environmental Ethic Based on the Concepts of Ukama and Ubuntu," in *African Ethics: An Anthology of Comparative and Applied Ethics*, ed. Munyaradzi Felix Murove (Pietermaritzburg: University of Kwazulu-Natal Press, 2009), 316.

49. Ibid., 317.

50. Bénézet Bujo, *Foundations of an African Ethic: Beyond the Universal Claims of Western Morality* (New York: The Crossroad Publishing Company, 2001), 22–23.

51. Godfrey B. Tangwa, "Some African Reflections on Biomedical and Environmental Ethics," in *Companion to African Philosophy*, ed. Kwasi Wiredu. (Malden, MA: Blackwell, 2004), 389.

52. Kofi A. Opuku, "African Traditional Religion: An Enduring Heritage," in *Religious Plurality in Africa*, ed. Jacob K. Olupona and Sulayman S. Nyang (Berlin: Mouton de Gruyter, 1993), 77.

53. Magobe B. Ramose, "Ecology through Ubuntu," in *African Ethics: An Anthology of Comparative and Applied Ethics*, ed. Munyaradzi F. Murove (Pietermaritzburg: University of KwaZulu-Natal Press, 2009), 308–309.

54. For a more detailed discussion on Ubuntu, environment and education, see Lesley Le Grange, "Ubuntu, Ukama, Environment and Moral Education," *Journal of Moral Education* 41 no. 3 (2012b); and Lesley Le Grange, "Ubuntu, Ukama and the Healing of Nature, Self and Society," *Educational Philosophy and Theory* 44(Supplement 2) (2012a): 56–57.

55. Braidotti, *The Posthuman*, 37.

56. Martha C. Nussbaum, *Cultivating Humanity: A Classical Defense of Reform in Liberal Education* (Cambridge, MA: Harvard University Press, 1999).

57. Braidotti, *The Posthuman*, 37.

58. Ibid.

59. Ibid., 39.

60. Sarah Franklin, Celia Lury, and Jackie Stacey, *Global Nature, Global Culture* (London: Sage Publications, 2000), 26.

61. Braidotti, *The Posthuman*, 40.

62. Ibid.

63. Nikolas Rose, *The Politics of Life Itself: Biomedicine, Power and Subjectivity in the Twentieth-First Century* (Princeton, NJ: Princeton University Press, 2007).

64. Braidotti, *The Posthuman*, 41.

65. Peter-Paul Verbeek, *Moralizing Technology: Understanding and Designing the Morality of Things* (Chicago, IL: University of Chicago Press, 2011).

66. Braidotti, *The Posthuman*, 42.

67. Ibid.

68. Ibid.

69. Ibid.

70. Ibid., 43.

71. Ibid.

72. Autonomy of technologies relates to the ability of machines to self-correct and reproduce. This is not the same as moralizing technology, which is to give technologies human qualities.

73. Braidotti, *The Posthuman*, 44.

## 58  Lesley le Grange

74. Ibid.
75. Frantz Fanon, *Black Skins, White Masks* (New York: Grove Press, 1967).
76. Aimé Césaire, *Discours Sur Le Colonialism* (Paris: Présence Africaine, 1955).
77. Braidotti, *The Posthuman*, 46.
78. Paul Gilroy, *Against Race: Imaging Political Culture beyond the Colour Line* (Cambridge, MA: Routledge, 2000).
79. Braidotti, *The Posthuman*, 47–48.
80. Maria Mies and Vandana Shiva, *Ecofeminism* (London: Zed Books, 1993).
81. Ramose, "Ecology through Ubuntu," 308.
82. Franklin et al., *Global Nature, Global Culture*.
83. Le Grange, *Ubuntu, Ukama, Environment and Moral Education*, 329–340; Le Grange, *Ubuntu, Ukama and the Healing of Nature*, 56–57; Le Grange, *Currere's Active Force and the Concept of Ubuntu*.
84. Rose, *The Politics of Life Itself*.
85. Verbeek, *Moralizing Technology*.
86. Deleuze, *Spinoza*.
87. For a more detail account, see Lesley Le Grange, "Environmental Education after Sustainability," 93–107.
88. Braidotti, *The Posthuman*.
89. I used "cultivated" and "cultivate" in quotation marks because developing (post)human sensibilities involves an unfolding, a releasing of what is immanent—a releasing of that which exists prior to thought.
90. Keith Ansell-Pearson, *Deleuze and New Materialism: Naturalism, Norms and Ethic*, 2016, accessed March 12, 2017, www.academia.edu/.
91. William Doll, "Seeking a Method-beyond-Method" (keynote presented at the fifth triennial conference of the International Association for the Advancement of Curriculum Studies, University of Ottawa, 2015).
92. Le Grange, "Sustainability Education and (Curriculum) Improvisation," 34.
93. Wilson, *Research is Ceremony*.
94. Susanne Kappeler, *The pornography of Representation* (Cambridge: Polity Press, 1986), 30.

## Bibliography

Ansell-Pearson, Keith. *Deleuze and New Materialism: Naturalism, Norms and Ethics*, 2016. Accessed March 12, 2017. www.academia.edu/.
Battiste, Marie, ed. *Reclaiming Indigenous Voice and Vision*. Vancouver: University of British Columbia Press, 2000.
———. *Decolonising Education: Nourishing the Learning Spirit*. Vancouver: University of British Columbia Press, 2013.
Battle, Michael. "The *Ubuntu* Theology of Desmond Tutu." In *Archbishop Tutu: Prophetic Witness in South Africa*, edited by Leonard Dugmore Hulley and Louise Kretzschmar, 99–100. Cape Town: Human & Rousseau, 1996.
Biesta, Gert. *Beyond Learning: Democratic Education for a Human Future*. London: Paradigm Publishers, 2006.
Bowers, Chet. "Curriculum as Cultural Reproduction: An Examination of the Metaphor as Carrier of Ideology." *Teachers College Record* 82 no. 2 (1980): 267–290.
Braidotti, Rosi. *The Posthuman*. Malden, MA: The Polity Press, 2013.
Bujo, Bénézet. *Foundations of an African Ethic: Beyond the Universal Claims of Western Morality*. New York: The Crossroad Publishing Company, 2001.
Byrant, Levi, Nick Srnicek, and Graham Harman. "Towards a Speculative Philosophy." In *The Speculative Turn: Continental Materialism and Realism*, edited by Graham Harman, Levi Bryant, and Nick Srnicek, 1–18. Melbourne: Re Press, 2011.

Césaire, Aimé. *Discours Sur le Colonialism*. Paris: Présence Africaine, 1955.

Chilisa, Bagele. *Indigenous Research Methodologies*. Los Angeles: Sage Publications, 2012.

Comaroff, Jean and John Comaroff. *Theory from the South: Or, How Euro-America Is Evolving toward Africa*. Boulder: Paradigm Publishers, 2012.

Connell, Raewyn. *Southern Theory*. Cambridge: Polity Press, 2007.

Coole, Diana and Samantha Frost. "Introducing the New Materialisms." In *New Materialisms: Ontology, Agency and Politics*, edited by Diana Coole and Samantha Frost, 1–46. Durham: Duke University Press, 2010.

Deever, Bryan. "If Not Now, When? Radical Theory and Systematic Curriculum Reform." *Journal of Curriculum Studies* 28 (1996): 171–191.

Dei, George J. Sefa. "Rethinking the Role of Indigenous Knowledges in the Academy." *International Journal of Inclusive Education* 4 no. 2 (2000): 111–132.

Deleuze, Gilles. *Spinoza: Practical Philosophy*. Translated by Robert Hurley. San Francisco: City Light Books, 1988.

Descartes, René. *A Discourse on the Method*. Translated by Ian Maclean. Oxford: Oxford University Press, 2006.

Doll, William. "Seeking Method-Beyond-Method." Keynote presented at the Fifth Triennial Conference of the International Association for the Advancement of Curriculum Studies, Ottawa: University of Ottawa, 2015.

Ellsworth, Elizabeth. "Why Doesn't This Feel Empowering? Working Through the Repressive Myths of Critical Pedagogy." *Harvard Educational Review* 59 no. 3 (1989): 297–324.

Enslin, Penny and Kai Horsthemke. "Can *Ubuntu* Provide a Model for Citizenship Education in African Democracies?" Paper presented at the 9th Biennial Conference of the International Network of Philosophers of Education. Madrid: Universidad Complutense, 2004.

Fanon, Frantz. *Black Skins, White Masks*. New York: Grove Press, 1967.

Foucault, Michel. *The Order of Things*. London: Tavistock Publications, 1970.

Franklin, Sarah, Celia Lury, and Jackie Stacey. *Global Nature, Global Culture*. London: Sage Publications, 2000.

Gilroy, Paul. *Against Race: Imaging Political Culture beyond the Colour Line*. Cambridge, MA: Harvard University Press, 2000.

Hroch, Petra. "Deleuze, Guattari, and Environmental Pedagogy and Politics: Ritournelles for a Planet-Yet-to-Come." In *Deleuze & Guattari, Politics and Education*, edited by Matthew Carlin and Jason Wallin, 3–75. New York: Bloomsbury, 2014.

Kappeler, Susanne. *The Pornography of Representation*. Cambridge: Polity Press, 1986.

Kovach, Margaret. *Indigenous Methodologies: Characteristics, Conversations, and Contexts*. Toronto: University of Toronto Press, 2009.

Le Grange, Lesley. "Ubuntu, Ukama and the Healing of Nature, Self and Society." *Educational Philosophy and Theory* 44(Supplement 2) (2012a): 56–67.

———. "Ubuntu, Ukama, Environment and Moral Education." *Journal of Moral Education* 41 no. 3 (2012b): 329–340.

———. "Curriculum Research in South Africa." In *International Handbook of Curriculum Research*, edited by William F. Pinar (2nd ed.), 466–475. New York: Taylor & Francis, 2014.

———. "Decolonising the University Curriculum." *South African Journal of Higher Education* 30 no. 2 (2016a): 1–12.

———. "Sustainability Education and (Curriculum) Improvisation." *Southern African Journal of Environmental Education* 32 (2016b): 26–36.

———. "*Currere's* Active Force and the Concept of Ubuntu." In *Understanding the Tasks of Curriculum Theorists: A Global Manifesto*, edited by Nicholas Ng-A-Fook, Awad Ibrahim, William F. Pinar, Bryan Smith, and Cristyne Herbert. New York: Palgrave MacMillan, 2017a. Forthcoming.

# 60  *Lesley le Grange*

———. "Environmental Education after Sustainability." In *Post-Sustainability: Remaking Education for the Future*, edited by Bob Jickling and Stephen Sterling, 93–107. New York: Palgrave MacMillan Publishers, 2017b.

Meillassoux, Quentin. *After Finitude: An Essay on the Necessity of Contingency*. Translated by Ray Brassier. Continuum: New York, 2008.

Metz, Thaddeus and Joseph B. R. Gaie. "The African Ethic of *Ubuntu/Botho*: Implications for Research on Morality." *Journal of Moral Education* 39 no. 3 (2010): 273–290.

Miles, Maria and Shiva Vandana. *Ecofeminism*. London: Zed Books, 1993.

Morton, Timothy. *Hyperobjects: Philosophy and Ecology after the End of the World*. Minneapolis, MN: The University of Minnesota Press, 2013.

Murove, Munyaradzi Felix. "An African Environmental Ethic Based on the Concepts of *Ukama* and *Ubuntu*." In *African Ethics: An Anthology of Comparative and Applied Ethics*, edited by Munyaradzi Felix Murove, 315–331. Pietermaritzburg: University of Kwazulu-Natal Press, 2009.

Nussbaum, Martha C. *Cultivating Humanity: A Classical Defense of Reform in Liberal Education*. Cambridge, MA: Harvard University Press, 1999.

Odora Hoppers, Catherine Alum, ed. *Indigenous Knowledge and the Integration of Knowledge Systems: Towards a Philosophy of Articulation*. Claremont: New Africa Books, 2002.

Opoku, Kofi Asare. "African Traditional Religion: An Enduring Heritage." In *Religious Plurality in Africa*, edited by Jacob K. Olupona and Sulayman Nyang, 67–82. Berlin: Mouton de Gruyter, 1993.

Ramose, Mogobe B. "Ecology through *Ubuntu*." In *African Ethics: An Anthology of Comparative and Applied Ethics*, edited by Munyaradzi Felix Murove, 308–314. Pietermaritzburg: University of KwaZulu-Natal Press, 2009.

Rose, Nikolas. *The Politics of Life Itself: Biomedicine, Power and Subjectivity in the Twentieth-First Century*. Princeton, NJ: Princeton University Press, 2007.

Santos, Boaventura de Sousa. *Epistemologies of the South: Justice against Epistemicide*. Boulder: Paradigm Publishers, 2014.

Smith, Linda Tuhiwai. *Decolonising Methodologies: Research and Indigenous Peoples*. London: Zed Books, 1999.

Tangwa, Godfrey. "Some African Reflections on Biomedical and Environmental Ethics." In *Companion to African Philosophy*, edited by Kwasi Wiredu, 387–395. Malden, MA: Blackwell, 2004.

Verbeek, Peter-Paul. *Moralizing Technology: Understanding and Designing the Morality of Things*. Chicago, IL: University of Chicago Press, 2011.

Wilson, Shawn. *Research Is Ceremony: Indigenous Research Methods*. Halifax & Winnipeg: Fernwood Publishing, 2008.

# 4 Indigeneity and African Education
## Cultivating Decolonized University Teaching and Learning

*Nuraan Davids and Yusef Waghid*

## Introduction

The question of what education should be for indigenous students, almost necessarily points to a set of other questions. Firstly, what is an indigenous student? Secondly, why would there be a need for an education that speaks specifically to indigenous students? And thirdly, if there is an education that ought to be geared at indigenous students, then should one be speaking about an indigenous education?

In South Africa—the context of this chapter—indigenous knowledge (which is not to be confused with indigenous education) is commonly understood to encompass local, traditional, non-Western beliefs and practices, as well as alternative, informal forms of knowledge.[1] Echoing the informal element of Horsthemke's description, Odora-Hoppers perceives indigenous knowledge as related to something natural, innate to a particular community, and therefore an integral part of culture.[2] From these two descriptions, and others, as suggested by Semali and Kincheloe, it is possible to conceive of indigenous knowledge, as understood in the African context, as being somehow aligned to conceptions of preservation, traditions, innateness, and in contrast to constructions of what it means to be Western—that is, non-indigenous to Africa.[3] But, of course, as already hinted at, while knowledge is necessary for the formation of education, knowledge is not synonymous with education. And while it might be that knowledge of a particular community is necessary to the understanding, and hence preservation of that community and its traditions, or ways of being and doing, that particular kind of knowledge is not to be confused with an education, in or of that particular community. Stated differently, teaching, for instance, involves knowledge of this or that, so that knowledge itself holds or enables the capacity to teach, but this does not mean that the knowledge being taught translates into an education. Of course, it is true, as scholars like Richard Rorty and Gert Biesta point out, that education is used to initiate children into particular traditions and existing ways of being, but it is equally true that education ought not to be about that which is traditional, and hence already known and familiar.[4]

## 62  Nuraan Davids and Yusef Waghid

In this regard, we are especially attracted to Rorty's conception of education as serving to reshape students into new self-images, which they themselves assist in creating. Following on this, we are equally drawn to conceptions of education which recognize and encourage individuation, which, to our minds, produce self-creating individuals through a reliance on criticism. Such an education, as will be discussed in this chapter, might not necessarily be commensurate with particular understandings of indigenous knowledge, which are seemingly focused on the preservation and reclamation of cultural and traditional heritage.[5] It is against this background of agitation between knowledge and education, between indigenously African and indigenously Western that we attempt to deal with the question of whether the education of the incredibly diverse and disparate communities of Africa might be addressed through an advocacy for indigeneity—an educational practice that integrates socialization and individuation. In this chapter, we argue that indigeneity is an educational practice aimed at cultivating, firstly, an integrated conception of African- and non-African-situated knowledges; and, secondly, a practice that evokes human understandings that relate to being reflectively loyal to local and global contexts and, simultaneously, being reflectively open to what is yet to come, more specifically, an unimaginable, fused understanding of knowledge, which integrates both local and global conceptions of knowledge.

## Making Sense of Indigeneity

This chapter departs from the premise that notions of indigeneity and indigenous people are thoroughly relational and situational, and most importantly, inherently and unambiguously political. To Ashcroft, Griffiths and Tiffin, indigeneity is among the most vexed and complex issues in postcolonial theory.[6] The way in which indigeneity intersects with notions of race, marginality, imperialism and identity, explains Ashcroft et al., "leads to a constantly shifting theoretical ground, a ground continually contested and subject to more heated debate than most."[7] Consequently, conceptions of indigeneity in Australia or Canada, for example, are quite different from those in India or Africa.

In examining the North American context, Whyte explains that there are numerous understandings of what indigeneity could mean, which cannot be systematized because they correspond to understandings of tribal identity, which are not necessarily connected to American colonial criteria, or to criteria of a specific indigenous political entity.[8] As such, states Whyte, being indigenous could have to do with being from a particular parentage, which identifies with a particular tribal band, clan or set of families, which are not necessarily constitutive of any political entity and the individuals in them are not formally enrolled.[9] In turn, being indigenous, continues Whyte could stem from being part of an urban community "in which one was identified as Native American by both outsiders based on visual interpretation and/or by others who identify as Native American in relation to their involvement in an urban Indian center."[10] In another example, reported by Alfred and Corntassel, many indigenous people have embraced the Canadian government's label of 'aboriginal', along with the concomitant and limited notion of post-colonial justice framed within the institutional construct of the state. The authors maintain, "this identity is purely a state construction that is instrumental to the state's attempt to gradually subsume Indigenous existences into its own constitutional system and body politic since Canadian independence from Great Britain."[11] Scholars like Alfred and Corntassel, however, are critical of what they describe as "state-imposed conceptions of indigenous identity." To indigenous people, rooted in their own cultures and languages, state-imposed conceptions of supposedly indigenous identity, contend Alfred and Corntassel, are interpreted not as moves towards justice and positive integration, "but as indicators of an on-going colonial assault on their existence, and signs of the fact that they remain, as in earlier colonial eras, occupied peoples who have been dispossessed and disempowered in their own homelands."[12]

Following on the above, Waldron explains that a people may be described as "indigenous" in relation to a certain land or territory, meaning that they are its original inhabitants.[13] Or, sometimes, continues Waldron, the concept is treated as doubly relative, so that a people are called indigenous, firstly in relation to a certain land or territory, and secondly, in relation to some other people, who arrived in the land at a time subsequent to the people now called "indigenous."[14] While, according to Waldron, these two descriptions might be coextensive, it remains necessary to understand the distinction between the two, since indigeneity, conceived as doubly relational, may evoke different claims to indigeneity, understood as original inhabitancy.[15] South Africa, for example, has multiple ethnic tribes, of which the most commonly known are the Zulus, Xhosas, Sothos, Tswanas, Pedis, Vendas, Ndebeles, Tsongas, Swazis and the Pondos. These tribes will lay claim to being the indigenous people of Africa, as they are the true Africans. Yet, others maintain that the San or Bushmen, and the Nama are the only original indigenous people of South Africa. Both the San and the Nama were part of the Khoikhoi, but except for the Nama, the overwhelming majority of the San people are no longer in existence.

Belaboring the contested terrain of the claim to indigeneity in South Africa, is the term "African," particularly, as Higgs points out, when the discussion pertains to "African."[16] In this regard, Ramose explains that, in terms of the interaction and relations between the Greeks and the Romans, on the one hand, and the people of north Africa, on the other hand, it is evident that the name 'Africa' is a description of the Greek and Roman experience, respectively, of the climate of the particular region.[17] It does not, he continues, directly and immediately refer to the inhabitants of the African region and their philosophy. Rather, "It is a description based upon the Roman conquest of 'north Africa'. It is therefore reasonable to infer that the name Africa does not arise from the indigenous conquered inhabitants of the region, let alone the whole continent."[18] To Ramose, therefore, the terms "Africa" and "African" were not conferred by the indigenous people of Africa on themselves.

While the history of African indigeneity has been long, and dates back to the times of ancient Greek explorations, as Masolo brings to our attention, the emergence of the notion of 'indigeneity' in relation to the practice of African philosophy

> has only recently appeared on the academic scene through the historical analysis, or the need for one, to outline the mobility of ideas, schools, and movements of thought in their contribution to the formation of African philosophy as a separate intellectual endeavour.[19]

In addition, Higgs posits:

> the name Africa(n) does not by definition refer to the particular histories of the indigenous peoples inhabiting various parts of the continent from time immemorial. In other words, the term is geographically significant but, historically, its meaning is questionable from the point of view of the indigenous African peoples. Today South Africa is home not only to a host of indigenous people, which include the ‡Khomani San; the Khwe; the !Xun [with the symbols referring to certain clicking sounds]; the Koranna; and the Griquas, as well as the African tribes, but also inhabitants from Malaysian, Indian, and European descent—all of whom might lay claim to being indigenous to South Africa—on the basis of being related to descendants.[20]

Following on the aforementioned discussion, it would appear that whether a people are indigenous or not, is neither juxtaposed against, nor irreconcilable with a people who are non-indigenous. For whatever reason notions of non-indigenous people are uncritically associated with notions of being "Western"—creating the dichotomy, that if a people are not indigenous, then they must be Western. Horsthemke, for example, attaches being indigenous to "nonwestern beliefs, practices, customs and world views."[21] Yet, it is our argument that indigenous has to do with what is contextually relevant, at times, and valuable, to a particular people. To argue that a people are Western, if they are not indigenous, or by implication, that they are indigenous, if they are not Western, does not offer any insight into the ways of understandings of those people. In a similar fashion, the mere association of indigenous knowledge with what is non-Western and grounded in custom and tradition does not justify dismissing such forms of knowledge as indigenous as every and any form of knowledge has a commitment to critical consciousness forged through people's actions and dialogical relations with other human beings.[22] Ocholla, for instance, describes indigenous knowledge as "a dynamic archive of the sum total of knowledge, skills and attitudes belonging to, and practised by, a community over generations, and is expressed in the form of action, objects and sign language for sharing."[23] In turn, Hountondji cautions against people being tempted to "overvalue" their heritage. Such actions, he states, amount to people closing themselves "into the heritage without any critical approach, without any attempt to update and renew the intellectual legacy, in a way that allows a higher degree of rationality and, as a consequence, a steadier march towards efficiency towards self-reliance."[24] Hountondji contends that, if indigenous people are to develop a critical and free relationship to their cultural heritage as well as the exogenous culture, then they would have to rid themselves of the obsession of the "Other."[25] More exactly, he continues, is the realization "that the so-called exogenous culture is, in a way, part and parcel of our heritage today, and we will develop a pluralistic and dynamic view of our heritage, as opposed to static and simplistic approach."[26]

Hence, inasmuch as notions of indigenous people cannot be reduced to non-Western peoples, notions of indigenous knowledge cannot be confined to a pseudo-dichotomous juxtaposition between Western and other forms of knowledge. In relation to indigeneity in Africa, Pelican states that defining "which groups may count as indigenous is much more problematic and controversial, as there are long and ongoing histories of migration, assimilation, and conquest."[27] Furthermore, he continues, "African societies tend to reproduce themselves at their internal frontiers, thus continuously creating and re-creating a dichotomy between original inhabitants and latecomers along which political prerogatives are negotiated."[28] This recurrent process, argues Pelican, does not allow for a permanent and clear-cut distinction of first nations versus dominant societies, as implied by the universal notion of "indigenous peoples."[29] To this end, the multiple and diverse communities one encounters in South Africa—whether Khoikhoi, Zulus, Swazis, Cape Malays, Chinese, Afrikaners or Indians—are all indigenous to that context. It is the particularities, peculiarities and idiosyncrasies of a people which define their indigeneity, and not, as Waldron contends, "original inhabitancy."[30] And indigeneity is certainly not a bifurcation to that which is considered as "Western" or "non-Western." That indigeneity is embedded in intersectional histories and stories of identities, and hence, rights and belonging, offers particular insights into our ensuing argument that it (indigeneity) is at once concerned with the individual, and his or her connectedness and socialization to a particular way of thinking and being, as well as his or her individuation to act and think autonomously.

## Indigenous Knowledge and Education in South Africa

It is possible, state Semali and Kincheloe, to conceive of indigenous knowledge, as understood in the African context, as being somehow aligned to conceptions of preservation, traditions, innateness.[31] Similarly, Odora-Hoppers perceives indigenous knowledge as related to something natural, innate to a particular community, and therefore an integral part of culture.[32] She describes indigenous knowledge as being characterized by its "embeddedness in the cultural web and history of a people including their civilization and forms the backbone of the social, economic, scientific and technological identity of such a people."[33] In this sense, indigenous knowledge, Semali and Kincheloe explain, reflects the dynamic way in which the residents of an area or community have come to understand themselves in relationship to their natural environment, and how they have organized that knowledge to enhance their lives.[34] Further distinguishing indigenous knowledge, according to Maila and Loubser is that it is embedded in the cultural milieu of all people, irrespective of race.[35] What indigenous knowledge hopes to achieve, according to Horsthemke, is "decolonisation of mind; recognition of self-determining development; appropriation; legitimation of indigenous practices" and condemnation of, or at least caution against, "the subjugation of nature and general oppressiveness of non-indigenous rationality, science and technology."[36] As raised by Davids and Waghid, Horsthemke's reference to the "oppressiveness of non-indigenous rationality", however, is concerning in that it seemingly ignores the fact that rationality cannot exist as a non-indigenous entity, since pluralist forms of rationality are in abundance.[37] In this regard, we are especially drawn to Karl Popper's humanist conception of rationality, which he refers to as being connected to an "imaginative intervention" of the human mind.[38] To Popper, to be both imaginative and to intervene, has some relation to what it means for humans to act responsibly, morally and intellectually—that is, to act rationally.[39] When humans act rationally, argues Popper, they "contemplate and adjudicate, and . . . discriminate between, competing theories."[40] To discount, therefore the depth of interpretation and receptivity of indigenous knowledge forms, is to bring into question the capacity of indigenous people to have an "imaginative intervention", and to act rationally.[41]

Offering a more restrained understanding of indigenous knowledge, Masuku-van Damme describes indigenous knowledge as local and traditional because it is constructed in a local context for resolving local challenges in the environment, creating the impression that indigenous knowledge might not be applicable or useful beyond the confines of its particular context.[42] Other scholars like Flavier, De Jesus and Navarro interpret indigenous knowledge or indigenous information systems as "dynamic and continually influenced by internal creativity and experimentation, as well as by contact with external systems."[43] To Flavier et al., indigenous knowledge systems are science that is user-derived, not scientifically derived, and the use of such systems complement and enhance the gains made by modern-day innovations.[44] Yet, as Vilakazi points out, Africa and its myriad communities cannot be excluded from global influences, and neither should Africa be guided only by her past because no civilization (culturally) can manage to develop and prosper in isolation from the "others."[45] In other words, communities, no matter how seeped they might be

*Indigeneity and African Education* 67

in the preservation of particular practices or traditions, cannot withstand "outside" ways of thinking and being.

Consider, for example, the young Xhosa men who have to participate in a boy-to-man initiation ritual, known as *Ulwaluko*. *Ulwaluko* involves young men spending time at traditional initiation schools where they are circumcised and initiated into manhood. Until Xhosa boys undergo this ritual, they are referred to as *amakhwenkwe* (boys), regardless of their age, and as such, are not allowed to participate in particular tribal and cultural practices. In signifying their transition to manhood, the new Xhosa initiates or *amakrwala*, adhere to a strict dress code after initiation for a period of six months. Traditionally, animal skins and animal skin sandals formed an important part of this dress code. Over time, the animal skin became a cloak or a blanket. Today, it is common to see Xhosa initiates wearing a hat, a tailored jacket (suede or tweed), including a silk handkerchief in the top pocket, smart trousers, and a shirt with the top button tied. What happens in relation to this depiction is that the knowledge of a particular indigenous system does not preclude its enactment from being influenced by other ways of being, or in this instance, dressing. Seemingly, the enactment of knowledge, as made visible through particular cultural practices, takes on different forms in relation to those who become the agents of that particular understanding. Knowledge, therefore, whether indigenous or not, is inextricably dyadic or relational.

According to Davids and Waghid—

> the construction of knowledge in relation to culture is dyadically intertwined, that is, inasmuch as knowledge of a community is (re)constructed in relation to their ever-evolving culture, so their culture in turn remains open to the vicissitudes of itself and knowledge system. In other words, human beings are permanently open to life and their thoughts, feelings, curiosity and desires are enveloped in a critical consciousness that gives form to their knowledge.[46]

Likewise, scholars like Alfred and Corntassel argue, "indigenousness is an identity constructed, shaped and lived in the politicized context of contemporary colonialism". In other words, what gives indigenous people their distinctiveness is not the fact that they come from a particular land or community.[47] What distinguishes indigenous people, according to Alfred and Corntassel, is that while they live alongside others in centers of communities and societies, they are in opposition to those centers.[48] To Alfred and Corntassel, "it is this oppositional, place-based existence, along with the consciousness of being in struggle against the dispossessing and demeaning fact of colonization by foreign peoples, that fundamentally distinguishes Indigenous peoples from other peoples of the world."[49]

Significantly, while Alfred and Corntassel describe the living relationship between indigenous communities and the "demeaning fact of colonization

68 *Nuraan Davids and Yusef Waghid*

by foreign peoples of the world" as an "oppositional, place-based existence," the example of the Xhosa initiate wearing the "colonizer's" clothing suggests an assimilatory place-based existence, rather than an "oppositional" one.[50] What we wish to highlight here, is that while we agree with Alfred and Corntassel's description of indigenous people as being dispossessed, and that their existence is to a large extent part lived "as determined acts of survival against colonizing states' efforts to eradicate them culturally, politically and physically," notions of survival should not necessarily be understood as being in opposition to other hegemonies.[51] In other words, the co-existence of indigenous and other communities should not necessarily be couched in a language of opposition, for the simple reason that the dynamics of an indigenous knowledge system is not only made visible through particular cultural practices and rituals, but the indigenous knowledge itself is also given impetus in relation to how it is practiced. As such, knowledge, as an informal experience, has to take shape through formal enactments and manifestations, if that knowledge is to survive. It is for this reason, that scholars like Battiste are critical of reducing conceptions of indigenous knowledge to mere forms of "traditional" knowledge.[52] Representing indigenous knowledge as "traditional," argues Battiste, suggests a body of relatively old data that has been handed down from generation to generation.[53]

To Battiste, indigenous knowledge is far more than the binary opposite of Western knowledge:

> As a concept, indigenous knowledge benchmarks the limitations of Eurocentric theory—its methodology, evidence, and conclusions—reconceptualises the resilience and self-reliance of Indigenous peoples, and underscores the importance of their own philosophies, heritages, and educational processes. Indigenous knowledge fills the ethical and knowledge gaps in Eurocentric education, research, and scholarship. By animating the experiences and voices of the cognitive 'other', and integrating them into the educational process, it creates a new, balanced centre and a fresh vantage point from which to analyse Eurocentric education and its pedagogies.[54]

## Towards a Distinction between Indigenous Knowledge and Indigenous Education

This brings us to our next point, namely that indigenous knowledge should not be construed as indigenous education. While knowledge is necessary for the formation of education, knowledge is not synonymous with education. And while it might be that knowledge of a particular community is necessary to the understanding, and hence preservation of that community and its traditions, or ways of being and doing, that particular kind of knowledge is not to be confused with an education, in or of that particular community. Stated differently, teaching, for instance, involves knowledge of this

*Indigeneity and African Education*  69

or that, so that knowledge itself holds or enables the capacity to teach, but this does not mean that the knowledge being taught translates into an education. It is uncontroversial, pre-philosophically, states Harvey Siegel that "education aims at the imparting of knowledge: students are educated in part so that they may come to *know* things."[55] What students might come to know—whether about this or that—observes Carr, plays a significant role in the social and political spheres of society in relation to inducting learners into the culture, practices and social relationships of their society—indigenous or not.[56] But, it is the educational process itself which determines how that knowledge is understood, and hence enacted. In other words, one might know about this or that—for example, one might know that young Xhosa men are expected to undergo a ritual, known as *Ulwaluko*. Or, one might know that young Zulu women participate in an annual Swazi and Zulu tradition, known as *Umhlanga*, or the Reed Dance. But, unless one is socialized, and beyond, into one that knows about these two traditions, one has not participated in the educational process thereof. Of course, as Biesta argues, the socialization dimension of education has its own risks.[57] While education initiates children and young people into particular traditions and ways of being and doing, continues Biesta, it has shown to work also behind the backs of learners and teachers, for example, in the ways in which education reproduces existing social structures, divisions and inequalities.[58] And hence, to be immersed in indigenous education, or any other form of education, necessarily implies both a commitment and endeavor towards that which is not immediately evident or known. It implies a continuous shift towards that which is yet to be known.

When we consider what an educated individual is, or what education ought to bring out, we are entering into a particular assessment, even judgment. Michael Oakeshott, for example, describes education as both an engagement between two individuals or learners, and what others have said and done.[59] As such, education symbolizes both that which has already occurred and what is already known, as well as that which is yet to be encountered through the "engagement." Oakeshott likens education to a conversation—that is, "an endless unrehearsed intellectual adventure in which, in imagination, we enter into a variety of modes of understanding the world and ourselves."[60] What we can draw from Oakeshott's "variety of modes of understanding the world and ourselves," is that education demands "unrehearsed" encounters with diverse understandings of ways of acting and being. As such, education is unconcerned with predictability or that which is already known; rather, it is immersed in the adventure of the "unrehearsed," and hence, the impulsiveness of being human.

In the previous section, we argued that because indigeneity is located in and shaped by intersectional histories and stories of identities, and hence, rights and belonging, indigeneity is as concerned with the socialization of an individual as it is with his or her individuation—that is, to think, to engage in critical self-reflection, and to reflect upon the world in which he or she

## 70 Nuraan Davids and Yusef Waghid

finds him- or herself. In this sense, the practice of indigeneity covers two simultaneous processes, namely socialization and individuation. As an educational practice, therefore, indigeneity is as concerned with particularities of an individual in relation to a particular context, as it is with recognizing the individual's capacity to think for him- or herself. In this regard, it is up to the individual to decide the extent to which he or she attaches to the particularities of a context or detaches him- or herself from it. This does not mean that the individual has to extract him- or herself from a particular context before he or she might act autonomously. Rather, what indigeneity, as an educational practice, does is to socialize the individual into certain particularities, while simultaneously inviting him or her to reflect on those particularities. Such a practice, in itself, speaks to a certain type of introduction or initiation, which cultivates within the individual or learner a curiosity to reflect upon that into which he or she has been socialized, while also looking towards that which is not immediately evident. At this point, we are reminded of R. S. Peters's seminal ideas on initiation, in which he argues that education is a human activity whereby an individual is initiated into "something worthwhile," on the grounds that the individual is committed to the human activity of education.[61]

Now that we have shown that notions of knowledge are not necessarily reconcilable with what it means to be educated, we turn our attention to Richard Rorty's argument of education as serving to reshape students into new self-images, which they themselves assist in creating.[62]

## Indigenous Education in Relation to Socialization and Individuation

In his essay, "Education as socialization and individualization," Richard Rorty suggests that the conservative political right and radical left are in agreement conceptually that while both accept "the identification of truth and freedom with the essentially human," they seemingly discount that education involves two distinct and interrelated processes.[63] To Rorty, the term "education" covers two entirely distinct, and equally necessary, processes— socialization and individuation. Because he describes the two processes as "entirely distinct," he refers to the first phase of education as socialization, or acculturation, and to the second phase, as individuation or edification.[64] He explains,

> There is only the shaping of an animal into a human being by a process of socialization, followed (with luck) by the self-individualization and self-creation of that human being through his or her own later revolt against that very process.[65]

Following on this, Peters and Ghiraldelli explain that the idea developed by Rorty is that, given the choice between freedom and truth, the Left is

# Indigeneity and African Education   71

right in seeking truth.[66] However, this does not mean that the Left should not assume that freedom is an element of "human essence."[67] According to Peters and Ghiraldelli,

> If education is socialization and individualization, and socialization is the moment of acceptance of consensus, and individualization is the moment of freedom and scepticism based on such consensus, the teachers could use the first moment to help the second moment.[68]

First, when students are initiated into the inherited discourses (that is, traditions, culture, language and ethical conduct) of a given community, they are said to be socialized without having to challenge or take into critical scrutiny what such discourses have to offer. Becoming socialized within existing traditions of thought and practice implies that students are educated on account of their initiation into modes of action that constitute communal norms and practices. For instance, being socialized into African communal practices, such as norms and traditions of African cultures, is a matter of being educated with what can be considered as indigenous to such practices. The point we are making, is that socialization is a form of education that envelops practices of indigenization. In the main, to be socialized within what is constitutive of a particular community is to be indigenized, and, by implication to be educated in light of the inherited traditions of a community.

Second, education, argues Rorty is also connected to a process of individuation. To be individuated into a discourse of particular communities provokes people to question and challenge the thoughts and practices with which they are confronted and within which they are immersed.[69] It is not enough for students merely to experience socialization uncritically. They should also be subjected to processes of criticality and deep questioning whereby they take into controversy the assumptions and prejudices of communal norms and practices. Thus, to be individuated into a particular communal discourse is to learn to put into question that with which one is confronted and to show dissent through contesting the assumptions of a particular communal discourse. For instance, when Africans are socialized with an inherited norm of offering *lobola*—that is, a marriage gift—to newly wedded brides, the contestation of the extravagance associated with such a wedding gift could be questioned by those who have been individuated into the traditional practice. And, when people begin to challenge and subvert the thoughts and practices into which they have been initiated, they have been individuated and hence, educated. The point is, indigenization implies that people have become critical about their understandings without just accepting things at face value.

Following on our arguments that education is an inter-threaded process of socialization and individuation, it becomes apparent, as Noaparast points out, that, perhaps, the dichotomies, which Rorty draws between socialization

72  *Nuraan Davids and Yusef Waghid*

(or acculturation) and individuation (or edification), might, in fact, be unnecessary.[70] Smeyers and Burbules (2006, 442), for instance, maintain—

> Because humans are cultural beings whose use of concepts presupposes a prereflective familiarity, a context of cultural practices is necessary even to communicate and interact with each other—one cannot not be initiated into such practices, for this would imply the lack of any human relationship at all. Yet such essential practices are learned foremost by doing rather than by teaching.[71]

Practice, according to Smeyers and Burbules, offers important insight into understanding education: Another dimension of the relationship that a practice encourages or discourages through different ways of learning or enacting, is how a practice is intertwined with oneself and one's sense of identity, on the one hand, and our relationships and ways of interacting with other people, on the other hand. Here, the way we identify with particular practices, and to which extent, are at stake. Some practices thrive on the possibility of multiple or alternative identities; others exemplify and enforce a more static identity. In both cases, our relationships with others and with ourselves will be changed. Practices transform the self, but at the same time, there may be subversions of a practice that give opportunities to the self. This account is intended to strike a balance between an excessive boundlessness and an inherent conservatism. Sometimes the way the practice is enacted encourages a particular "interpretation;" sometimes it helps to distance oneself from it. As practices have the potential to deepen one's engagement with them, they clearly have educational relevance and potential. As modes of engagement, it becomes clear how central they are for education. What for one person is a practice may for someone else merely be a ritual. Whereas practices are those traditions that are enacted with some understanding, rituals are merely ways of uncritical doing. At the heart is the issue of how practices are reproduced and sustained over a period of time.[72]

Following on the above, Noaparast states that the narrative comes to play an important role in interpreting practice because some narratives can provide one with a more critical and reflective relationship to practice.[73] To Smeyers and Burbules, there are those

> narratives that can give rise to a more critical or reflective relation to a practice"—that is, "education about a practice", rather than simply "education into a practice"—and how these can "revitalize practices and promote a more liberating relation to them.[74]

Smeyers and Burbules contend that

> processes of narrativization create the possibility of framing practices in relatively static or dynamic terms; they can influence who gets to

# Indigeneity and African Education   73

adjudicate or interpret the rules (implicit or explicit) of a practice—and who gets to propose new rules or norms.[75]

Furthermore, continue Smeyers and Burbules, these

> processes of narrativization play a crucial role in how one views the practice itself: whether, on the one hand, they are viewed as historical, cultural constructs and conventions, or whether, on the other hand, they are seen as necessary, natural, inevitable—and hence as unquestionable.[76]

The upshot of the non-bifurcationist relationship between socialization and individuation as different forms of education that happen during different stages in people's lives is connected to what they experience as indigenous education. The point is, indigenous education is linked to both socialization and individuation and not necessarily related to the specific location in which such educational experiences unfold. Put differently, for us, indigenous education is not merely about validating and utilizing relevant knowledge from local people's cultural histories as Asebere-Ameyaw, Anamuah-Mensah, Sefa Dei and Raheem would argue.[77] Rather, indigenous education involves practicing socialization and individuation in relation to traditions, cultural histories and scientific knowledge of various (African) communities. That is, when Africans assert their own representations of identity, history, culture sense of self, community and social interdependence of local and global forms of knowledge on the basis of socialization and individuation, they engage in indigenous education. It seems rather parochial to associate indigenous education exclusively with understandings of knowledge situated locally as education in itself involves humans engaging with one another on account of their contextual and epistemological embeddedness. In this sense, speaking about indigenous education and merely foregrounding local peoples' agency in relation to their communal activities is an implausible idea. Instead, indigenous education integrates local and global understandings of knowledge when humans exercise their creativity, imagination, ingenuity and resourcefulness vis-à-vis socialization and individuation.

Now that we have given an account of indigenous education, as enframed by socialization and individuation, it would be apposite to ascertain why and how such a form of education can be considered a way to decolonize education on the African continent.

## Decolonizing African Education through Indigeneity

Undeniably the global hegemonic agenda of colonization on the African continent has stripped local people's agency, their power of imagination and their ability to design their own futures because "Western" scientific knowledge has been perceived as the only legitimate science worthy of pursuit.[78] Together with the imposition of colonized knowledge systems on Africa's peoples was an erroneous presumption that by far the majority of Africans are powerless, exploited, oppressed and uneducated.[79] And, if global hegemony were to hold sway on the African continent, the peoples of Africa had to be denied their legitimate rights to assert their own representations of culture, identity and history. In this way, colonization was aimed at curtailing indigenous human agency—that is, African peoples' needs and aspirations and their sense of individual and collective autonomy constituted in Africa's "cultural knowledge[s] and . . . rich legacies of intellectual tradition."[80]

In our view, colonization could not have been an authentic educational strategy as it excluded the knowledges, life experiences and intellectual pursuits of Africa's peoples. How could colonization have been perceived as an educational agenda, if education is constituted in the first place within the local and global life experiences of people? Any form of education is constituted by people's knowledge, experiences and other aspects of their social, economic, ideological and political connectedness to what is considered as indigenous, and by implication of relevance to their life worlds. The point is colonization only advanced the life worlds and expectations of dominant imperialist powers at the exclusion and denial of localized and context-specific knowledges. What followed was that education on the African continent was prejudiced towards a global "Western" perspective that was oblivious about indigenous human aspirations related to the African continent. Considering that African education has been subjected to colonialism, the possibility of an authentic form of education functioning on the continent was always contestable. How could African education have functioned authentically if colonialism disrupted the potential engagement of different peoples with one another's self-understandings? The very act of invoking human self-understandings in relational situations is an educational discourse. And, when legitimate participants are already excluded beforehand, the possibility for any credible form of human engagement would not be forthcoming. Such a situation, as has been the case with colonial education, has been overtly exclusionary and, therefore, could not have been considered a credible educational discourse.

The question is: how can indigeneity, as educational practice, contribute towards enhancing a decolonized education discourse? Indigeneity, following Kwase Wiredu, offers two action procedures. First, African thought should be divested from modes of conceptualization which emanate from the colonial past that cannot withstand rigorous critical reflection.[81] In other words, not everything and every concept that has a colonial provenance should be repudiated for that in itself would deny other modes of thought from being considered equally and in relation to indigenous thoughts. Second, integration of human understandings, whether indigenously African or indigenously European, should be considered equally and if of relevance to African education, should be examined critically and collectively. That is, everything "Western" cannot be deemed irrelevant to African education. Rather, indigeneity advocates for the examination of a fused Afro-European notion of education of relevance to Africa's local communities. Decolonizing African indigeneity through education calls for a re-assertion of the self—one in which the individual critically reflects on his or her own identity and practices in relation to others, and narrates his or her own story, not through the lenses and experiences of others, but through his or her understandings. In this sense, a decolonized education has less to do with re-designing curricula, or with the question of what education should be for indigenous students, or not. A decolonized education has to do with, and is connected to an "imaginative intervention" of the human mind.[82] As an "imaginative intervention," a decolonized education implies acting humanely, responsibly, morally and rationally. Next we analyze how a fused understanding of knowledge can affect pedagogic encounters in African university classrooms.

## Conclusion: towards Indigeneity and Its Implications for Teaching and Learning

Earlier we have argued that a demand for indigeneity is always implicitly connected to the cultivation of socialization and individuation. Africans cannot lay claim to indigeneity without intrinsically making a case for an initiation into processes of socialization and individuation. To be initiated into inherited traditions, beliefs, values and cultures of an African community, and subsequently to be individuated into such communal discourses is tantamount to practicing indigeneity. Such a view of indigeneity—one constituted and guided by socialization and individuation—construes university teaching and learning in reasonably distinctive ways. We now examine three ways in which indigeneity potentially guides university teaching and learning.

First, attuned to an intertwined relationship between socialization and individuation, indigeneity requires that teaching and learning be enacted critically. To develop critical attitudes through teaching and learning requires of one to look at things discerningly and intuitively—that is, critically. The point about discernment and intuition involves looking at things with care and the possibility that one would be able to imagine things as if they could be otherwise. For instance, teaching with care requires that one connects with students in ways that one has perhaps not thought about previously— what Maxine Greene refers to as "teaching with imagination whereby students make their own attempts to interpret the significance of their learning such as for them to take initiatives, and move thoughtfully (intelligently) in the direction of new openings and possibilities."[83]

Second, indigeneity requires that teachers and students examine local understandings vis-à-vis global understandings of concepts and practices. This means that those teachers and students enacting on indigeneity do not simply abandon one set of beliefs and traditions for another. Rather, they bring such divergent understandings in proximity to one another and then ascertain how such concepts and practices cohere, diverge or become attached or detached from one another. Put differently, teachers and students act disruptively whereby they "carve a space in which we [they] [teachers and students] can break peculiar silences and choose."[84] In this way, teaching and learning become disruptive in the sense that teachers and students stimulated by their interest to engender indigeneity become attentive and vigilant as they proceed to open up pedagogical spaces that would provoke one another to experience moments of recognition (attachment) and moments of doubt (detachment).

Third, indigeneity also provokes teachers and students to engage in pedagogic encounters on the basis of a reflexive loyalty to the known (that is, African ways of thinking, acting and being) fused with a reflective openness to the new.[85] Being reflectively loyal to the known implies that teachers and students would honor that with which they are familiar in such a way that they subject their "known" understandings to conjecture, argumentation and refutation. This implies that teaching and learning ought to unfold deliberatively, which requires a willingness to wait and see, a capacity to listen and a desire to understand otherness, which is crucial to the practice of indigeneity.[86] And to be reflectively open to the new implies that potentially fused understandings of local and global knowledges or perhaps aspects thereof would be prioritized as pedagogic spaces underscored by meanings that come into the world—that is, teachers and students develop a sense grasping inconclusive truths that remain subjected to change. In the end, indigeneity is an educational practice that is intrinsically linked to cultivating socialization and individuation. And, enacting indigeneity occurs along at least three practices: criticality, diversity and reflexivity. By implication any talk of indigeneity ought to be open to critical, diverse and reflexive understandings and or reconceptualizations of educational practices.

## Notes

1. Kai Horsthemke, "'Indigenous Knowledge': Conceptions and Misconceptions," *Journal of Education* 32 (2004): 32–33.
2. Catherine Alum Odora-Hoppers, "Indigenous Knowledge and the Integration of Knowledge Systems: Towards a Conceptual and Methodological Framework," in *Indigenous Knowledge and the Integration of Knowledge Systems: Towards a Philosophy of Articulation*, ed. Catherine Alum Odora-Hoppers (Claremont: New Africa Books, 2002), 8.
3. Ladislaus Semali and Joe L. Kincheloe, "What Is Indigenous Knowledge and Why Should We Study It?," in *What Is Indigenous Knowledge? Voices from the Academy*, ed. Ladislaus M. Semali and Joe L. Kincheloe (New York: Falmer Press, 1999), 5.
4. Richard Rorty, *Philosophy and Social Hope* (London: Penguin Books, 1999).
5. Ibid.

## Indigeneity and African Education    77

6. Bill Ashcroft, Gareth Griffiths, and Helen Tiffin, *The Post-Colonial Studies Reader* (London: Routledge, 1995), 213.
7. Ibid.
8. Kyle P. Whyte, "Indigeneity and US Settler Colonialism," in *Oxford Handbook of Philosophy and Race*, ed. Naomi Zack (Oxford: Oxford University Press, 2016), 95.
9. Ibid.
10. Ibid.
11. Taiaiake Alfred and Jeff Corntassel, "Being Indigenous: Resurgences against Contemporary Colonialism," *Government and Opposition* 40 no. 4 (2005): 598.
12. Ibid.
13. Jeremy Waldron, "Indigeneity? First Peoples and Last Occupancy," *New Zealand Journal of Public Law* 1 no. 1 (2003): 62.
14. Ibid.
15. Ibid., 63.
16. Philip Higgs, "African Philosophy and the Decolonisation of Education in Africa: Some Critical Reflections," *Educational Philosophy and Theory* 44 no. 2 (2012): 39.
17. Mogobe B. Ramose, "I Doubt, Therefore African Philosophy Exists," *South African Journal of Philosophy* 22 no. 2 (2003): 114.
18. Ibid.
19. Dismis A. Masolo, "Philosophy and Indigenous Knowledge: An African Perspective," *Africa Today* 50 no. 2 (2003): 25.
20. Higgs, "African Philosophy," 40.
21. Horsthemke, "'Indigenous Knowledge'," 32–33.
22. Nuraan Davids and Yusef Waghid, "Beyond the Indigenous/Non-Indigenous Knowledge Divide: The Case of Muslim Education and Its Attenuation to Cosmopolitanism," *South African Journal of Higher Education* 28 no. 5 (2014).
23. Dennis N. Ocholla, "Marginalised Knowledge: An Agenda for Indigenous Knowledge Development and Integration with Other Forms of Knowledge," *International Review of Information Ethics* 7 (2007): 1.
24. Paulin J. Hountondji, "Knowledge Appropriation in a Post-Colonial Context," in *Indigenous Knowledge*, ed. Catherine Alum Odora-Hoppers (Claremont: New Africa Books, 2002), 25.
25. Ibid.
26. Ibid., 25–26.
27. Michaela Pelican, "Complexities of Indigeneity and Autochthony: An African Example," *American Ethnologist* 36 no. 1 (2009): 56.
28. Ibid.
29. Ibid.
30. Jeremy Waldron, "Indigeneity? First Peoples and Last Occupancy," *New Zealand Journal of Public Law* 1 no. 1 (2003): 62.
31. Semali and Kincheloe, *What Is Indigenous Knowledge*.
32. Odora-Hoppers, "Indigenous Knowledge,", 8.
33. Catherine Alum Odora-Hoppers, *Indigenous Knowledge and the Integration of Knowledge Systems: Towards a Conceptual and Methodological Framework* (Pretoria: HSRC Press, 2001), 4.
34. Semali and Kincheloe, *What Is Indigenous Knowledge*, 3.
35. Mago W. Maila and Carl Pauw Loubser, "Emancipatory Indigenous Knowledge Systems: Implications for Environmental Education in South Africa," *South African Journal of Education* 23 no. 4 (2003): 276.
36. Horsthemke, "'Indigenous Knowledge'," 33.
37. See: Davids and Waghid, "Beyond the Indigenous," 1488; Horsthemke, "'Indigenous Knowledge',".

38. Karl Popper, *Conjectures and Refutations* (London: Routledge, 1963), 515.
39. Ibid., 516.
40. Ibid.
41. Ibid.
42. Lynette Masuku-van Damme, "Indigenous Knowledge within Environmental Education Processes," *EnviroInfo* (1997).
43. Juan Manuel Flavier, Antonio De Jesus, and Conrado S. Navarro, "Regional Program for the Promotion of Indigenous Knowledge in Asia," in *The Cultural Dimension of Development: Indigenous Knowledge Systems*, ed. Dennis M. Warren, David Brokensha, and Leendert J. Slikkerveer. (London: SRP, 1999), 479.
44. Ibid.
45. Herbert W. Vilakazi, "The Problem of African Universities," in *African Renaissance*, ed. Malegapuro William (Cape Town: Mafube-Tafelberg, 1999), 203.
46. Davids and Waghid, "Beyond the Indigenous," 1486–1487.
47. Alfred and Corntassel, "Being Indigenous: Resurgences," 597.
48. Ibid.
49. Ibid.
50. Ibid.
51. Ibid.
52. Marie Ann Battiste, "Indigenous Knowledge and Pedagogy in First Nations Education: A Literature Review and Recommendations" (prepared for the National Working Group on Education and the Minister of Indian Affairs, Ottawa: Indian and Northern Affairs, 2002), 10.
53. Ibid.
54. Ibid., 5.
55. Harvey Siegel, "Knowledge, Truth and Education," in *Education, Knowledge and Truth: Beyond the Postmodern Impasse*, ed. David Carr (London: Routledge, 1998), 20.
56. Wilfred Carr, "The Curriculum in and for a Democratic Society," *Curriculum Studies* 6 no. 3 (1998): 325.
57. Gert Biesta, "What Is Education for? On Good Education, Teacher Judgement, and Educational Professionalism," *European Journal of Education* 50 no. 1 (2015): 77.
58. Ibid.
59. Michael Oakeshott, *Experience and Its Modes* (Cambridge: University of Cambridge Press, 2010).
60. Ibid., 28.
61. Richard S. Peters, *Ethics and Education* (London: George Allen & Unwin, 1966).
62. Rorty, *Philosophy and Social Hope*.
63. Ibid., 122.
64. Ibid.
65. Ibid., 117.
66. Michael A. Peters and Paulo Ghiraldelli, *Richard Rorty: Education, Philosophy, and Politics* (Maryland: Rowan and Littlefield, 2001), 10.
67. Ibid.
68. Ibid.
69. Rorty, *Philosophy and Social Hope*.
70. Khosrow Bagheri Noaparast, "Richard Rorty's Conception of Philosophy of Education," *Educational Theory* 64 no. 1 (2014): 90.
71. Paulus Smeyers and Nicholas Burbules, "Education as Initiation into Practices," *Educational Theory* 56 no. 4 (2006): 442.
72. Ibid., 448–449.

*Indigeneity and African Education* 79

73. Noaparast, "Richard Rorty's Conception," 96.
74. Smeyers and Burbules, "Education as Initiation into Practices."
75. Ibid., 449.
76. Ibid.
77. Akwasi Asebere-Ameyaw, Jophus Anamuah-Mensah, George J. Sefa Dei, and Kolawole Raheem, *Indigenist African Development and Related Issues: Towards a Transdisciplinary Perspective* (Rotterdam: Sense, 2014), 4.
78. George J. Sefa Dei, *Teaching Africa: Towards a Transgressive Pedagogy* (New York: Springer, 2010).
79. Asebere-Ameyaw et al., *Indigenist African Development*, 11.
80. Ibid., 1.
81. Kwasi Wiredu, "Truth and the Akan Language," in *African Philosophy: An Akan Collection*, ed. Safro Kwame (Lanham: University Press of America, 1995), 15.
82. Popper, *Conjectures and Refutations*, 516.
83. Maxine Greene, *Releasing the Imagination: Essays on Education, the Arts, and Social Change* (San Francisco: Jossey-Bass, 1995), 14.
84. Ibid., 117.
85. David Hansen, *The Teacher and the World: A Study of Cosmopolitanism as Education* (London: Routledge, 2011), 86.
86. Ibid., 23.

## Bibliography

Alfred, Taiaiake and Jeff Corntassel. "Being Indigenous: Resurgences against Contemporary Colonialism." *Government and Opposition* 40 no. 4 (2005): 597–614.

Asebere-Ameyaw, Akwasi, Jophus Anamuah-Mensah, George J. Sefa Dei, and Kolawole Raheem. *Indigenist African Development and Related Issues: Towards a Transdisciplinary Perspective*. Rotterdam: Sense, 2014.

Ashcroft, Bill, Gareth Griffiths, and Helen Tiffin. *The Post-Colonial Studies Reader*. New York: Routledge, 1995.

Battiste, Marie Ann. "Indigenous Knowledge and Pedagogy in First Nations Education: A Literature Review and Recommendations." Prepared for the National Working Group on Education and the Minister of Indian Affairs. Ottawa: Indian and Northern Affairs, 2002.

Biesta, Gert. "What Is Education for? On Good Education, Teacher Judgement, and Educational Professionalism." *European Journal of Education* 50 no. 1 (2015): 75–87.

Carr, Wilfred. "The Curriculum in and for a Democratic Society." *Curriculum Studies* 6 no. 3 (1998): 323–340.

Davids, Nuraan and Yusef Waghid. "Beyond the Indigenous/Non-Indigenous Knowledge Divide: The Case of Muslim Education and Its Attenuation to Cosmopolitanism." *South African Journal of Higher Education* 28 no. 5 (2014): 1485–1496.

Flavier, Juan Manuel, Antonio De Jesus, and Conrado S. Navarro. "Regional Program for the Promotion of Indigenous Knowledge in Asia." In *The Cultural Dimension of Development: Indigenous Knowledge Systems*, edited by Dennis M. Warren, David Brokensha, and Leendert J. Slikkerveer, 479–493. London: SRP, 1999.

Greene, Maxine. *Releasing the Imagination: Essays on Education, the Arts, and Social Change*. San Francisco: Jossey-Bass, 1995.

Hansen, David. *The Teacher and the World: A Study of Cosmopolitanism as Education*. London: Routledge, 2011.

Higgs, Philip. "African Philosophy and the Decolonisation of Education in Africa: Some Critical Reflections." *Educational Philosophy and Theory* 44 no. 2 (2012): 37–55.

Horsthemke, Kai. "'Indigenous Knowledge': Conceptions and Misconceptions." *Journal of Education* 32 (2004): 31–48.

Hountondji, Paulin J. "Knowledge Appropriation in a Post-Colonial Context." In *Indigenous Knowledge and the Integration of Knowledge Systems: Towards a Philosophy of Articulation*, edited by Catherine Alum Odora Hoppers, 23–38. Claremont: New Africa Books, 2002.

Maila, Maila W. and Carl Pauw Loubser. "Emancipatory Indigenous Knowledge Systems: Implications for Environmental Education in South Africa." *South African Journal of Education* 23 no. 4 (2003): 276–288.

Masolo, Dismis A. "Philosophy and Indigenous Knowledge: An African Perspective." *Africa Today* 50 no. 2 (2003): 21–38.

Masuku-van Damme, Lynette. "Indigenous Knowledge within Environmental Education Processes." *EnviroInfo* (1997): 26–28.

Noaparast, Khoswow Bagheri. "Richard Rorty's Conception of Philosophy of Education." *Educational Theory* 64 no. 1 (2014): 75–98.

Oakeshott, Michael. *Experience and Its Modes*. Cambridge: University of Cambridge Press, 2010.

Ocholla, Dennis N. "Marginalised Knowledge: An Agenda for Indigenous Knowledge Development and Integration with Other Forms of Knowledge." *International Review of Information Ethics* 7 (2007): 1–10.

Odora-Hoppers, Catherine Alum. *Indigenous Knowledge and the Integration of Knowledge Systems: Towards a Conceptual and Methodological Framework*. Pretoria: HSRC Press, 2001.

———. "Indigenous Knowledge and the Integration of Knowledge Systems: Towards a Conceptual and Methodological Framework." In *Indigenous Knowledge and the Integration of Knowledge Systems: Towards a Philosophy of Articulation*, edited by Catherine Alum Odora-Hoppers, 2–22. Claremont: New Africa Book, 2002.

Pelican, Michaela. "Complexities of Indigeneity and Autochthony: An African Example." *American Ethnologist* 36 no. 1 (2009): 52–65.

Peters, Michael A. and Paulo Ghiraldelli, eds. *Richard Rorty: Education, Philosophy, and Politics*. Maryland: Rowan and Littlefield, 2001.

Peters, Richard S. *Ethics and Education*. London: George Allen & Unwin, 1966.

Popper, Karl. *Conjectures and Refutations*. London: Routledge, 1963.

Ramose, Mogobe B. "I Doubt, Therefore African Philosophy Exists." *South African Journal of Philosophy* 22 no. 2 (2003): 110–121.

Rorty, Richard. *Philosophy and Social Hope*. London: Penguin Books, 1999.

Sefa Dei, George J. *Teaching Africa: Towards a Transgressive Pedagogy*. New York: Springer, 2010.

Semali, Ladislaus M. and Joe L. Kincheloe. "What Is Indigenous Knowledge and Why Should We Study It?" In *What Is Indigenous Knowledge? Voices from the Academy*, edited by Ladislaus M. Semali and Joe L. Kincheloe, 3–58. New York: Falmer Press, 1999.

Siegel, Harvey. "Knowledge, Truth and Education." In *Education, Knowledge and Truth: Beyond the Postmodern Impasse*, edited by David Carr, 19–36. London: Routledge, 1998.

Smeyers, Paulus and Nicholas Burbules. "Education as Initiation into Practices." *Educational Theory* 56 no. 4 (2006): 439–449.

Vilakazi, Herbert W. "The Problem of African Universities." In *African Renaissance*, edited by Malegapuro William Makgoba, 37–51. Cape Town: Mafube-Tafelberg, 1999.

Waldron, Jeremy. "Indigeneity? First Peoples and Last Occupancy." *New Zealand Journal of Public Law* 1 no. 1 (2003): 55–82.

Whyte, Kyle P. "Indigeneity and US Settler Colonialism." In *Oxford Handbook of Philosophy and Race*, edited by Naomi Zack, 91–101. Oxford: Oxford University Press, 2016.

Wiredu, Kwasi. "Truth and the Akan Language." In *African Philosophy: An Akan Collection*, edited by Safro Kwame, 125–145. Lanham: University Press of America, 1995.

# 5 The Deaf as an Indigenous Community

## Philosophical Considerations

*Timothy Reagan*

Recently, studies of deafness have adopted more complex sociocultural perspectives, raising issues of community identity, formation and maintenance, and language ideology. Anthropological researchers have approached the study of d/Deaf communities from at least three useful angles. The first, focusing on the history of these communities, demonstrates that the current issues have roots in the past, including the central role of education in the creation and maintenance of communities. A second approach centers on emic perspectives, drawing on the voices of community members themselves and accounts of ethnographers. A third perspective studies linguistic issues and how particular linguistic issues involving deaf people articulate with those of their hearing societies.[1]

There has been a growing international recognition that Deaf[2] people constitute a unique linguistic and cultural community.[3] Deaf people perceive themselves as fundamentally different from the hearing population around them, utilize signed languages as their vernacular languages,[4] and operate within a distinctive culture, in English typically called the "Deaf culture," but in American Sign Language (ASL),[5] signed the DEAF-WORLD.[6] At the same time, they live surrounded by hearing people,[7] and are educated in and served by institutions designed, managed and staffed by hearing people.[8] Further, since most Deaf people have hearing parents,[9] both the language and culture of the DEAF-WORLD are largely transmitted *intragenerationally* rather than *intergenationally*. This "sociocultural" view of d/Deafness can be contrasted with the common medical and pathological view most typically found in the hearing world. It is thus hardly surprising that the hearing world and DEAF-WORLD often come into conflict, a conflict that Deaf people see as evidence of the rejection of their worldview and the domination of their world by the dominant hearing world's perspective of "deafness as disability."[10] The difference between the two ways of thinking about d/Deafness is neither a minor nor a trivial one; it is fundamental to how d/Deafness is conceived, what it means to be d/Deaf, and how and by whom decisions should be made about d/Deafness educationally, medically and socially. At the heart of the sociocultural conception of the

## The Deaf as an Indigenous Community    83

DEAF-WORLD is the rejection of an audiological view of deafness, the idea that "Deafness is not merely the absence of hearing."[11] Thus, it also entails a rejection of efforts to "remediate" or "cure" deafness.[12] As Lane, Hoffmeister and Bahan note,

> when hearing people think about Deaf people, they project their ... subtractive perspective onto Deaf people. The result is an inevitable collision with the values of the DEAF-WORLD, whose goal is to promote the unique heritage of Deaf language and culture. The disparity in decision-making power between the hearing world and the DEAF-WORLD renders this collision frightening for Deaf people.[13]

One interesting example that makes clear this fundamental distinction is the way in which "hard of hearing" is understood: in English, the phrase "*very* hard of hearing" refers to individuals who have *little* residual hearing, while in ASL to say that a person is VERY HARD-OF-HEARING is to indicate that s/he has *substantial* residual hearing. The key difference here is in what the speaker assumes to be normative: for hearing people, being able to hear is the fundamental baseline by which "normal" is evaluated, while for the Deaf, it is d/Deafness that is the normative baseline.[14] Nor do Deaf people see themselves simply as a *distinctive* cultural and linguistic community; they are also aware of their community and language as historically dominated, marginalized, and oppressed.[15]

A common misunderstanding about the signed languages is the belief that "sign language" is in some sense universal,[16] with Deaf people around the world sharing a single sign language. Not only is this not the case, but hundreds of different signed languages have been documented;[17] Skutnabb-Kangas has suggested that "there probably are something between 6,500 and 10,000 spoken (oral) languages in the world, and a number of sign languages which can be equally large."[18] Although this claim is almost certainly hyperbolic, her fundamental claim is valid: there are almost certainly a substantial number of signed languages about which we are completely ignorant. These signed languages are, for the most part, different and distinct languages, although it is true that many share certain generic features (such as their gestural and visual nature, their use of space for linguistic purposes, etc.), and some are genetically related to others (just as there are spoken language families, so too are there sign language families).[19] Finally, there has been extensive and detailed linguistic research on a few signed languages (especially ASL,[20] Australian Sign Language,[21] and British Sign Language[22]—each of which has a distinctive phonology, vocabulary, and syntax), and considerable linguistic research on many others.[23] Finally, for many lesser-known signed languages, we have limited information and evidence, albeit often anecdotal.[24] Many signed languages are being used in deaf education programs, others have received some degree of legal or constitutional recognition at the national

## 84   *Timothy Reagan*

level, and the linguistic rights of users of signed languages are increasingly being recognized.[25]

Just as there are many different signed languages, there are many distinctive Deaf cultures which vary from place to place. Although there are certainly many similarities from one Deaf community to another, Deaf cultures are no more universal than signed languages.[26] There are also distinctive Deaf sub-cultures in many countries, such as Black Deaf culture in the U.S. The case of Black Deaf culture in the U.S. is reflected in the distinctive "Black ASL" used by many Deaf African Americans, which is characterized by 2-handed versus 1-handed signs, the use of repetition, the size of the "signing space," the amount of mouthing, the incorporation of African American English into "Black ASL," forehead versus lowered location, and vocabulary differences. Such sub-cultures may perceive themselves to be oppressed or marginalized *both* by the hearing world *and* by the dominant Deaf community in their own society.[27] And yet, this diversity of Deaf cultures co-exists with a general sense of a common DEAF-WORLD that crosses regional and national borders, and which largely unites Deaf people regardless of their country of origin. To some extent, this is similar to the concept of the "English-speaking world"—there are certainly many core cultural and linguistic characteristics shared through the English-speaking world, but at the same time, there are a large number of very significant differences among different groups of English-speaking people and societies.

## The DEAF-WORLD as Indigenous

If the DEAF-WORLD is a distinctive cultural community with its own vernacular language, does this mean that it is also an *indigenous* community? Recently, a number of authors writing about the Deaf have chosen to use this term,[28] and there are certainly similarities between Deaf people and indigenous populations. The question of whether the DEAF-WORLD can accurately be described as *indigenous*, though, is complex, and does not have an easy answer. Commonly, when we use the term *indigenous* we are referring to a group that has special historical (and typically linguistic) ties to a particular geographic territory, and which has been subjected to various kinds of exploitation, marginalization, assimilation (both forced and voluntary), and often even genocide, by colonizing groups.[29] Indigenous populations are thus most often associated with *native, tribal, aboriginal*, or *First Nations* populations in the Americas, Asia, Africa, Australia, and Oceania, and even in parts of Europe. Used in a narrow sense, the Deaf community does not easily fit within such a framework; it is not tied to any specific geographic area, nor is it, for the most part, comparable to an ethnic community whose language, culture, and values are passed from parents to children. However, Deaf people nevertheless *do* belong to a closely related set of cultures, characterized by all of the features that are normally associated with specific cultures: an in-group vernacular language, a shared awareness of group identity and members, distinctive behavioral norms, fairly endogamous marital patterns, cultural artifacts, a shared historical awareness, a network of voluntary social organizations, a distinctive worldview, literature, theater and poetry in signed languages, visual art grounded in and devoted to the DEAF-WORLD, and even a body of jokes and humorous stories.[30] Further, both as individuals and as community members, Deaf people have been, and continue to be, subjected to discrimination, marginalization, social and educational efforts to assimilate them into the hearing world, to deny their language, and in many cases to impose state-sanctioned programs to sterilize or even kill them as less than fully human. Deaf people are also commonly victims of an overwhelming kind of audism, comparable in many ways to racism, sexism, and so on.[31] Indeed, some scholars and activists have begun to refer to Deaf people as "Sign Language Peoples":

> [There are] strong parallels between Sign Language Peoples (SLPs) and First Nation peoples. ... SLPs (communities defining themselves by shared membership in physical and metaphysical aspects of language, culture, epistemology, and ontology) can be considered indigenous groups in need of legal protection in respect of educational, linguistic, and cultural rights accorded to other First Nation indigenous communities. We challenge the assumption that SLPs should be primarily categorised within concepts of disability. The disability label denies the unique spatial culturolinguistic phenomenon of SLP collectivist identity by replicating traditional colonialist perspectives, and actively contributing to their ongoing oppression. Rather, SLPs are defined spatially as a locus for performing, building, and reproducing a collective topography expressed through a common language and a shared culture and history.[32]

In short, there is a compelling case to be made for conceptualizing Deaf people as an indigenous community, though there is also an ambiguity in the use of the term *indigenous* when applied to sign language minorities: on the one hand, it can be used to refer to all members of the DEAF-WORLD, which is how I am using it here. At the same time, though, it can also be employed to refer to individuals and groups who are *both* Deaf *and* members of minority, local Deaf cultures. Examples for such groups include Deaf people who are *also* aboriginal Australians, Māoris, Bedouins, and so on.[33]

## The Epistemology of the DEAF-WORLD

Epistemology, the philosophical study of matters of knowledge, justification, and the rationality of belief has typically taken place within a profoundly western context, but in cases in which we are concerned with understanding the worldviews and epistemological frameworks of indigenous groups, it is more appropriate to talk about *ethnoepistemology*. Ethnoepistemology is *a posteriori* rather than *a priori* in nature (unlike

## 86  *Timothy Reagan*

traditional approaches to epistemology), and is grounded to a much greater extent in anthropology rather than philosophy.[34] The idea that in the DEAF-WORLD there are core differences in epistemology that would impact, among other things, teaching and learning, is hardly a radical one, though it is somewhat more complex than many educators might suppose. To be sure, auditory differences between hearing and d/Deaf children and young adults will inevitably impact learning and teaching, but the difference goes well beyond this:

> Deaf epistemology constitutes the nature and extent of the knowledge that deaf individuals acquire growing up in a society that relies primarily on audition to navigate life. Deafness creates beings who are more visually oriented compared to their auditorily oriented peers. How hearing individuals interact with deaf individuals shapes how deaf individuals acquire knowledge and how they learn. Aspects of the Deaf episteme, not caused by deafness but by Deafhood, have a positive impact on how deaf individuals learn, resist audism, stay healthy, and navigate the world.[35]

Epistemologically Deaf perspectives will impact opinions about a number of key issues and concepts impacting the d/Deaf community: cochlear implants, Deaf culture, Deafhood, DEAF-WORLD, "Deaf brain," "Deaf mind," and the "psychology of d/Deafness." Characterizing epistemological Deafness is the reliance on personal testimony, personal experiences, and personal accounts in constructing knowledge. What is most interesting in this regard is that the nature of the Deaf epistemological framework is grounded *both* in the dominance of visual over auditory input *and* in the resistance of audism and audist perspectives on d/Deafness.[36] Thus, an ethnoepistemological approach is *both* physical *and* cultural in nature.

## Segregation and Inclusion

The relationship between the DEAF-WORLD and the hearing world is in many ways a paradoxical one. Not only do d/Deaf people live their lives interacting with hearing people, but the vast majority have hearing parents and children. At the same time, they believe that both they and their language and culture are marginalized by the hearing world. The paradox that this tension creates is, as Padden and Humphries note, one between the drive for separation and the desire for inclusion:

> The idea of culture offers the possibility of separation and inclusion at the same time. Culture provides a frame for Deaf people to separate themselves from an undefined group of those with hearing impairments, but at the same time, they are included in the world of human communities that share long histories, durable languages, and common

The Deaf as an Indigenous Community   87

social practices. Separation allows Deaf people to define political goals that may be distinct from other groups. Inclusion allows Deaf people to work toward humanist goals that are common to other groups such as civil rights and access. In this way, the idea of culture is not merely an academic abstraction, but very much a "lived" concept.[37]

An additional aspect of the paradox of separation and inclusion is the way that it is manifested in contemporary educational practice in many parts of the world. We have seen that there have been significant improvements with respect to the recognition and acknowledgement of Deaf culture and the role of signed languages in the education of d/Deaf children and young adults in recent decades, but as these positive changes have been taking place, another well-intentioned set of major shifts in educational practice has also been occurring: from the 1980s, there has been a paradigm shift in public education, originally toward "mainstreaming" and increasingly toward "inclusive education." The rise of inclusive education has had major impacts on virtually all aspects of public schooling, and has created challenges with respect to teacher education, teaching methods, curricula, assessment, classroom management, not to mention for the funding needs of public schooling. For the most part, they have been seen as positive developments for both "special needs" students and "regular" (*sic*) students,[38] but for d/Deaf students, the picture is considerably more complex.

Public Law 94–142 ("The Education for All Handicapped Children Act"), passed by the 94th U.S. Congress and signed by President Gerald Ford in 1975, was widely seen as landmark legislation addressing the needs and rights of children with disabilities.[39] The philosophical foundation for inclusive education is based upon the premise that:

> Research to date provides a solid foundation on which to expand inclusive schooling. Legally and ethically, students should not be segregated unless there is clear evidence for superiority for segregated classes and programs. The most important research questions for the future are not *whether* we should seek to build inclusive schools but *how* we may do so well. . . . For us, inclusive teaching is quite simply: We seek to educate *all children together well*. For us, "all" really does mean "all" . . . teaching all children together is a cornerstone of good teaching and schooling.[40]

Such a position is, in many ways and for many groups of children, an admirable one. When the case of the d/Deaf population is considered, however, a number of problematic issues arise. The major challenge facing d/Deaf children is that it is abundantly clear that the proper and healthy cognitive and social development of every child is dependent on his or her access to communication with peers. For the d/Deaf child, this is unlikely to take place in an inclusive classroom, in which most children will not be able to

## 88   *Timothy Reagan*

communicate in a signed language. The presence of signed language interpreters does not really address this problem, either, first because of the shortage of such interpreters, second, because of the well-documented problems with respect to the linguistic and communicative competencies of signed language interpreters, and third, because of the need for children to interact with peers in non-mediated settings. In short, the inclusive classroom for the d/Deaf child is all too often anything except "inclusive," nor can it be taken to represent the "least restrictive environment" for the d/Deaf child in any meaningful way, a point that has been made repeatedly by d/Deaf adults reflecting on their childhood educational experiences in mainstreamed and inclusive settings.[41]

Historically, large numbers of d/Deaf children and young adults have been educated in residential schools for the deaf; most states had a residential school serving all of the d/Deaf children in the state. Public Law 94–142 did not on its own result in the decline in residential schools in the United States but it clearly accelerated a trend that was already underway,[42] and the rise of "inclusive education" further increased this trend:

> In the past decade or so several residential schools have been closed, others transformed into day programs, and others now serve a relatively small number of residential students on-site while providing statewide support services. Many day school programs in large cities also have been closed and students served in areas closer to home to meet least restrictive environment (LRE) and inclusion mandates.[43]

This decline in both the number of residential schools for the deaf and in the numbers of d/Deaf students served by such schools is extremely important, since it has been in residential schools that d/Deaf children "were extensively exposed to Deaf people and signed language."[44] The importance of residential schools for the deaf in the maintenance and transmission of Deaf culture cannot be overstated:

> At a residential school, all students are deaf or hard of hearing, so deaf students are not looked at as different. They have "a common heritage . . . a common language, . . . and a set of customs and values." People at deaf schools help pass on 'Deaf folklore and folklife (jokes, legends, games, riddles, etc.)' from one generation to the next. Deaf parents of deaf children often send their children to residential schools so that they may participate in the Deaf community and culture.[45]

The rise of mainstreaming and inclusive education, whatever their benefits for other groups, have constituted a major transformation in the education of d/Deaf children, and one consequence of this transformation has been that the identification of many of these children with the Deaf community

## The Deaf as an Indigenous Community    89

may be weaker than that found in students attending residential schools.[46] As a consequence, many educators concerned with the education of d/Deaf children, as well as many d/Deaf adults, have been critical of mainstreaming and inclusive education for d/Deaf students, in some instances going so far as to discuss such programs as examples of "epistemic violence." Branson and Miller, for instance, have argued that mainstreaming and inclusive education are, "oriented not towards the educational needs of the Deaf but towards the reinforcement of the dominant ideology of equality of access to educational resources, an ideology which is in fact the foundation for the reproduction of structured inequalities."[47]

## Toward a Deaf Philosophy of Deaf Education

At the heart of any philosophy of Deaf education must be a recognition that, "without special arrangements, students who are deaf constitute an oppressed minority similar to a variety of language minority groups for whom standard education is inaccessible."[48] This means that any philosophical approach to the education of d/Deaf children and young adults must have the goal of empowering such students, or, more accurately and appropriately, assisting such students to empower themselves, both as individuals and as members of a larger community.[49] This is no easy matter:

> The term "empowerment" is used to describe a process which is aimed at implementing the sense of an ability to make a difference or participate in change at the individual, group, and community levels. While leading towards this goal, empowerment should be treated carefully in a way that does not entail paternalism nor lead to another form of social control over minorities and disadvantaged groups.[50]

As this focus on empowerment suggests, a key component of empowerment in deaf education is to recognize the historical power relations in the field.[51] Institutions designed to educate d/Deaf children and young adults have largely been founded and managed *by* hearing people *for* the deaf. Important decisions about policy, teaching methods, curricula, and so on have been controlled by hearing people. To a considerable extent, d/Deaf people were not allowed to become teachers of the d/Deaf, and there has been a decided lack of d/Deaf professionals serving the d/Deaf community. There has also been an almost complete "lack of voice" (or, on some accounts, a "denial of voice") about key issues affecting the d/Deaf, especially in education. As Komesaroff has argued,

> The system of education for deaf people has been dominated by, and suited to, the needs of most hearing educators. Control has been maintained over deaf people through official language policies and a system that is structured to advantage hearing teachers.[52]

90    *Timothy Reagan*

In short, in the case of the education of the d/Deaf, the people who arguably have the best understanding of what being d/Deaf means for everyday life, and who have developed the skills necessary for survival in the hearing world, have not been consulted at all about how d/Deaf children should be prepared for life.

In recent decades, this situation has begun to change, for the most part in positive ways. As early as the mid-1970s, there were calls for bilingual-bicultural education programs which would utilize both ASL and English for d/Deaf children, and which would include curricular content devoted to Deaf culture, such as the inclusion of ASL literature, Deaf history, prominent Deaf individuals and groups, Deaf clubs, the Deaf Olympics, the role of the World Federation of the Deaf, and so on.[53] By the 1980s, a full-blown movement for bilingual-bicultural education for such children was underway in the United States,[54] and today such programs exist in many parts of the country, as well as overseas in a number of countries. There is a growing body of research that seems to suggest the effectiveness of such programs,[55] though the extent to which this research is empirically sound has been questioned by some researchers.[56] Bilingual-bicultural education programs for d/Deaf children are similar to bilingual education programs for other language minority children in many ways, but are also distinctive in several extremely important ways.[57] For example, unlike hearing children, a large percentage of d/Deaf children arrive in educational institutions without a clearly identified "native language."[58]

As Gregory has suggested, bilingual education programs for d/Deaf children involve four major goals:

- to enable d/Deaf children to become linguistically competent;
- to provide access to a wide content and skill curriculum;
- to facilitate strong literacy skills; and
- to provide d/Deaf students with a positive sense of their own identity.[59]

The underlying principles of these goals make clear both the similarities and differences of bilingual-bicultural education for deaf students:

- The signed language of the Deaf community is used as the first language and as the medium of instruction;
- The dominant spoken language is introduced only *after* students have begun to develop skills in the signed language;
- Deaf culture and Deaf role models are an important part of the educational program; and
- Parents as well as students are actively introduced to the culture and community of Deaf people, and are supported in the learning/acquisition of signed language.[60]

Finally, in order to implement bilingual-bicultural programs for d/Deaf children effectively, a final change has to do with the willingness to employ

The Deaf as an Indigenous Community 91

Deaf teachers and other educators, a practice that was common prior to the Congress of Milan,[61] but which declined as oralism[62] became increasingly dominant in the United States.

## Summary

In this chapter, I have argued that the Deaf, as a linguistic and cultural community, can be considered an indigenous population, comparable in many ways to other indigenous groups around the world. Further, I have suggested that there is a distinctive epistemology associated with the DEAF-WORLD, and that this epistemology has significant implications for how, where, and by whom d/Deaf children should be educated. Among the concepts that are related to or grounded in Deaf epistemology are:

- Individuals who are d/Deaf are visual learners.
- All d/Deaf children/adolescents should be taught d/Deaf culture/history.
- Individuals who are d/Deaf learn differently from hearing individuals.
- Anything based on sound/speech is not appropriate for d/Deaf learners.
- Most of deaf education is focused on deficits, not cultural or individual proclivities.
- Students who are d/Deaf should be taught mostly by Deaf teachers.
- Models for teaching should be based solely or predominantly on patterns of interactions involving sign language dyads such as Deaf mothers/teachers and d/Deaf children.
- American Sign Language (or any sign language) is the natural language of d/Deaf individuals.
- The Deaf brain or the Deaf mind is different from the hearing brain or the hearing mind.
- There is no psychology of the Deaf or of deafness.
- Mainstream theories and research are inappropriate or not sufficient for understanding d/Deaf individuals.[63]

Finally, I have used the growth of bilingual-bicultural education programs for d/Deaf children which involve both signed language and Deaf culture and the language and culture of the surrounding hearing community as an example of the way in which the needs of d/Deaf children can be met.

## Notes

1. Richard Senghas and Leila Monaghan, "Signs of Their Times: Deaf Communities and the Culture of Language," *Annual Review of Anthropology* 31 (2002): 69.
2. A common distinction made in writing about deafness is between 'deaf' and 'Deaf': the former refers to deafness solely as an audiological condition, while the latter to Deafness as a linguistic and cultural condition. Although this is a valuable distinction, it oversimplifies and dichotomizes d/Deafness. I have chosen to follow the common usage when either purely audiological deafness is

92  *Timothy Reagan*

intended or when purely sociocultural deafness is intended. When a more inclusive sense in intended, or where the meaning is ambiguous, I use d/Deaf and d/Deafness.

3. See Carol Baker, "Sign Language and the Deaf Community," in *Handbook of Language and Ethnic Identity*, ed. Joshua Fishman (New York: Oxford University Press, 1999), 122–139; Robert Hoffmeister, "Language and the Deaf World: Difference not Disability," in *Language, Culture, and Community in Teacher Education*, ed. María Brisk (New York: Lawrence Erlbaum Associates, 2008), 71–98; Thomas Holcomb, *Introduction to Deaf Culture* (Oxford: Oxford University Press, 2012); Megan Jones, "Deafness as Culture: A Psychological Perspective," *Disability Studies Quarterly* 22 (2002): 51–60; Paddy Ladd, *Understanding Deaf Culture: In Search of Deafhood* (Clevedon: Multilingual Matters, 2003); Paddy Ladd, "Deafhood: A Concept Stressing Possibilities, Not Deficits," *Scandinavian Journal of Public Health* 33(Supplement 66) (2005): 12–17; Irene Leigh, *A Lens on Deaf Identities* (New York: Oxford University Press, 2009); Kristen Lindgren, Doreen DeLuca, and Donna Jo Napoli, eds., *Signs and Voices: Deaf Culture, Identity, Language, and Arts* (Washington, DC: Gallaudet University Press, 2008); Carol Padden and Tom Humphries, *Deaf in America: Voices from a Culture* (Cambridge, MA: Harvard University Press, 1988); Carol Padden and Tom Humphries, *Inside Deaf Culture* (Cambridge, MA: Harvard University Press, 2005); Lillian Tomkins, "Cultural and Linguistic Voice in the Deaf Bilingual Experience," in *Literacy and Deaf People: Cultural and Contextual Perspectives*, ed. Brenda Jo Brueggemann (Washington, DC: Gallaudet University Press, 2004), 139–156.

4. See Timothy Reagan, "The DEAF-WORLD and Competence in ASL: Identity and Language Issues," in *Readings in Language Studies*, Volume 3, ed. Paul C. Miller, John Watzke, and Miguel Mantero (Lakewood Ranch, FL: International Society for Language Studies, 2012), 233–246.

5. ASL is the dominant signed language used in the United States and Anglophone Canada. It has also had a disproportionate influence on many other signed languages around the world, especially through lexical borrowing, and dialects and creoles based on ASL are used in many parts of the world, especially in Africa and Asia.

6. I have followed the normal practice of indicating a particular sign by writing its English gloss in capital letters (e.g., BOY). In many cases, a single sign in ASL requires multiple English words to represent it; in these instances, the words are linked together with a hyphen to indicate that they are a single sign (as in I-ASK-YOU). The sign used here, DEAF-WORLD, is the one used in ASL to indicate the Deaf cultural community. There are a number of terms used in English to express the concept of DEAF-WORLD; the two most common are "d/Deaf culture" and "d/Deafhood."

7. For an excellent discussion of this phenomenon, see Jerome Schein, *At Home among Strangers: Exploring the Deaf Community in the United States* (Washington, DC: Gallaudet University Press, 1989).

8. Linda Komesaroff, *Disabling Pedagogy: Power, Politics and Deaf Education* (Washington, DC: Gallaudet University Press, 2008); Harlan Lane, Robert Hoffmeister, and Ben Bahan, *A Journey into the DEAF-WORLD* (San Diego: DawnSign Press, 1996); Harry Lang, "Perspectives on the History of Deaf Education," in *Oxford Handbook of Deaf Studies, Language, and Education*, ed. Marc Marschark and Patricia Spencer (Oxford: Oxford University Press, 2003), 9–20.

9. In most developed societies, only approximately 10% of the deaf population are the children of d/Deaf parents. See Ladd, *Understanding Deaf Culture: In Search of Deafhood*, 35; Rachel McKee, "Connecting Hearing Parents with the Deaf World," *Sites: A Journal of Social Anthropology and Cultural Studies* 3 (2006):

The Deaf as an Indigenous Community    93

143–167; Jenny Singleton and Matthew Tittle, "Deaf Parents and Their Hearing Children," *Journal of Deaf Studies and Deaf Education* 5 (2000): 221–236.

10. See Harlan Lane, "Do Deaf People Have a Disability?," *Sign Language Studies* 2 (2002): 356–379.

11. Senghas and Monaghan, "Signs of Their Times," 69.

12. There are several conflicting approaches to understanding d/Deafness. The most common is the audiological, which sees deafness in pathological and medical terms. The alternative is the sociocultural perspective, which suggests that Deaf people are best conceived as members of a cultural and linguistic community. Efforts to remediate deafness technologically or surgically are thus appropriate and reasonable for those presupposing the former perspective, but are seen as deeply misguided and even offensive for those holding the latter perspective. See Timothy Reagan, "Toward an 'Archeology of Deafness': Etic and Emic Constructions of Identity in Conflict," *Journal of Language, Identity, and Education* 1 (2002): 41–66.

13. Lane, Hoffmeister, and Bahan, *A Journey into the DEAF-WORLD*, 371.

14. See Lennard Davis, *Enforcing Normalcy: Disability, Deafness and the Body* (London: Verso, 1995).

15. Len Barton, "Blaming the Victims: The Political Oppression of Disabled People," in *The Politics, Sociology and Economics of Education: Interdisciplinary and Comparative Perspectives*, ed. Russell Farnen and Heinz Sünker (Houndsmills, Hampshire: Macmillan, 1997), 63–72; H. Dirksen Bauman, "Audism: Exploring the Metaphysics of Oppression," *Journal of Deaf Studies and Deaf Education* 99 (2004): 239–246; Jan Branson and Don Miller, *Damned for Their Difference: The Cultural Construction of Deaf People as Disabled* (Washington, DC: Gallaudet University Press, 2002); Richard Eckert and Amy Rowley, "Audism: A Theory and Practice of Audiocentric Privilege," *Humanity & Society* 37 (2013): 101–130; Halvor Hanisch, "Frontiers of Justice: Disability, Nationality, Species Membership," *Scandinavian Journal of Disability Research* 9 (2007): 133–136; Linda Komesaroff, "Linguistic Rights of the Deaf: Struggling against Disabling Pedagogy in Education," *Australian Journal of Human Rights* 6 (2000): 59–78; Harlan Lane, *The Mask of Benevolence: Disabling the Deaf Community*, new ed. (San Diego: DawnSign Press, 1999).

16. To say that signed languages are not universal does not mean that there may not be linguistic universals that apply to signed languages, just as they apply to spoken languages. See Wendy Sandler and Diane Lillo-Martin, *Sign Language and Linguistic Universals* (Cambridge: Cambridge University Press, 2006).

17. Ethnologue, for instance, includes specific identifications of 141 signed languages.

18. Tove Skutnabb-Kangas, *Linguistic Genocide in Education: Or Worldwide Diversity and Human Rights?* (Mahwah, NJ: Lawrence Erlbaum Associates, 2000), 30.

19. Henri Wittmann, "Classification Linguistique des Langues Signées Non Vocalement," *Revue Québécoise de Linguistique Théorique et Appliquée* 10 (1991): 215–288.

20. See Scott Liddell, *Grammar, Gesture, and Meaning in American Sign Language* (Cambridge: Cambridge University Press, 2003); Carol Neidle, Judy Kegl, Dawn Maclaughlin, Benjamin Bahan, and Robert Lee, *The Syntax of American Sign Language: Functional Categories and Hierarchical Structure* (Cambridge, MA: MIT Press, 2000); Clayton Valli, Ceil Lucas, Kristein Mulrooney, and Miako Villanueva, *Linguistics of American Sign Language: An Introduction*, 5th ed. (Washington, DC: Gallaudet University Press, 2011).

21. It should be stressed here that each of these signed languages is a distinct and different "language" in its own right—these are not varieties of a single common

94   *Timothy Reagan*

language or signing system, but fully self-contained languages. For Australian Sign Language, see Trevor Johnston and Adam Schembri, *Australian Sign Language (AUSLAN): An Introduction to Sign Language Linguistics* (Cambridge: Cambridge University Press, 2007).

22. See Margaret Deuchar, *British Sign Language* (London: Routledge, 2013); Rachel Sutton-Spence and Bencie Woll, *The Linguistics of British Sign Language: An Introduction* (Cambridge: Cambridge University Press, 1999).

23. See Diane Brentari, ed., *Sign Languages* (Cambridge: Cambridge University Press, 2010).

24. Of course, the same situation is found with respect to spoken languages. Linguists believe that there are somewhere between 6,000 and 7,000 languages currently in the world, but of these, of the vast majority we know very little indeed, and in some cases, only the name of the language or its speakers.

25. See Jan Branson and Don Miller, "Nationalism and the Linguistic Rights of Deaf Communities: Linguistic Imperialism and the Recognition and Development of Sign Languages," *Journal of Sociolinguistics* 2 (1998): 3–34; Hilde Haualand and Collin Allen, *Deaf People and Human Rights* (Helsinki: World Federation of the Deaf, in Collaboration with the Swedish National Association of the Deaf, 2009); Tom Humphries, Raja Kushalnagar, Gaurav Mathur, Donna Jo Napoli, Carol Padden, Christian Rathmann, and Scott Smith, "The Right to Language," *The Journal of Law, Medicine and Ethics* 41 (2013): 872–884; Markku Jokinen, "The Linguistic Human Rights of Sign Language Users," in *Rights to Language: Equity, Power, and Education*, ed. Robert Phillipson (Mahwah, NJ: Lawrence Erlbaum Associates, 2000), 203–213; Rachel McKee and Victoria Manning, "Evaluating Effects of Language Recognition on Language Rights and the Vitality of New Zealand Sign Language," *Sign Language Studies* 15 (2015): 473–497; Joseph Murray, "Linguistic Human Rights Discourse in Deaf Community Activism," *Sign Language Studies* 15 (2015): 379–410; Timothy Reagan, "Ideological Barriers to American Sign Language: Unpacking Linguistic Resistance," *Sign Language Studies* 11 (2011): 594–624; Lawrence Siegel, *The Human Right to Language: Communication Access for Deaf Children* (Washington, DC: Gallaudet University Press, 2008).

26. See Carol Erting, Robert Johnson, Dorothy Smith, and Bruce Snider, eds., *The Deaf Way: Perspectives from the International Conference on Deaf Culture* (Washington, DC: Gallaudet University Press, 1994); Harvey Goodstein, ed., *The Deaf Way Reader II: Perspectives from the Second International Conference on Deafness* (Washington, DC: Gallaudet University Press, 2006); Leila Monaghan, Constanze Schmaling, Karen Nakamura, and Graham Turner, eds., *Many Ways to be Deaf: International Variation in Deaf Communities* (Washington, DC: Gallaudet University Press, 2003); Toya Stremlay, ed., *The Deaf Way II Anthology: A Literary Collection by Deaf and Hard of Hearing Writers* (Washington, DC: Gallaudet University Press, 2002).

27. Ceil Lucas and her colleagues have been investigating Black ASL for a number of years, and their work has provided fascinating insights into variation in ASL. See Ceil Lucas and Robert Bailey, "Variation in Sign Languages: Recent Research on ASL and Beyond," *Language and Linguistics Compass* 5 (2011): 677–690; Carolyn McCaskill, Ceil Lucas, Robert Bailey, and Joseph Hill, *The Hidden Treasure of Black ASL: Its History and Structure* (Washington, DC: Gallaudet University Press, 2011).

28. See Sarah Batterbury, Paddy Ladd, and Mike Gulliver, "Sign Language Peoples as Indigenous Minorities: Implications for Research and Policy," *Environment and Planning* 39 (2007): 2899–2915; Tom Humphries, "The Modern Deaf Self: Indigenous Practices and Educational Imperatives," in *Literacy and Deaf People: Cultural and Contextual Perspectives*, ed. Brenda Jo Brueggemann

The Deaf as an Indigenous Community 95

(Washington, DC: Gallaudet University Press, 2004), 29–46; Tove Skutnabb-Kangas, "Bilingual Education and Sign Language as the Mother Tongue of Deaf Children," in *English in International Deaf Communication*, ed. Cynthia Kellett Bidoli and Elana Ochese (Bern: Peter Lang, 2008), 75–96.

29. See S. James Anaya, *Indigenous Peoples in International Law*, 2nd ed. (Oxford: Oxford University Press, 2004); Marie Battiste and James Youngblood, *Protecting Indigenous Knowledge and Heritage: A Global Challenge* (Saskatoon: Purich Publishing, 2000); Dawn Chatty and Marcus Colchester, eds., *Conservation and Mobile Indigenous Peoples: Displacement, Forced Settlement, and Sustainable Development* (New York: Berghahn, 2002); Glen Coulthard, "Subjects of Empire: Indigenous Peoples and the 'Politics of Recognition' in Canada," *Contemporary Political Theory* 6 (2007): 437–460; Gillette Hall and Harry Patrinos, eds., *Indigenous Peoples, Poverty, and Human Development in Latin America* (New York: Palgrave Macmillan, 2006).

30. See Lois Bragg, ed., *DEAF-WORLD: A Historical Reader and Primary Sourcebook* (New York: New York University Press, 2001); Susan Gregory and Gillian Hartley, eds., *Constructing Deafness* (London: Pinter Publishers, in Association with the Open University, 1991); Jennifer Harris, *The Cultural Meaning of Deafness: Language, Identity and Power Relations* (Aldershot: Ashgate, 1995); Laurene Simms and Helen Thumann, "In Search of a New, Linguistically and Culturally Sensitive Paradigm in Deaf Education," *American Annals of the Deaf* 152 (2007): 302–311.

31. See H. Bauman, "Audism: Exploring the Metaphysics of Oppression." Model eugenic legislation in the United States in the early twentieth century sought "the sterilization of feebleminded, insane, criminalistic ... epileptic, inebriate, diseased, blind deaf, deformed, and dependent people"; by the First World War, such legislation had been enacted into law in sixteen states, and by 1940, thirty states had such laws. The goal was to "eliminate" such groups from the human stock, and even today there are d/Deaf individuals who were subjected to such procedures in this country. The American experience provided an important part of the rationale for the development of similar programs in Nazi German. For the U.S. case, see Lane, *The Mask of Benevolence: Disabling the Deaf Community*, 215; for the case of Nazi Germany, see Horst Biesold, *Crying Hands: Eugenics and Deaf People in Nazi Germany* (Washington, DC: Gallaudet University Press, 2002); Donna Ryan and John Schuchman, eds., *Deaf People in Hitler's Europe* (Washington, DC: Gallaudet University Press, 2002).

32. Batterbury, Ladd, and Gulliver, "Sign Language Peoples as Indigenous Minorities: Implications for Research and Policy," 2899.

33. See Anne Hynds, Susan Faircloth, Clint Green, and Helen Jacob, "Researching Identity with Indigenous d/Deaf Youth," *New Zealand Journal of Educational Studies* 49 (2014): 176–190; Shifra Kisch, "'Deaf Discourse': The Social Construction of Deafness in a Bedouin Community," *Medical Anthropology* 27 (2008): 283–313; Des Power, "Australian Aboriginal Deaf People and Aboriginal Sign Language," *Sign Language Studies* 13 (2013): 264–277; Ulrike Zeshan and Connie De Vos, *Sign Languages in Village Communities: Anthropological and Linguistic Insights* (Berlin: Walter de Gruyter, 2012).

34. See Michael Christie, "Transdisciplinary Research and Aboriginal Knowledge," *The Australian Journal of Indigenous Education* 35 (2006): 78–89; Claude Gélinas, "An Epistemological Framework for Indigenous Knowledge," *Revista de Humanidades de Valparaíso* 4 (2014): 47–62; Michael Hannon, "The Universal Core of Knowledge," *Synthese* 192 (2015): 769–786.

35. Peter Hauser, Amanda O'Hearn, Michael McKee, Anne Steider, and Denise Thew, "Deaf Epistemology: Deafhood and Deafness," *American Annals of*

## 96 Timothy Reagan

*the Deaf* 154 (2010): 486–492. See also Thomas Holcomb, "Deaf Epistemology: The Deaf Way of Knowing," *American Annals of the Deaf* 154 (2010): 471–478.

36. See Margery Miller, "Epistemology and People Who Are Deaf: Deaf Worldviews, Views of the Deaf World, or My Parents Are Hearing," *American Annals of the Deaf* 154 (2010): 479–485; Donald F. Moores, "Epistemologies, Deafness, Learning, and Teaching," *American Annals of the Deaf* 154 (2010): 447–455; Donald F. Moores and Peter V. Paul, "Summary and Prologue: Perspectives on Deaf Epistemologies," *American Annals of the Deaf* 154 (2010): 493–496; Peter V. Paul and Donald F. Moores, "Perspectives on Deaf Epistemologies," *American Annals of the Deaf* 154 (2010): 417–420; Ye Wang, "Without Boundaries: An Inquiry into Deaf Epistemologies through a Metaparadigm," *American Annals of the Deaf* 154 (2010): 428–434.

37. Padden and Humphries, *Inside Deaf Culture*, 160–161.

38. For example, see Peter Mittler, *Working Towards Inclusive Education: Social Contexts* (London: Routledge, 2012). It is worth noting, though, that in recent years many of the core (and largely unquestioned) assumptions underlying inclusive education have been critiqued. See, for instance, Geoff Lindsay, "Inclusive Education: A Critical Perspective," *British Journal of Special Education* 30 (2003): 3–12; Susie Miles and Nidhi Singal, "The Education for All and Inclusive Education Debate: Conflict, Contradiction or Opportunity?," *International Journal of Inclusive Education* 14 (2010): 1–15; Roger Slee, *The Irregular School: Exclusion, Schooling and Inclusive Education* (London: Routledge, 2011); Roger Slee and Julie Allan, "Excluding the Included: A Reconsideration of Inclusive Education," *International Studies in Sociology of Education* 11 (2001): 173–192.

39. See Tiina Itkonen, "PL 94–142: Policy, Evolution, and Landscape Shift," *Issues in Teacher Education* 16 (2007): 7–17; Robert Osgood, *The History of Inclusion in the United States* (Washington, DC: Gallaudet University Press, 2005).

40. J. Micael Peterson and Mishael Marie Hittie, *Inclusive Teaching: Creating Effective Schools for All Learners* (Boston: Allyn and Bacon, 2003), 41–42.

41. For a powerful example of such a work, see Gina Oliva, *Alone in the Mainstream: A Deaf Woman Remembers Public School* (Washington, DC: Gallaudet University Press, 2004).

42. Donald F. Moores, "Residential Schools for the Deaf and Academic Placement Past, Present, and Future," *American Annals of the Deaf* 154 (2009): 3–4.

43. Ibid., 3.

44. Padden and Humphries, *Deaf in America: Voices from a Culture*, 5.

45. Judith Gilliam and Susan Easterbrooks, *Educating Children Who Are Deaf or Hard of Hearing: Residential Life, ASL, and Deaf Culture*. ERIC Digest #558. Washington, DC: Education Resources Information Center, ERIC Clearinghouse on Disabilities and Gifted Education, August 1997.

46. See Timothy Reagan, "Cultural Considerations in the Education of the Deaf," in *Research in Educational and Developmental Aspects of Deafness*, ed. Donald Moores and Kay Meadow-Orlans (Washington, DC: Gallaudet University Press, 1990), 78.

47. Jan Branson and Don Miller, "Sign Language, the Deaf and the Epistemic Violence of Mainstreaming," *Language and Education* 7 (1993): 21. See also Stephen Powers, "From Concepts to Practice in Deaf Education: A United Kingdom Perspective on Inclusion," *Journal of Deaf Studies and Deaf Education* 7 (2002): 230–243.

48. Joan B. Stone, "Minority Empowerment and the Education of Deaf People," in *Cultural and Language Diversity and the Deaf Experience*, ed. Ila Parasnis (Cambridge: Cambridge University Press, 1998), 171–180.

The Deaf as an Indigenous Community   97

49. Empowerment is always a complex and difficult goal, but this is arguably especially so in the case of indigenous populations. One serious challenge is the risk of what Zhenzhou Zhao has called "imagined empowerment." See Zhenzhou Zhao, "Trilingual Education for Ethnic Minorities: Toward Empowerment?," *Chinese Education and Society* 43 (2010): 70–81. See also Ismael Abu-Saad and Duane Champagne, eds., *Indigenous Education and Empowerment: International Perspectives* (Lanham, MD: Rowman & Littlefield, 2006).

50. Majid Al-Haj and Rosmarie Mielke, "Introduction: Education, Multiculturalism, and Empowerment of Minorities: An Overview," in *Cultural Diversity and Empowerment of Minorities*, ed. Majid Al-Haj and Rosmarie Mielke (New York: Berghahn, 2007), 2; Katherine A. Jankowski, *Deaf Empowerment: Emergence, Struggle, and Rhetoric* (Washington, DC: Gallaudet University Press, 1997).

51. See Linda Komesaroff, "Politics of Language Practices in Deaf Education" (PhD diss., Geelong, Victoria, Australia: Deakin University, 1998). The same phenomenon has been documented with respect to First Nations peoples; see Ceila Haig-Brown, *Taking Control: Power and Contradiction in First Nations Adult Education* (Vancouver: University of British Columbia Press, 1995).

52. Komesaroff, *Disabling Pedagogy*, 5.

53. Carol Erting, "Language Policy and Deaf Ethnicity in the United States," *Sign Language Studies* 19 (1978): 139–152; Barbara Kannapel, "Bilingualism: A New Direction in the Education of the Deaf," *Deaf American* 26 (June 1974): 9–15.

54. See, for example, Martha Barnum, "In Support of Bilingual/Bicultural Education for Deaf Children," *American Annals of the Deaf* 129 (1984): 404–408; Danielle Bouvet, *The Path to Language: Toward Bilingual Education for Deaf Children* (Clevedon: Multilingual Matters, 1990); Carol Padden, "The Deaf Community and the Culture of Deaf People," in *Sign Language and the Deaf Community: Essays in Honor of William C. Stokoe*, ed. Charlotte Baker and Robbin Battison (Silver Spring, MD: National Association of the Deaf, 1980), 89–103; Timothy Reagan, "The Deaf as a Linguistic Minority: Educational Considerations," *Harvard Educational Review* 55 (1985): 265–278; Michael Strong, "A Bilingual Approach to the Education of Young Deaf Children: ASL and English," in *Language Learning and Deafness*, ed. Michael Strong (Cambridge: Cambridge University Press, 1938), 113–129.

55. Melissa DeLana, Mary Anne Gentry, and Jean Andrews, "The Efficacy of ASL/English Bilingual Education: Considering Public Schools," *American Annals of the Deaf* 152 (2007): 73–87; Doreen DeLuca and Donna Jo Napoli, "A Bilingual Approach to Reading," in *Signs and Voices: Deaf Culture, Identity, Language, and Arts*, ed. Kristen Lindgren, Doreen DeLuca, and Donna Jo Napoli (Washington, DC: Gallaudet University Press, 2008), 150–159; Erik Drasgow, "Bilingual/Bicultural Deaf Education: An Overview," *Sign Language Studies* 80 (1993): 243–266, Ruth Swanwick and Susan Gregory, *Sign Bilingual Education: Policy and Practice* (Coleford, Gloucestershire: Douglas McLean, 2007).

56. See Marc Marschark, Gladys Tang, and Harry Knoors, eds., *Bilingualism and Bilingual Deaf Education* (Oxford: Oxford University Press, 2014); Connie Mayer and C. Tane Akamatsu, "Bilingual-Bicultural Models of Literacy Education for Deaf Students: Considering the Claims," *Journal of Deaf Studies and Deaf Education* 4 (1999): 1–8. It is important to note here that the fundamental argument for bilingual-bicultural education for d/Deaf students is not an empirical one; it is, rather, grounded in what are taken to be the basic human rights of such children.

57. See Robert Johnson, Scott Liddell, and Carol Erting, *Unlocking the Curriculum: Principles for Achieving Access in Deaf Education* (Gallaudet Research Institute Working Paper 89-3) (Washington, DC: Gallaudet University Press, 1989).

98    *Timothy Reagan*

58. The question of the "native language" of the deaf child is both complex and sometimes controversial. For d/Deaf children whose parents are Deaf, and who are raised in a home in which ASL (or some other signed language) is used as the vernacular language, then that signed language is without question the child's native language. However, as noted above, such children constitute only about 10% of the deaf population; some 90% of deaf children have hearing parents, whose language is a spoken language, most of whom do not sign, or begin learning to sign only once the child is identified as deaf. This means that normally these children cannot typically be said to speak their parents' spoken language as a native language, nor, prior to acquisition of a signed language, is a signed language really their "native language" (though it might well be considered to be their "natural language"' or even "first language," in spite of its generally late acquisition).
59. See Susan Gregory, "Bilingualism and the Education of Deaf Children" (paper presented at the 'Bilingualism and the Education of Deaf Children: Advances in Practice,' Leeds, UK: University of Leeds, June 29, 1996).
60. Neita Israelite, Carolyn Ewoldt, and Robert Hoffmeister, *Bilingual/Bicultural Education for Deaf and Hard-of-Hearing Students* (Ontario: Ministry of Education, 1992).
61. The Congress of Milan (technically, the "Second International Congress on Education of the Deaf"), which was held in 1880, has traditionally been blamed for the large-scale replacement of manual approaches to deaf education and the growing dominance of oral ones. The Congress was certainly a political fiasco in many ways, and the pro-manual Americans were outmanned in a variety of ways. Further, the only Deaf member in attendance was not even allowed to vote. Nevertheless, while the Congress of Milan clearly had a huge impact on the education of deaf students in Europe, its actual impact in the United States seems to have been both more limited and more gradual in nature. It was not until 1926, for example, that the Conference of Superintendents and Principals of American Schools for the Deaf "officially voted to eliminate the language of signs from all departments as a means of instruction," and in fact the preceding half-century had been one in which the Combined System remained largely dominant in American deaf education. Nor, in spite of common beliefs and claims to the contrary, does it seem that the Congress of Milan resulted in either an immediate purging of deaf instructors in schools for the deaf or an unwillingness to hire such teachers. According to Nover, the number of deaf teachers in schools for the deaf nearly doubled during this period, increasing from 132 in 1880 to 243 in 1899. See Stephen Nover, "History of Language Planning in Deaf Education: The 19th Century" (PhD diss., Tuscon, AZ: University of Arizona, 2000), 140–142.
62. Two terms that have been important historically in the modern history of deaf education are "manualism" and "oralism." These terms reflect a fundamental philosophical distinction both in terms of teaching methodologies and with respect to the underlying goals of education for deaf students. "Manualism" accepts the use of some sort of visual/gestural communication system in teaching d/Deaf students (though not always a natural signed language), while "oralism" has traditionally rejected the use of any such visual/gestural system, and focuses on the development of skills such as lip-reading, speech, and so on. The debate between "manualists" and "oralists" in deaf education began with the development for formal schools for deaf children, but became especially heated from the late nineteenth and through the mid-twentieth century. See Timothy Reagan, "Nineteenth-Century Conceptions of Deafness: Implications for Contemporary Educational Practice," *Educational Theory* 39 (1989): 39–46; Richard Winefield, *Never the Twain Shall Meet: Bell, Gallaudet, and the Communications Debate* (Washington, DC: Gallaudet University Press, 1987).
63. Paul and Moores, "Perspectives on Deaf Epistemologies," 417.

## Bibliography

Abu-Saad, Ismael and Duane Champagne, eds. *Indigenous Education and Empowerment: International Perspectives*. Lanham, MD: Rowman & Littlefield, 2006.

Al-Haj, Majid and Rosmarie Mielke. "Introduction: Education, Multiculturalism, and Empowerment of Minorities: An Overview." In *Cultural Diversity and Empowerment of Minorities*, edited by Majid Al-Haj and Rosmarie Mielke, 1–7. New York: Berghahn, 2007.

Anaya, S. James. *Indigenous Peoples in International Law* (2nd ed.). Oxford: Oxford University Press, 2004.

Baker, Carol. "Sign Language and the Deaf Community." In *Handbook of Language and Ethnic Identity*, edited by Joshua Fishman, 122–139. New York: Oxford University Press, 1999.

Barnum, Martha. "In Support of Bilingual/Bicultural Education for Deaf Children." *American Annals of the Deaf* 129 (1984): 404–408.

Barton, Len. "Blaming the Victims: The Political Oppression of Disabled People." In *The Politics, Sociology and Economics of Education: Interdisciplinary and Comparative Perspectives*, edited by Russell Farnen and Heinz Sünker, 63–72. Houndsmills, Hampshire: Macmillan, 1997.

Batterbury, Sarah, Paddy Ladd, and Mike Gulliver. "Sign Language Peoples as Indigenous Minorities: Implications for Research and Policy." *Environment and Planning* 39 (2007): 2899–2915.

Battiste, Marie and James Youngblood. *Protecting Indigenous Knowledge and Heritage: A Global Challenge*. Saskatoon: Purich Publishing, 2000.

Bauman, H. Dirksen. "Audism: Exploring the Metaphysics of Oppression." *Journal of Deaf Studies and Deaf Education* 99 (2004): 239–246.

Biesold, Horst. *Crying Hands: Eugenics and Deaf People in Nazi Germany*. Washington, DC: Gallaudet University Press, 2002.

Bouvet, Danielle. *The Path to Language: Toward Bilingual Education for Deaf Children*. Clevedon: Multilingual Matters, 1990.

Bragg, Lois, ed. *DEAF-WORLD: A Historical Reader and Primary Sourcebook*. New York: New York University Press, 2001.

Branson, Jan and Don Miller. "Sign Language, the Deaf and the Epistemic Violence of Mainstreaming." *Language and Education* 7 (1993): 21–41.

———. "Nationalism and the Linguistic Rights of Deaf Communities: Linguistic Imperialism and the Recognition and Development of Sign Languages." *Journal of Sociolinguistics* 2 (1998): 3–34.

———. *Damned for Their Difference: The Cultural Construction of Deaf People as Disabled*. Washington, DC: Gallaudet University Press, 2002.

Brentari, Diane, ed. *Sign Languages*. Cambridge: Cambridge University Press, 2010.

Chatty, Dawn and Marcus Colchester, eds. *Conservation and Mobile Indigenous Peoples: Displacement, Forced Settlement, and Sustainable Development*. New York: Berghahn, 2002.

Christie, Michael. "Transdisciplinary Research and Aboriginal Knowledge." *The Australian Journal of Indigenous Education* 35 (2006): 78–89.

Coulthard, Glen. "Subjects of Empire: Indigenous Peoples and the 'Politics of Recognition' in Canada." *Contemporary Political Theory* 6 (2007): 437–460.

Davis, Lennard. *Enforcing Normalcy: Disability, Deafness and the Body*. London: Verso, 1995.

DeLana, Melissa, Mary Anne Gentry, and Jean Andrews. "The Efficacy of ASL/English Bilingual Education: Considering Public Schools." *American Annals of the Deaf* 152 (2007): 73–87.

DeLuca, Doreen and Donna Jo Napoli. "A Bilingual Approach to Reading." In *Signs and Voices: Deaf Culture, Identity, Language, and Arts*, edited by Kristen

100　*Timothy Reagan*

Lindgren, Doreen DeLuca, and Donna Jo Napoli, 150–159. Washington, DC: Gallaudet University Press, 2008.

Deuchar, Margaret. *British Sign Language*. London: Routledge, 2013.

Drasgow, Erik. "Bilingual/Bicultural Deaf Education: An Overview." *Sign Language Studies* 80 (1993): 243–266.

Eckert, Richard and Amy Rowley. "Audism: A Theory and Practice of Audiocentric Privilege." *Humanity and Society* 37 (2013): 101–130.

Erting, Carol. "Language Policy and Deaf Ethnicity in the United States." *Sign Language Studies* 19 (1978): 139–152.

———, Robert Johnson, Dorothy Smith, and Bruce Snider, eds. *The Deaf Way: Perspectives from the International Conference on Deaf Culture*. Washington, DC: Gallaudet University Press, 1994.

Gélinas, Claude. "An Epistemological Framework for Indigenous Knowledge." *Revista de Humanidades de Valparaíso* 4 (2014): 47–62.

Gilliam, Judith and Susan Easterbrooks. *Educating Children Who Are Deaf or Hard of Hearing: Residential Life, ASL, and Deaf Culture*. ERIC Digest #558. Washington, DC: Education Resources Information Center, ERIC Clearinghouse on Disabilities and Gifted Education, August 1997.

Goodstein, Harvey, ed. *The Deaf Way Reader II: Perspectives from the Second International Conference on Deafness*. Washington, DC: Gallaudet University Press, 2006.

Gregory, Susan. "Bilingualism and the Education of Deaf Children." Paper presented at the Conference of 'Bilingualism and the Education of Deaf Children: Advances in Practice', Leeds, UK: University of Leeds, June 29, 1996.

——— and Gillian Hartley, eds. *Constructing Deafness*. London: Pinter Publishers, in Association with the Open University, 1991.

Haig-Brown, Ceila. *Taking Control: Power and Contradiction in First Nations Adult Education*. Vancouver: University of British Columbia Press, 1995.

Hall, Gillette and Harry Patrinos, eds. *Indigenous Peoples, Poverty, and Human Development in Latin America*. New York: Palgrave Macmillan, 2006.

Hanisch, Halve. "Frontiers of Justice: Disability, Nationality, Species Membership." *Scandinavian Journal of Disability Research* 9 (2007): 133–136.

Hannon, Michael. "The Universal Core of Knowledge." *Synthese* 192 (2015): 769–786.

Harris, Jennifer. *The Cultural Meaning of Deafness: Language, Identity and Power Relations*. Aldershot: Ashgate, 1995.

Haualand, Hilde and Collin Allen. *Deaf People and Human Rights*. Helsinki: World Federation of the Deaf, in Collaboration with the Swedish National Association of the Deaf, 2009.

Hauser, Peter, Amanda O'Hearn, Michael McKee, Anne Steider, and Denise Thew. "Deaf Epistemology: Deafhood and Deafness." *American Annals of the Deaf* 154 (2010): 486–492.

Hoffmeister, Robert. "Language and the Deaf World: Difference Not Disability." In *Language, Culture, and Community in Teacher Education*, edited by María Brisk, 71–98. New York: Lawrence Erlbaum Associates, 2008.

Holcomb, Thomas. "Deaf Epistemology: The Deaf Way of Knowing." *American Annals of the Deaf* 154 (2010): 471–478.

———. *Introduction to Deaf Culture*. Oxford: Oxford University Press, 2012.

Humphries, Tom. "The Modern Deaf Self: Indigenous Practices and Educational Imperatives." In *Literacy and Deaf People: Cultural and Contextual Perspectives*, edited by Brenda Jo Brueggemann, 29–46. Washington, DC: Gallaudet University Press, 2004.

———, Raja Kushalnagar, Gaurav Mathur, Donna Jo Napoli, Carol Padden, Christian Rathmann, and Scott Smith. "The Right to Language." *The Journal of Law, Medicine and Ethics* 41 (2013): 872–884.

# The Deaf as an Indigenous Community    101

Hynds, Anne, Susan Faircloth, Clint Green, and Helen Jacob. "Researching Identity with Indigenous D/deaf Youth." *New Zealand Journal of Educational Studies* 49 (2014): 176–190.

Israelite, Neita, Carolyn Ewoldt, and Robert Hoffmeister. *Bilingual/Bicultural Education for Deaf and Hard-of-Hearing Students*. Ontario: Ministry of Education, 1992.

Itkonen, Tiina. "PL 94–142: Policy, Evolution, and Landscape Shift." *Issues in Teacher Education* 16 (2007): 7–17.

Jankowski, Katherine A. *Deaf Empowerment: Emergence, Struggle, and Rhetoric*. Washington, DC: Gallaudet University Press, 1997.

Johnson, Robert, Scott Liddell, and Carol Erting. *Unlocking the Curriculum: Principles for Achieving Access in Deaf Education*. Gallaudet Research Institute Working Paper 89-3. Washington, DC: Gallaudet University Press, 1989.

Johnston, Trevor and Adam Schembri. *Australian Sign Language (AUSLAN): An Introduction to Sign Language Linguistics*. Cambridge: Cambridge University Press, 2007.

Jokinen, Markku. "The Linguistic Human Rights of Sign Language Users." In *Rights to Language: Equity, Power, and Education*, edited by Robert Phillipson, 203–213. Mahwah, NJ: Lawrence Erlbaum Associates, 2000.

Jones, Megan. "Deafness as Culture: A Psychological Perspective." *Disability Studies Quarterly* 22 (2002): 51–60.

Kannapel, Barbara. "Bilingualism: A New Direction in the Education of the Deaf." *Deaf American* 26 (June 1974): 9–15.

Kisch, Shifra. "'Deaf Discourse': The Social Construction of Deafness in a Bedouin Community." *Medical Anthropology* 27 (2008): 283–313.

Komesaroff, Linda. "Politics of Language Practices in Deaf Education." PhD diss., Geelong, Victoria, Australia: Deakin University, 1998.

———. "Linguistic Rights of the Deaf: Struggling Against Disabling Pedagogy in Education." *Australian Journal of Human Rights* 6 (2000): 59–78.

———. *Disabling Pedagogy: Power, Politics and Deaf Education*. Washington, DC: Gallaudet University Press, 2008.

Ladd, Paddy. *Understanding Deaf Culture: In Search of Deafhood*. Clevedon: Multilingual Matters, 2003.

———. "Deafhood: A Concept Stressing Possibilities, Not Deficits." *Scandinavian Journal of Public Health* 33(Supplement 66) (2005): 12–17.

Lane, Harlan. *The Mask of Benevolence: Disabling the Deaf Community* (new ed.). San Diego, CA: DawnSign Press, 1999.

———. "Do Deaf People Have a Disability?" *Sign Language Studies* 2 (2002): 356–379.

———, Robert Hoffmeister, and Ben Bahan. *A Journey into the DEAF-WORLD*. San Diego: DawnSign Press, 1996.

Lang, Harry. "Perspectives on the History of Deaf Education." In *Oxford Handbook of Deaf Studies, Language, and Education*, edited by Marc Marschark and Patricia Spencer, 9–20. Oxford: Oxford University Press, 2003.

Leigh, Irene. *A Lens on Deaf Identities*. New York: Oxford University Press, 2009.

Liddell, Scott. *Grammar, Gesture, and Meaning in American Sign Language*. Cambridge: Cambridge University Press, 2003.

Lindgren, Kristen, Doreen DeLuca, and Donna Jo Napoli, eds. *Signs and Voices: Deaf Culture, Identity, Language, and Arts*. Washington, DC: Gallaudet University Press, 2008.

Lindsay, Geoff. "Inclusive Education: A Critical Perspective." *British Journal of Special Education* 30 (2003): 3–12.

Lucas, Ceil and Robert Bailey. "Variation in Sign Languages: Recent Research on ASL and Beyond." *Language and Linguistics Compass* 5 (2011): 677–690.

## 102 Timothy Reagan

Marschark, Marc, Gladys Tang, and Harry Knoors, eds. *Bilingualism and Bilingual Deaf Education*. Oxford: Oxford University Press, 2014.

Mayer, Connie and C. Tame Akamatsu. "Bilingual-Bicultural Models of Literacy Education for Deaf Students: Considering the Claims." *Journal of Deaf Studies and Deaf Education* 4 (1999): 1–8.

McCaskill, Carolyn, Ceil Lucas, Robert Bailey, and Joseph Hill. *The Hidden Treasure of Black ASL: Its History and Structure*. Washington, DC: Gallaudet University Press, 2011.

McKee, Rachel. "Connecting Hearing Parents with the Deaf World." *Sites: A Journal of Social Anthropology and Cultural Studies* 3 (2006): 143–167.

——— and Victoria Manning. "Evaluating Effects of Language Recognition on Language Rights and the Vitality of New Zealand Sign Language." *Sign Language Studies* 15 (2015): 473–497.

Miles, Susie and Nidhi Singal. "The Education for All and Inclusive Education Debate: Conflict, Contradiction or Opportunity?" *International Journal of Inclusive Education* 14 (2010): 1–15.

Miller, Margery. "Epistemology and People Who Are Deaf: Deaf Worldviews, Views of the Deaf World, or My Parents Are Hearing." *American Annals of the Deaf* 154 (2010): 479–485.

Mittler, Peter. *Working towards Inclusive Education: Social Contexts*. London: Routledge, 2012.

Monaghan, Leila, Constanze Schmaling, Karen Nakamura, and Graham Turner, eds. *Many Ways to be Deaf: International Variation in Deaf Communities*. Washington, DC: Gallaudet University Press, 2003.

Moores, Donald F. "Residential Schools for the Deaf and Academic Placement Past, Present, and Future." *American Annals of the Deaf* 154 (2009): 3–4.

———. "Epistemologies, Deafness, Learning, and Teaching." *American Annals of the Deaf* 154 (2010): 447–455.

——— and Peter V. Paul. "Summary and Prologue: Perspectives on Deaf Epistemologies." *American Annals of the Deaf* 154 (2010): 493–496.

Murray, Joseph. "Linguistic Human Rights Discourse in Deaf Community Activism." *Sign Language Studies* 15 (2015): 379–410.

Neidle, Carol, Judy Kegl, Dawn Maclaughlin, Benjamin Bahan, and Robert Lee. *The Syntax of American Sign Language: Functional Categories and Hierarchical Structure*. Cambridge, MA: MIT Press, 2000.

Nover, Stephen. "History of Language Planning in Deaf Education: The 19th Century." PhD diss., Tucson, AZ: University of Arizona, 2000.

Oliva, Gina. *Alone in the Mainstream: A Deaf Woman Remembers Public School*. Washington, DC: Gallaudet University Press, 2004.

Osgood, Robert. *The History of Inclusion in the United States*. Washington, DC: Gallaudet University Press, 2005.

Padden, Carol. "The Deaf Community and the Culture of Deaf People." In *Sign Language and the Deaf Community: Essays in Honor of William C. Stokoe*, edited by Charlotte Baker and Robbin Battison, 89–103. Silver Spring, MD: National Association of the Deaf, 1980.

——— and Tom Humphries. *Deaf in America: Voices from a Culture*. Cambridge, MA: Harvard University Press, 1988.

———. and Tom Humphries. *Inside Deaf Culture*. Cambridge, MA: Harvard University Press, 2005.

Paul, Peter V. and Donald F. Moores. "Perspectives on Deaf Epistemologies." *American Annals of the Deaf* 154 (2010): 417–420.

Peterson, J. Michael and Mishael Marie Hittie. *Inclusive Teaching: Creating Effective Schools for All Learners*. Boston: Allyn and Bacon, 2003.

Power, Des. "Australian Aboriginal Deaf People and Aboriginal Sign Language." *Sign Language Studies* 13 (2013): 264–277.

Powers, Stephen. "From Concepts to Practice in Deaf Education: A United Kingdom Perspective on Inclusion." *Journal of Deaf Studies and Deaf Education* 7 (2002): 230–243.

Reagan, Timothy. "The Deaf as a Linguistic Minority: Educational Considerations." *Harvard Educational Review* 55 (1985): 265–278.

———. "Nineteenth-Century Conceptions of Deafness: Implications for Contemporary Educational Practice." *Educational Theory* 39 (1989): 39–46.

———. "Cultural Considerations in the Education of Deaf Children." In *Educational and Developmental Aspects of Deafness*, edited by Donald F. Moores and Kay Meadow-Orlans, 73–84. Washington, DC: Gallaudet University Press, 1990.

———. "Toward an 'Archeology of Deafness': Etic and Emic Constructions of Identity in Conflict." *Journal of Language, Identity, and Education* 1 (2002): 41–66.

———. "Ideological Barriers to American Sign Language: Unpacking Linguistic Resistance." *Sign Language Studies* 11 (2011): 594–624.

———. "The DEAF-WORLD and Competence in ASL: Identity and Language Issues." In *Readings in Language Studies*, Volume 3, edited by Paul C. Miller, John Watzke, and Miguel Mantero, 233–246. Lakewood Ranch, FL: International Society for Language Studies, 2012.

Ryan, Donna and John Schuchman, eds. *Deaf People in Hitler's Europe*. Washington, DC: Gallaudet University Press, 2002.

Sandler, Wendy and Diane Lillo-Martin. *Sign Language and Linguistic Universals*. Cambridge: Cambridge University Press, 2006.

Schein, Jerome. *At Home among Strangers: Exploring the Deaf Community in the United States*. Washington, DC: Gallaudet University Press, 1989.

Senghas, Richard and Leila Monaghan. "Signs of Their Times: Deaf Communities and the Culture of Language." *Annual Review of Anthropology* 31 (2002): 69–97.

Siegel, Lawrence. *The Human Right to Language: Communication Access for Deaf Children*. Washington, DC: Gallaudet University Press, 2008.

Simms, Laurene and Helen Thumann. "In Search of a New, Linguistically and Culturally Sensitive Paradigm in Deaf Education." *American Annals of the Deaf* 152 (2007): 302–311.

Singleton, Jenny and Matthew Tittle. "Deaf Parents and Their Hearing Children." *Journal of Deaf Studies and Deaf Education* 5 (2000): 221–236.

Skutnabb-Kangas, Tove. *Linguistic Genocide in Education: Or Worldwide Diversity and Human Rights?* Mahwah, NJ: Lawrence Erlbaum Associates, 2000.

———. "Bilingual Education and Sign Language as the Mother Tongue of Deaf Children." In *English in International Deaf Communication*, edited by Cynthia Kellett Bidoli and Elana Ochese, 75–96. Bern: Peter Lang, 2008.

Slee, Roger. *The Irregular School: Exclusion, Schooling and Inclusive Education*. London: Routledge, 2011.

——— and Julie Allan. "Excluding the Included: A Reconsideration of Inclusive Education." *International Studies in Sociology of Education* 11 (2001): 173–192.

Stone, Joan B. "Minority Empowerment and the Education of Deaf People." In *Cultural and Language Diversity and the Deaf Experience*, edited by Ila Parasnis, 171–180. Cambridge: Cambridge University Press, 1998.

Stremlay, Toya, ed. *The Deaf Way II Anthology: A Literary Collection by Deaf and Hard of Hearing Writers*. Washington, DC: Gallaudet University Press, 2002.

Strong, Michael. "A Bilingual Approach to the Education of Young Deaf Children: ASL and English." In *Language Learning and Deafness*, edited by Michael Strong, 113–129. Cambridge: Cambridge University Press, 1988.

## 104 *Timothy Reagan*

Sutton-Spence, Rachel and Bencie Woll. *The Linguistics of British Sign Language: An Introduction.* Cambridge: Cambridge University Press, 1999.

Swanwick, Ruth and Susan Gregory. *Sign Bilingual Education: Policy and Practice.* Coleford, Gloucestershire: Douglas McLean, 2007.

Tomkins, Lillian. "Cultural and Linguistic Voice in the Deaf Bilingual Experience." In *Literacy and Deaf People: Cultural and Contextual Perspectives*, edited by Brenda Jo Brueggemann, 139–156. Washington, DC: Gallaudet University Press, 2004.

Valli, Clayton, Ceil Lucas, Kristein Mulrooney, and Miako Villanueva. *Linguistics of American Sign Language: An Introduction* (5th ed.). Washington, DC: Gallaudet University Press, 2011.

Wang, Ye. "Without Boundaries: An Inquiry into Deaf Epistemologies through a Metaparadigm." *American Annals of the Deaf* 154 (2010): 428–434.

Winefield, Richard. *Never the Twain Shall Meet: Bell, Gallaudet, and the Communications Debate.* Washington, DC: Gallaudet University Press, 1987.

Wittmann, Henri. "Classification Linguistique des Langues Signées Non Vocalement." *Revue Québécoise de Linguistique Théorique et Appliquée* 10 (1991): 215–288.

Zeshan, Ulrike and Connie De Vos. *Sign Languages in Village Communities: Anthropological and Linguistic Insights.* Berlin: Walter de Gruyter, 2012.

Zhao, Zhenzhou. "Trilingual Education for Ethnic Minorities: Toward Empowerment?" *Chinese Education and Society* 43 (2010): 70–81.

# 6 Transformational Leadership in Chinese Schools

## An Analysis from the Perspective of the Confucian Idea of Transformation

*Jing Ping Sun, Xinping Zhang, and Xuejun Chen*

## Introduction

Organization and management theories in North American in the twentieth century have been significantly influenced by men like Frederick Taylor, Henry Ford, Abraham Maslow and, more recently, Peter Drucker and Tom Peters.[1] Although there are differences in theories between European and U.S. scholars Western functionalist rhetoric about management and leadership are relatively uniform in its character, it being mostly North American with evolving variants of British and other European thinking.[2] Under this broad umbrella, this branch of educational leadership inquiry is fairly new. Educational leadership theories and models started to emerge in the 1950s and in the last 60 years a number of leadership models have been developed with school contexts in mind; for instance, models variously labeled instructional,[3] moral and constructivist[4] have been constructed. Other leadership models aimed to span organizational types and sectors, such as servant, authentic, contingent and situational models.[5] Transformational leadership (TL) models are among the most-studied of this second group.

The evolution of TL concepts for schools over the years reflected the broadening of leadership responsibilities from vision building and the empowering of followers to engaging school stakeholders to improve teaching and learning by developing both teachers' collective capacity and school organizational capacity towards a shared vision.[6] The values associated with Western TL are aligned with the major themes of modern Western ethical agenda, such as, liberty, utility, distributive justice, value congruence, agency and cooperative action, which establish the strategic and moral foundations of authentic transformational leadership.[7] These values fit into the culture characterized as low power distance (less powerful individuals that are unwilling to accept an unequal distribution of power and regard it as normal), low uncertainty avoidance (People that are not nervous about uncertain or unpredictable situations and don't try to avoid such situations by adopting strict codes of behavior or believing in absolute truths.), low individuality (valuing group membership and less individual identity) and medium masculinity (different expectations for men and women of their

## 106  *Jing Ping Sun et al.*

roles in a culture).[8] It appears that low individuality might be contradictory to the high individualism of North American thought but the emergence and advocacy of TL in North America may reflect the wish to place high value on collaboration and team work that can counteract the negative effects of individualism.

Since the development of TL in North America, the notion and examination of this type of leadership quickly extended to other countries, for example, England, Hong Kong, Korea, the Philippines and Tanzania,[9] and more recently Mainland China. Gathering from major English journals in the field of educational administration, a majority of the studies used theoretical frameworks or instrumentations developed in North America to study TL. In China, empirical studies on school leadership models began to appear in Chinese academic journals at the turn of the twenty-first century following the inquiry of TL in the fields of business and psychology in late 1990s. A recent search using the nation's largest database, the Chinese National Knowledge Infrastructure, presented transformational leadership as the most studied leadership model in K-12 settings. Three types of approaches to TL appeared in journals and dissertations: conceptual or reviews introducing the concept and theories of TL developed in North America, survey research using Western instruments, or case studies through a Western theoretical framework, portraying what a school transformational leader may look like.

These approaches to TL and their dominance are, arguably, manifestations of Western theory imperialism—a condition of dominance by one nation over others resulting from an unequal distribution of power, usually associated with economic and technological superiority.[10] Such imperialism is often results in the transferring of knowledge to the periphery through publications in a dominant language (English) and through international students or visiting scholars.[11] While the transplanting of Western theories has provided certain benefits to the advancement of disciplinary inquiry in less developed countries, it has obscured the development of indigenous theories that may have been more suitable for the domestic culture. Given the current convergence in understanding and developing school leadership globally, especially through unveiling distinctive features of leadership particularly effective in specific cultures,[12] we believe the study of indigenous leadership models contextualized within its indigenous culture can add to global understanding and inquiry into leadership.

Indigenous education, focused on teaching indigenous knowledge, models, methods and content, are viable and legitimate. Efforts have been made to embrace special cultural practices and revive indigenous languages and traditions, and in so doing, have improved the educational well-being of indigenous students while ensuring the survival of their culture.[13] Such philosophy towards indigenous education justifies the pursuit for indigenous philosophies on education. Instead of using the term "indigenous" to mean "native" or originating naturally in a particular place in Mainland China, we use "indigenous" to connote a broader meaning of "native" or originating naturally from China. By applying indigenous CTSL, we mean the TSL is unique or native to Chinese culture verses using borrowed leadership models from the West.

Chinese culture is dramatically different from North America with leader legitimacy maintained by intra- and extra-organizational structural arrangements, or in some cases, by historical roots and by higher levels of power distancing.[14] Hierarchy is viewed as a natural way to order social relations with "conformity to the 'natural' order of power relations existing as the norm."[15] It is therefore surprising to have TSL as conceptualized in Western ways existing in Chinese schools. This leads to the following questions: Why does such a type of TSL exist in China? Is it *indigenous*? What should indigenous CTSL look like in current China? How can CTSL adapt to meet the demands stemming from the rapid development in education and modernization while being effective in the environment of current policies ideology? In the ensuing texts, we briefly review the development of TSL in the West, followed by a review of findings on TSL empirical research in Mainland China. We then strive to understand the existence of CTSL in Chinese educational contexts and explain its indigenousness from the perspective of Confucian idea of transformation. Finally, we discuss how Confucianism can infuse CTSL to adapt to ever-changing society, how to foster this type of school leadership practice in Mainland China, and how the study on indigenous Chinese school leaders informs further understanding and development of TSL with a global view and application.

## The Concept of TL as Developed in North America

The term TL was first introduced and systematically discussed by Downton.[16] The conceptualization of TL as a notable approach is commonly considered as beginning with Burns's[17] classic work, *Leadership*. According to Burns, the nature of influence stemming from transformational leadership is the elevation of motivation and morality that both the leader and the followers attain, in particular, the heightened efforts from subordinates. In a non-educational context, the model of TL was developed in its most mature form from Bass and his associates.[18] They developed a "two-factor theory", with transformational and transactional leadership being at the ends of a continuum with most leaders doing some or both.

Referring back to education, the concept of transformational school leadership was first introduced as a promising leadership model to meet the needs of school restructuring.[19] A few reviews[20] of research on TSL from 1996 to 2016 revealed that seven models of transformational leadership have been developed. These include Bass and Avolio's[21] two-factor theory, Kouzes and Posner's[22] *Leadership Practices Inventory* (LPI), Sashkin's visionary leadership, Leithwood's TSL model measured with Principal Leadership Questionnaire (PLQ)[23] and early versions of the Nature of School Leadership

108  *Jing Ping Sun et al.*

survey.[24] Developed initially from business or non-educational settings (see Bass's models), transformational leadership models[25] evolved as including more leadership practices that typically fit school settings. Leithwood and his associates[26] fully developed a leadership model for educational settings that included more than a dozen leadership practices classified into four domains. A more recent review of research evidence in the last ten years[27] identifies 14 TSL practices. Four of them are related to Bass's four "I"s, i.e., inspirational motivation or shared vision, idealized influence or modeling, providing individual support, and providing intellectual stimulation but with variations and additions of new leadership practices that suit school contexts. The other ten practices are related to school cultural building, enlisting support from parents and community, and improving instruction that are uniquely related to school settings.

Empirical studies have so far shown significant large impacts of TSL on teachers' satisfaction with their jobs, their perceptions of their leaders' effectiveness, and their commitment.[28] This type of leadership is also very influential in shaping school culture, school cohesion, developing shared visions and goals in schools, and has positive impact of TL on student learning through various school conditions and teacher variables.[29]

## Transformational Leadership in Mainland China

In the field of education in Mainland China, the concept of transformational leadership was first introduced by a few scholars[30] in major academic journals. Dr. Zhang[31] introduced TL as being more comprehensive and effective compared with transactional leadership. The former inspires and motivates followers by helping them realize higher order needs on Maslow's need ladder, while the latter uses contracts and/or contingent reward and management by exception. A few years after the introduction from the likes of Zhang,[32] empirical research published in academic journals in China has grown. Our search showed that TL has also become the most studied and empirically tested form of leadership in mainland China.[33] Collectively, these studies suggest three findings. First, TSL did exist in Chinese schools because the means of TSL aggregate or individual practices measured by Western instruments were above the average. Second, Chinese principals demonstrated similar leadership practices as conceptualized in Western or adapted Western models (13 in total), which can be classified in four groups: Setting Directions, Developing People, Redesigning School Organizations, and Managing Instruction. The most frequently examined leadership practices are:

- Developing a widely shared vision/goals for the school/ Building consensus /inspirational motivation
- Providing individualized support/consideration/developing an atmosphere of caring and trust/concerned about teachers' existence such as work stress

- Modeling behavior/idealized influence—attribute, behavior or total/ Symbolization/ Charisma
- Providing intellectual stimulation/developing teachers through school visits, training, academic activities and learning from experts and encouraging the consideration of new ideas for teaching
- Moral modeling/modeled behavior/appropriate model

The mean of principals' providing intellectual stimulations to teachers was lower than those of the other four practices.[34] These findings are similar to those reported from North American studies.[35]

Third, we found one unique feature of Chinese TSL, the separation of moral modeling from modeling behaviors. It reflects the emphasis and expectations of Chinese transformation leaders being an ethical change agent, holding and demonstrating high level of values, avoiding the pursuit of personal benefits, putting the organization or others' interests in front of oneself, being devoted to the job without the concern about rewards, working as hard as staff, not attributing staff's corporate accomplishments to oneself and not taking revenge or taking it personally if staff do not agree.[36] This is consistent with the original conceptualization of TL by Burns,[37] who indicated that the nature of influence of transformational leadership is the elevation of motivation and morality both in the leader and followers with the outcome of heightened efforts from subordinates. Finally, TSL had strength in influencing teachers' perceptions of leader effectiveness, teacher emotions (e.g., commitment), and their work engagement. This is also consistent with those reported in previous reviews[38] of studies in the North American context emphasizing TL.

## Why Did Chinese Principals Demonstrate TSL?

Personal factors, or internal antecedents and external antecedents (e.g., organizational factors, policy contexts and national culture) give rise to TSL.[39] Given the rare empirical studies on the former, we explored external factors, including educational reform and policy contexts, organizational development and educational philosophy or national culture that may foster the emergence of CTSL. First, at the national level, Chinese TSL suits the call for continuous improvement of Chinese compulsory education. Since the 1980s, "change" has become the key to continuous development of Chinese compulsory education. Under changing times, transformational leadership, with its unique strength in influencing followers was believed to be the most promising type of leadership as principals could not lead the school by executive orders or just maintain the status quo. They had to be transformational, building relationship with teachers, and morale.[40]

TSL matched the new professional standards for school leaders. In mainland China, the Ministry of Education released the first standards for school leaders in February, 2013.[41] There were six standards structured around five dimensions of school leadership: goal setting and planning, developing cultures, leading instructional programs, developing teachers and optimizing internal structures and management, and adapting to external environment. These standards are consistent with the research rationale underpinning the school leadership standards in North America and overlapped to a large extent with the major TSL practices conceptualized in Liu's[42] model and Leithwood and Louis's[43] model. Such policy contexts fostered the emergence of TSL in China.

Transformational leadership also suited the call for quality schools as envisioned by practitioners and scholars,[44] characterized by highly qualified teachers and school leaders, excellent instructional programs and structure, positive school culture and adequate resources. Concerning human capacity, school leaders should be of high moral, committed and conscientious professionals who have leadership knowledge, management skills, a set of principles for education, model instruction, inspire teachers and build a school into a happy family or community. He or she is charismatic, willing to try new methods, has educational dreams and makes efforts to realize those dreams. Teachers should be a model of morality, experts in disciplinary knowledge and teaching pedagogies, care about students, committed to teaching and willing to sacrifice for the good of others. Quality schools should be a happy place for students and teachers, fostering student (e.g., academically, emotionally, physically) and teacher development (professionally) with students and teachers being respected and engaged, teachers having a say in the decision-making process vs. centralized control, and a shared vision pursuing academic excellence, democracy, harmony, a collaborative and appreciative culture emphasizing shared values, collaboration and an appreciative culture with parents and school community. In these school cultures, capacity building, mindset of "continuous growth", and adapting to external change and environment are emphasized. These are all the school, teacher and student outcomes that TSL has strength to achieve as reflected from research evidence in North America and argued by Chinese scholars.[45]

Research evidence in North America, for example, consistently demonstrate the positive impacts of TSL on developing shared visions, achieving cohesions in schools, developing teachers and instructional capacity in schools and enlisting support from parents and communities (e.g., Leithwood and Sun). Hence, TSL meets the expectations of teachers, principals and professors' imaginations of what ideal school leaders should look like.

Second, at the school level, Chinese TSL meets the needs for capacity building of the school organization and to adapt to changes. Effective educational changes under such transforming times in the Chinese context requires changes in teachers' beliefs and attitudes, their commitment to change, enhanced collective capacity to implement changes, and their wiliness to take risks to try and experiment new things. For teachers' autonomy

_Transformational Leadership_ 111

a collaborative school environment is needed, in which teachers grow professionally, reflect, learn from each other and develop innovative teaching. TSL has the ability to nurture such school cultures, cultivate teachers, promote teacher professionalism, motivate teachers to learn and empower teachers.[46] In such school environments, teachers are more satisfied with their jobs and consider their leaders as being effective.[47]

Finally, we argue that TSL has roots in the Confucian idea of transformation. Confucian philosophy remained a major influence on Chinese culture and shaped the value orientation of Chinese scholars and leaders until the Revolution of 1911, though at some periods giving way or competing with other philosophies such as Daoism and Buddhism. The Confucian tradition suffered a severe setback during the Cultural Revolution (1966–76) and resumed as a formal line of inquiry ever since 1978.

One major way in which Confucianism shaped the value orientation of Chinese scholars and leaders was through the Civil Service Examinations which integrated a canon of classical texts that Confucius, his disciples and Confucian scholars formed and developed (e.g., the Four Books). These canons were considered to be of utmost importance, influential and long-lasting readings for all examinees over a long period of Chinese history.[48] It was largely through this system that Confucianism influenced education and governance and that Confucian ideology was passed down from generation to generation. It is from this perspective and the consideration of its longlasting influence that the Confucian idea of transformation, a main part of the Confucian doctrines, can be regarded as a theory for leadership.

Since the birth of Chinese universities, it may seem that there have not been any connections between Confucian heritage and educational management. However, in contemporary China, the influence of Confucian transformation on educational administration occurs more through the leadership of educators who were influenced by the Confucian tradition, rather than, through domination in formally recognized textbooks or field theories. "Confucianism has played a key role in influencing the nature of school leadership in China which remains overwhelmingly male, with a balance of hierarchy and collectivism".[49] Ribbons and Zhang[50] studied selected head teachers in rural China and found that they highly valued Confucianism even though it was abandoned officially decades ago. They believed Confucianism remained relevant to this day at all levels of society including the nation, the school and the family. Some of the head teachers argued that this could be explained by its emphasis on the need for self-cultivation and the search for ethical and moral perfection. They were deeply influenced by Confucianism and were guided by the sayings of Confucius in their leadership practice.

Confucian idea of transformation can be found in the Four Books, the most representative books of Confucian philosophy. Tu Wei-ming,[51] a Confucian Humanist, retrieves and examines the three core concepts in _The Analects_, namely, "tao" (the Way), "hsüeh" (learning) and "cheng" (politics) of the

## 112 *Jing Ping Sun et al.*

classical period (sixth to third century). According to Tu's interpretation of *Analects*, Confucius believes in the transformability of human beings and in their roles as guardians of human civilization. Morals and virtues transcend life and death and endless self-cultivation is the ultimate goal of human existence, or tao. Self-cultivation, though seemingly an individual matter, "is not the private possession of a single individual, but a shared experience that underlies common humanity".[52] The transformation is creative by actively practicing rituals and interacting with other people. One becomes fully human through continuous interaction with other human beings, communal participation and the active practice of rituals (e.g., the Confucian six arts). During this process, the culture is guarded and transmitted. Confucians not only aim to transform themselves but also strive to transform society into a moral community, either by fulfilling official positions or by undertaking the roles of teachers and advisers. Confucians contend that the transformative power of a benevolent government depends on the self-cultivation of an ethical ruler. The rulers need to transform themselves first and then can transform the state. Confucius imparted *root metaphors* and *framing narratives* of the moral person as a transforming person that have guided philosophical discourse ever since, in the East.[53] Confucius himself was a practitioner of transformational leadership.[54] Hence, we can understand the existence of Chinese TSL in contemporary China if we trace its root to Confucian idea of transformation.

### Indigenous Chinese Transformational School Leadership

The previous sections have exhibited the similarities between CTSL and Western TSL and the uniqueness of Indigenous CTSL. So, what should indigenous CTSL look like? To answer this question, we examine the national context or major philosophies which CTSL roots in, and identify possible features of CTSL that are indigenous. Although traditionally, Confucian educational philosophy has been influencing Chinese education for years,[55] many competing philosophies or factors currently influence school leaders' thinking and behaviors as well, such as: rapid political ideological demands, Marxism and Chinese socialism, school leaders' professional context, modernization and Western new thoughts. Marxism is a required text for all students in Mainland China from middle schools to colleges. For Marxists, the worker is alienated from his or her productive activity, from other human beings and from the distinctive potential for creativity and community. Given private ownership of the means of production, the laborer is forced to sell his labor power to survive. In so doing, he is exploited, creating surplus value for the capitalist.[56] The class struggle between workers and capitalist involves everything that these two major classes do to promote their incompatible interests and can only be solved through revolution (Marx, Karl, *Wage Labor and Capital;* Engels, Friedrich, *Socialism: Utopian and Scientific).* Out of the revolution would emerge a socialist society, which would fully utilize and develop much further the productive potential inherited from capitalism through democratic planning, directing products to serving social needs and abolishing alienation, the attainment of this goal "communism". Built upon this are more recent Chinese Socialist theories developed by presidents and their advisors, including for example, Deng's open door policy, Jiang's Three Representatives, Hu's Three Harmonies, and more recently Xi's "Four Comprehensives". These political theories reflect Chinese Communist Party (CCP) members' efforts to incorporate various philosophies and theories in the hope to move the society forward and influence what educational leaders do at the local level as most principals in public schools in China are CCP members. Under such constant changing political environment, school leaders must be change agents. This political ideology impacts school leaders' leadership style. For example, Hu's three Harmonies (seeking peace in the world, reconciliation with Taiwan and harmony in Chinese society), consistent with one emphasis of ancient Confucian classics, sent a central message to school leaders to maintain the status quo and continue good relationships with school stakeholders, with the former hindering the exercising of TSL and the latter facilitating the enactment of it. In another example, among Xi's Four Comprehensives,[57] "building a moderately prosperous society" and "deepening reform" promote the emergence of TL (as transformational leaders are change agents) while "strictly governing the CCP" may enhance educational leaders' conformity and compliance with the acts and agenda set by the central government. Therefore, Chinese transformational school leaders are change agents, who implement changes that are aligned with the political ideology that governs their behaviors. The compliance with the central government's agenda relates to the shared vision building in schools, a central component of CTSL. This is different from developing a shared vision in a school conceptualized in Western TSL, which is a vision collective designed by stakeholders.

In such a political ideology, school leaders give strong preferences for elements of the Confucian Authority Chain (e.g., establishing order and obedience among staff, demanding their staff to strictly follow school rules) and hold strong belief in the importance of faithfully implementing government policy.[58] Regardless of school leaders' political affiliation, school leaders are required to implement the CCP's political will.[59] The first national criterion for appointing school principals is that they support the CCP's leadership, loving the nation and diligently studying Marxism, and their first fundamental duty is to persistently implement the directives, politics and regulations of the CCP.[60]

In Chinese society, relationship (*Guanxi*) plays an important role in determining leader appointment and what school leaders do. Though school leaders prefer performance-based over relationship-based promotions, principals' appointment and promotion are closely related to which leaders they interact with and build trust and good relationship.[61] Principals rely on *Guanxi* in managing both internal and external school relations and to resolve problems. For instance, school leaders grasp every opportunity to report their school's achievements to officials, put forward their views and bring their schools' needs and problems to officials' attention.[62] Though building relationship and developing teachers is the backbone of TSL in Western concept, *Guanxi* building goes beyond Western conceptions, and is a distinct indigenous component of CTSL.

In the hierarchy of the power along principal, assistant principal, department or division chairs, and teachers, Chinese school leaders welcome the delegation of leadership, but they delegate tasks to those who are moral in their eyes (or holding the similar values as they do), and have good *Guanxi* with them and other external and internal stakeholders.[63] They monitor closely how they execute delegated tasks, and intervene immediately whenever they feel is needed. This is different from fostering collaboration among school staff and encouraging professionals such as teachers to make instructional decisions, as conceptualized in Western TSL. Moreover, due to the unclear division of power among the three parties, (i.e., principal responsible for administration, the school secretary concentrating on ideology, political work and supporting the principal in administration, and the congress of professional teachers to ensure democratic management and supervision over school leadership) power is largely still in the principals' hands,[64] with teachers having little say in decision-making. This is another key feature of indigenous CTSL, task distribution, rather than distributed, or shared leadership, as conceptualized in Western TL.

Besides the influence from internal sources, the school leaders' way of educating and leading are also influenced by Chinese Modernization and the new thoughts the process brought in. The May Fourth Movement in 1919 served as a decisive cultural turning point for Chinese modernity. During that period, Chinese educationalists employed an eclectic array of American, German, French and Russian theories and practices. Chinese universities flourished intellectually. Chiang launched the New Life Movement in 1934, blending elements of Confucianism, Social Darwinism, and fascism with Sun's ideas being suggested theories and guiding practices.[65] Western ideas and practices again dominated the academic world. Works by Marx, Lenin, Gorky and an array of native social critics were widely read. After Deng's Open Door Policy, China experienced the third wave of incorporating Western theories in almost all disciplines, including economy, business and psychology, for instance, which influenced the early content of curriculum in educational management science in China. More recently, Western management and leadership theories are the major sources of required readings for students in the programs of Educational Administration in many Chinese universities.

While boosting China's economy, modernization has also promoted the detachment from tradition, and resulted in the loss of foundational philosophies in education. Rapid modernization, political ideological demands and adoption of Western philosophies in education in hopes of moving the country forward without challenging their suitability to the Chinese context have now led to a situation where China presently appears to have no clear philosophical foundation.[66] In the process of modernization, the current moral climate in China becomes more focused on getting and spending, with the spirit of entrepreneurialism having developed into rampant materialism.[67] In such circumstances, CTSL serves as a promising model and heuristic guide for school principals.

In addition, Confucian philosophical principals such as the integration of humanity with the universe, balancing individuals, society and the natural environment, the integration of learning with life, balancing individual goals with national and global ones, the integration of morality with knowledge, and the integration of knowing and doing[68] about how to get insights from Confucian culture to support modernism, can be used for school leaders to solve problems, lead change, and be creative when short of effective leadership strategies. bounded by *Guanxi*, and pressed with conformity in bureaucracy. The foremost purpose is to maximize the remarkable capacity of Confucian culture and the high degree of integration in Chinese epistemology to accommodate the TSL models developed in Western cultures, absorb some of their best elements into itself and develop a Chinese indigenous model. Tu Wei-ming[69] considers the Confucian faith in the betterment of the human condition through individual effort; commitment to family ethics as the foundation of social stability; trust in the intrinsic value of moral education; belief in self-reliance, the work ethic and mutual aid; and a sense of an organic unity with an ever-exchanging network of relationships all provide rich culture resources for East Asian democracies to develop their own distinctive features. According to him, the process of a country becoming more modern is a process of finding its cultural identity.

The distinctive feature of CTSL, as discussed in previous sections, moral modeling, can help prevent school leaders from becoming "business oriented", "position oriented", "student scores oriented" and even coercive to push teachers to work hard with external incentives available in their hands, an emerging phenomenon in the current Chinese schools.[70] The emphasis of moral excellence is consistent with the initial Western conception of TL.[71] In Confucian philosophy, a pair of essential principles is humanity (*ren*) and propriety (*li*).[72] The nature of human transformation is the development of virtues until moral excellence is reached. The process of self-cultivation and the moralization of governance is a process of transmitting values and culture. The central morality and root of the Confucian culture is "ren" (humanity), symbolizing a holistic manifestation of humanity in its most common and highest state of perfection in Confucianism.[73] For Confucius, a superior person is a moral leader, which is the source of their leadership transformation, hence the strength of CTSL. As well, Confucius's leadership comes from a transcendent vision of fulfillment, justice and peace based upon the right order of relationships.[74] This strength in Confucianism,

## 116   *Jing Ping Sun et al.*

if incorporated in CTSL, can help school leaders to cope with the bound *Guanxi* while make balanced use of it to develop supportive, harmonious environments in and out of schools.

## Discussion

This chapter examined the status of research on TSL in Mainland China and found Chinese principals do exercise TSL but the level is only moderately high. We found that school leadership standards, continuous educational reform contexts, calls for quality schools and needs for capacity building in schools, as well as a Confucian transformation culture, foster the emergence of CTSL. Further, we also identified six distinct features of indigenous CTSL. In addition to providing the four "I"s as conceptualized in Western TSL, Chinese transformational school leaders are change agents and at the same time conform to government mandates; they develop a shared vision aligned with government ideology; they distribute tasks to others but closely monitor them to make sure they complete the tasks in the way they wish and they build relationships with people as one of their central leadership activities. They model moral excellence, the source of their leadership. A sustained educational process of re-examining the legacy of Confucianism in light of modernism, Chinese political ideology and educational operation systems can help find Chinese indigenous TSL. Intentional reflection, through rational reasoning[75] and critical thinking[76] could be a fruitful process in developing a unique CTSL. Reflecting without regard for cultural tradition, on the other hand, will have a consequence that one fails to grasp the appropriate ways of dealing with situations and will therefore endanger oneself and/or others in the sense of losing one's foothold in reality, a reality that can only be adequately apprehended through the categories shared by one's culture.[77]

CTSL appears to be one of the most promising school leadership models that suits the Chinese current educational reform contexts. Change has become the key to continuous development of Chinese compulsory education and how to make schools successful during the process of constant change.[78] As a result, some scholars propose that school leaders must be transformational, relational and moral as they cannot maintain the status quo anymore or resort to executive orders to guide school activities[79] and must lead under a high level of uncertainty.[80] Due to the concentration of power in principals, school staff loses interest and motivation to adapt to change. Breakthrough must be made in school leadership so that school leaders can be more motivational and effective for continuous school improvement.[81] Tang[82] points out that the success of some Shanghai schools is due to TSL, with leaders who are charismatic, believe in change as the solution to future development and teacher engagement as the ultimate source of change. Typical CTSL strategies such as inspiring school staff by appealing visions, developing team spirit and facilitating teachers' professional development are important tools for school leaders.[83]

We noticed that most Chinese principals demonstrated TSL, but at a moderate level, especially when providing intellectual stimulation. Their impacts on teacher perceived leader effectiveness[84] and teacher commitment[85] were relatively lower when compared to results reported from North America.[86] These results may owe to two issues. One is about research factors. For example, translated instruments for measuring Chinese TSL and outcome variables may not be satisfactory in terms of reliability and validity to capture the strength of CTSL. The application of more rigorous research designs, indigenous instruments and more sophisticated statistical analysis and qualitative approaches have the potential to unveil the strengths of and impacts of CTSL. As well, it may be worthwhile developing CTSL into a relational process, due to its strength in relationship building.

The second issue is about school leaders' TSL capacity. The level of TSL Chinese school leaders exhibited may indicate that their grasp of this type of leadership needs to be improved. In particular, principals need help or professional training in order to provide intellectual stimulation and provide needed, effective teacher professional development to teachers. Most principals have found themselves ill-prepared to navigate school-wide transformation of strategic planning, curriculum, instruction, teacher development, performance review and other key components of school management.[87] The development of indigenous knowledge about school leadership in these regards is urgently needed.

Leadership preparation programs in China will have to take on more responsibilities to train and coach principals, explore and develop indigenous knowledge and theories about leadership, interpret multiple influencers on school leadership, define indigenous knowledge concerning indigenous leadership and create theoretical frameworks on implementation. New or updated leadership models and theories will bring forth what school leaders, teachers and students long for, that is, a more harmonious connection with political ideology, while at the same time, remaining true to traditional Confucian philosophies.

There is a gap between acknowledgement and prosperity of this type of leadership. To fill the gap, besides the development of indigenous CTSL and training, sound implementation of this type of leadership also matters. To implement TL in Chinese schools, the following four ideas may prove to be useful:

- When developing a shared vision, it is essential to consult all stakeholders, tap into the hearts, reconcile the values of all stakeholders and construct an agenda. Only by this, the shared vision can be the "lighthouse" for the school,[88] can be motivational and increase the school's potential to improve and adapt to change.[89]
- School leaders are encouraged to build partnerships with teachers rather than being at the opposite spectrum to them.[90] This can be done through understanding and respecting teachers' work and opinions,

118  *Jing Ping Sun et al.*

helping teachers to realize their higher order of needs by fostering organizational change and capacity building, and fostering collaboration, in which teachers make shared decisions and learn from each other. This would foster real transformation of school and changes in teachers' beliefs and behaviours.[91]

- School leaders are encouraged to improve their charisma by providing teachers with individualized support and building harmonious relationships with them rather than using contingent reward, salary incentives and positional power. This would turn control into empowerment and encouragement.[92]
- School leaders are encouraged to nurture collective and distributive leadership to an array of stakeholders to foster the collective efforts of teachers, parents and students as a means to work together and grow interdependently, avoiding the only "great man" role in schools.
- School leaders shall make leadership a process of moral excellence; and not only to meet the needs of organizational goals, school goals that are under the accountability policy context but also the authentic needs of teachers and students while moving forward to a common cause.[93] Teachers should be the most important resource in school organizations.

In conclusion, transformational leadership has been considered as a promising type of leadership that suits the needs of Chinese schools as they adapt to transforming times in contemporary China. The knowledge initiated from Mainland China would contribute to our knowledge base and global understanding of this type of leadership, therefore avoiding being the "photocopier" of Western research or "silence"[94] situation of Chinese research. More indigenous leadership knowledge developed in non-Western contexts, combined with Western leadership theories, would eventually help us to understand and develop leadership theories with a global view and application. School leaders are encouraged to engage in critical thinking, deep learning, lifelong and life-wide learning to look for insights and inspirations from Confucianism.[95] This will, in turn, assist Chinese principals to cope with demands from multiple philosophical, professional, societal and political sources and lead schools forward to help each student succeed.

## Notes

1. Peter Blunt and Jones Merrick, "Exploring the Limits of Western Leadership Theory in East Asia and Africa," *Personnel Review* 1 no. 2 (1997): 6–23.
2. Chris Brewster and Henning Larsen, "Human Resources Management in Europe: Evidence from Ten Countries," *International Journal of Human Resource* 3 no. 3 (1992): 409–432; Blunt and Merrick, "Exploring the Limits of Western Leadership Theory in East Asia and Africa," 6–23.
3. Philip Hallinger, "The Evolving Role of American Principals: From Managerial to Instructional to Transformational Leaders," *Journal of Educational Administration* 30 no. 3 (1992): 35; Philip Hallinger, Wen-Chung Wang, and Chia-Wen

Chen, "Assessing the Measurement Properties of the Principal Instructional Management Rating Scale," *Educational Administration Quarterly* 49 (2013): 272–309; Philip Hallinger and Ronald H. Heck, "Exploring the Principal's Contribution to School Effectiveness: 1980–1995," *School Effectiveness and School Improvement* 9 (1998): 157–191.

4. Kenneth Leithwood and Daniel Duke, "A Century's Quest for a Knowledge Base, 1976–1998," in *Handbook of Research on Educational Policy*, ed. Joseph Murphy and Karen Seashore Louis (San Francisco: Jossey-Bass, 1999), 45–72.

5. John Antonakis, Anna T. Cianciolo, and Robert Sternberg, *The Nature of Leadership* (Washington, DC: Sage Publications, 2004).

6. Kenneth Leithwood and Jingping Sun, "The Nature and Effects of Transformational School Leadership: A Meta-Analytic Review of Unpublished Research," *Educational Administration Quarterly* 48 (2012): 387–423.

7. Bernard M. Bass and Paul Steidlmeier, "Ethics, Character, and Authentic Transformational Leadership Behavior," *The Leadership Quarterly* 10 no. 2 (1999): 181–217.

8. Blunt and Merrick, "Exploring the Limits of Western Leadership Theory in East Asia and Africa," 6–23.

9. Leithwood and Sun, "The Nature and Effects of Transformational School Leadership," 387–423.

10. Blunt and Merrick, "Exploring the Limits of Western Leadership Theory in East Asia and Africa," 6–23.

11. Mary McLean, "Educational Dependency: A Critique," *Compare* 13 no. 1 (1983): 25–42.

12. Allan Walker and Phillip Hallinger, "International Perspectives on Leader Development," *Educational Management Administration & Leadership* 41 no. 4 (2013): 401–404.

13. Stephen May and Sheila Aikman, "Indigenous Education: Addressing Current Issues and Developments," *Comparative Education* 39 no. 2 (May 1, 2003): 139–145.

14. Geert Hofstede, *Culture's Consequences*: *Cross-Cultural Research and Methodology Series* (Beverly Hills: Sage Publication, 1980).

15. Blunt and Merrick, "Exploring the Limits of Western Leadership Theory in East Asia and Africa," 6–23.

16. James V. Downton, *Rebel Leadership: Commitment and Charisma in a Revolutionary Process* (New York, NY: Free Press, 1973).

17. James Burns, *Leadership* (New York, NY: Harper & Row, 1978).

18. Bernard Bass, *Leadership and Performance Beyond Expectations* (New York: The Free Press, 1985); Bernard Bass and Bruce Avolio, *Multifactor Leadership Questionnaire* (Palo Alto: Mind Garden, 1995).

19. Kenneth Leithwood, *Contributions of Transformational Leadership to School Restructuring* (Paper presented at the Annual Meeting of the University Council for Educational Administration. Houston, TX, October 29–31, 1993); Phillip Podsakoff, Scott MacKenzie, Robert Moorman, and Richard Fetter, "Transformational Leader Behaviors and Their Effects on Followers' Trust in Leader, Satisfaction, and Organizational Citizenship Behaviors," *The Leadership Quarterly* 1 no. 2 (1990): 107–142.

20. Kenneth Leithwood and Doris Jantzi, "A Review of Transformational School Leadership Research 1996–2005," *Leadership and Policy in Schools* 4 (2005): 177–199; Kenneth Leithwood and Jingping Sun, "The Nature and Effects of Transformational School Leadership: A Meta-Analytic Review of Unpublished Research," *Educational Administration Quarterly* 48 (2012): 387–423; Jose Weinstein, ed., *Educational Leadership in Schools: Nine Perspectives* (Santiago, Chilies: University Diego Portales Press, 2016).

120  *Jing Ping Sun et al.*

21. Bernard Bass and Bruce Avolio, *MLQ—Multifactor Leadership Questionnaire* (Palo Alto, CA: Mind Garden, 1990); Bruce Avolio, Bernard Bass, and Dong I. Jung, "Reexamining the Components of Transformational and Transactional Leadership using the Multifactor Leadership Questionnaire," *Journal of Occupational & Organizational Psychology* 72 (1999): 441–462.
22. James M. Kouzes and Barry Zane Posner, *Leadership Practices Inventory: A Self-Assessment and Analysis* (San Francisco, CA: Jossey-Bass, 1993); James M. Kouzes and Barry Zane Posner, *The Leadership Challenge: How to Keep Getting Extraordinary Things Done in Organizations* (San Francisco, CA: Jossey-Bass, 1995).
23. Doris Jantzi and Kenneth Leithwood, "Toward an Explanation of Variation in Teachers' Perceptions of Transformational School Leadership," *Educational Administration Quarterly* 32 (1996): 512–538; Kenneth Leithwood and Doris Jantzi, "Explaining Variation in Teachers' Perceptions of Principals' Leadership: A Replication," *Journal of Educational Administration* 35 (1997): 312–331; Kenneth Leithwood and Doris Jantzi, "Transformational School Leadership Effects: A Replication," *School Effectiveness and School Improvement* 10 (1999): 451–479.
24. Kenneth A. Leithwood, Robert Aitken, and Doris Jantzi, *Making Schools Smarter*, 3rd ed. (Thousand Oaks, CA: Corwin Press, 2006); Leithwood and Sun, "The Nature and Effects of Transformational School Leadership," 387–423.
25. Kouzes and Posner, *Leadership Practices*, 5; Marshall Sashkin, "Transformational Leadership Approaches: A Review and Synthesis," in *The Nature of Leadership*, ed. John Antonakis, Anna T. Cianciolo, and Robert J. Sternberg (Thousand Oaks, CA: Sage Publications, 2004), 171–196; Leithwood and Sun, "The Nature and Effects of Transformational School Leadership," 387–423.
26. Leithwood and Jantzi, "Transformational School Leadership Effects," 451–479.
27. Jose Weinstein, ed., *Educational Leadership in Schools: Nine Perspectives* (Santiago, Chilies: University Diego Portales Press, 2016).
28. Leithwood and Jantzi, "Transformational School Leadership Effects," 451–479; Leithwood and Sun, "The Nature and Effects of Transformational School Leadership," 387–423.
29. Jingping Sun and Ken Leithwood, "Transformational School Leadership Effects on Student Achievement," *Leadership & Policy in Schools* 11 no. 4 (2012): 418–451; Leithwood and Sun, "The Nature and Effects of Transformational School Leadership," 387–423; Jingping Sun and Kenneth Leithwood, *Leadership Effects on Student Learning Mediated by Teacher Emotions* (Basel: MDPI AG, 2015).
30. XinPing Zhang, "Burns' Transformational Leadership Theory and Principal's Role Transformation," *Research in Educational Development* 5–6 (2008): 44–50; N.-K. Lo, X.-L. Li, and M.-H. Lai, "Transformational Leadership Theory and Its Implications for School Reform in China," *Fudan Education Forum* 8 (2010): 25–30; Xinzhong Yao, *An Introduction to Confucianism*, 1st. publ. ed. (Cambridge: Cambridge University Press, 2000).
31. Xinping Zhang, "Burns' Transformational," 44–50.
32. Ibid.
33. Variations of the translations of transformational leadership were used as the keywords to search empirical studies on TL in Chinese National Knowledge Infrastructure, the largest database in the field of education. The search yielded 363 published articles in a wide range of disciplines: business, management, human resource, health, psychology, tourism, economics, science, and engineering, social science, nursing, industry, humanities, higher education, finance, statistics, as well as K-12 education.
34. Cao, "The Relationship"; Li (2008); Wi Liu, "The Research on Transformative Curriculum Leadership Behavior of the Principal in Senior Middle-School in

Xinjiang" (MA thesis., Xinjiang Normal University, 2010); Liu, "The Research on Transformative Curriculum Leadership Behavior of the Principal in Senior Middle-School in Xinjiang"; Liu, "Motivating Teachers."

35. Leithwood and Louis, *Linking Leadership*, 12.
36. Han (2008).
37. Burns, *Leadership*, 4.
38. Leithwood and Jantzi, "Transformational School Leadership Effects," 451–479; Leithwood and Sun, "The Nature and Effects of Transformational School Leadership," 387–423.
39. Leithwood and Jantzi, "Transformational School Leadership Effects," 451–479.
40. Zhong Jing Huang, "How School Leaders Transform Schools," *Educational Development Research* 18 (2009).
41. Chen, "The Relationship."
42. Liu, "Motivating Teachers."
43. Leithwood and Louis, *Linking Leadership*, 12.
44. Zhang (2015).
45. Zhang, "Burns' Transformational": Wen Hui Zhu and Yu Le Jin, "K-12 Educational Administration under the Vision of Transformational Leadership," *Modern Educational Administration* 5 (2014): 15–19.
46. Li, Li, and Lu, "An Analysis," 11.
47. Xin Zhuo Zhang, "An Analysis of Teachers' Perception and Job Satisfaction on Principal Behaviors: With the Example of Junior High Schools in Yanbian Area" (MA thesis., Jilin: Yanbian University, 2012).
48. Hayhoe, *China's Universities*, 8.
49. Tony Bush and Qiang Haiyan, "Leadership and Culture in Chinese Education," *Asia Pacific Journal of Education* 20 (2000): 58–67.
50. Peter Ribbins and Junhua Zhang, "Culture, Societal Culture and School Leadership: A Study of Selected Head Teachers in Rural China," *International Studies in Educational Administration* 34 no. 1 (2006): 71–88.
51. Wei-ming Tu, *The Way, Learning, and Politics: Essays on the Confucian Intellectual*. SUNY Series in Chinese Philosophy and Culture (Albany: State University of New York Press, 1993).
52. Wei-ming Tu, *Confucian Thought: Selfhood as Creative Transformation* (New York: SUNY Press, 1985).
53. Bernard Bass, "Two Decades of Research and Development in Transformational Leadership," *European Journal of Work and Organizational Psychology* 8 no. 1 (1999): 9–32.
54. Bernard Bass, *Multifactor Leadership Questionnaire* (Palo Alto: Consulting Psychologists Press, 1996).
55. Ruth Hayhoe, *China's Universities 1895–1995* (Hong Kong: CERC, University of Hong Kong, 1999).
56. Bertell Ollman, *Alienation: Marx's Conception of Man in Capitalist Society* (Cambridge: University Press, 1971).
57. The four Comprehensives are: Comprehensively building a moderately prosperous society, comprehensively deepening reform, comprehensively governing the nation according to law, and comprehensively strictly governing the CCP. BBC News. Retrieved 2016–04–08.
58. Lam (2009).
59. Ibid.
60. Ministry of Education (1991)
61. Lam (2009).
62. Ibid.
63. Ibid.
64. Ibid.

## 122  *Jing Ping Sun et al.*

65. Batchelor, Randall Shon, *Borrowing Modernity: A Comparison of Educational Change in Japan, China, and Thailand from the Early Seventeenth to the Mid-Twentieth Century* (2005). Bozeman, MT: Montana State University.
66. Carsten Schmidtke and Peng Chen, "Philosophy of Vocational Education in China: A Historical Overview," *Journal of Philosophy of Education* 46 no. 3 (2012): 432–448.
67. W. O. Lee, David Grossman, Kerry Kennedy, and Gregory Fairbrother, eds., *Citizenship Education in Asian and the Pacific Concpets and Issues* (New York: Springer, 2004).
68. Ming-Yuan Gu; Ying-jie Wang, cited in Ruth Hayhoe, *Portraits of Influential Chinese Educators* (Berlin: Springer, 2006).
69. Wei-Ming Tu, "Confucian Traditions in East Asian Modernity," *Bulletin of the American Academy of Arts and Sciences* 50 no. 2 (1996): 12–39.
70. Zhang, "Burn's Transformational," 7.
71. Burns, *Leadership*, 4; Bass, "Two Decades of Research and Development in Transformational Leadership," 9–32.
72. Herbert Fingarette, *Confucius, the Secular as Sacred* (New York: Harper & Row, 1972).
73. Tu, *Confucian Thought*, 26.
74. Bass, "Two Decades of Research and Development in Transformational Leadership," 9–32.
75. Chi-Ming Lam, "Confucian Rationalism," *Educational Philosophy and Theory* 46 no. 13 (2014): 1450–1461.
76. Sigurðsson (2017).
77. Ibid.
78. Huang, "How School Leaders Transform School," 70–73.
79. Ibid.
80. Tao Zhang and Hong Li, "The Enlightenment of Transformational Leadership on Principals," *Teaching and Management* 2 (2005): 3–4.
81. Huang, "How School Leaders Transform School," 70–73.
82. Zong-Qing Tang, "Transformational Leadership and Leadership Strategies," *Elementary and Middle School Educational Administration* 8 (2006).
83. Zong-Qing Tang (2006).
84. Peng Li and De Quan Zhu, "Multidimensional Measurement of the Effectiveness of Transformational Leadership in School," *Education Science* 31 no. 1 (2015): 26–32.
85. Li, "Relationships."
86. Leithwood and Jantzi, *A Review*, 5; Leithwood and Sun, *The Nature*, 4.
87. Chu and Fu (2011).
88. Zhu and Jin, "K-12 Educational Administration under the Vision of Transformational Leadership."
89. Zhang and Hong, "The Enlightenment of Transformational Leadership on Principals," 3–4.
90. Zhang, "Burn's Transformational," 7.
91. Nai Gui Lu, Xiao Lei Li, and Wan Hong Li. "The Enlightenment of Transformational Leadership on China's School Reform," *Fudan Education Forum* 5 (2010): 25–30.
92. Zhang, "Burn's Transformational," 7: 44–50.
93. James McGray Burns, *Leadership*, trans. Jiang Chang, Haiyan Sun, et al. (Beijing: Remin University of China Press, 2006).
94. Zheng, Kangsheng; Huan, Jialiang 2012. People Forum.
95. Janette Ryan and Kam Louie, "False Dichotomy? 'Western' and 'Confucian' Concepts of Scholarship and Learning," *Educational Philosophy and Theory* 39 no. 4 (2007): 404–417.

## Bibliography

Antonakis, John, Anna T. Cianciolo, and Robert Sternberg. *The Nature of Leadership*. Washington, DC: Sage Publications, 2004.

Avolio, Bruce, Bass Bernard, and Dong I. Jung. "Reexamining the Components of Transformational and Transactional Leadership Using the Multifactor Leadership Questionnaire." *Journal of Occupational & Organizational Psychology* 72 (1999): 441–462.

Bass, Bernard M. *Leadership and Performance Beyond Expectations*. New York: The Free Press, 1985.

———. "Two Decades of Research and Development in Transformational Leadership." *European Journal of Work and Organizational Psychology* 8 (1999): 9–32.

——— and Bruce Avolio. *MLQ—Multifactor Leadership Questionnaire*. Palo Alto, CA: Mind Garden, 1990.

———. and Bruce Avolio. *Multifactor Leadership Questionnaire*. Palo Alto, CA: Mind Garden, 1995.

———. and Bruce Avolio. *Multifactor Leadership Questionnaire*. Palo Alto, CA: Shi, 1996.

——— and Paul Steidlmeier. "Ethics, Character, and Authentic Transformational Leadership Behavior." *The Leadership Quarterly* 10 no. 2 (1999): 181–217.

Blunt, Peter and Merrick Jones. "Exploring the Limits of Western Leadership Theory in East Asia and Africa." *Personnel Review* 1 no. 2 (1997): 6–23.

Brewster, Chris and Henning Larsen. "Human Resources Management in Europe: Evidence from Ten Countries." *International Journal of Human Resource* 3 no. 3 (1992): 409–432.

Burns, James McGray. *Leadership*. New York, NY: Harper & Row, 1978.

———. *Leadership*. Translated by Jiang Chang, Haiyan Sun, et al., Beijing: Remin University of China Press, 2006.

Bush, Tony and Qiang Haiyan. "Leadership and Culture in Chinese Education." *Asia Pacific Journal of Education* 20 (2000): 58–67.

Cai, Jin Xiong. "The Relationships between School Effectiveness and Transformational Leadership, Transactional Leadership and School Culture." PhD diss., Taibei: Taiwan Normal University, 2000.

Cao, Ke Yan. "The Relationship between Transformational Leadership and the Teachers' Organizational Commitment in the Junior Middle School." MA thesis, Guangzhou: South China Normal University, 2007.

Chen, Hao Ting. "The Impact of Transformational Leadership on the Organizational Citizenship Behavior and Turnover Intention of Kindergarten Staff." MA thesis, Kaifeng: Henan University, 2013.

Chen, Lei. "The Relationship of Personalities, Self-Efficacy and Leadership Styles of Middle School Leaders." MA thesis, Jinan: Shandong Normal University, 2006.

Chen, Yao. "An Analysis of Gender Difference among Principals under Transformational Leadership." MA thesis., Beijing: Nanjing Normal University.

Downtown, James V. *Rebel Leadership: Commitment and Charisma in the Revolutionary Process*. New York: The Free Press, 1973.

Fingarette, Herbert. *Confucius, the Secular as Sacred*. New York: Harper & Row, 1972.

Geovanni, Thomas J. *A Practice on Reflection*. Translated by Hong Zhang. Shanghai: Shanghai Education Press, 2004.

Hallinger, Philip. "The Evolving Role of American Principals: From Managerial to Instructional to Transformational Leaders." *Journal of Educational Administration* 30 no. 3 (1992): 35. doi:10.1108/09578239210014306. http://search.proquest.com/docview/220458343.

## 124 *Jing Ping Sun et al.*

——— and Kenneth Leithwood. "Culture and Educational Administration: A Case of Finding Out What You Don't Know You Don't Know." *Journal of Educational Administration* 34 no. 5 (1996): 98–116.

——— and Ronald H. Heck. "Exploring the Principal's Contribution to School Effectiveness: 1980–1995." *School Effectiveness and School Improvement* 9 (1998): 157–191.

———, Wen-Chung Wang, and Chia-Wen Chen. "Assessing the Measurement Properties of the Principal Instructional Management Rating Scale." *Educational Administration Quarterly* 49 (2013): 272–309.

Hayhoe, Ruth. *China's Universities 1895–1995*. Hong Kong: CERC, University of Hong Kong, 1999.

———. *Portraits of Influential Chinese Educators*. Berlin: Springer, 2006.

Hofstede, Geert. *Culture's Consequences: Cross-Cultural Research and Methodology Series*. Beverly Hills: Sage Publications, 1980.

Huang, Zhong Jing. "How School Leaders Transform Schools." *Educational Development Research* 18 (2009): 70–73.

Jantzi, Doris and Kenneth Leithwood. "Toward an Explanation of Variation in Teachers' Perceptions of Transformational School Leadership." *Educational Administration Quarterly* 32 (1996): 512–538.

Ji, Meng. "The Kindergarten Principal Transformational Leadership Behavior and Its Influencing Factors." MA thesis, Chongqing: Southwest University, 2014.

Klitgaard, Robert. "Taking Culture into Account: From 'Let's' to 'How'." In *Culture and Development in Africa*, edited by Ismail Serageldin and June Taboroff, 75–120. Washington, DC: World Bank, 1994.

Kluckhohn, Clyde. *Navaho Witchcraft*. Boston: Beacon Press, 1967.

Kouzes, James M. and Barry Zane Posner. *Leadership Practices Inventory: A Self-Assessment and Analysis*. San Francisco, CA: Jossey-Bass, 1993. http://catalog. hathitrust.org/Record/004536097.

———. *The Leadership Challenge: How to Keep Getting Extraordinary Things Done in Organizations*. San Francisco, CA: Jossey-Bass, 1995.

Lam, Chi-Ming. "Confucian Rationalism." *Educational Philosophy and Theory* 46 no. 13 (2014): 1450–1461.

Leithwood, Kenneth. *Contributions of Transformational Leadership to School Restructuring*. Paper presented at the Annual Meeting of the University Council for Educational Administration. Houston, TX, October 29–31, 1993.

———, Robert Aitken, and Doris Jantzi. *Making Schools Smarter* (3rd ed.). Thousand Oaks, CA: Corwin Press, 2006.

——— and Daniel L. Duke. "A Century's Quest for a Knowledge Base, 1976–1998." In *Handbook of Research on Educational Policy*, edited by Joseph Murphy and Karen Seashore Louis, 45–72. San Francisco: Jossey Bass, 1999.

——— and Doris Jantzi. "Explaining Variation in Teachers' Perceptions of Principals' Leadership: A Replication." *Journal of Educational Administration* 35 (1997): 312–331. doi:10.1108/09578239710171910. http://search.proquest. com/docview/220459223.

——— and Doris Jantzi. "Transformational School Leadership Effects: A Replication." *School Effectiveness and School Improvement* 10 (1999): 451–479. doi:10.1076/sesi.10.4.451.3495. www.tandfonline.com/doi/abs/10.1076/sesi. 10.4.451.3495.

——— and Doris Jantzi. "A Review of Transformational School Leadership Research 1996–2005." *Leadership and Policy in Schools* 4 (2005): 177–199. doi:10.1080/15700760500244769. www.tandfonline.com/doi/abs/10.1080/157 00760500244769.

——— and Karen Seashore-Louis. *Linking Leadership to Student Learning*. US: Jossey-Bass, 2012. http://ebooks.ciando.com/book/index.cfm/bok_id/486677.

———— and Jingping Sun. "The Nature and Effects of Transformational School Leadership: A Meta-Analytic Review of Unpublished Research." *Educational Administration Quarterly* 48 (2012): 387–423. http://search.proquest.com/docview/1022966000.

Li, Chaoping and Kan Shi. "The Structure and Measurement of Transformational Leadership in China." *Frontiers of Business Research in China* 2 (2008): 571–590. www.econis.eu/PPNSET?PPN=589088807.

Li, Dong-Jia. "Relationship Analysis between Principals' Transformational Leadership, Teachers' Organizational Commitment and Teachers' Job Satisfaction of Rural Middle School." MA thesis, Suzhou: Soochow University, 2010.

Li, Peng and De Quan Zhu. "Multidimensional Measurement of the Effectiveness of Transformational Leadership in School." *Education Science* 31 no. 1 (2015): 26–32.

Li, Wei. "An Analysis of Transformational Behaviors among Xinjiang High School Principals." MA thesis, Xinjiang: Xinjiang Normal University.

Li, Xiao Lei, Wan Hong Li, and Nai Gui Lu. "An Analysis of Principal Leadership That Promotes Teacher Development: An Exemplary of Two Junior High School Principals." *Educational Development Research* 4 (2012): 70–74.

Liu, Peng. "Motivating Teachers' Commitment to Change by Transformational School Leadership in Urban Upper Secondary Schools of Shenyang City, China." EdD diss., University of Toronto, 2013. http://hdl.handle.net/1807/35883.

Liu, Wi. "The Research on Transformative Curriculum Leadership Behavior of the Principal in Senior Middle-School in Xinjiang." MA thesis, Urumqi, Xingjang: Xinjiang Normal University, 2010.

Lo, Nai-Kwai, Li, Xiao-Lei, and Lai, Man-Hong. "Transformational Leadership Theory and Its Implications for School Reform in China." *Fudan Education Forum* 8 (2010): 25–30.

Lu, Nai Gui, Li Xiao Lei, and Li Wan Hong. "The Enlightenment of Transformational Leadership on China's School Reform." *Fudan Education Forum* 5 (2010): 25–30.

May, Stephen and Sheila Aikman. "Indigenous Education: Addressing Current Issues and Developments." *Comparative Education* 39 no. 2 (May 1, 2003): 139–145.

McLean, Mary. "Educational Dependency: A Critique." *Compare* 13 no. 1 (1983): 25–42.

Peters, Michael A. "The Humanist Bias in Western Philosophy and Education." *Educational Philosophy and Theory* 47 no. 11 (2015): 1128–1135.

Podsakoff, Philip M., Scott B. MacKenzie, Robert H. Moorman, and Richard Fetter. "Transformational Leader Behaviors and Their Effects on Followers' Trust in Leader, Satisfaction, and Organizational Citizenship Behaviors." *The Leadership Quarterly* 1 no. 2 (1990): 107–142.

Reed, Gay Garland. "Multidimensional Citizenshship, Confucian Humanism and the Imagined Community: South Korea and China." In *Citizenship Education in Asian and the Pacific Concpets and Issues*, edited by W. O. Lee, David Grossman, Kerry Kennedy, and Gregory Fairbrother, 239–255. New York: Springer, 2004.

Ribbins, Peter and Junhua Zhang. "Culture, Societal Culture and School Leadership: A Study of Selected Head Teachers in Rural China." *International Studies in Educational Administration* 34 no. 1 (2006): 71–88.

Ryan, Janette and Kam Louie. "False Dichotomy? 'Western' and 'Confucian' Concepts of Scholarship and Learning." *Educational Philosophy and Theory* 39 no. 4 (2007): 404–417.

Sashkin, Marshall "Transformational Leadership Approaches: A Review and Synthesis." In *The Nature of Leadership*, edited by John Antonakis, Anna T. Cianciolo, and Robert J. Sternberg, 171–196. Thousand Oaks, CA: Sage Publications, 2004.

# 126  Jing Ping Sun et al.

Sun, Jingping. "The Nature, Impacts and Antecedents of Transformational School Leadership: A Review." In *Educational Leadership in Schools: Nine Perspectives*, edited by Jose Weinstein. Santiago, Chilies: University Diego Portales Press, 2016a.

———— "The Nature, Impacts and Antecedents of Transformational Leadership: A Review." In *Educational Leadership in Schools: Nine Perspectives*, edited by Jose Weistein. Santiago: University Diego Portales Press, 2016b: 81–120.

———— and Kenneth Leithwood. "Transformational School Leadership Effects on Student Achievement." *Leadership & Policy in Schools* 11 no. 4 (2012): 418–451.

———— and Kenneth Leithwood. *Leadership Effects on Student Learning Mediated by Teacher Emotions*. Basel: MDPI AG, 2015.

Tang, Zong-Qing. "Transformational Leadership and Leadership Strategies." *Elementary and Middle School Educational Administration* 8 (2006): 25–27.

Tian, Li-Li. *A Study on Transformational Leadership of Middle School Principal and Its Relationship with Leadership Effectiveness*. Henan: Henan University, 2005.

Tu, Wei-Ming. *Confucian thought: Selfhood as Creative Transformation*, New York: SUNY, 1985.

————. *The Way, Learning, and Politics: Essays on the Confucian Intellectual*. SUNY Series in Chinese Philosophy and Culture. Albany: State University of New York Press, 1993.

————. "Confucian Traditions in East Asian Modernity." *Bulletin of the American Academy of Arts and Sciences* 50 no. 2 (1996): 12–39.

Walker, Allan and Clive Dimmock. *School Leadership and Administration: Adopting a Cultural Perspective*. Reference Books in International Education. London: Routledge, 2012.

———— and Philip Hallinger. "International Perspectives on Leader Development." *Educational Management Administration & Leadership* 41 no. 4 (2013): 401–404.

Yao, Xinzhong. *An Introduction to Confucianism* (1st. publ. ed.). Cambridge: Cambridge University Press, 2000.

Zhang, Tao and Hong Li. "The Enlightenment of Transformational Leadership on Principals." *Teaching and Management* 2 (2005): 3–4.

Zhang, Xingping. "Thoughts on Burns' Transformational Leadership." *Education Development Study* 2008 (2009): 5–6.

Zhang, Xin Ping. "Burns' Transformational Leadership Theory and Principal's Role Transformation." *Research in Educational Development* 5–6 (2008): 44–50.

Zhang, Xin Zhuo. "An Analysis of Teachers' Perception and Job Satisfaction on Principal Behaviors: With the Example of Junior High Schools in Yanbian Area." MA thesis, Yanjing: Yanbian University, 2012.

Zheng, Hang Sheng and Jia Liang Huang. "'Chinese Story' Expects Academic Discourse Support: An Exemplary of Chinese Sociology." *People's Forum* 8 (2012): 59–61.

Zhu, Wen Hui and Yu Le Jin. "K-12 Educational Administration under the Vision of Transformational Leadership." *Modern Educational Administration* 5 (2014): 15–19.

Part 2

# Understanding Indigenous Cultures and Education

# 7 Indigenous Education Reform
## A Decolonizing Approach

*John P. Hopkins*

## Introduction

Indigenous peoples throughout the United States have endured a contentious history of education reform. Since the late nineteenth century the federal government has utilized education as a strategy to colonize Indigenous minds and bodies. These colonizing strategies have compelled Indigenous peoples to assert their status as sovereign nations in an effort to revitalize their cultures and languages within both public and tribal schools. The States of Montana and Washington are attempting to address this contentious history by passing legislation that has the potential to transform the relationship between Indigenous peoples and mainstream education. Montana passed *Indian Education For All* (IEFA), which mandates mainstream educators to include Native culture and history into the curriculum.[1] In Washington, Governor Jay Inslee recently signed into law Senate Bill 5433. This law mandates public schools to include the newly designed tribal sovereignty curriculum, called *Since Time Immemorial*.[2]

The new legislations in Washington and Montana promote what I call an *inclusive conversation* between tribal communities and mainstream educators. An inclusive conversation brings different persons or groups together into dialogue for the purpose of finding common ground on a shared goal or issue. In the context of these legislations, an inclusive conversation brings tribal communities into the decision-making process over Indigenous education reform—curricular developments, policy decisions, and pedagogical initiatives—where historically they have been excluded from the process. An inclusive conversation helps tribal communities and mainstream educators break down barriers and reach consensus over curricular and policy matters. Inclusive conversations thus seek to remedy historically exclusive practices of Indigenous peoples by bringing tribal communities and mainstream educators to the conversation as equals. *But can inclusive conversations sufficiently reform Indigenous education?*

On the surface, it might appear that inclusive conversations would facilitate reform of Indigenous education. After all, inclusion brings all groups to the table of conversation. Yet, given that Indigenous peoples historically have been *systematically excluded* from conversations about educational

130  *John P. Hopkins*

reform, an inclusive conversation misses a critical philosophical problem. It fails to account for how mainstream educators and Indigenous groups already stand in unequal relations within public education. Because of this inequality, there exists a climate of distrust. These legislations sidestep the issue of distrust by centering the conversation on *inclusion*. On some level, these legislations recognize that trust has not existed. If trust already exists, then it can be promoted—but if trust does not already exist, then it cannot be promoted without addressing the reasons why distrust exists. The problem is that inclusive reforms bring these groups together in conversation without directly and explicitly addressing why trust does not exist between them. To examine distrust, these groups must turn towards colonizing history.

In this chapter, I will argue that what is required in Indigenous education reform is a *decolonizing conversation* between tribal communities and mainstream educators, not an inclusive conversation. By decolonization, I mean the political and cultural revival strategies utilized by Indigenous peoples to challenge the domination and exploitation of tribal lands and communities, what I call in this chapter the *decolonization of lived-experience*. The decolonization of lived-experience seeks to overturn colonizing systems and structures, to realize the liberation of Indigenous groups. A decolonizing conversation recognizes the need for groups to engage in conversations that directly and explicitly confront colonization and its enduring effects in the lived-experience of tribal communities. Basing the interactions of these groups on decolonizing conversations rather than inclusive conversations brings colonization and its enduring effects to the foreground of the reform process. My aim is to develop a meaning of decolonizing conversation by analyzing key concepts in the politics of reconciliation. Reconciliation, I argue, is not about minimizing the past as obsolete or irrelevant. Rather, reconciliation turns toward the past as the basis upon which oppressed groups can realize social justice. The reconciliation process that I propose requires dominant groups to acknowledge, repair, and take responsibility for the historical and continued oppression of certain social groups. In the context of Indigenous education, I argue that reconciliation establishes a political framework in which tribal communities and mainstream educators can engage in more authentic conversations over educational reform.

However, the politics of reconciliation does not say much about the role of colonized tribal communities. Utilizing postcolonial and Indigenous studies literature, I will show how reconciliation requires what Gerald Vizenor calls *survivance*.[3] Survivance is a resistance and survival strategy utilized by Indigenous peoples to assert their sovereign right to remain Indigenous, as the original inhabitants of *this* land and of *these* places. As an Indigenous voice of survival and resistance, survivance becomes a concept to examine how Indigenous peoples have been historically opposed to and in isolation from the colonizing agenda of the dominant group. I integrate survivance with reconciliation to propose a way for tribal communities to participate in decolonizing conversations with mainstream educators rather than being

*Indigenous Education Reform*    131

in opposition to and isolation from them. In decolonizing conversations, these groups are able to build alliances that can transform public schools to reflect Indigenous aims and interests, thus bringing mainstream educators and tribal communities into a more equal partnership.

The chapter proceeds in the following way. I begin by examining the recent scholarship in the politics of reconciliation. Specifically, I articulate the necessary conditions that help inform political engagements between democratic nations seeking reconciliation with Indigenous peoples. I then describe how the postcolonial and Indigenous studies scholarship defines decolonization. This definition focuses on what I refer to as the decolonization of lived-experience. Drawing on the insights from these sections, I explain how reconciliation facilitates conversations centered on decolonization. Finally, I introduce the concept of survivance and integrate it with reconciliation. I show that reconciliation requires survivance and survivance also is enhanced by reconciliation. This integration of reconciliation and survivance brings mainstream educators and Indigenous peoples into equal relations.

## Justice and the Politics of Reconciliation

Reconciliation is playing a prominent role within contemporary political theory and practice. But political theorists debate what reconciliation actually means. In "Accommodating Historical Oppressed Social Groups: Deliberative Democracy and the Politics of Reconciliation," Bashir Bashir offers a meaning of reconciliation that surfaces the historical injustices committed against what he describes as *historically oppressed social groups*. Certain racial, ethnic, and immigrant groups require a politics of reconciliation that allows them to publicly voice their historical and contemporary experiences of oppression. Traditional political theories, argues Bashir, have failed to adequately account for injustices of these oppressed groups. A politics of reconciliation emphasizes the link between "past wrongs and the present political and social inequalities" in order for these groups to attain justice.[4] Rather than minimizing the past as obsolete or irrelevant in contemporary political contexts, this conception of reconciliation turns toward the past as the basis upon which oppressed groups can realize justice.

According to Bashir, the politics of reconciliation must entail three principles to guide political engagement between dominant and historically oppressed social groups in order to realize justice: the historically oppressed social group's story of exclusion, the dominant group's acknowledgement of historical injustices and willingness to repair them, and the dominant group's offering of an apology. The first principle recognizes "the significance of the collective memory and history of exclusion."[5] Dominant groups, argues Bashir, erase and suppress the stories of historically oppressed social groups and "[downplay] the occurrences of past harms . . . and [portray] the dominant group as not responsible for causing these harms."[6] This principle takes seriously the stories of historically oppressed social groups and situates them

132 *John P. Hopkins*

as counter-discourses to the dominant group's legitimacy in the national story. It allows for a public space in which historically oppressed social groups can voice their stories of exclusion. These counter-discourses challenge the meta-narrative of historical amnesia and offer a counter-narrative to the dominant group's preeminence in society. Historically oppressed social groups will remain skeptical, writes Bashir, of "any conception of democratic inclusion that requires them to set aside these memories of oppression and exclusion."[7]

Bashir's first principle of reconciliation extends to issues that are relevant to Indigenous peoples and their colonizing experiences. This principle complicates the easy solution that democratic nation-states use to smooth over the historical injustices of colonization committed against Indigenous peoples. There is something superficial about democratic engagement without an honest and truthful conversation of historical oppression and its current impact on the lives of oppressed peoples. Bashir's first principle shows that unless stories of colonization come into public consciousness, the colonizing history will continue without examination. This minimizes the need to address past wrongs. Bashir's first principle establishes the condition for democratic nation-states to confront their colonizing past and its continued legacy. It does so directly by creating a public space in which Indigenous peoples can voice their stories of colonization.

Bashir's second principle of reconciliation emphasizes the need for dominant groups to "[acknowledge] the occurrence of historical injustice and seek to repair them."[8] Unless the dominant group recognizes that historical injustices are not accidental occurrences but instead are central to its national story, it will be unlikely that historically oppressed social groups would want to participate in the democratic process. States Bashir:

> As long as these past injustices are denied or portrayed as accidental historical incidents, and not as an integral part of the national narratives, the achievement of democratic accommodation is hardly attainable from the perspective of the historically oppressed social group.[9]

Bashir refers to the examples of Native Americans and African Americans who will remain distrustful of any attempts of democratic inclusion until "the past wrongs against their ancestors are acknowledged as an integral part of American history."[10] What this suggests is that the nation-state cannot, morally speaking, offer one hand of democratic inclusion towards Indigenous peoples without also offering the other hand of reparations. Indigenous peoples, for example, demand language revitalizations, land reclamations, and sovereignty recognitions that have been denied by the dominant group. Thus, seeking their inclusion within the broader social and political structure without repairing the damages wrought by colonization and its ongoing effects misunderstands their unique experiences and struggles for justice.

This second principle of reconciliation resonates with several Indigenous scholars who criticize reconciliation processes that exclude reparations

## Indigenous Education Reform    133

towards Indigenous peoples. Gerald Taiaiake Alfred argues that reconciliation without reparations pacifies Indigenous peoples and seduces them into accepting their colonized position within liberal democracies.[11] States Alfred: "I see reconciliation as an emasculating concept, weak-kneed and easily accepting of half-hearted measures of a notion of justice that does nothing to help Indigenous peoples regain their dignity and strength."[12] To regain the dignity and strength of Indigenous peoples, Alfred contends that governments need to undergo a reparations process prior to any movement towards reconciliation with Indigenous peoples. Reparations, Alfred argues, center primarily on land reclamations and financial restitutions for past injustices. Without reparations, reconciliation "would permanently enshrine colonial injustices and is itself a further injustice."[13]

Bashir's third principle of reconciliation emphasizes the complicity of dominant groups in the historical injustices of oppressed social groups. It places the burden on dominant groups "to take responsibility for causing these injustices and offer a public apology."[14] Public apologies can take on multiple forms and activities—memorials, museums, or holidays—and they must be perceived by historically oppressed social groups as authentic acts of atonement on the part of the dominant group as opposed to being symbolic gestures devoid of sincerity, redress, or compensation. According to Bashir, a formal apology "is not to romanticize or perpetuate guilt or victimhood . . . [but rather to] help citizens . . . understand differently their history and its connection to current political, social, and economic inequalities."[15] Apologies serve as a means to repair relationships between dominant and historically oppressed social groups.

Bashir addresses the problem of whether current generations can apologize for the injustices committed by their ancestors. For Bashir, we cannot *personally* blame individuals or hold them *personally* responsible for injustices caused by their ancestors. But "it is not unreasonable to hold them politically (not personally) responsible."[16] Political responsibility recognizes that the inequalities currently experienced by historically oppressed social groups are tied to past injustices. As a result the current generation benefits in material and economic ways from these historical injustices caused by their ancestors.[17] What dominant groups apologize for is the fact that they have not apologized for the continued legacy and current forms of injustices affecting oppressed groups. On this account, dominant groups offer apologies for how past injustices have carried into the present and have perpetuated inequalities.

We can see how the politics of reconciliation might differ from inclusive conversations in the context of the States of Washington and Montana. An inclusive conversation in these contexts brings mainstream educators and Indigenous groups together with the aim of reaching consensus on a shared goal. In Washington, for example, tribal groups and state legislators collaborated on making the *Since Time Immemorial* curriculum a mandate to be incorporated by public schools; and in Montana mainstream educators and tribal communities worked cooperatively in designing and implementing

134 *John P. Hopkins*

an indigenized curriculum in public schools. While an inclusive conversation might recognize power distinctions between dominant and historically oppressed social groups, it does not explicitly or directly address these power relations. It aims to find common ground between groups, such that productive conversations can emerge. By contrast, Bashir's meaning of reconciliation situates power relations at the center of political interactions between mainstream educators and Indigenous groups. The reason is because Indigenous groups present unique challenges and demands that inclusion policies cannot fully accommodate. Their claims of justice, writes Bashir, go "beyond familiar multiculturalist mantras of recognizing or accommodating 'diversity'."[18] Thus, seeking their inclusion within the broader social and political structure without accounting for their unique experiences of historical oppression misunderstands their struggles for justice.

## Reconciliation: A Decolonizing Conversation

The politics of reconciliation offers a political framework to accommodate historically oppressed social groups. Here I want to examine how reconciliation can address the aims of decolonization among Indigenous peoples. According to Pramod Nayar, decolonization is a *process* that seeks "freedom from colonial forms of thinking [and] to revive native, local, and vernacular forms of knowledge by questioning and overturning European categories and epistemologies."[19] Through colonization, European nations constructed a colonial discourse that essentialized Native peoples and identities. Colonial discourses defined the "native . . . as primitive, depraved, pagan, criminal, immoral, vulnerable and effeminate."[20] European nations utilized colonial discourses to relegate Indigenous peoples to a subordinated status within their own lands and territories. The process of decolonization thus seeks freedom from the colonizing discourses that have essentialized Native identity and have prevented Indigenous groups from expressing their cultures, languages, epistemologies, and values in traditional ways.

The decolonization process is complicated by the fact that the legacy of colonization persists in the lives of Indigenous peoples. Two concepts—*colonialism* and *coloniality*—help explain this complication. Nelson Maldonado-Torres refers to colonialism as the political, cultural, and economic power of one nation over a particular group through acts of violence, domination, and possession. Coloniality, he writes, refers to the "longstanding patterns of power that emerged as a result of colonialism."[21] It survives in the everyday discourses, experiences, and structures of colonized peoples. It also distorts Indigenous peoples' self-images and aspirations, such that "as modern subjects, we [colonized peoples] breathe coloniality all the time and everyday."[22] The project of decolonization entails the recovery of colonized peoples, what Maldonado-Torres calls the *damnés*, "condemned of the earth,"[23] from these everyday discourses and structures, restoring their full humanity and being in the world.

*Indigenous Education Reform*   135

The pervasiveness of coloniality is due to the continued systematic suppression and erasure of Indigenous cultures, languages, and epistemologies. The suppression has had deleterious effects on Indigenous peoples and communities. Explains Brian Brayboy:

> Colonization has been so complete that even many American Indians fail to recognize that we are taking up colonialist ideas when we fail to express ourselves in ways that may challenge dominant society's ideas about who and what we are supposed to be, how we are supposed to behave, and what we are supposed to be within the larger population.[24]

For Brayboy, Indigenous peoples manifest coloniality by the fact that they have internalized the colonizer's ideologies and domination, as well as their own subordination and inferiority as subjugated peoples. This suggests that Indigenous peoples will maintain their own colonized status unless they interrogate and challenge the ways in which they have internalized dominant ways of thinking and being in their lived-experiences.

The decolonization process begins by raising the consciousness of Indigenous peoples about their lived-experience in coloniality. In order for Indigenous peoples to articulate specific strategies that challenge colonizing discourses, it is critical for them to interrogate coloniality and its impact on Indigenous communities. In short, it requires them to decolonize lived- experience. As Waziyatawin and Michael Yellow Bird state, decolonization is the "meaningful and active resistance to the forces of colonialism that perpetuate the subjugation and/or exploitation of our minds, bodies, and lands."[25] Decolonization includes "creating, restoring, and birthing various strategies to liberate oneself [and] adapt to or survive oppressive conditions."[26]

I want to position the decolonization of lived-experience as an essential political strategy for Indigenous peoples. Two points become critical. First, the decolonization of lived-experience immerses Indigenous peoples within their own traditions, languages, and worldviews. This can be achieved by creating spaces in which Indigenous peoples can reclaim their sense of humanity. Decolonizing lived-experience allows them to think and speak from their own cultural, linguistic, and epistemological perspectives. The more Indigenous peoples are able to think and speak from their own perspectives the more they are able to interrogate the *colonizer within*. To interrogate the colonizer within is to awaken to coloniality. Indigenous peoples do this by developing critical consciousness, understanding how they have unwittingly adopted dominant modes of thinking and being. Gregory Cajete writes that "the effects of internalized colonization—manifested most profoundly as hopelessness and powerlessness—must be understood and remedied."[27] Decolonizing lived-experience seeks to recover from the deep wounds of colonization, surfacing and challenging internalized colonization.

Second, decolonizing lived-experience allows Indigenous peoples to build the necessary foundation to realize other decolonization projects. The more

136  *John P. Hopkins*

Indigenous peoples awaken to the pervasiveness of coloniality in their own lived-experiences the more they are able to challenge the *colonizer without*. To interrogate the colonizer without is to critically examine the historical and current strategies of colonization that are interwoven throughout the broader social and political structure. Writes Cajete: "we must especially understand the ways in which colonialism continues to function in hidden forms in educational, institutional, economic, and political structures."[28] Insofar as Indigenous peoples interrogate colonization, they are in a better position to see how to transform the broader social and political structure that perpetuates colonizing policies and practices. This allows them to move forward with other decolonization projects. These decolonizing projects include the restitution of stolen lands, the recovery of suppressed cultures and languages, or the restoration of tribal communities. Thus, the decolonization of lived-experience serves as an essential first step in the overall process of decolonization.

We are now in a position to see how the politics of reconciliation can facilitate decolonizing conversations. Inclusive conversations seek consensus between different groups on a given topic or issue. They also presume equality between conversers and expect conversers to be willing and able to engage in conversation. This suggests that inclusive conversations are sufficient to overcome historical and current injustices committed against Indigenous peoples. *Consequently, colonization and coloniality remain in the background of the conversation.* On this account, inclusion allows mainstream educators and tribal communities to move forward from the legacy of colonization and find common ground over curricular and policy matters in Indigenous education reform. By contrast, decolonizing conversations begin with the assumption that mainstream educators and tribal communities do not stand as equals in the conversation. Nor are they necessarily willing or able to engage in conversation. This is due to the longstanding process of colonization and pervasiveness of coloniality, which have created and maintained a climate of distrust. The aim of decolonizing conversations is to engage in conversations that directly and explicitly confront colonization and its enduring effects. *Consequently, colonization and coloniality come forward in decolonizing conversations.* Recognizing the inequalities and a climate of distrust between mainstream educators and tribal communities, decolonizing conversations compel groups to question the legitimacy of colonization and seek to transform it. It is only through decolonizing conversations that historically authentic conversations between these groups can emerge.

We can see how reconciliation can facilitate decolonizing conversations. It does so in two ways. First, Bashir's emphasis on historical injustices and their enduring effects facilitates the decolonizing strategy for Indigenous peoples to interrogate the *colonizer within*. To interrogate the colonizer within implies that there exist opportunities for Indigenous peoples to question the legitimacy of colonization and awaken to coloniality. It presumes a context in which Indigenous peoples can actually engage in the decolonization of lived-experience.

Reconciliation facilitates the decolonization of lived-experience by linking past injustices to current forms of inequality between dominant and historically oppressed social groups. As Bashir explains, the "historical character of the oppression shapes identities in terms of conflict and opposition, and this raises profound challenges for any conception of democratic inclusion that must be addressed head on."[29] For Bashir, there is a direct link between how the historical occurrences of injustices have shaped the identity of oppressed groups. Rather than relegating colonization to the past or minimizing it in contemporary political interactions, reconciliation can help us recognize that in order to accommodate the unique demands of Indigenous peoples we must bring colonization and its effects forward in the conversation. Native groups and mainstream educators engaged in conversation over Indigenous education reform cannot minimize historical oppression, but rather see it as the starting point of their interaction. On this account, these groups must look backward in order to move forward in political partnership. "What matters to group members," writes Bashir, "is not simply that they are oppressed but also how they came to be oppressed."[30] It is thus through reconciliation that Indigenous peoples would be able to interrogate colonization and question its legitimacy.

Second, Bashir's emphasis on reparations and taking responsibility facilitates the decolonizing strategy for Indigenous peoples to challenge the colonizer without. The decolonization of lived-experience recognizes that Indigenous groups have internalized colonization. Other decolonization strategies become possible only when Indigenous peoples begin to recover from the deep wound of colonization. To challenge the colonizer without implies that Indigenous peoples have opportunities to reclaim their sense of humanity. It also implies that the broader social and political structures need to be transformed to help facilitate this process.

Reconciliation fulfills this decolonizing strategy by requiring dominant groups to repair the damages caused by historical injustices. Reparations are not merely symbolic, Bashir explains, but must include "practical concerns such as the redistribution of material resources."[31] But reparations are not only financially or materially based. For Bashir, repairing the damages caused by historical injustices requires dominant groups to help historically oppressed social groups recover and reclaim their sense of humanity. This is important for Indigenous peoples because it recognizes that financial restitutions or land reclamations are not the only issues in helping them attain greater recognition or equality. Transformations related to Indigenous identity are needed by both the dominant and subordinate group because they help change the stigmatization that Indigenous peoples endure in the broader culture. On this account, the dominant group transforms its negative perceptions of Indigenous peoples that are pervasive in mainstream culture. Indigenous peoples transform how they have internalized dominant perceptions of their own identities resulting from reductionist, colonizing discourses. As Bashir states, "taking responsibility and offering an apology

138  *John P. Hopkins*

are incomplete . . . [if they are] disconnected from efforts to change national narratives or identities."[32]

My analysis of reconciliation and decolonization shows that the politics of reconciliation is in a better position to facilitate the aims of decolonization rather than inclusive conversations. An inclusive conversation might recognize historical injustices committed against Indigenous peoples. But because it does not foreground these historical injustices in the conversation, it lacks the framework to facilitate conversations that directly and explicitly interrogate colonization and its enduring effects. Inclusion assumes that different groups can overcome historical injustices and thus make partners in the conversation more equal. This is what we might describe as the *business-as-usual* kind of conversations between mainstream educators and tribal communities. Business-as-usual conversations maintain the status quo in education and minimize what is central to Indigenous experiences. Reconciliation challenges the business-as-usual engagements between these groups by facilitating a new kind of conversation. It does so by making historical injustices explicit in mainstream educators and Native interactions.

## Reconciliation and Survivance

Thus far, I have shown how reconciliation is a promising political framework that can facilitate decolonizing conversations between mainstream educators and tribal communities. But reconciliation is not without its critics. Critics of reconciliation contend that Indigenous peoples need to separate themselves from the dominant group and resist any attempt to reconcile with non-Natives. This claim does not mean that Indigenous peoples should seek absolute separation from the nation-state: it means that they must realize decolonization without partnering with the dominant group. Resistance to colonization and the aim of decolonization are exclusively Indigenous projects that can be accomplished apart from the dominant group. This critical assessment of reconciliation reflects what I call the *Indigenous voice of survivance*.

Survivance brings together two concepts, *survival* and *resistance*, to describe Indigenous responses to colonization. As Gerald Vizenor describes, "Survivance is not just survival but also resistance, not heroic or tragic, but the tease of tradition, and my sense of survivance outwits dominance and victimry."[33] Survivance becomes possible through deliberate acts of resistance towards colonization. It illuminates the fact that Native peoples have always resisted the colonizing agendas that would seek to limit tribal sovereignty and transform indigeneity through various assimilation strategies. Springing from an Indigenous "standpoint, a worldview, and a presence," survivance can be understood as a decolonizing strategy to "live, write, and think" from specific Indigenous positions, places, and traditions.[34] The Indigenous voice of survivance interrogates and challenges colonialism and coloniality, standing *in opposition to* and *isolation from* the dominant

*Indigenous Education Reform* 139

group. Put simply, survivance means the continual realization by Indigenous peoples to assert their sovereign right to remain Indigenous, as the original inhabitants of *this* land and of *these* places.

Contrary to the critics of reconciliation, which articulate an Indigenous voice of survivance, my contention is that the politics of reconciliation remains a useful political framework that can further decolonizing strategies. Although I recognize that not all decolonizing strategies require a partnership between Indigenous peoples and dominant groups, the primary reason is that reconciliation can facilitate opportunities for Indigenous groups to partner with the dominant group on certain decolonizing strategies.

My argument does not center on decolonization strategies that Indigenous groups need to undergo in their own tribal communities. These decolonization strategies include the reclamations of stolen lands, the resurgence of tribal sovereignty, and the revitalization of Indigenous languages and cultures. Rather, my argument centers on decolonization strategies in the context of Indigenous education reform. I argue that a political partnership between tribal communities and mainstream educators is in the best interest of Indigenous peoples within the context of public schools. My argument is particularly important in public education contexts that educate high numbers of Native students. It is also important given the fact that the vast majority of Native students across the United States attend public schools.[35] In these public schools, Native students are primarily taught by white, non-Indigenous educators using a Eurocentric curriculum. Rather than rejecting partnerships between mainstream educators and tribal communities, my argument presents an opportunity for tribal communities to partner with mainstream educators in an effort to transform public education to reflect Indigenous aims and interests.

This argument builds upon Victoria Freeman's idea of reconciliation and its ability to help realize the decolonizing aims of Indigenous peoples. Reconciliation, according to Freeman, "is an ongoing process of building the relationships, alliances, and social understandings that are necessary to support the systematic changes that are true decolonization."[36] For Freeman, political relationships with members of the dominant group are essential for Indigenous peoples because the colonizer is here to stay. States Freeman: "because the colonizers never leave they must be transformed."[37] In order for Indigenous peoples to further the aims of decolonization, it is necessary to transform how the colonizer thinks about Indigenous peoples and their concerns. This transformation of the colonizer does not mean that the colonizer and Indigenous peoples resolve deep-seated issues of inequality or distrust. As Freeman describes, reconciliation is not about "seeking forgiveness . . . or 'getting over colonization' or simply 'making friends'."[38] Rather, it is about building alliances that help serve the interests of Indigenous peoples.

Thus, Indigenous peoples should not jettison the idea of reconciliation, but instead should utilize it as a political framework to transform colonizing policies and practices in order to serve Indigenous interests. This utilization of reconciliation requires partnerships and alliances between Indigenous peoples and dominant groups, especially in contexts where mainstream educators and policy-makers oversee the education of Native students in public schools. Through reconciliation, mainstream educators and tribal communities can work collaboratively to transform public education institutions that reflect and promote the aims of decolonization.

But collaboration between mainstream educators and tribal communities is challenging. We saw how survivance voices talk back to the dominant group's colonizing agenda. Speaking from distinctive tribal perspectives, experiences, and traditions, the Indigenous voice of survivance promotes a decolonizing strategy that advances and strengthens tribal sovereignty. As a decolonizing strategy, survivance awakens Indigenous peoples to internalized colonization and challenges the existing colonizing structure that seeks to suppress tribal sovereignty. Survivance shows us what is central to decolonization: *it is the ongoing struggle of Indigenous peoples to remain sovereign peoples of their places and communities.*

This characterization of survivance shows why collaboration between tribal communities and mainstream educators is challenging. Survivance is undertaken in opposition to and isolation from the dominant group. However, given my analysis of reconciliation it is now possible to consider survivance in a new way. I want to transition from thinking about survivance as an Indigenous strategy in opposition to and isolation from the dominant group to thinking about survivance as an opportunity for mainstream educators and tribal communities to engage in decolonizing conversations. The politics of reconciliation can facilitate this new way of thinking about survivance. Because reconciliation can facilitate decolonizing conversations between tribal communities and mainstream educators and the Indigenous voice of survivance is a decolonizing strategy, reconciliation can therefore facilitate the Indigenous voice of survivance. My argument suggests that reconciliation allows the Indigenous voice of survivance to be in partnership with mainstream educators. What reconciliation adds that survivance alone cannot provide is a political framework in which mainstream educators and tribal communities can partner on decolonizing strategies in the context of public education.

We are now in a position to see how Bashir's three principles of reconciliation integrate with survivance in the context of Indigenous education reform. First, we saw that Bashir's first principle requires dominant groups to create public space for historically oppressed social groups to offer counter-narratives to the dominant group's preeminence in the national story. In the context of Indigenous education reform, this first principle suggests that non-Natives need to create public spaces for Indigenous peoples to bring the Indigenous voice of survivance to the foreground of the conversation. Because these are voices of survivance, Indigenous peoples are able to articulate meanings of Native identity and tribal sovereignty in contrast to the dominant group's beliefs about Indigenous peoples. Reconciliation creates public spaces for Indigenous peoples to speak from a position of sovereignty.

*Indigenous Education Reform* 141

By sovereignty, I mean the right of Indigenous peoples to determine and decide for themselves the direction of their own present and future circumstances. As David Wilkins explains, tribal sovereignty is "a tribe's right to retain a measure of independence from outside entities and the power of regulating one's internal affairs."[39]

The Indigenous voice of survivance begins with the assumption that Indigenous groups are the sovereign peoples of the land. While survivance voices might understand tribal sovereignty differently, the basic claim among survivance voices is that the aim of Indigenous peoples is to assert and strengthen tribal sovereignty. Bashir's first principle, then, is not merely a way for Indigenous groups to offer counter-narratives to the dominant group. It creates a public space for Indigenous peoples to speak as sovereign peoples. Indigenous peoples are not merely expressing their collective story of injustice. Through survivance, Indigenous peoples are asserting the claim that they are sovereign nations but that this sovereignty has been suppressed because of colonizing policies and practices. Thus, because of reconciliation, the Indigenous voice of survivance becomes explicit and articulates the ongoing presence of indigeneity.

Second, we saw that Bashir's second principle of reconciliation requires dominant groups to hear, acknowledge, and repair the historical injustices committed against historically oppressed social groups. In the context of Indigenous education reform, Bashir's second principle requires mainstream educators to acknowledge and take seriously the Indigenous voice of survivance. Without this principle, they may or may not acknowledge survivance voices. Historically, mainstream educators have not been required to listen to the Indigenous voice of survivance. Bashir's second principle directs mainstream educators towards the voices of survivance and requires them to acknowledge Native claims. Equally important, mainstream educators must not simply acknowledge that survivance voices are counter-narratives: they must also recognize that the survivance voice poses a legitimate claim of tribal sovereignty. If mainstream educators hear the story of exclusion and injustice, but fail to hear the claim of sovereignty, they miss the point. In acknowledging survivance voices, mainstream educators can come to recognize that Indigenous peoples are speaking from positions of sovereignty to determine their own present and future affairs and interests. Put differently, to truly hear the voices of survivance is to acknowledge the sovereign status of Indigenous peoples.

Third, Bashir's third principle requires dominant groups to take responsibility and apologize for historical and current injustices committed against historically oppressed social groups. In the context of Indigenous education reform, Bashir's third principle requires that both mainstream educators and tribal communities come to terms with the fact that both have a role to play in taking responsibility for colonization and its enduring legacy. The Indigenous voice of survivance shows what these responsibilities might entail for both groups. For Natives, the survivance voice awakens Indigenous peoples to the fact that they have internalized colonization and

142   *John P. Hopkins*

at times replicated the same oppressive practices of the dominant group. One example is the ongoing issues of determining Native identity within Indigenous groups. Hilary Weaver states the issue this way:

> Internalized oppression, a by-product of colonization, has become common among Indigenous peoples. We fight among ourselves and often accuse each other of not being 'Indian enough' based on differences in politics, religion, or phenotype. . . . Such fighting among ourselves only serves to divide communities.[40]

Survivance offers a way for Native groups to take responsibility for transforming the oppressive meanings of identity that show up in their own communities. By reminding Indigenous peoples that they are the sovereign peoples of the land, survivance shows Native groups that they need to take responsibility for their complicity in colonizing practices *and* claim their sovereign status, thereby resisting the deep insidious power of colonial thinking and being.

The goal of the integration between reconciliation and survivance is to show what mainstream educators need to take responsibility and apologize for. We have already seen that Bashir's third principle requires dominant groups to take responsibility and apologize for historical injustices committed against historically oppressed social groups. By claiming tribal sovereignty, Indigenous peoples are now showing mainstream educators that taking responsibility for colonization requires them to acknowledge sovereignty and apologize for their role in denying that sovereignty in the context of public education.

In making this claim about the integration of the politics of reconciliation with survivance, I am disputing Indigenous scholars who contend that reconciliation is a failed political strategy for Indigenous peoples. We saw how various Indigenous scholars, such as Gerald Taiaiake Alfred, see reconciliation as another colonizing agenda of Indigenous peoples. But in the context of public education, I am claiming that we need a different way of thinking about Indigenous education reform. Tribal communities and mainstream educators need the other in order to sufficiently reform Indigenous education in the States of Washington and Montana, among other places nationally or internationally with similar histories of oppression. Thus, the integration of reconciliation and survivance brings these groups into a decolonizing conversation in which the Indigenous claim to sovereignty becomes central to their engagement. In this decolonizing conversation, Indigenous peoples are able to articulate their sovereign ways of being in the world, while mainstream educators are compelled to acknowledge these ways of being in the world. *In a decolonizing conversation, with the integration of reconciliation and survivance, tribal communities can authentically speak from a position of sovereignty and mainstream educators can authentically listen to the voice of sovereignty.*

*Indigenous Education Reform*    143

Integrating the Indigenous voice of survivance with Bashir's three principles of reconciliation leads me to claim that the politics of reconciliation can position tribal communities and mainstream educators in a more equal relationship. By equality, I mean that these groups recognize the power differences between them and acknowledge the importance of Indigenous sovereignty in their conversations. My claim leads to a more robust notion of equality than inclusion implies. Inclusion suggests that equality means *sameness* between these groups. An inclusive conversation presumes that these groups come to the conversation on the same level of contribution over curricular and policy matters. On this account, each voice counts the same on what an inclusive curriculum entails and how it should be implemented.

But inclusion misses the role that history has played in situating these groups is unequal power relations. Since the late nineteenth century, with the federal policies of boarding schools, no relationship of equality has existed between Natives and the dominant group in education. For example, tribal groups in both Washington and Montana have been recipients of colonizing boarding schools, whose legacy endures within Indigenous communities. Given the history of colonization, we can thus describe the historical and contemporary relationship between the dominant group and Natives as a relationship of inequality rather than equality. The American school system, for example, embodies and promotes a mainstream dominant culture that is built on Euro-American values, beliefs, and epistemologies. This culture creates a context in which schools privilege mainstream, dominant cultures and values at the expense of Native cultures and values. Mainstream educators are caught up within this colonizing education system, unwittingly maintaining and reproducing the dominant education structure in the classroom. More equality is thus possible when mainstream educators and tribal groups *both* recognize the unequal power differences in the American school system *and* when they acknowledge the sovereignty of tribal communities.

Equality does not mean that structural equality between mainstream educators and Indigenous peoples has been achieved. Alfred is correct when he states that in order for the relationship between nation-state and Indigenous peoples to improve the broader political structure needs to be radically transformed. He writes: "For justice to be achieved out of a colonial situation, a radical rehabilitation of the state is required. Without radical changes to the state itself, all proposed changes are ultimately assimilative."[41] Given that the broader social and political structure is ultimately assimilative, equality would only be possible when "settlers are forced into a reckoning of who they are, what they have done, and what they have inherited."[42]

Alfred's claim is helpful when we consider the question of equality on the broader social and political structural level. But I want to think of equality in the context of everyday interactions between mainstream educators and tribal communities, specifically as they occur in Washington and Montana's public schools. My idea of equality draws on Freeman's claim about the need to build alliances between the dominant group and Natives in everyday

## 144   John P. Hopkins

contexts. Decolonization is not only a broader social and political struggle, but is "necessarily a bottom-up process involving individuals, families, communities and relationships to communities."[43] When mainstream educators and tribal communities build alliances, they begin the important work of breaking down the divisions in order to realize necessary social and political changes in their communities. These local alliances, although replete with "misunderstandings, serious differences, and learnings," are important because they lay the foundation for broader social and political changes.[44] Freeman refers to local alliances as "a laboratory for processes of personal decolonization, the development of alliances, and any successful nation-to-nation relationship."[45] Thus, transforming the relationship between mainstream educators and tribal communities in the localities of Washington and Montana makes it possible to transform the relationship on the broader social and political structural level.

Building alliances on the local level allows us to think about the possibility of equality between mainstream educators and tribal communities. As these groups interact with each other in public schools, local communities, or political organizations, the integration of reconciliation and survivance allows them to recognize each other as equals and treat each other with mutual respect. Insofar as mainstream educators acknowledge the sovereign position of Natives in decolonizing conversations, they can engage tribal communities in conversation as sovereign peoples of this land and of these places. Certainly inequality still characterizes the relationship between these groups on the broader political level. But equality becomes possible when we consider it on the local level in the everyday interactions between these groups in public schools.

## Concluding Remarks

The legislations in Washington and Montana offer innovative and bold strategies to address the systemic problems of Indigenous education. While I recognize the important contributions of these reforms, my assessment of their assumptions about inclusion has been critical. Rather than promoting inclusive conversations, I have argued that these reforms need to promote decolonizing conversation between mainstream educators and tribal communities. These reforms, I believe, can lead the way in Indigenous education reform not only in Montana and Washington but also in international locales with similar colonizing histories. For these reforms to materialize, mainstream educators and tribal communities need to promote decolonizing strategies based on the integration of reconciliation and survivance. Previously I claimed that it is necessary to transform how the colonizer thinks about Indigenous peoples and their concerns. Transforming the colonizer benefits Indigenous groups in promoting decolonizing strategies. My framework suggests who is responsible for this transformation in the context of Indigenous education reform. When tribal communities

## Indigenous Education Reform   145

authentically speak from a position of sovereignty and mainstream educators authentically listen to the voice of sovereignty, it is the responsibility of mainstream educators to transform their thinking about Indigenous peoples. This transformation is made possible because the reconciliation framework provides the space for Indigenous peoples to voice their story of exclusion and injustice. In the relationship between reconciliation and survivance the Indigenous voice of survivance has spoken. Now mainstream educators must take responsibility to listen *and change*. My hope is that this chapter can offer insights into how all stakeholders in Indigenous education reform can engage in more authentic conversations that create an educational system by and for Indigenous peoples.

## Notes

1. Jioanna Carjuzaa, Mike Jetty, Michael Munson, and Teresa Veltkamp, "Montana's Indian Education for All: Applying Multicultural Education Theory," *Multicultural Perspectives* 12 no. 4 (2010): 192–198.
2. In 2005, Washington State passed HB1495, entitled Since Time Immemorial (STI), which brought together the Office of Indian Education and tribal and educational representatives to develop a state-wide curriculum inclusive of Indigenous cultures and histories. This bill only "encouraged" school districts to adopt STI. With SB5433, school districts seeking to change its social studies curriculum are now "required" to include STI. The STI curriculum focuses on the history and understanding of tribal sovereignty of the 29 federally recognized tribes in Washington State. Unlike previous social science curriculum, which provided general knowledge of Native American culture and history, STI derives from the perspectives, cultures, and traditions of local tribal communities, particularly those within a school district's geographical area. STI is gaining momentum in a number of public school districts that serve high numbers of Native students. Several tribal schools have now incorporated STI into its curriculum. For more details, see: Richard Walker, "'Since Time Immemorial' Training Gets a 600K Boost," *Indian Country Today*, accessed April 20, 2017, https://indiancountrymedianetwork.com/education/native-education/since-time-immemorial-training-gets-a-600k-boost/. Also see: Washington Office of Superintendent of Public Instruction, Indian Education, www.k12.wa.us/IndianEd/TribalSovereignty/.
3. Gerald Vizenor and Robert Lee, *Postindian Conversations* (Lincoln, NE: University of Nebraska Press, 1999).
4. Bashir Bashir, "Accommodating Historically Oppressed Social Groups: Deliberative Democracy and the Politics of Reconciliation," in *The Politics of Reconciliation and Multicultural Societies*, ed. Will Kymlicka and Bashir Bashir (Oxford: Oxford University Press, 2008), 59.
5. Ibid., 55.
6. Ibid., 56.
7. Ibid.
8. Ibid., 57.
9. Ibid.
10. Ibid.
11. Gerald Taiaiake Alfred, "Restitution Is the Real Pathway to Justice for Indigenous Peoples," in *Response, Responsibility and Renewal: Canada's Truth and Reconciliation Journey*, ed. Gregory Younging, Jonathan Dewar, and Mike DeGagné (Ottawa: Aboriginal Healing Foundation, 2009): 179–187.

146  *John P. Hopkins*

12. Ibid., 181.
13. Ibid., 152.
14. Bashir, "Accommodating Historically Oppressed Social Groups," 58.
15. Ibid.
16. Ibid.
17. For a basic analysis of economic inequalities between racial/ethnic groups, see: Chuck Collins and Felice Yeskel, *Economic Apartheid in America: A Primer on Economic Inequality & Insecurity*, Rev. and Updated, 2nd ed. (New York: New Press: Distributed by W.W. Norton & Company, 2005); Michael J. Vavrus, *Diversity & Education: A Critical Multicultural Approach*. Multicultural Education Series (New York, NY: Teachers College Press, 2015).
18. Bashir, "Accommodating Historically Oppressed Social Groups," 54.
19. Pramod K. Nayar, *Postcolonialism: A Guide for the Perplexed* (London: Continuum Press, 2010), 1–2.
20. Ibid., 3.
21. Nelson Maldonado-Torres, "On the Coloniality of Being: Contributions to the Development of a Concept," *Cultural Studies* 21 nos. 2–3 (2007): 243.
22. Ibid.
23. Ibid.
24. Bryan M. Brayboy, "Toward a Tribal Critical Race Theory in Education," *Urban Review* 37 no. 5 (2005): 431.
25. Waziyatawin and Michael Yellow Bird, "Introduction: Decolonizing Our Minds and Actions," in *For Indigenous Minds Only: A Decolonization Handbook*, ed. Waziyatawin and Michael Yellow Bird (Santa Fe, NM: School for Advanced Research Press, 2012), 3.
26. Ibid.
27. Gregory Cajete, "Decolonizing Indigenous Education in a Twenty-First Century World," in *For Indigenous Minds Only: A Decolonization Handbook*, ed. Waziyatawin and Michael Yellow Bird (Santa Fe, NM: School of Advanced Research Press, 2012), 148.
28. Ibid.
29. Bashir, "Accommodating Historically Oppressed Social Groups," 53.
30. Ibid., 54.
31. Ibid., 57.
32. Ibid.
33. Vizenor and Lee, *Postindian Conversations*, 93.
34. Brian Brayboy, "'Yakkity Yak' and 'Talking Back': An Examination of Sites of Survivance in Indigenous Knowledge," in *Indigenous Knowledge and Education: Sits of Struggle, Strength, and Survivance*, ed. Malia Villegas, Sabina Rak Neugebauer, and Kerry R. Venegas (Cambridge, MA: Harvard Educational Review, 2008), 341.
35. Approximately 90% of students attend public education. See the National Indian Education Association website for detailed statistics, www.niea.org/Research/Statistics.aspx#Discipline.
36. Victoria Freeman, "In Defense of Reconciliation," *Canadian Journal of Law and Jurisprudence* 27 no. 1 (2014): 216.
37. Ibid.
38. Ibid.
39. David Wilkins, *American Indian Politics and the American Political System*, 2nd ed. (Lanham, MD: Rowman and Littlefield Publishers, Inc., 2002), 48.
40. Hilary Weaver, "Indigenous Identity: What Is It, and Who Really Has It?," *American Indian Quarterly* 25 no. 2 (2001): 250.
41. Alfred, "Restitution," 184.
42. Ibid.

43. Freeman, "In Defense of Reconciliation," 220.
44. Ibid.
45. Ibid.

## Bibliography

Alfred, Gerald Taiaiake. "Restitution is the Real Pathway to Justice for Indigenous Peoples." In *Response, Responsibility and Renewal: Canada's Truth and Reconciliation Journey*, edited by Gregory Younging, Jonathan Dewar, and Mike DeGagné, 179–187. Ottawa: Aboriginal Healing Foundation, 2009.

Banks, James A. "Multicultural Education: Dimensions and Paradigms." In *The Routledge International Companion to Multicultural Education*, edited by James A. Banks, 9–32. New York and London: Routledge, 2009.

Bashir, Bashir. "Accommodating Historically Oppressed Social Groups: Deliberative Democracy and the Politics of Reconciliation." In *The Politics of Reconciliation and Multicultural Societies*, edited by Will Kymlicka and Bashir Bashir, 48–69. Oxford: Oxford University Press, 2008.

Brayboy, Brian. "'Yakkity Yak' and 'Talking Back': An Examination of Sites of Survivance in Indigenous Knowledge." In *Indigenous Knowledge and Education: Sites of Struggle, Strength, and Survivance*, edited by Malia Villegas, Sabina Neugebauer, and Kerry Venegas, 339–346. Cambridge, MA: Harvard Educational Review, 2008.

Brayboy, Bryan. "Toward a Tribal Critical Race Theory in Education." *Urban Review* 37 no. 5 (2005): 425–446.

Cajete, Gregory. "Decolonizing Indigenous Education in a Twenty-First Century World." In *For Indigenous Minds Only: A Decolonization Handbook*, edited by Waziyatawin and Michael Yellow Bird, 145–156. Santa Fe: School for Advanced Research Press, 2012.

Carjuzaa, Jioanna, Mike Jetty, Michael Munson, and Teresa Veltkamp. "Montana's Indian Education for All: Applying Multicultural Education Theory." *Multicultural Perspectives* 12 no. 4 (2010): 192–198.

Freeman, Victoria. "In Defense of Reconciliation." *Canadian Journal of Law and Jurisprudence* 27 no. 1 (2014): 213–223.

Maldonado-Torres, Nelson. "On the Coloniality of Being: Contributions to the Development of a Concept." *Cultural Studies* 21 nos. 2–3 (2007): 240–270.

Nayar, Pramod. *Postcolonialism: A Guide for the Perplexed*. London: Continuum Press, 2010.

Rouhana, Nadim. "Reconciling History and Equal Citizenship in Israel: Democracy and the Politics of Historical Denial." In *The Politics of Reconciliation in Multicultural Societies*, edited by Will Kymlicka and Bashir Bashir, 70–93. Oxford: Oxford University Press, 2008.

Vizenor, Gerald and Robert Lee. *Postindian Conversations*. Lincoln: University of Nebraska Press, 1999.

Waziyatawin and Michael Yellow Bird. "Introduction: Decolonizing Our Minds and Actions." In *For Indigenous Minds Only: A Decolonization Handbook*, edited by Waziyatawin and Michael Yellow Bird, 1–14. Santa Fe: School for Advanced Research Press, 2012.

Weaver, Hilary. "Indigenous Identity: What Is It, and Who Really Has It?" *American Indian Quarterly* 25 no. 2 (2001): 240–255.

Wilkins, David E. and Heidi Kiiwetinepinesiik Stark. *American Indian Politics and the American Political System* (3rd ed.). Lanham: Rowman and Littlefield Publishers, 2011.

# 8 Untamed Education
## The Philosophical Principles Behind the Kokama School

*Edison Hüttner and Alexandre Guilherme*

## Introduction

Brazil possesses one of the greatest ethnic and linguistic diversities in the world. *The UNESCO Atlas of World Languages in Danger* states that in its territory there are 220 indigenous peoples and some 178 languages.[1] In *Línguas Brasileiras: Para o conhecimento das línguas indígenas* A. D. Rodrigues notes that all of these languages are divided into distinct families, such as Tupi, Macro-Jê, Aruak, Karib, Pano, Maku, Yanomama.[2] There are dozens of other families of languages, most of which have only a few members. These less popular languages do not belong to any of the classified languages; further, it should be noted here that these are language families, and that cultural divisions sometimes emerge between groups that speak the same language, which is evidence of the rich linguistic and cultural heritage of these native peoples. According to the *Atlas* the cultural situation of most of these native peoples in Brazil is very precarious as some 12 languages have disappeared recently (i.e. Amanayé; Arapáso; Huitoto; Krenjê; Máku; Múra; Nukiní; Torá; Umutina; Urupá; Xakriabá; Yuruti) because all speakers have either died or become culturally assimilated by other groups. And a number of others are considered in danger on a scale that goes from vulnerable to definitely in danger as the number of speakers is either diminishing rapidly or becoming culturally assimilated. This is a worldwide phenomenon, the phenomenon of "language-death and rapid cultural change",[3] that appears to be accelerating.[4]

Adding to this troublesome situation faced by indigenous and minority communities in Brazil and across the world, is the fact that during the colonial period (c. 1530–1825), indigenous communities were decimated by disease or massacred by white settlers. In the 20th century, the Brazilian government introduced strong integrationist policies, which aimed to locate native populations and integrate them into mainstream society. These integrationist policies were implemented through education, especially formal schooling, and the opening of new agricultural frontiers, where these populations worked as labourers. However, in the last quarter of the 20th century, these integrationist policies were replaced by an approach valuing

Untamed Education 149

diversity and the right to a differentiated educational system for indigenous communities to choose at their own discretion. This was a much welcomed paradigm shift.

In striking contrast with this scenario of language-death and the disappearance of ethnic groups, we find a very interesting case that might be a glimmer of hope for indigenous populations. The Kokama tribe of Brazil re-emerged in the 1980s as an ethnic group by becoming both politically active and achieving official governmental recognition. The Kokama were hiding for security, possibly in response to the former integrationist policies, amongst other indigenous groups, most notably the Tikuna. Their experience with indigenous education is somewhat new, but it has been crucial for the re-establishment of the tribe, fostering the learning of their language and encouraging the continuation of their history and worldview by teaching their myths, their dances, their cultural heritage. Thus, in this article, we characterise Kokama education, defined as a form of *untamed education*, identifying the philosophical principle behind it, namely *imperfection*. Thus, the first part of this chapter provides an overview of the past and current situation of indigenous education in Brazil, leading to the recently gained right to a differentiated educational system, if indigenous communities so choose. The second part discusses the Kokama case and their experiences with education, which have benefited greatly from this new right. *Untamed education*, based on this principle of *imperfection*, stands for the kind of education that is essentially indigenous and that does not try to 'normalise' indigenous peoples into the 'white man's society.'

## Indigenous Education in Brazil[5]

Within this context, the current situation of indigenous education in Brazil is complex and problematic despite the fact that Brazil appears to have one of the most advanced legislations on native Indians in the world. This is to say, in 1988 when a new constitution was promulgated in Brazil following the process of re-democratisation after twenty years under a military administration, the relationship between the state and indigenous communities changed. Until 1988, this relationship was guided by the Estatuto do Índio[6] which understood indigenous peoples as 'relatively capable', treating them as under the protection of the state and trying to force their integration into the 'white man's society'; however, the new constitution abandoned this idea, replacing it with an understanding based on the importance of diversity, allowing indigenous peoples autonomy in various issues, including education, language and culture, if they so choose.

Thus, on the one hand, as we have already mentioned, the process of colonisation and integrationist ideologies have decimated many peoples and cultures in Brazil and throughout the world (e.g. United States, Canada and Australia). But, on the other hand, the new Brazilian legislation allowed some indigenous peoples to gain an understanding of their rights and to safeguard

150  *Edison Hüttner and Alexandre Guilherme*

some of their culture because it gave them a special status, allowing them to choose a differentiated educational system. As a local individual from the Alto Rio Negro area in the Amazon region of Brazil commented on the historical consequences of their schooling experiences, which were provided in the past by religious missionaries and more recently by the state: "They [missionaries and state employees] took away half of our culture, but at the same time they taught us how to defend the other half against the Whites."[7] Thus, in spite of a schooling system that historically did not value their culture and language, indigenous communities gained through it the tools for continuing to protect some of their traditions and knowledge.

The category 'indigenous schools' was officially recognised by the Brazilian Ministry of Education and Culture in 1991. As a consequence of this, the schools in indigenous villages could be neither categorised as 'schools of missionary work', as it happened from colonial times and until the middle of the 20th century, nor as 'schools of Indian reserves', which took over the 'missionary schools' in the second part of the 20th century and were administered by the FUNAI (Brazilian National Indian Foundation), a federal government agency for the protection of Native Indians. In the Indian village or in urban areas, the 'indigenous school' became part of the official national framework of education. These indigenous schools are now categorised as either state or municipal schools. However, they have a differentiated calendar, teaching and learning workload, methodology and curriculum; and, they are no longer in the shadows of the dominant educational system as was the case when they were 'missionary schools' or 'indigenous reserve schools.' They are now growing and flourishing. Genuine indigenous schools opened their doors over the past decades in Brazil with support at either state (e.g. Escola Estadual Indígena *Índio Macuxi* (RR), *Nitotu Eif* (PR), Cacique Timóteo (MG)) or municipal levels (e.g. Escola Municipal Indígena *Tengatuí Marangatú* (MS), São José (AM)), changing permanently the scenario of indigenous education in Brazil.

According to the last Brazilian National Census of 2010, there are 821 thousand Native Indians in Brazil, representing about 0.4% of the current Brazilian population.[8] This population is distributed in 688 native indigenous reserves throughout the country and in some urban areas. In addition to these, another 160 areas are still being demarcated and claimed by indigenous peoples. These reserves represent a great victory for native peoples of Brazil, who have managed to survive 500 years of colonization, enabling them to retain cultural traditions and a different way of being-in-the-world.[9] In the past, native communities could flee mainstream society's encroachment by going further inland; however, this appears to be no longer possible as 'civilisation' has reached the depths of the country through the fast development of agro-business, hydroelectric power dams, mining, opening of new roads and the establishment of new towns. As such, the reserves are safe-heavens for these indigenous communities because no

*Untamed Education*   151

exploitation of natural resources can take place in them. Incidentally, these reserves also help to protect important areas of unique biodiversity.

These pro-indigenous developments were only possible due to recent historical developments. As previously noted, in 1988 Brazil proclaimed a new constitution, which replaced old integrationist policies towards Native Indians with ones forged on respect for their ethnicity and recognising the importance of cultural diversity. Article 231 of the Constitution of 1988 states:

> Indians shall have their social organization, customs, languages, creeds and traditions recognized, as well as their original rights to the lands they traditionally occupy, it being incumbent upon the Union to demarcate them, protect and ensure respect for all of their property.[10]

Moreover, this new constitution secured the right to a differentiated educational system. It was only ten years later, in 1998, that Brazilian educationists and officials from the Ministry of Education started to develop new national policies for indigenous education, culminating in a report that was distributed to all native communities throughout Brazil in 2004.[11] Traditionally, the educational provision for most 'contacted groups' (i.e. groups that maintain some sort of contact with mainstream society)[12] was in the hands of missionaries, such as Jesuits, Franciscans, and Salesians, who provided formal schooling in a somewhat haphazard manner, especially in the Amazon region of Brazil.[13] The post-1998 developments placed the issue of indigenous education at the top of the agenda for many indigenous communities, directing Native Indians' grassroots movements and the work of non-governmental organisations (NGOs).[14]

Given this recent paradigm change, Brazil conducted a School Census in 2005, which identified that there were 2,323 indigenous schools in the country. However, the last figures from the Brazilian Ministry of Education and Culture estimate that there are 2,819 schools, which demonstrates a remarkable increase of provision. These schools are present in all 27 states of the federation, except for the states of Piauí and Rio Grande do Norte. Most of these schools are administered at either municipal (52.39%) or state (46.66%) level, and a very small proportion is privately run (0.95%). However, there are some very significant regional differences. Whilst in the North (62.08%) and Centre (83.93%) regions of the country municipal schools predominate (and these are the regions that have by far the largest numbers of indigenous peoples), in the other regions of Brazil, namely, Northeast (83.93%), Southeast (77.55%) and South (71.30%) state schools appear to be the norm. The reasons for these regional differences and the possible impact they might have on indigenous education are not clear and more research is required into this area.[15]

The census also established that 8,431 teachers worked in these schools and it is estimated that about 90% of them are of a Native Indian

## 152  Edison Hüttner and Alexandre Guilherme

background. These teachers work mostly in elementary school education (7-years to 15-years old; 72.01%) and another significant number work in nursery and pre-school (14.60%). This means that only 13.39% work in secondary education, which might have an impact on the secondary school provision and standards. Perhaps, more worryingly, is the fact that the census determined that only 13.17% of teachers have a degree, 64.83% have only a secondary school qualification, and 12.05% have only an elementary education; therefore, the impact of this on the quality of the education provided might be quite substantial in some schools.[16] That said, most of them know the local language and culture, which is something crucial for indigenous schools and there are a number of educational ventures supporting this that go back to the 1980s and 1990s.[17] In connection with this, it is important to note that the Universidade Estadual do Mato Grosso (UNEMAT) has recently implemented teacher-training courses aimed solely at forming Native Indian teachers and this has been replicated by other institutions such as the Universidade Federal de Minas Gerais (UFMG) and the Universidade Federal de Santa Catarina (UFSC). This is a welcome development as it strengthens the education provision for native communities, tackling the issue of quality in education.[18] Also, a recent law (Law 11.096) safeguards a number of university places to persons with a Native Indian background and it is now expected that some 5000 individuals have taken up this opportunity.[19]

The 2005 census also found that 163,773 students attended indigenous schools in Brazil.[20] However, in 2010 it was verified that 246,793 students were matriculated in primary school (7 years to 14 years), indicating that the number of places for Indian students and the number of Indian students attending schools had increased dramatically in just a few years. Unfortunately, high drop-out rates are an issue.[21] It is arguable that there is an urgent need to try to establish the reasons for such high drop-out rates amongst students of Native Indian background, and the Brazilian government has to take concrete actions to solve this issue so to fulfil its responsibilities under the United Nations Convention on the Rights of the Child, which states:

> State parties recognize the right of the child to education, and with a view to achieving this right progressively and on the basis of equal opportunity, they shall, in particular: [. . .] (e) take measures to encourage regular attendance at schools and the reduction of drop-out rates.[22]

Further, an important question was asked in the census of 2005, that is: what language is used as the medium of learning at the school? It was established that 78.26% of the schools (i.e. 1818 schools) employed either the native language solely or a bilingual approach (i.e. native language and Portuguese) as their medium of teaching and learning. More striking is the fact that some schools (i.e. 8.57%) did not declare Portuguese as a taught

*Untamed Education* 153

language, which indicates that they only taught and employed native languages. It is interesting to note that multilingualism is a feature of many indigenous communities in Brazil and that by the time a child reaches school-age she might be able to speak four or more different indigenous languages. Early missionaries found it difficult to understand this multilingualism, preferring to force on indigenous communities a reductionist monolingual perspective causing great cultural and social damage to communities.[23] It thus becomes very important that educators are given the power and opportunity to create educational spaces that draw on the multilingual abilities and resources of their students and communities. This said, only 41.54% of these schools employed or had access to pedagogical materials in their own language.[24]

This is a very worrying situation demonstrating that there is an urgent need to develop pedagogical materials to be used specifically by these Native Indian schools. In response to this, in some schools in the Alto Rio Negro area of the Amazon region, which borders Colombia and Peru, both teachers and students are actively engaged in writing books and other materials in the local language, which is something that was previously unavailable to them since they were being forced to learn and speak Portuguese. These are not translations, but genuine materials focusing on and valuing their culture and language. Moreover, these books and new materials will be used in their teaching and learning activities, which will provide further support for the learning of their language and culture by the younger generations, ensuring the continuity of their communities.

These are examples of *untamed education*, which we discuss in detail below, because it is the kind of education that focusses on the Indian context and civilisation, breaking away from the previously imposed educational system that aimed at their full integration to the "white man's society."[25] It is arguable that this process helps them to strengthen their command of their own language and deepens the connection to their culture and community. Thus, the impact of switching to their own native language has not only revitalised the language but also the culture and community because when the child learns the language she also learns the culture bonding herself to the community. However, Hüttner emphasises that there are major challenges to this approach. For instance: i) there are very few studies about the grammar of some languages, and others do not have a unified alphabetical system; ii) the Brazilian publishing industry lacks the capacity to produce textbooks with the kind of alphabetical signs used by native languages; iii) there is a certain preoccupation that the research into language and culture resulting from the interaction between scholars and the elders of native communities only generates outputs for academics.[26] This situation seems to reflect the well-known argument that schools alone cannot save endangered languages.[27] Schools cannot turn back the language loss that has been going on for hundreds of years, but a school-based revitalisation programme needs to work with individuals and the community, looking

## 154 Edison Hüttner and Alexandre Guilherme

for viable and appropriate options.[28] There must also be support at the macro level, with fitting policies, financial support and logistic provision, if indigenous schools are to be as effective as they can for their respective communities.

Another problem faced by Indian schools concerns logistics and infrastructure. The 2005 census also ascertained that 65.78% of schools functioned in its own premises, whilst the remaining 34.22% were either located in warehouses, or the teacher's house, or churches, or other schools—237 schools reported 'other locations.' This means that more than a third of indigenous schools are based in locations that are not ideal for the functioning of a school. Moreover, out of 2323 schools, 23 reported that they had computer rooms, three as possessing a sciences lab, 55 as holding playing fields, 85 as having a library *in situ*, 307 as having a TV set, 238 a VCR, 177 a satellite dish, and only 23 confirmed that they have access to the internet. These figures suggest that the inclusion of indigenous schools with their own requirements and curriculum intact into the Brazilian educational system faces major structural and logistical problems that must be addressed soon if they are to rise to the challenge of providing indigenous communities with the same standard of schooling in mainstream society, whether in rural or urban areas. Given the scale of the problem, all spheres of government, namely federal, state and municipal, must not turn a blind eye to this issue and provide their full support.[29] Moreover, the new indigenous schools face not only logistical and structural problems, but also conceptual ones; for instance, the Brazilian government need to establish ways through which it can support indigenous cultures, evaluate the quality of their teaching and learning, and help indigenous communities develop a pedagogy that is appropriate to their respective contexts.[30]

## Kokama People

Against this background, the case of the Kokama people is an interesting one. The Kokama of Brazil, also called Cucamas, are present in Colombia and Peru, and according to recent data there are 11,274 Kokamas Indians.[31] Figure 8.1 shows their location in Brazil.

Gre Urban has traced the origins of this tribe and states that between two and three thousand years ago the first expansion of the Tupi-Guarani took place, causing the migration of the Kokama and Omágua,[32] who belong to this family, to the north and towards the Amazon region.[33] Thus, the Kokama language is identified as belonging to the family "of the Tupi or in general of the Tupi-Guaranis, having close affinities with the general language spoken in the Upper Amazonas and Upper Solimões." Historically speaking, with the invading colonization of the Iberian Crowns in the 1500s, the Kokama advanced to the mouth of the Putamayo River, also populating the Marañón, Middle and Lower Ucayali, Huallaga, Baixo Napo and Tigre

*Untamed Education* 155

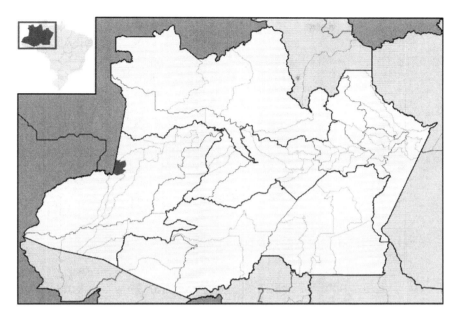

*Figure 8.1*

shores.[34] The historian Antonio Porro studied Paul Marcoyalong, an artist and adventurer, who travelled in the middle of 1847 along the Amazon River, and points out:

> Going alone on the Ucayali he arrived at Nauta, at the confluence with the Maranon or Amazonas, where he changed his vessel; he took a Brazilian *igarité* (canoe) with six Cocamas rowers and a pilot, passing through Iquitos and the Falls of Napo and arrived in Pevas.[35]

Despite these brief historical accounts about the Kokama, according to the anthropologist Ana Suelly Arruda Câmara Cabral, working and researching in the Upper Solimões, the organization of the Kokama Indians in Brazil is recent. In the community of Sapotal, in the municipality of Tabatinga, Antônio Januario Samias stands out as the first leader to fight for the rights of the Kokamas in the 1980s. Cabral recounts a beautiful statement by the leader:

> *Ta awa, ta Kukama, ta tapìya Kinkin. Ta papa tapì ya Kinkin, ta amuy tapìya kinkin, ya ra puranu tapìya kinkin* (Translation: I am a people, I am Kokama, I am a real Indian. My father was a real Indian, my grandfather was a real Indian, just like those who have died).[36]

## 156  Edison Hüttner and Alexandre Guilherme

It was only in the 1980s that the Kokama resurfaced from within another ethnic group, the Tikuna.[37] They lived in the lands of the Tikuna, but they knew that they were different, expressing themselves with language and symbols of their own traditional paintings. When they came to realise their identity, they sought through the National Indian Foundation (FUNAI) the recognition of their ethnicity and the right to land, health care and differentiated education. In 1995 Antônio Januario Samias, who was the first Kokama leader, died. On his deathbed, he passed on his position to Francisco Samias. Edison Hüttner, a co-author of this article, notes that,

> In 1996 I was living in Benjamin Constant (state of Amazonas, Brazil), I met Franscisco Samias, the new Kokama leader on the banks of the Solimões River. He was on one of his travels seeking Kokama speakers and identifying the Kokama people in other villages, who were mixed with the Tikuna Indians. At that moment I began to help with this, and started working alongside the Kokama in the area.[38]

In that same year, the National Indian Foundation (FUNAI) made the decision to recognise the Kokama people, based on the work of the anthropologist and ethnolinguist Ana Suelly Arruda Câmara Cabral, whom we have already mentioned.[39] Currently the Kokama ethnic group of Alto Solimões is present in: Tabatinga, Benjamin Constant, São Paulo de Olivença, Amaturá, Santo Antonio do Içá, Tonantins, Jutaí, Fonte Boa and Tefé. The Kokama are also present in Manaus. The Sapotal village, which is the centre of the community and located in the municipality of Tabatinga, received a governmental declaration confirming their property rights to their lands in 2006. The Kokama represent the resurgence of ethnic groups, forgotten by society and researchers. However, they themselves realized the value of their traditions and culture, and of saying that they are a people.

## Kokama Education

The principle of Kokama Education is the maintaining and appreciation of their culture and identity. In their community meetings there is always singing and dancing, and traditional garments. In January of 2002, Edison Hüttner returned to work with the Kokamas. Francisco Samias, then leader of the Kokama and director of the Sapotal Community School, taught classes but with few resources and didactic material because these were still being designed. On February 12, 2002, in Tabatinga, the Marist Education Center (Edison Huttner is a member of the Marist Order) celebrated the recognition of the Kokama people by the Brazilian State.[40] Traditional dances and handicrafts were integral to the event. In 2002 a representative of the Kokama and president of the organization, Cristóvão Macedo Moçambite reported in this meeting that: "Our main objective is a rescue of the people,

*Untamed Education* 157

their roots and their language. We are 3,300 Indians scattered in villages in Upper Solimões."[41]

Two days later, on February 14, in the same place, they had another meeting with tribal chiefs (i.e. *caciques*) and representatives from some Kokama villages where a debate about the needs of the villages took place. The first commitment was to build a headquarters and Kokama House or Cultural Center in Sapotal village belonging to the municipality of Tabatinga. On February 21 I (Huttner) visited Sapotal village and in meeting with Francisco Samias, we organized a project for the construction of the Kokama Cultural Center.

The construction of the Kokama Cultural Center was conceived of and built by the Indians themselves with the donation of resources acquired by the FMSI (Marist Foundation for International Solidarity in Rome, Italy). Francisco Samias in the Sapotal village in Tabatinga in an interview (9/2/2006) makes an import statement concerning the Kokama people:

> We are finalizing our Kokama Cultural Center. But it was very difficult at first. We had to drive through the large wooden beams. All of the Kokama helped. And today each time we affirm our identity. [. . .] We are united. Here in the Center we will dance and sing songs in our language, paint our clothes, eat our food. We are a brave people.
> (Samias, interview, 9/2/2006)

Figure 8.2 shows the construction of the Kokama Cultural Centre.

*Figure 8.2*

In the Sapotal village Francisco Samias on February 10, 2006 spoke enthusiastically about the place where the Kokama Culture Center would be built:

> The Kokama people are a brave people. Today everyone comes and embraces us ... before it was not like that. We are concerned to know where the other Kokamas are, because the basis of everything is our communities, and there is always someone who speaks the original language. Today Okaa Grande [Uka nuan; i.e. Big House] is the place to learn, teach and make plant remedies, make hunting and fishing weapons, dance, train the body to fight with weapons and no weapon, a place to play, a place of festivities, a place of Prayer, a meeting place. Our great oka is a traditional place to keep alive our ancient knowledge.

Figure 8.3 shows children performing a Kokama traditional dance in the Cultural Centre.

In Kokama culture, in addition to schools and churches, the Kokama Cultural Centers have become a reference for formal education with an adapted curriculum, as well as 'informal' education covering the entire tradition of the Kokama. In 2006, the teaching of the Kokama language became part of a degree course for indigenous teachers in Filadélfia, Benjamin Constant, in Upper Solimões.[42] The project was coordinated by the linguist Ana Suely Arruda Camara Cabral; she and her team collected important material for the study of the Kokama language. They recorded on

Figure 8.3

CD Traditional and Audiovisual Songs, the DVDs being called Material to Support the Kokamas teachers—adding three volumes of materials with the copyright of the Laboratory of Indigenous Languages / LALI of the Institute of Letters of the University of Brasilia:

A) Volume 1. Makatipa na utsu? Where are you going? Published in July 2009.
B) Volume 2. Ritamaka ini utsu. Let's go to the community. Published in July 2010.
C) Volume 3. Kokáma Kumitsa. Lala Kokáma. These materials were used in the villages and not in the classroom.[43]

These courses stimulated the teaching of the Kokama language. According to Rubin, in a study concerning the Kokama schools in the Upper Solimões and Manaus regions, 211 Kokama teachers in 105 schools with 5,058 students[44] are currently registered in the department of education of the counties. However, there is another textbook for children that is being used in the Sapotal Kokama school connected to the Cultural Center, and which was conceived by Altaci Correa Rubin: the *Yawati Tini* (volume 1). The book is suitable for children from 4 to 8 years old and has, as part of its content, Kokama food, traditional knowledge of fishing and hunting, traditional forms of planting, presentations of dances and songs of the ancestors and authors, as well as the knowledge of tribal markings and drawings of the Kokama people.[45]

In addition to this, the Kukumi/kamira-Portugues is a bilingual dictionary, which was conceived of and produced by the Kokama for their schools. An important detail in the making of the dictionary was its cover, which carries images of the building of the Kokama Cultural Center. The bilingual dictionary reveals the identity of the Kokama people—a history in the process of being understood. In the beginning, Francisco Guerra Samais was assisted by *Gramatica Cocama, Lecciones para el aprendizaje del idioma cocama* published in Peru (1972).[46] In the early 1980s he made translations of the Kokama language, into Spanish then to Portuguese. Over time the Kokamas gained experience and proficiency in the language with courses and conversation in the villages. As the introduction of the dictionary says:

> The mother-speakers Maria Januário Samias, Inocêncio Silva Arimuia, Augustinho Samias, Antonio Januário Samias (In memory) and Francisco Guerra Samias (In memoria) were the driving force in the first translations into Portuguese.[47]

All these developments enabled the Kokama community to develop that which is called *untammed education*, the kind of education that does not aim at integrating indigenous communities into the 'white man's society'; rather, it is a type of education centred on indigenous values and culture.

## 160 Edison Hüttner and Alexandre Guilherme

### Untammed Education: A Kokama Perspective

As we stated before, in 2002, and with the already mentioned changes in the Brazilian educational system, the Kokama started to see the benefit of differentiated schools and started to build a Cultural Center, which was constructed with fallen trees from the forest and that took four years to be completed. While the Center was being built, dances, rituals and festivals were performed in that locality, turning it into a converging point for the Kokama people. This is *untamed education* being encouraged and practiced by the community.

Thus, the elders praised this as a form of *untamed education*, keeping and encouraging their traditions, which was something that had suffered a great deal under the previous *civilisatory paradigm of education*. In this sense, *untamed education* is not savage or wild education, but an education that opposes the previous *civilisatory education* that tried to normalise individuals, forcing indigenous communities to fit into the white man's society. *Untamed education* is *indigenous education*. The idea of *untamed education* is not particular to the Kokama and is very prominent in other Brazilian indigenous communities; however, given that the Kokama were a hidden ethnic group and that there is little written about them, they provide us with an interesting philosophical case study. In this respect, *untamed education* seeks to strengthen the ethnic identities and is defined by four characteristics: i) by and large, it adopted a bilingual approach to education (e.g. Kokama and Portuguese; Tupi and Portuguese); ii) it is centred around a symbolic centre in the Indian village (e.g. Cultural Centre; School); iii) this context fosters values and perceptions that are lived by the community (e.g. the concepts of beauty and of being good are deeply connected in Indigenous peoples, so that what is beautiful is also good and vice versa. This is an interesting aspect of Kokama culture because Westerners might find someone or something not aesthetically pleasing, but still consider this individual or object as good; however, in Kokama culture, these concepts merge, so that what is beautiful is good and what is good is beautiful. There is no differentiation between these concepts in their culture); and supports the local mythology, which is part and parcel of the school curriculum (e.g. their Gods are painted using natural local dyes, the class enables the environmental consciousness of students because the trees and other entities of the jungle speak, have personalities, and are part of their worldview); iv) it encourages the use of technologies so that the *virtual world* is used as a cultural space for teaching content that is relevant to the community. This idea of *untamed education* is connected to these populations' heritage, supporting their culture and values, and consequently their 'worldview' and 'way-of-life.' Without the benefit of *untamed education*, these populations would be again at the mercy of the kind of education provided by integrationist policies that aimed at assimilating them into the "white man's society."[48] Perhaps even the term *untamed education*

# Untamed Education    161

(Brazilian *Educação Selvagem*) should be replaced, which seems to somehow hint at an inferiority.

An important philosophical principle guiding all this is *imperfection*, which is sourced in shamanism. The shaman, a central figure in Indian societies, seeks constantly to bring balance to imperfections; for instance, an illness is an unbalance of energies, an imperfection, which needs to be rebalanced. This mode of thinking is essential to indigenous schools, manifesting itself in the pedagogy and curriculum. This means that in indigenous schools, students learn through their imperfections to seek a balanced connection to their parents, their families, the village and the whole, and this means that everything is much more malleable and fluid. For instance, when the teacher says that it is break and play time, this ends up being a suggestion rather than command, and many children continue to work on whatever they were doing. Likewise, they can be in class sitting at their desks or on the floor. That is, this means that there is no *perfect* timetable, no *perfect* way of being in the classroom or school.

Thus, the indigenous school mirrors the reality in indigenous villages, being deeply connected to the continuous tension between perfection, imperfection and harmony. In this respect, the Indian worldview is complex and differs a great deal from Western understanding. For instance, when indigenous populations build a hut, this hut is not just a heap of branches and stones, rather it represents certain cosmic ideas. To enter the darkness of the hut and to re-emerge from it and into the light is an important and meaningful experience, representing creation and re-creation, and the imbalances these movements create. And this movement of creation and re-re-creation is full of imbalances, imperfections that need to be accepted and embraced rather than overlooked or suppressed. Darkness (and Light) does not stand for nothingness, but for the recreation of the night (and of the day), its creation and continuous re-creation. The indigenous schools embrace this movement, the flow of their reality and worldview, so that imbalances and *imperfections* are respected and accepted rather than disregarded or overcome within the educational setting. Guilherme notes some practical consequences of this with regards to indigenous schools in Brazil:

> the school calendar has become more flexible as each of these communities has a specific social and economic context, which is taken into account during the school year; for instance, the calendar takes note of traditional festivities and the period of preparations leading to these; and the calendar may be modified for economic reasons (e.g. people need to help with the harvest). This allows for the school to work with the community and not against it, as was the case in the past (e.g. forming individuals ill equipped to live in rural native communities) . . . the community has become an extension of the classroom as it welcomes teachers and students (some are members of the community, others come from surrounding communities), provides them with

162   *Edison Hüttner and Alexandre Guilherme*

school meals, is considered a learning environment and participates in the assessment of students. For instance, when food for school meals is short, teachers and students can go fishing (boys) or harvesting (girls), which becomes a learning experience that prepares them to live locally. As such, they learn not just how to fish, but the kinds of local fish that are available; they learn not just how to harvest, but the fruits and vegetables of the area, and through this a sense of community and interdependence is reinforced in them. When the time for assessment comes, the teacher, student, parents and wider community are involved in establishing the student's progress.[49]

All these changes are of great benefit to the community and are only possible because of *untamed education*, which provides a greater integration between community and school, and between what is learned and what is required and useful to the community. This provides a glimmer of hope to these communities, which were disappearing under integrationist policies that threatened their language, culture, values and 'way-of-life.'

## Conclusion

To conclude this chapter, as one can gather, the current situation of 'contacted Indians', such as the Kokama, in Brazil is very problematic, despite all the recent progress that has been made. The full implementation of the rights of indigenous peoples still faces a number of political, social and economic challenges. The Brazilian government has gone to great lengths to fulfil its duty to provide elementary education (i.e. "elementary education shall be compulsory") and higher levels of education are also available (i.e. "technical and professional education shall be made . . . available and higher education shall be equally accessible . . . on the basis of merit").[50] However, in the light of the evidence provided by the various school censuses and work by commentators in the field of indigenous education, there remains many pedagogical, structural and logistical problems that must be resolved, if Native Indian communities are to be provided with the same standard of education present in mainstream Brazilian society.

We wish also to refer to the political dimension of indigenous education, drawing attention to its importance for issues concerning the rights of indigenous peoples. May and Aikman note that

[i]n the increasingly prominent articulation of minority rights worldwide, indigenous peoples have been at the forefront in arguing for better treatment, recognition of, and restitution for historical injustices and . . . the recognition of greater *self-determination* . . . within nation-states. Where nation-states have ignored, or derided their claims, indigenous peoples have turned instead to supra-national organisations, and international law, with surprisingly successful results.[51]

*Untamed Education* 163

Incidentally, when 'contacted indigenous' peoples complain and raise awareness of the problems they face through international and national organisations, trying to make their rights good, they are forcing the country and its citizens to reflect upon the problems faced by them, qua citizens of the country. This strengthens the democratic processes of the country and should not be viewed, as it is in more nationalistic quarters, as a form of meddling with internal affairs.[52] Further, Native Indians still face prejudices from mainstream society, perhaps as a consequence of inaccurate literary works and pedagogical texts, and this needs to be addressed.[53] In order to tackle these issues, education is crucial for both indigenous communities, which need to be able to access information and articulate their demands,[54] and mainstream society, which needs to become aware of its own misconceptions about the Other and gain a better understanding of indigenous communities. Hence, the Kokama case, which is unique in many ways, provides us with food for thought. The pressures of historical processes forced this people to hide amongst others, and their re-emergence as a people occurred when more auspicious circumstances emerged. It can be argued that their success or failure in re-establishing themselves as a people will be a reflection on us as a society that has learned, or not, to live with the Other.

## Notes

1. Atlas of the world's languages in danger. Accessed January 14, 2012, www.unesco.org/culture/languages-atlas/index.php.
2. Aryon D. Rodrigues, *Línguas Brasileiras: Para o conhecimento das línguas indígenas* (São Paulo, Brazil: Loyola, 1986).
3. Atlas of the world's languages in danger. Accessed January 14, 2012, www.unesco.org/culture/languages-atlas/index.php; UNESCO (2012b). Endangered languages. Accessed January 14, 2012, www.unesco.org/new/en/culture/themes/cultural-diversity/languages-and-multilingualism/endangeredlanguages/; Alex Guilherme, "Language Death: A Freirean Solution in the Heart of the Amazon," *Educational Philosophy and Theory* 45 1 (2013): 63–76.
4. Vaz notes that it is estimated that some 1300 languages were spoken, and some six million individuals divided into 1000 different peoples lived in the current territory of Brazil when the Portuguese first arrived in 1500. The majority of these peoples and their languages were first decimated by disease and slavery, and later by integrationist policies, which were in place until the 1980s. The situation in Brazil is not particular to the country and is an example of what happened throughout the world (e.g. US, Canada, Australia). (Vaz, A. (2011). Isolados no Brasil—Política de Estado: Da Tutela a Política de Direitos—Uma Questão Resolvida? (Informe 10). IWGIA, accessed December 21, 2013, http://servindi.org/pdf/informe_10.pdf).
5. This section draws on two previous published articles Alex Guilherme and Edison Huttner, "Exploring the New Challenges for Indigenous Education in Brazil: Some Lessons from Ticuna Schools," *International Review of Education* 61 no. 4 (2015): 481–501; and Alex Guilherme, "Indigenous Education in Brazil: The Issue of Contacted Native Indians," *Diaspora, Indigenous, and Minority Education* 9 no. 4 (2015): 205–220.

# 164 *Edison Hüttner and Alexandre Guilherme*

6. Estatuto do Indio, Law 6001, which was promulgated in 1973, and followed previous similar laws (Available on www.planalto.gov.br/ccivil_03/leis/L6001. htm; Last access on 29/05/2017).
7. Georg Grünberg, "Indigene Rechte, Ôkologie und die entwicklungspolitische Praxis im tropischen Waldland. Beispiele aus Brasilien und Guatemala," in *Tierra—indigene Volker, Umwelt und Recht*, ed. Doris Cech, Elke Mader, and Stefanie Reinberg (Frankfurt: Brandes und Apsel/Südwind, 1994), 159–174. Cited and translated by Gabriele Brandhuber, "Why Tukanoans Migrate? Some Remarks on Conflict on the Upper Rio Negro (Brazil)," *Journal de la Societe´ des Ame´ricanistes* 85 (1999): 261–280.
8. Instituto Brasileiro de Geografia e Estatística, "População residente, por cor ou raça, segundo o sexo, a situação do domicílio e os grupos de idade," accessed December 21, 2013, http://ftp.ibge.gov.br/Censos/Censo_Demografico_2010/ Caracteristicas_Gerais_Religiao_Deficiencia/tab1_2.pdf.
9. Antenor Vaz, *Isolados no Brasil—Política de Estado: Da Tutela a Política de Direitos—Uma Questão Resolvida?* (2011), 9.
   (Informe 10). IWGIA, accessed December 21, 2013, http://servindi.org/pdf/ informe_10.pdf.
10. Brazil, "Constituição Federal de 1988," English version accessed December 13, 2013, http://pdba.georgetown.edu/constitutions/brazil/english96.html# mozTocId506170.
11. Marta M. Azevedo, *Indigenous Education in Brazil: History and Recent Developments: In Schools in the Rainforest: Innovative Indigenous Education in the Amazon* (Oslo, Norway: Rainforest Foundation Norway, 2009), 16–19.
12. There are also so-called 'non-contacted groups.' The majority of noncontacted peoples in the world are found in jungle regions in South America, Papua New Guinea and the Andaman Islands of India. These groups are also sometimes referred to as 'isolated peoples' or 'lost tribes.' In South America, these groups are found in Paraguay, Bolivia, Peru, Ecuador, Venezuela, Colombia, French Guiana, Guiana, Suriname and Brazil. Survival International (2013), an NGO focused on raising awareness of noncontacted tribes, suggests that there are about 100 noncontacted tribes in the world and that about half of these are in Brazil and Peru. However, these figures may be an underestimation as the FUNAI (the Brazilian National Indian Foundation), which is a federal government agency for the protection of Native Indians, reported in 2013 that 82 communities have been reported, and 32 of these have now been confirmed, which suggests that Brazil is home to the largest number of these groups in the world. (Alex Guilherme, "Indigenous Education in Brazil: The Issue of Contacted Native Indians," *Diaspora, Indigenous, and Minority Education* 9 no. 4 (2015): 205–220).
13. Cristiane Lasmar, "Conhecer para transformar: Os índios do rio Uaupés (Alto Rio Negro) e a educação escolar," *Tellus* 9 no. 16 (2009): 11–33; Guilherme (2013), Ibid.
14. Luís D. B. Grupioni "Introdução. Instituto Socioambiental," 2013a, accessed December 21, 2013, http://pib.socioambiental.org/pt/c/politicas-indigenistas/ educacao-escolar-indigena/introducao.
15. Grupioni, ibid.; L. D. B. Grupioni, "Censo Escolar Indigena. Instituto Socioambiental," 2013b, accessed December 21, 2013, http://pib.socioambiental. org/pt/c/politicas-indigenistas/educacao-escolar-indigena/censo-escola-indigena; Edison Hüttner, "Educação Indígena Brasileira," *Revista Anec, Edição 03*, Ano II, 2009, pp. 20–21.
16. Grupioni, ibid.
17. Flora D. Cabalzar, and Luís A. A. Oliveira, "Novas Práticas na Educação Escolar Indígena do Rio Negro," in *Educação Escolar Indígena do Rio Negro*

*Untamed Education* 165

*1998–2011*, ed. Flora D. Cabalzar (São Paulo, Brazil: Instituto Socioambiemtal and FOIRN, 2012), 26–49.

18. Hüttner, ibid, 19–20; Januário, E. (2002). Ensino superior para índios: Um novo paradigma na educação. Cadernos de Educação Escolar Indígena, 1(1), 15–24.
19. Hüttner, "Educação Indígena Brasileira," 20.
20. Grupioni, ibid.
21. Instituto Brasileiro de Geografia e Estatística, "Censo Escolar 2010," 2010, accessed December 21, 2013, http://portal.mec.gov.br/index.php?option=com_docman&task=doc_details&gid=7272&Itemid=.
22. United Nations, "Promoción y protección de todos los derechos humanos, civiles, políticos, económicos, sociales y culturales, incluido el derecho al desarrollo," 2009, accessed December 21, 2013, www.acnur.org/biblioteca/pdf/8057.pdf?view=1.
23. Luis E. López, *Reaching the Unreached: Indigenous Intercultural Bilingual Education in Latin America* (Paris, France: UNESCO, 2009), http://unesdoc.unesco.org/images/0018/001866/186620e.pdf; Bruna Franchetto, "Preservação de línguas minoritárias. A experiência kuikuro" (Lecture given at the Seminario International sobre Revitalización de lenguas indígenas, Universidad del Cauca. Colombia: Fondo Indígena, GTZ, June 11 and 12, 2008).
24. Grupioni, ibid.
25. Guilherme, Alexandre, ibid., 71; Eva M. Johannssen, *Schools in the Rainforest: Innovative Indigenous Education in the Amazon* (Oslo, Norway: Rainforest Foundation Norway, 2009); Justino S. Rezende, "Repensando a Educação Indígena. Inspetoria Salesiana Missionária da Amazônia," 2004, accessed March 15, 2012, www.isma.org.br/artigos/educacao_indigena.pdf; Lilia A. Sumiya, "Projeto Educação Indígena no Alto Rio Negro AM," in *20 Experiências de Gestão Pública e Cidadania*, ed. M. A. C. Teixeira, M. G. de Godoy, and R. Clemente (São Paulo, Brazil: Programa Gestão Pública e Cidadania, 2005), 117–125.
26. Hüttner, Edison, "Educação Indígena Brasileira," 19–21; cf. also Hugo A. Camacho Gonzáles, "Escuela, Tradición oral y Educación propria entre los Tikuna de Trapecio Amazónico Colombiano," in *Os Ticuna Hoje, No. 5. Manaus* (Brazil: Editora da Universidade do Amazonas, 1999), 88.
27. Nancy H. Hornberger, *Can Schools Save Indigenous Languages?* (New York, NY: Palgrave, 2008). Nancy H. Hornberger, "Language and Education: A Limpopo Lens," in *Sociolinguistics and Language Education*, ed. Nancy H. Hornberger and S. L. McKay (Toronto, Canada: Multilingual Matters, 2010), 549–564.
28. Teresa L. MacCarthy, *Language Planning and Policy in Native America: History, Theory and Praxis* (Toronto, Canada: Multilingual Matters, 2013), XX; Dick Littlebear, "Effective Language Education Practices and Native Language Survival," in *Effective Language Education Practices and Native Language Survival*, ed. I. Reyhner (Choctaw, OK: Native American Language Issues, 1990), 1–8.
29. Grupioni, ibid.
30. Hüttner, "Educação Indígena Brasileira," 20–21.
31. Instituto Brasileiro de Geografia e Estatística, "Censo Escolar 2010."
32. Greg A. Urban, *A História da Cultura Brasileira segundo as Línguas Nativas: Histórias dos índios no Brasil* (São Paulo: Companhia das Letras, 1992), 92–100.
33. The Tupi-Guarani is the most widely subgroup and language spoken in South America.
34. Alfred Metraux, *Religión y magias indígenas de América del Sur* (Madrid: Ed. Aguilar, 1973), 11.
35. Paul Marcoy, *Viagem pelo rio Amazonas*. trans. Bras Antonio Porro (Manaus: Gov. Est.Secret. Est. Cult, EDUA, 2001), 5.
36. Ana S.A.C. Cabral, Relatório de levantamento preliminar da comunidades Kokáma do Alto Solimões, Instruções Executivas: DAF/FUNAI, nn. 124/97 e 154/97/, Brasília, 1998, 1.

## 166 Edison Hüttner and Alexandre Guilherme

37. The Tikuna (i.e. the *black nose*) are an Amerindian people, who currently live in the border region of Brazil, Peru and Colombia. They form a society of about 50 thousand individuals, of which 36 thousand live in Brazil, eight thousand in Colombia and seven thousand in Peru. They are the most numerous people in the Brazilian Amazon region. The Tikuna have a long tradition insofar as experiences with education and indigenous schools are concerned, and we can learn a great deal from them. (cf. Beto Ricardo and Fanny Ricardo, *Povos Indigenas no Brasil: 2006/2010* (São Paulo: Instituto Socioambiental, 2011), 11).
38. Personal statement.
39. Deise Silva Rubim, "Traçando novos caminhos: ressignificação dos kokama em Santo Antonio do Içá, Alto Solimões—Am" (Dissertação apresentada ao Programa de Pós-Graduação em Antropologia Social (PPGAS) da Universidade Federal do Amazonas (UFAM), Museu Amazônico, Manaus (AM), 2016), 52.
40. The Marist Brother of Schools, commonly known as the Marists, is an international community of Catholic Religious Institute of Brothers, founded by Marcellin Champagnat in 1817 in France.
41. Personal statement.
42. Chandra Wood Viegas, "Línguas em rede: para o fortalecimento da língua e da cultura Kokama, 2014" (Tese submetida ao Programa de Pós-Graduação em Linguística, Departamento de Linguística, Português e Línguas Clássicas, Instituto de Letras, Universidade de Brasília, 2014), 53.
43. Rubim, "Traçando novos caminhos," 111–113.
44. Altaci Correa Rubin, "O Reordenamento Político E Cultural Do Povo Kokama: A Reconquista Da Língua E Do Território Além Das Fronteiras Entre O Brasil E O Peru" (Tese de Doutoramento apresentada ao curso de Pós-Graduação em Linguística do Departamento de Linguística, Português e Línguas Clássicas do Instituto de Letras da Universidade de Brasília, 2016), 80.
45. Rubim, "Traçando novos caminhos," 167.
46. Norma Faust W. Gramatica Cocama, *Lecciones para el aprendizaje del idioma cocama*, Ministerio de Educación—Serie Lingüística peruana n° 6. Instituto Lingüístico de Verano, Primera edición 1972, Segunda edición, 1978—Versión española de Ezequiel Romero, revisada por Walter del Aguila e Irma Inugai, Centro Amazónico de Lenguas Autóctonas Peruanas "Hugo Pesce", Yarinacocha, Pucallpa, Perú, p. 11. 1978.
47. Samias, Edney da Cunha (Org.), *Dicionário. Kukami / Kukamiria Português*, 1ª Edição (Tawa Tini—AM, 2015), 7.
48. There are Indians in the Amazon without contact with the current society—these are the so called 'uncontacted Indians.' It could be argued that even in their case these principles apply, and that 'contacted Indians' are trying to maintain a 'worldview' and 'way-of-life' alive. They are not savages, brutes or violent peoples—they live in harmony with nature, with other forms of learning and relationships. We know very little about noncontacted groups. The information about these peoples is always very heterogeneous and often provided by contacted Native Indians, or by individuals inhabiting adjacent areas who came into contact with them accidentally, or by researchers who found evidence for their existence in the form of objects (e.g. arrows) in provisional settlements, or through aerial photographs. It is not uncommon for us not to know the name of the tribe and the language spoken by them. It is estimated that there are 82 such communities in Brazil, and 32 have been confirmed (cf. Guilherme, "Indigenous Education in Brazil."
49. Guilherme (2013), ibid., 10–11.
50. United Nations, "The Universal Declaration of Human Rights," 2013, accessed December 13, 2013, www.un.org/en/documents/udhr/.

51. Stephen May and Sheila Aikman, "Indigenous Education: Addressing Current Issues and Developments," *Comparative Education* 39 no. 2 (2003): 139.
52. Érika M. Yamada, "Os Direitos Humanos e o Estado Brasileiro. Instituto Socioambiental," 2013, accessed December 21, 2013, http://pib.socioambiental.org/pt/c/direitos/internacional/os-direitos-humanos-e-o-estado-brasileiro.
53. Hüttner, "Educação Indígena Brasileira," 20–21.
54. NB. 'Contacted Indian' communities are aware of this, especially when they reflect back upon their experiences prior to the 1980s when integrationist policies were in full force and missionary schools were the norm. For instance, a local individual from the Alto Rio Negro area in the Amazon region of Brazil commented that: "They took away half of our culture, but at the same time they taught us how to defend the other half against the Whites" (Grünberg, "Indigene Rechte, Ôkologie und die entwicklungspolitische Praxis im tropischen Waldland. Beispiele aus Brasilien und Guatemala." Cited and translated by Brandhuber, "Why Tukanoans Migrate?"

# 9 Home Within

## Locating a Warlpiri Approach to Developing and Applying an Indigenous Educational Philosophy in Australian Contexts

*Aaron Corn with Wantarri Jampijinpa Patrick*

### Introduction

Opportunities for students to learn through Indigenous epistemologies within the formal curricula of schools and universities are, all too often, rare and fleeting in Australia. Even remote Indigenous communities that have only been extended government services within the past century have repeatedly fought public education policies to prevent, within their local schools, the systemic marginalisation of their own languages and knowledge traditions. This centre–periphery dynamic between the enduring Anglocentrism of Australia's publically-regulated education system and the holders of Australia's rich Indigenous knowledge traditions perpetuates a colonising construct, which is itself echoed in an entrenched post-colonial paradigm of knowledge production and dissemination that continues, on a global scale, to normalise the values and perspectives of the affluent Trans-Atlantic metropole over equally legitimate alternatives found in other societies.

In this chapter, I explore the work of the Warlpiri educator, artist and scholar, Steven Wantarri Jampijinpa Pawu-Kurlpurlurnu Patrick, also known as Wanta, in his development and application of Indigenous educational philosophies amid the Australian contexts of the public school in his hometown, Lajamanu, in the Northern Territory's remote Tanami Desert (see Figure 9.1), and our collaborative design and teaching of the course, Indigenous Music and Media, in Canberra at the Australian National University (ANU). I demonstrate the genesis of Wanta's educational philosophy and approach to youth engagement in his development of ideas and content drawn from Warlpiri law and public ceremony for use in the Milpirri Festival at Lajamanu, and examine how his approach aims to ensure the survival of Warlpiri ways of being and knowing while simultaneously championing their legitimacy as a means of learning that can hold intrinsic value and beneficial outcomes for all.[1]

Wanta's innovative work as an Indigenous educator striving to promote bicultural balance through his engagements with Australia's inherently

*Home Within* 169

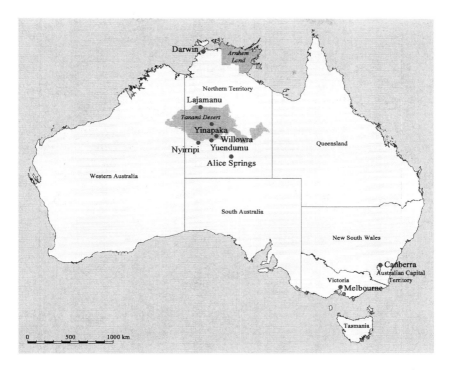

*Figure 9.1* Map of the Tamani Desert and other cited locations within Australia

Anglocentric education system exemplifies ontological paradoxes observed on a global intercultural scale by sociologist Raewyn Connell and philosopher Hamid Dabashi.[2] Beyond this specifically Warlpiri context, this Anglocentric bias has also been challenged by a range of Australian Indigenous scholars working predominantly from within universities with the goals of more broadly improving educational outcomes for Indigenous Australians and establishing Indigenous knowledges as a distinct field within the academy.[3] Martin Nakata has warned that it is

> important to understand what happens when Indigenous knowledge is documented in ways that disembodies it from the people who are its agents, . . . [and] to consider what disintegrations and transformations occur when it is redistributed across Western categories of classification.[4]

The Yolŋu Studies program at Charles Darwin University in the Northern Territory's capitol, Darwin, which is primarily taught by Yolŋu educators from the remote Northern Territory communities of northeast Arnhem Land,[5] nonetheless provides an excellent example of how Indigenous educators can work in partnership with the academy to share their knowledges with students from a diverse range of backgrounds.[6] I therefore ask whether Australians should complacently accept that our educational institutions do little more than echo received epistemologies and pedagogies from the Trans-Atlantic metropole as a consequence of our nation's colonial history of 230 years or simultaneously seek to embrace Indigenous epistemologies and pedagogies that have been shaped by the Australian continent over scores of millennia and, in doing so, support Australian Indigenous communities in their efforts to maintain their knowledge traditions amid the contemporary challenges of cultural survival.

## Background

Lajamanu is a remote community with a population of some 1200 people of whom the overwhelming majority are Aboriginal Australians of Warlpiri descent as distinct from other Australian Indigenous peoples.[7] Warlpiri is the community's main language and English is usually only spoken in dealings with outsiders.[8] In 2016, 189 students, 99% of whom were Aboriginal Australians and 98% of whom were from a language background other than English, were enrolled at Lajamanu School.[9]

In 1982, Lajamanu School established a bilingual education program, which was adequately resourced with trained staff and printing facilities to teach literacy in both Warlpiri and English, and was widely considered to be highly successful.[10] This program was largely defunded and began to gradually decline with its primary emphasis shifted to enabling English literacy, under the guise of "two-way" learning, following two decades of adverse Northern Territory Government policies from 1998 onwards.[11] Subsequently, between October 2008 and September 2012, all vestiges of bilingual education in Northern Territory schools were effectively suspended when the Northern Territory Government mandated that the first four hours of education during each school day must be conducted only in English.[12]

Like other Australian Indigenous peoples, the Warlpiri possess a rich intellectual tradition that demands high levels of cultural literacy in reading country and its living environments, relationships and obligations among different groups and individuals, and complex canons of ancestrally-given ceremonial language, songs, dances and designs.[13] The Warlpiri have been strongly involved in systemic education since the first Warlpiri–English bilingual education program was established in the school of the Warlpiri community at Yuendumu in 1974. Since 1984, Warlpiri educators and residents in the communities of Yuendumu, Willowra, Lajamanu and Nyirrpi have shared their views on education and learning matters through regular meetings of the Warlpiri Triangle network of the Warlpiri-patu-kurlangu Jaru association.[14]

I first became aware of Wanta's work at Lajamanu late last decade through a mutual colleague at ANU, the ethnomusicologist Stephen A. Wild, who had begun recording Wanta's father, Jerry Jangala Patrick, and his contemporaries singing traditional Warlpiri songs at Lajamanu in 1970.[15] After commencing work on his Australian Research Council (ARC) Linkage Project on traditional Warlpiri songs with linguist Mary Laughren and anthropologists Nicolas Peterson and Anna Meltzer in 2005,[16] Wild returned to Lajamanu to find Wanta working as an Assistant Teacher at Lajamanu School, and introducing traditional ideas and content drawn from Warlpiri law and public ceremonies to new generations of Warlpiri children through his work as Creative Director of the Milpirri Festival. Wanta then became employed as a Research Associate on Wild's ARC Linkage Project, and a doctoral student of Wild's, Yukihiro Doi, who later I also supervised, undertook a doctoral thesis on the Milpirri Festival.[17]

In 2012, Wanta, Wild and I subsequently commenced work on an ARC Discovery Indigenous project on public collections of Warlpiri heritage in Australia, which provided Wanta with three years of full-time employment at ANU as Research Fellow in receipt of an ARC Discovery Indigenous Award.[18] This was the first time that a Warlpiri investigator would lead an ARC project of any kind, and it afforded me the opportunity to collaborate with Wanta in the design and teaching of our course, Indigenous Music and Media, which we offered at ANU to seven cohorts of students from 2012 to 2014.

Delivered over five days of intensive classes, Indigenous Music and Media was a second-year undergraduate elective course.[19] It contributed towards Major and Minor programs in both Music and Australian Indigenous Studies, yet having no prerequisite course requirement, it attracted a much broader cohort of students pursuing undergraduate majors and minors in Anthropology, Development Studies, History, Languages, Linguistics, Pacific Studies, Philosophy and Political Science as well. It further attracted postgraduate students pursuing topics in Australian Indigenous Studies, Creative Writing, Music, Linguistics and Law, who either audited it voluntarily or secured permission to undertake it towards fulfilling their postgraduate coursework requirements. Among those who participated, only two undergraduate Music students and one auditing doctoral candidate studying Law identified as Indigenous Australians.[20]

As Wanta and I designed and delivered Indigenous Music and Media for the first time in July 2012,[21] I came to recognise him to be a pedagogue of exceptional vision. This was even more evident when I travelled to Lajamanu to witness his creative direction of the Milpirri Festival later that year.[22] Students were so enthused by Wanta's teaching that some subsequently funded themselves to make the 5000 kilometre journey from Canberra to Lajamanu to attend the Milpirri Festival, while others found ways to extend their learning with Wanta via a combination of voluntary side-projects and elective courses supporting independent studies. These included formally-assessed internships working with recordings of Warlpiri song archived at the Australian Institute for Aboriginal and Torres Strait Islander Studies, and voluntarily collaborating with Wanta to create a mixed-media art installation called *Wirntaru [Great Story]: Hear the Elements Talk*.[23]

## Carrying Home Within

Wanta's vision for Indigenous Music and Media was to offer our students, all but one of whom held no direct knowledge of Warlpiri society and culture, an immersive learning environment that was grounded in Warlpiri law, and an Australian Indigenous pedagogy of knowing through doing that simulated, over the course's five days, an experience of participating in Warlpiri ceremony as a key modality through which Warlpiri knowledge is traditionally encountered and taught. Wanta's teaching style aimed to instill in our students an embodied understanding that knowing comes through doing, and that knowledge must be earnt through active engagement. His approach to teaching and the Warlpiri educational philosophy that underpins it remain important to this day because they challenge racialised notions about the broader value of Indigenous knowledges beyond Australian Indigenous communities.

Rather than teaching our students *about* Warlpiri knowledge from a detached and distanced perspective of ethnographic curiosity, Wanta's key pedagogical approach was instead to encourage our students to understand themselves and their place in the cosmos *through* the frame of Warlpiri knowledge. To this end, he extended the complex logic of Warlpiri social organisation into our interactions with our students, taught them how to perform ceremonial song and dance repertoires that he had selected for presentation at the Milpirri Festival, encouraged them to actively hunt for knowledge on their own initiative, and admitted them to greater levels of knowing and responsibility in reward for educational aptitude and attainment. Through these processes, Wanta demonstrated to our students how Warlpiri knowledge can hold intrinsic value for everyone, irrespective of heritage, as a framework of understanding and living in Australia that has enabled humans to inhabit the Tanami Desert for scores of millennia.

Far removed from the knowledge and experiences of most students in Australia, the Warlpiri people understand themselves to be the descents of the original ancestors who shaped the Tanami Desert and inscribed into its living environment their *jukurrpa*, or "dreamings," as a system of law for living in balance with the natural order. Each Warlpiri person is an inheritor of a discrete country or estate within the Tanami Desert that was shaped and populated by the original ancestors and has been passed from father to child intergenerationally to the present day. Extensive ceremonies structured around the ritual application of sacred repertoires of songs, dances and designs frame the traditional process of formal learning through which young males and females are separately inducted into this system of law and transitioned into adulthood. By pursuing subsequent levels of gendered ceremonial initiation, men and women can also gain gradual access to deeper and deeper esoteric knowledge, and become qualified to take on leadership roles in ceremonies, contribute to making decisions for their respective countries, and participate in public debate as respective elders within their communities.[24]

Fundamental to Wanta's educational philosophy and his means of introducing students to Warlpiri knowledge is his *Ngurra-kurlu* schema for working with Warlpiri people.[25] *Ngurra-kurlu* can be translated into English as

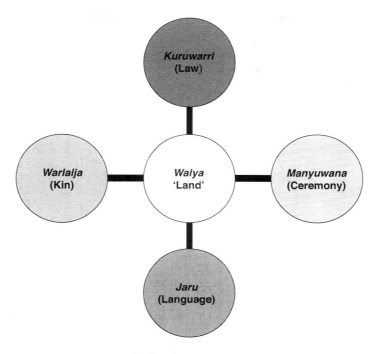

*Figure 9.2* Wantarri's *Ngurra-kurlu* schema.

"about home," "with home" and the carriage of "home within." It circumscribes five interrelated fundaments of classical Warlpiri knowledge that Wanta identifies as essential for knowing and being in the world as a Warlpiri person, and for epistemologically framing and communicating this worldview to others. These five fundaments of Warlpiri knowledge circumscribe principles for living in the world that were given to the Warlpiri by their original ancestors. They are *Walya* (Land), *Kuruwarru* (Law), *Warlalja* (Kin), *Jaru* (Language) and *Manyuwana* (Ceremony). Wanta theorises *Ngurra-kurlu* as a framework for understanding one's place in the world within the environment of the Warlpiri homelands, and depicts it as a cross made of five points connected by two intersecting perpendicular lines (see Figure 9.2). Land is the central point, and radiating out from it at respective ends of the four spokes anti-clockwise from the bottom are Law, Kin, Language and Ceremony.

The central point, Land, is an eternal present that binds humans to their ancestors through a shared environment onto which the original ancestors inscribed their dreamings. The top point, Law, is the means through which these dreamings are observed as a body of law for maintaining balance within society and nature. The right-hand point, Kin, is a complex system of social organisation that binds all individuals in Warlpiri society, and regulates their rights and obligations among ancestors, country and each other. The bottom point, Language, represents the utterances spoken by the

174  *Aaron Corn with Wantarri Jampijinpa Patrick*

original ancestors and recorded in the ceremonial songs they passed to their living descendants. Finally, the left-hand point, Ceremony, is the cooperative process for observing Warlpiri law through the ritual performance of sacred repertoires of songs, dances and designs. Together, as *Ngurra-kurlu*, these five fundaments of Warlpiri knowledge provide a template for being and knowing, as established by the original ancestors, that has enabled the *yapa* (people) of the Tanami Desert to read country as an ever-changing living entity, to deduce the patterns in natural forms and functions, and to live in balance with the natural order since long before European contact.

Warlpiri society consists of four patrifilial ceremonial groups named *Wanya-parnta* or *Yankirri* (Emu), *Parra* (Day), *Wawirri* (Kangaroo), and *Munga* (Night). Each of these four groups comprises the hereditary owners of multiple non-contiguous estates dotted throughout the Tanami Desert. Wanta's *Ngurra-kurlu* schema therefore also represents the respective winds that blow from the four cardinal directions, *Yatitjarra* (North), *Kakarrara* (East), *Kurlirra* (South) and *Karlarra* (West), to bring the four ceremonial groups together for shared ceremonies (see Figure 9.3). Along the North–South axis of this schema, the Kangaroo and Emu groups form a patrimoiety that performs a fire purification ceremony called *Jardiwarnpa* (Deep Sleep),

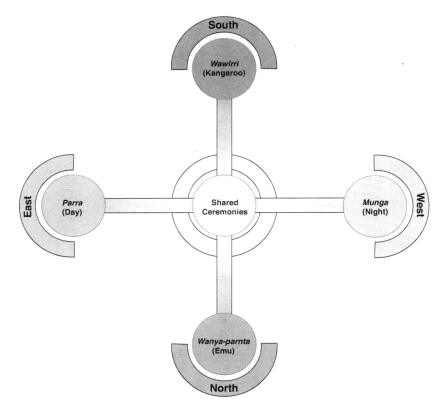

*Figure 9.3* The four Warlpiri ceremonial groups.

*Home Within* 175

which functions to restore balance and social order by laying to rest all disagreements, enmities and hostilities of the year gone past.[26] The Day and Night groups form a second patrimoiety along the schema's East–West axis that performs the *Kurdiji* (Shield) ceremony through which women hand their boys over to men for the process of their initiation into adulthood.[27] As each boy is handed over, he faces four shields, which are inscribed with the respective dreamings of the countries of his *warringi* (father's father), *jinngardi* (father's mother), *jaja* (mother's mother), and *jamirdi* (mother's father).

## The Flying Emu's Crown

As a patrilineal member of the Emu group, Wanta's pedagogical approach is guided by the *jukurrpa* relationship between emu and water that can be observed in the night sky. The Warlpiri term for the Milky Way, *Pirli-mangkuru*, can be translated as 'Sea of Stones'. But on the night of a new moon, dark nebulae can also be seen amid this expansive sea of stars (see Figure 9.4). Crux, the Southern Cross, is the most iconic of southern hemisphere constellations, and adjoining this is the Coalsack Dark Nebula, which can be seen to form the head of an emu. Following the silhouette of an emu in profile, the Coalsack joins a long, thin neck of dark nebulae that stretches past the Pointers, and into a greater dark nebulae body bisected by Scorpio. The legs of this celestial emu also are comprised of dark nebulae and both stretch backwards behind his tail to the sidereal constellation Scutum. This composite constellation of dark nebulae is known as the Flying Emu, and like the single white feather

*Figure 9.4* The Warlpiri Flying Emu constellation.

176    *Aaron Corn with Wantarri Jampijinpa Patrick*

worn as a headdress in Warlpiri ceremonies, the South Cross is his Crown. This Flying Emu taught the soaring *Warlawurru* (Wedge-tailed Eagle) how to fly before this bird of prey then taught all the other birds at Yinapaka (Lake Surprise). From his vantage among the stars, the Flying Emu is considered to be the ultimate teacher and a paragon of knowledge for all to aspire towards.

In the series of songs held and performed by the Emu group for the *Jardiwarnpa* ceremony, the four seasons are designated as stations of the Flying Emu. It commences with songs that locate the Emu in his eternal ancestral state before moving through each of the four seasons in turn. The Wet season is that of the Emu group, and this is when the Emu rests, submerged beneath the water. The Cool season is that of the Day group, and this is when the Emu wakes and propels himself out of the water. The Dry season is that of the Kangaroo group when the Emu, in full flight, is astonished to see both of his legs stretched backwards behind him. Finally, the Hot season is that of the Night group when the Emu loses altitude and dives back into the water. In this final Hot season, the Digging Stick Pointers touch the horizon, and the Southern Cross hides behind the curvature of the Earth to mark the commencement of annual ceremonies starting with the *Jardiwarnpa* ceremony. In this position, the Southern Cross becomes a *Yarla* (Great Yam) of knowledge on which all who gather for ceremonies can feast.

The Crown of the Flying Emu, the Great Yam of knowledge, and Wanta's *Ngurra-kurlu* schema are each an expression of the constellation Crux, the Southern Cross, which comprises five main stars in the approximate shape of a five-point cross. The four seasonal stations of the Flying Emu, the cardinal directions of their respective winds, and the four Warlpiri ceremonial groups are attributed to the four outer stars of this constellation, starting clockwise from the bottom at Alpha Crusis ($\alpha$ Cru), its brightest star (see Figure 9.5). The fifth inner star, however, is always attributed to the fixed ancestral eternity of *jukurrpa* around which revolves the natural cycles of the physical world, the sentient ancestors that reside eternally within country, and the Warlpiri social order in which everyone is bound together by balanced ceremonial relationships. In the night sky, this fifth star is left purposefully off centre as a reminder that life must be lived in balance with the natural order lest the Warlpiri become homeless in their own lands.

Wanta vested this organisational logic of the Southern Cross, as expressed through his *Ngurra-kurlu* schema, when programming of our five-day course at ANU, Indigenous Music and Media (see Figure 9.6). Days One and Two traced the East–West *Kurdiji* axis, and Days Three and Four followed the North–South *Jardiwarnpa* axis with Day Five coming to rest on the central fifth star ($\varepsilon$ Cru). Lectures over these five days spanned topics and readings on Australian Indigenous epistemologies, languages, environmental management, collections, music, visual arts, digital media, public policy, and native title legislation. However, Wanta also assigned a unique theme to each of these five days to incrementally scaffold our students' engagements with Warlpiri knowledge and culture, and to gradually introduce them to new ceremonial repertoires as an applied means of knowing through doing.

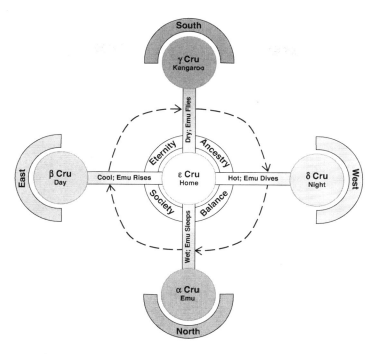

*Figure 9.5* Polysemic Warlpiri interpretations of the Southern Cross constellation.

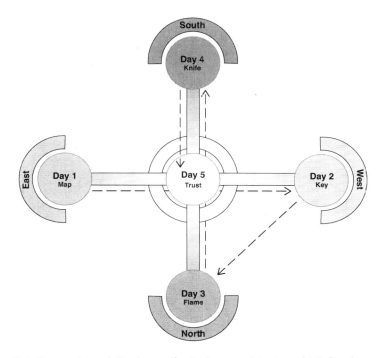

*Figure 9.6* Overarching daily themes for Indigenous Music and Media classes.

178    *Aaron Corn with Wantarri Jampijinpa Patrick*

At the commencement of Day One, themed *Kuyu Ngurru* (Map), Wanta purified students with a traditional smoking ceremony before we overviewed various traditions of Indigenous music and dance across Australia, and introduced them to the concept of *Ngurra-kurlu*. On Day Two, themed *Yukurruku* (Key), he assigned each student to one of the four Warlpiri ceremonial groups and explained how this related us all to each other through the Warlpiri kinship system. For this exercise, he applied an educational technique that he had developed for use with Warlpiri children during the Milpirri Festival. Students were given gel wristbands, their keys, in colours that corresponded to their respective ceremonial groups: red for Kangaroo representing blood, green for Day representing vegetation, blue for Emu representing water, and yellow for Night representing flame. That afternoon, he taught our students dances for two songs of the Day group: *Kanakurlangu* (Digging Stick Pointers) through which women hand over their boys for the *Kurdiji* initiation ceremony, and Wantarri (Sun) which is alternatively known as *Warlu* (Fire) and symbolizes new growth. On Day Three, themed *Jarra* (Flame), students learnt about the Flying Emu constellation, and Wanta taught them dances to five songs from the Emu group's *Jardiwarnpa* repertoire about the seasonal stations of the Flying Emu. By the end of Day Four, themed *Junma* (Knife), when Wanta taught our students dances to songs from the Emu group's *Yankirri* (Emu) repertoire, our students had grown into their roles as active hunters of knowledge through their explorations of the myriad semantic linkages surrounding the concepts and materials that had been presented to them in class. These included a side-excursion to Australia's Parliament House, where the forecourt, designed by Michael Jakamara Nelson,[28] depicts a *Jardiwarnpa* ceremony in a classical Warlpiri expression constitutional polity. Finally, on Day Five, themed *Wala* (Trust), Wanta acknowledged each student's achievements in recognition of their learning with the gift of a traditional design aligned with their respective ceremonial groups, and taught them one final dance to a song of the Day and Night groups called *Warntarritarri* (Celestial Road) or *Wulpararru* (The Milky Way).

Wanta's orchestration of this educational process was masterful. From his use of coloured wristbands to enable students to identify with the Warlpiri social structure and the heightened biochemistry of their active participation in ceremonial dances to the esteem they earned by demonstrating that they could hunt for knowledge themselves, each element that Wanta introduced to Indigenous Music and Media brought our students closer to an understanding of how Warlpiri knowledge can hold intrinsic value for everyone, irrespective of heritage, as a framework for understanding and living in Australia, and for understanding themselves and their place in the cosmos.

## The Milpirri Festival

The organisational logic of the Southern Cross within Wanta's *Ngurra-kurlu* schema and its cycle of five fundaments of Warlpiri knowledge also runs though the programming of the Milpirri Festival at Lajamanu. Launched in

2005 in partnership with Tracks Dance Company and Lajamanu School, the Milpirri Festival was founded in response to a tragic youth suicide at Lajamanu as a means of bringing the awe and wonder of traditional Warlpiri culture back into the lives of local children. Wanta hoped that the exposure of local school children to Warlpiri culture and ceremonial themes during school hours would also improve their educational outcomes by improving their overall attendance and engagements with learning while at school.[29]

Produced in collaboration with Tracks Dance Company in Darwin,[30] the first cycle of five Milpirri Festivals was held in 2005, 2007, 2009, 2011 and 2012, and each of these performances focused on a discrete theme drawn from traditional Warlpiri ceremonies. In order of presentation, these themes were the *Jardiwarnpa* fire purification ceremony in 2005; the *Kurdiji* first initiation ceremony for boys in 2007; the Jurntu *purlapa* (public) ceremony, which teaches how people are bound by Warlpiri law and must face the consequences of their actions, in 2009; a *yawulyu* (women's) ceremony that recounted how the birds gathered at Yinapaka to learn to fly in 2011; and *Pulyaranyi* (Windblown Path), which describes how the winds from the four cardinal directions carry people of the four ceremonial groups together for ceremony, in 2012.[31] This same cycle of five themes recommenced for a second time with the sixth and seventh Milpirri Festivals of 2014 and 2016.

Each Milpirri Festival usually takes place in October when, traditionally, the Digging Stick Pointers touch the horizon and annual ceremonies are due to commence. It typically consists of a single evening's performance of music and dance staged outdoors by a cast of more than 200 performers. The event is usually preceded by some eight weeks of intensive preparation and regular rehearsals led by Wanta and Tracks Dance Company, mostly during school hours, with children at Lajamanu School, local elders and other performers.

To bring students into a deeper understanding of Land, Law, Kin, Language and Ceremony as explicated through *Ngurra-kurla*, the Milpirri Festival, since its inception, has employed an innovative array of pedagogical methods for simultaneously engaging Warlpiri youths with Warlpiri traditions and formal schooling via a novel intergenerational and intercultural performance context. Children engage with local elders and work within their own hereditary ceremonial groups to create new content for the festival. But rather than framing old and new expressive practices as separate cultural domains, the festival seamlessly incorporates ceremonial repertoires into a unified program alongside contemporary items. This allows school children the freedom to create and perform their own hip-hop dances based on the themes of traditional song and dance items that are led by their elders during each performance.

The Milpirri Festival exists within a rich continuum of innovative practice and engagements with new media technologies that has been developing since the introduction of local television to the Tanami Desert in the 1980s.[32] In conceiving the Milpirri Festival, Wanta also drew inspiration from the Garma Festival at Gulkula in Arnhem Land, and the pedagogical ideas of the Yolŋu educator and musician, Mandawuy Yunupiŋu, who drew on his own ceremonial traditions to theorise *Gaṉma* (Converging Currents) as an Indigenous model for bicultural education and exchange.[33] *Gaṉma* is a meeting of freshwater and saltwater currents that creates a pungent yellow foam on the surface of certain tropical estuaries in Arnhem Land, and serves as a traditional framework for forging peaceful cooperation between different patrifilial groups of equal social standing. In the 1980s, Yunupiŋu further developed this *Gaṉma* concept into a model for the bicultural schooling of Yolŋu children, and into an ideal for balanced relations between Indigenous and other Australians that he expressed through the influential music of his rock band, Yothu Yindi.[34]

As there is nowhere that saltwater and freshwater currents meet in the Tanami Desert, Wanta looked to Warlpiri law to find a similarly balanced model of two complementary natural forces. Drawn from ceremonial law of his own inheritance within the Emu ceremonial group, *Milpirri* is a lofty Thundercloud that forms along the path of the great Rain *jukurrpa* through the meeting of hot air rising from the Earth's surface and cold air falling from the sky. It can be a turbulent space full of thunder and lightning, but one that nourishes the desert floor with its life-giving Wet-season rains.[35]

The Milpirri Festival that I attended in 2012, themed *Pulyaranyi*, was structured around an overarching sequence of ceremonial items sung by elders and danced by adults of each of the four Warlpiri ceremonial groups in an overarching order of Emu, Day, Kangaroo, and Night. This took place against a visually-striking backdrop of children wearing t-shirts and gel wristbands in the blue, green, red and yellow colours of the four ceremonial groups, and twenty-seven towering banners coded with the same four colours that, like the shields displayed in a *Kurdiji* ceremony, depicted the dreamings of numerous Warlpiri homelands.[36] The Emu group performed *Yankirri* (Emu) first, symbolising parental teachings. This was followed by a medley of Yinapaka *yawulyu* items on the subjects of *Jipilyaku* (Duck), *Pinparlajarrpa* (Wood Swallow), *Kurlukuku* (Diamond Dove), and *Ngatijirri* (Budgerigar) that were danced solo and sung by senior women of each of the four ceremonial groups to denote their coming together for ceremony. *Warlu* (Fire) was then performed by the Day group, symbolising new growth; *Marlu* (Kangaroo) by the Kangaroo group, symbolising unchanging law; and *Witi* (Two Trees) by the Night group, symbolising the consequences of one's choices. *Wulpararri* (Milky Way) was jointly performed by the Day and Night groups to evoke the greater esoteric teachings embedded among the stars and, as the program concluded, large floating lanterns were released into the night sky to evoke the Milky Way, and leafy ceremonial *Witi* poles were lit ablaze to mark the commencement of all in attendance on a journey to greater understanding.

Interspersed amid this ceremonial repertoire, children danced together within their four groups as animals living in the desert landscape, and encircled each of the four senior women who danced the four Yinapaka *yawulyu* birds. A discrete hip-hop dance by each group of children then followed representing the four winds blowing everyone together for ceremony. The children's final dance was a massed chorus representing *Pulyaranyi*, the four winds of change, which preceded the program's *Wulpararri* finale.[37] Supported by a mobile sound-and-lighting rig supplied by Top End Sounds, the original hip-hop soundtrack heard throughout this program was set to lyrics and narration by Wanta, and co-composed with local children through the Red Sand Culture initiative.[38]

## Winds of Change

The Milpirri Festival is the now primary means at Lajamanu through which Warlpiri children are introduced to song and dance repertoires drawn from their hereditary ceremonial traditions. Building on ceremonial repertoires that are now rarely performed in their complete original formats, it has become a new Warlpiri tradition for a post-classical age in which Warlpiri communities seek to build upon their emerging intercultural engagements to develop innovative strategies for cultural survival.[39]

The Warlpiri system of law has informed a logic for living in the remote Tanami Desert that enabled the Warlpiri to survive there for scores of millennia. Yet the legacy of sustained exposure to adverse colonial policies and practices since the 1930s, including punitive massacres, forced removals of Aboriginal Australians from their families and homelands, government prohibitions against freedom of movement and association for Aboriginal people, the systemic suppression of Aboriginal languages and cultures, and rapid and radical changes to the socioeconomic circumstances of Aboriginal people, has brought Warlpiri ways of being and knowing under serious threat.[40] Over the past four decades, from a population of around 5500 people, the number of Warlpiri language speakers has dropped to around 3000 and, in its place, has emerged a hybridised form of Warlpiri, English and Kriol known as Light Warlpiri.[41]

Born in 1964, Wanta's first language is the classical Warlpiri through which esoteric ideas are conveyed and ceremonial songs are learnt. Today, however, Warlpiri children at Lajamanu are raised speaking Light Warlpiri instead, and receive much of their formal schooling in English.[42] Wanta attended school at Lajamanu mostly in the 1970s, when fewer government controls were imposed upon local teachers in remote communities and school children could readily be released from classes to participate in traditional ceremonies for extended periods. This momentum continued as Lajamanu School established its bilingual education program in 1982, which enabled students to retain contact with their culture, homelands and elders during school hours. In December 1998, the Northern Territory Government announced that it would phase out bilingual education programs to trim costs and better resource English language programs.[43] The Northern Territory Department of Education's subsequent review of Indigenous education in the Northern Territory in 1999 gave qualified

## 182   *Aaron Corn with Wantarri Jampijinpa Patrick*

support to continuing bilingual education under the new guise of "two-way" learning, which emphasised using local Indigenous languages to assist with teaching English literacy.[44]

This largely-defunded "two-way" learning program increasingly marginalised Indigenous languages within Northern Territory schools and, by 2000, the number of government schools that had initially offered bilingual education programs had dropped from sixteen to twelve.[45] With this decline of bilingual education programs, Wanta, through his role as an Assistant Teacher, became a key figure in helping Lajamanu School students make sense of their schooling as it drifted further and further from the surrounding context of Warlpiri society and cultural life.[46] In 2007, he received an Innovative Curriculum Award from the Australian Curriculum Studies Association for introducing to Lajamanu School his pedagogical conception of *Ngurra-kurlu*, and his application of the reconciliatory tenets of the *Jardiwarnpa* ceremony as the theme of the first Milpirri Festival in 2005.[47]

Further challenges arose in October 2008 when, in a move that flouted Article 30 of the United Nations *Convention on the Rights of the Child*,[48] the Northern Territory Government announced that the first four hours of education during each school day must be conducted solely in English.[49] This measure was ostensibly taken to improve Indigenous outcomes in National Assessment Program Literacy and Numeracy (NAPLAN) testing as well as the readiness of Indigenous students for work and further study,[50] yet it effectively abolished all remaining vestiges of bilingual education programs in Northern Territory schools.[51] In response to widespread public and professional outcry, the House of Representatives Standing Committee on Aboriginal and Torres Strait Islander Affairs mounted a federal inquiry into this matter,[52] and the Northern Territory Department for Education and Training repealed this policy two months before the release of the Standing Committee's findings in September 2012. It was amid these adverse policy conditions of 2008 to 2012 that Wanta's efforts as Creative Director of the Milpirri Festival became particularly important as, during this time, the 2009, 2011 and 2012 iterations of the Milpirri Festival provided most of the Warlpiri language and cultural content experienced by students at Lajamanu School.

During this episode, the Ministerial Council on Education, Employment, Training and Youth Affairs had simultaneously issued its *Melbourne Declaration on Educational Goals for Young Australians*, which placed the valuing of "Australia's Indigenous cultures as a key part of the nation's history, present and future."[53] Following the establishment of the Australian Curriculum, Assessment and Reporting Authority (ACARA) in 2008, the *Melbourne Declaration* would become the founding document of this new peak body's continuing development of the first national Australian Curriculum. As a result, "Aboriginal and Torres Strait Islander histories and cultures" were embedded within the Australian Curriculum as a cross-curriculum priority to be taught across all subjects.[54] Their inclusion was

## Home Within 183

decried by political conservatives for allegedly deemphasising Western values[55] and, following a *Review of the Australian Curriculum* in 2014,[56] the resourcing and delivery of this content has been sporadic with uneven results.

It has been largely left to a minority of individual teachers, irrespective of subject area, to draw upon their own personal interests in, experiences of and networks with Indigenous Australians to deliver Aboriginal and Torres Strait Islander histories and cultures content on behalf of their schools. This has meant that, in common practice, Aboriginal and Torres Strait Islander histories and cultures content can be delivered in some subject areas and not others at each year level. There is also a wide variety of approaches from teacher to teacher and from school to school as to what specific Aboriginal and Torres Strait Islander histories and cultures content is taught. This can range from very general overviews to deep exchanges that focus on a specific group of Indigenous Australians.

School teachers across the country have nonetheless sought new ways to implement Indigenous perspectives throughout the new Australian Curriculum, and Wanta himself became highly sought after interstate among elite independent schools and university teacher-training programs for his engaging workshops on Warlpiri knowledge and culture. Yet, at the same time, Warlpiri children in his own community were largely denied the educational opportunity of learning about their own language and culture as part of their formal schooling, which led to plummeting enrolments and attendance.[57]

Grounded in the pedagogical logic of Wanta's *Ngurra-kurlu* schema, the Milpirri Festival has not only worked to rebuild a social foundation for imparting classical Warlpiri concepts and ceremonial traditions from old to young, but has also improved school enrolment and attendance numbers. While all adults, including visitors, who wish to dance in the festival are generally welcome to do so, the message to local children throughout the rehearsals held at Lajamanu School is clear: no school, no Milpirri. The eight-week period of intensive rehearsals during school hours that typically precedes each festival, and co-creation with local children of new songs and dances for each show, offer Lajamanu School students an immersive learning experience focused on their own cultural heritage and values that enables them to feel more connected to the school's learning environment overall. More children want to attend school at these times, and are indeed told that they can only perform in the Milpirri Festival if they attend school regularly. As a result, school attendance has been shown to leap from some forty to sixty per cent during Milpirri Festival rehearsals, while fitness and overall personal efficacy among local children have also shown appreciable improvements due to the festival's regime of regular dance training.[58]

The festival has also inspired local children to embrace their Warlpiri heritage in other ways. They now wear their ceremonial-group colour-coded festival t-shirts and wristbands all year round. Thirsting for greater

## 184 Aaron Corn with Wantarri Jampijinpa Patrick

exposure to Warlpiri knowledge and culture, many have also sought more frequent instruction from Wanta between festivals outside school hours. Wanta devised an inventive new curriculum called *Yirtaki-mani* (Tracking) to meet this demand, which emphasised self-sufficient learning. Devised as a grand treasure hunt, *Yirtaki-mani* encouraged children to progress through a graded series of ever more demanding written clues left for them by Wanta that were based on traditional Warlpiri knowledge, but could only be deciphered by exercising reading literacy skills. Trialled by volunteers outside school hours, *Yirtaki-mani* proved highly popular. Entire families would spend their evenings together trying to decipher Wanta's clues, and Wanta was encouraged to see teenagers who had left school to raise families begin to show an interest in pursuing formal education again. Wanta had hoped that his new curriculum might be adopted by the Lajamanu School as a means of improving enrolment and attendance numbers in between Milpirri Festivals. However, given that the Northern Territory Government had just announced its first four hours in English education policy at that time, the political climate for this was not right. By the time this policy was abandoned in September 2012, Wanta had already begun his employment in Canberra on our ARC project at ANU.

Lajamanu School's original bilingual education program remains discontinued. However, since September 2012, traditional Warlpiri values have informed the positive values expected of children at school, and a team of Warlpiri support staff work with local elders to deliver a one-hour Warlpiri lesson each week and two extended trips to remote Warlpiri homelands each term. Through this process, students have regained some opportunities to learn the sacred dances and designs of their respective ceremonial groups beyond the context of the Milpirri Festival.[59] Wanta has continued working to bring local children opportunities for experiencing Warlpiri culture within the Lajamanu School context and, as our ARC project drew to a close in early 2015, he became a resident of Lajamanu again. He remains Creative Director of the Milpirri Festival, which was presented most recently in 2016 and continues to introduce students to an understanding of *Ngurra-kurlu*. He has served on the Lajamanu School Council, which comprises representatives of each of the four Warlpiri ceremonial groups,[60] and his *Yirtaki-mani* curriculum was hosted by the school in April 2017 as a "Cultural Day" event to help celebrate Warlpiri culture and what remains of the "two-way" learning program.[61]

## Conclusions

Dabashi has questioned the Eurocentrism of the academy in persistently qualifying South Asian thinkers by their ethnos instead of considering them to be just "thinkers" in the way that European thinkers are.[62] Why is it, he asks, that Mozart's works simply qualify as music, while Indian music is the subject of ethnomusicology? Why is it that European philosophy as just philosophy, while the academy considers African philosophy to be ethnophilosophy? Dabashi's concerns echo those of Connell, who questions why the academy has continued to privilege social theorists of the affluent Trans-Atlantic metropole over knowledge and social theories produced by other societies.[63] Dabashi contends that European philosophers cannot read philosophy by non-Europeans without assimilating "it back into what they already know . . . and are thus incapable of projecting it forward into something they may not know and yet might be able to learn."[64]

The systemic Anglocentrism of the Australian education system and the marginalisation of Australian Indigenous knowledges within it mirror this paradox. Wanta's educational agency in Indigenous Music and Media indeed enabled our students to transcend this Anglocentrism, and to gain familiarity with an Indigenous worldview that taught them something new about themselves and their place in the cosmos. Yet, as soon as the externally-funded ARC grant that supported Wanta's salary ended, so too did our course, and a rare university curriculum grounded in Warlpiri epistemology ceased to be delivered. Similarly, at Lajamanu, school enrolments and attendance spike whenever rehearsals for the Milpirri Festival are underway, and local youths thirst for greater exposure to Warlpiri knowledge and culture in the years between festivals. Yet the gradual defunding and marginalisation of Australian Indigenous languages and culture within Northern Territory schools underscores the fragility of such Indigenous curriculum innovations, especially whenever adverse policy conditions arise.

These cases exemplify the needless polemic that persists within Australia between *philosophies of Indigenous education* that are designed to equip Indigenous students for work and further study, and *Indigenous educational philosophies* that aim to ground Indigenous children in their own intellectual and cultural traditions as a strategy for personal efficacy and cultural survival. The myriad positive outcomes of Wanta's educational approach across the delivery contexts explored in this chapter nonetheless exemplify why Indigenous educational philosophies deserve no longer to be relegated to the periphery of systemic education in Australia. What is missing from this equation, however, is trust, which was the theme of the final day of Indigenous Music and Media, and a state that Wanta seeks to engender in others through his educational endeavours. Through the application of Indigenous educational philosophies such as Wanta's *Ngurrakurlu*, we can learn to trust that Indigenous educators know how to select and adapt traditional pedagogies to engage local youths in the processes of their own learning, that these approaches can complement the attempts of schools to equip Indigenous students for work and further study, and that they can also be applied in broader intercultural contexts to facilitate learning opportunities that can hold intrinsic value and beneficial outcomes for all while simultaneously working to ensure the continuing survival of Indigenous ways of being and knowing in Australia.

## Notes

1. There is a sizable body of ethnography about the Warlpiri which, in brief, spans Olive Pink, *Warlpiri Material, Anthropological and Linguistic, Miscellaneous Notes and Correspondence* (Canberra: Australian Institute for Aboriginal and Torres Strait Islander Studies, 1932–48); Mervyn J. Meggitt, *Desert People* (Sydney: Angus, 1962); Adolphus P. Elkin, "Australian and New Guinea Musical Records," *Oceania* 27 (1957): 313–319; Nicolas Peterson, Patrick McConvell, Stephen A. Wild, and Rod Hagen, *A Claim to Areas of Traditional Land by the Warlpiri and Kartangarurru-Kurinji* (Alice Springs: Central Land Council, 1978); Nancy Munn, *Walbiri* [sic *Warlpiri*] *Iconography* (London: Ithaca, 1973); David Nash, "An Etymological Note on Warlpiri Kurdungurlu," in *Languages of Kinship in Aboriginal Australia*, ed. Jeffrey Heath, Francesca Merlan, and Alan Rumsey (Sydney: Oceania, 1982), 141–159; Stephen A. Wild, "Recreating the Jukurrpa," in *Songs of Aboriginal Australia*, ed. Margaret Clunies Ross, Stephen A. Wild, and Tamsin Donaldson (Sydney: Oceania, 1987), 97–120; Diane Bell, *Daughters of the Dreaming* (Melbourne: McPhee, 1983); Barbara Glowczewski, *Yapa* (Paris: Baudoin, 1991); Mary Laughren and Robert Hoogenraad, *A Learner's Guide to Warlpiri* (Alice Springs: IAD Press, 1996); Ken Hale, *An Elementary Warlpiri Dictionary*, rev. ed. (Alice Springs: IAD Press, 1995); Herbert C. Coombs, *Aboriginal Autonomy* (Cambridge: Cambridge University Press, 1995); Peter Sutton, *Country* (Canberra: Aboriginal History, 1995); Jane Simpson, "Perceptions of Meteorology in Some Aboriginal Languages," in *Windows on Meteorology*, ed. Eric Webb (Melbourne: CSIRO, 1997), 20–28; Sylvie Poirier, *A World of Relationships* (Toronto: University of Toronto Press, 2005); Jennifer Biddle, *Breasts, Bodies, Canvas* (Sydney: UNSW Press, 2007); Yasmin Musharbash, *Yuendumu Everyday* (Canberra: Aboriginal Studies Press, 2008); Kasia Gabrys and Petronella Vaarzon-Morel, "Aboriginal Burning Issues in the Southern Tanami," in *Desert Fire*, ed. Glenn Edwards and Grant Allan (Alice Springs: Desert Knowledge Cooperative Research Centre, 2009), 79–186; Stephen M. Swartz, comp., *Interactive Warlpiri—English Dictionary*, 2nd ed. (Darwin: AuSIL, 2012), accessed March 27, 2017, http://ausil.org/Dictionary/Warlpiri/lexicon/index.htm; and Miles Holmes and Wantarri J. Patrick, "Law for Country," *Ecology and Society* 18 no. 3 (2013), accessed March 27, 2017, www.ecologyandsociety.org/vol18/iss3/art19/.

2. Raewyn Connell, *Southern Theory* (Sydney: Allen, 2007); Hamid Dabashi, *Can Non-Europeans Think?* (London: Zed, 2015).

3. Aaron Corn and Joseph N. Gumbula, "Rom and the Academy Repositioned," in *Boundary Writing*, ed. Lynette Russell (Honolulu: University of Hawai'i Press, 2006), 170–197; Payi Linda Ford, *Aboriginal Knowledge Narratives and Country* (Brisbane: Post Pressed, 2010); Larissa Behrendt, Steven Larkin, Robert Griew, and Patricia Kelly, *Review of Higher Education Access and Outcomes for Aboriginal and Torres Strait Islander People Final Report* (Canberra: Australian Government, 2012); Tracey Bunda, Lew Zipin, and Marie Brennan, "Negotiating University 'Equity' from Indigenous Standpoints," *International Journal of Inclusive Education* 16 no. 9 (2012): 941–957; Zane Ma Rhea, Peter J. Anderson, and Bernadette Atkinson, *Improving Teaching in Aboriginal and Torres Strait Islander Education* (Melbourne: Australian Institute for Teaching and School Leadership, 2012); Zane Ma Rhea and Lynette Russell, "The Invisible Hand of Pedagogy in Australian Indigenous Studies and Indigenous Education," *Australian Journal of Indigenous Education* 41 no. 1 (2012): 18–25; Martin Nakata, Victoria Nakata, Sarah Keech, and Reuben Bolt, "Decolonial Goals and Pedagogies for Indigenous Studies," *Decolonization* 1 no. 1 (2012): 120–140; Peter Buckskin, "Engaging Indigenous Students," in *Big Fish, Little*

*Fish*, ed. Susan Groundwater-Smith and Nicole Mockler (Melbourne: Cambridge University Press, 2015), 155–174; Melitta Hogarth, "Speaking Back to the Deficit Discourse," *Australian Educational Researcher* 44 (2017): 21–34.

4. Martin Nakata, "The Cultural Interface," *Australian Journal of Indigenous Education* 36(Supplement) (2007): 7–14.

5. Charles Darwin University, "Yolŋu Studies," (Darwin: Darwin Charles University, 2017), accessed June 14, 2017, http://learnline.cdu.edu.au/yolngustudies/.

6. Michael Christie, "Yolŋu Studies," *Gateways* 1 (2008): 31–47.

7. Australian Curriculum, Assessment and Reporting Authority, "School Profile: Lajamanu School, Lajamanu, NT," (Sydney: Australian Curriculum, Assessment and Reporting Authority, 2017), accessed May 29, 2017, www.myschool. edu.au/SchoolProfile/Index/113213/LajamanuSchool/50060/2016.

8. Lajamanu School, *Annual Performance Report to the School Community 2014* (Lajamanu: Northern Territory Government Department of Education, 2015), accessed May 29, 2017, https://web.ntschools.net/w/antgsr/Annual%20 Reports/2014_ar_lajamcec.pdf.

9. Australian Curriculum, Assessment and Reporting Authority, "Lajamanu School."

10. Bob Gosford, "Remote NT Education Crisis," *Crikey*, January 18, 2011, accessed June 11, 2017, www.crikey.com.au/2011/01/18/remote-nt-education-crisis-lost-in-the-warlpiri-triangle/.

11. Australian Broadcasting Corporation, "Chronology," (Sydney: Australian Broadcasting Corporation, 2009), accessed June 11, 2017, www.abc.net.au/4corners/special_eds/20090914/language/chronology.htm.

12. Marion Scrymgour, "Education Restructure Includes Greater Emphasis on English," (Darwin, Northern Territory Government, 2008), accessed January 25, 2017, http://newsroom.nt.gov.au/mediaRelease/4656.

13. Jennifer Biddle, "When Writing Is Not Writing," *Australian Aboriginal Studies* 1996 no. 1 (1996): 21–33 contends that the Warlpiri possessed literacy in their own ceremonial designs well before the introduction of written English. I posit a similar argument with respect to ceremonial names, songs, dances and designs in Yolŋu culture in Aaron Corn, "'Nations of Song," *Griffith Review* (2014), accessed June 14, 2017, https://griffithreview.com/nations-of-song.

14. Warlpiri-patu-kurlangu Jaru, "Submission to the House of Representatives Sanding Committee on Aboriginal and Torres Strait Islander Affairs National Inquiry into Language Learning in Indigenous Communities," (Yuendumu: Warlpiri-patu-kurlangu Jaru, 2011), 4, accessed June 13, 2017, www.aph. gov.au/Parliamentary_Business/Committees/House_of_Representatives_ Committees?url=atsia/languages/subs/sub121.pdf.

15. Australian Institute of Aboriginal and Torres Strait Islander Studies, "Finding Aid, WILD_S05, Sound Recordings Collected by Stephen Wild, 1972," (Canberra: Australian Institute of Aboriginal and Torres Strait Islander Studies, 2010), accessed March 27, 2017, http://aiatsis.gov.au/sites/default/files/catalogue_resources/wild_s05_finding_aid.pdf.

16. Funded by the ARC for three years, this Linkage Project was called "Warlpiri Songlines: Anthropological, Linguistic and Indigenous Perspectives" (LP0560567).

17. Yukihiro Doi, "Milpirri at Lajamanu as an Intercultural Locus of Warlpiri Discourses with Others" (PhD thesis., Canberra: ANU, 2015).

18. Funded by the ARC for three years, this Discovery Indigenous project was called "Early Collections of Warlpiri Cultural Heritage and Resulting Community Access Needs in Remote Desert Australia" (IN120100008).

19. ANU, "Indigenous Music and Media," (Canberra: ANU, 2014), accessed March 27, 2017, http://programsandcourses.anu.edu.au/2014/course/MUSI2213.

20. The convention that an Indigenous person of Australia "is a person of Aboriginal or Torres Strait Islander descent who identifies as an Aboriginal or Torres Strait Islander and is accepted as such by the community in which he [or she] lives" was established in the Australian Government Department of Aboriginal Affairs, *Report on a Review of the Administration of the Working Definition of Aboriginal and Torres Strait Islanders* (Canberra: Commonwealth of Australia, 1981), 1.

21. Patrick and I have explained our collaborative approaches to designing and teaching in Indigenous Music and Media in Aaron Corn and Wantarri J. Patrick, "Singing the Winds of Change," in *Collaborative Ethnomusicology*, ed. Katelyn Barney (Melbourne: Lyrebird, 2014), 147–168; and Aaron Corn and Wantarri J. Patrick, "Pulyaranyi," *UNESCO Observatory* 4 no. 2 (2015), accessed January 25, 2017, http://education.unimelb.edu.au/__data/assets/pdf_file/0007/1391686/002_CORN_V2.pdf.

22. Tracks Dance Company, "Milpirri 2012 (Pulyaranyi)," (Darwin: Tracks Dance Company, 2015), accessed January 25, 2017, http://tracksdance.com.au/milpirri-2012-pulyaranyi.

23. Belconnen Community Service, *Wintaru* [sic *Wirntaru*], (Canberra: Belconnen Community Service, 2013), accessed January 25, 2017, http://new.bcsact.com.au/latest-news/wintaru-hear-the-elements-talk/; *Wintaru* [sic *Wirntaru*], performed by Wantarri J. Patrick (Canberra: Belconnen Community Service, 2013), YouTube video, accessed January 25, 2017, http://tracksdance.com.au/milpirri-2012-pulyaranyi; www.youtube.com/watch?v=QGWDnBIcZbc.

24. Françoise Dussart, *The Politics of Ritual in An Aboriginal Settlement* (Washington: Smithsonian Institution Press, 2000).

25. *Ngurra-kurlu*, directed by Wantarri J. Patrick (Yuendumu: PAW media, 2008), YouTube video, accessed January 25, 2017, www.youtube.com/watch?v=iFZq7AduGrc; Wantarri J. Patrick, Miles Holmes, and Alan Box, *Ngurra-kurlu* (Alice Springs: Desert Knowledge Cooperative Research Centre, 2008), accessed January 25, 2017, www.nintione.com.au/resource/DKCRC-Report-41-Ngurra-kurlu.pdf.

26. *Jardiwarnpa*, directed by Ned Lander (Sydney: Australian Film Finance Corporation, 1983), VHS.

27. Georgia Curran, "The 'Expanding Domain' of Warlpiri Initiation Ceremonies," in *Ethnography and the Production of Anthropological Knowledge*, ed. Yasmine Musharbash and Marcus Barber (Canberra: ANU E Press, 2011), 39–50.

28. Michael Jakamara Nelson, *Possum and Wallaby Dreaming* (Canberra: Parliament House, 1985).

29. *Milpirri*, directed by Wantarri J. Patrick (Fryerstown: People Pictures, 2014), SBS On Demand video, www.sbs.com.au/ondemand/video/344924739668/milpirri.

30. Tracks Dance Company, "Lajamanu Tracks Relationship," (Darwin: Tracks Dance Company, 2015), accessed January 25, 2017, www.tracksdance.com.au/lajamanu-tracks-relationship.

31. Doi, "Milpirri at Lajamanu" more fully chronicles this first cycle of five festivals.

32. Eric Michaels, *Aboriginal Invention of Television* (Canberra: Australian Institute of Aboriginal Studies, 1983); Faye Ginsburg, "Indigenous Media," *Cultural Anthropology* 6 no. 1 (1991): 92–112; Melinda Hinkson, "New Media Projects at Yuendumu," *Continuum* 16 no. 2 (2002): 201–220; Barbara Glowczewski, "Returning Indigenous Knowledge in Central Australia," in *The Power of Knowledge, the Resonance of Tradition*, ed. Graeme Ward and Adrian Muckle (Canberra: AIATSIS, 2005), 137–152; Andrew Stojanovski, *Dog Ear Café* (Melbourne: Hybrid, 2010); Inge Kral and Robert G. Schwab, *Learning Spaces* (Canberra: ANU E Press, 2012).

## Home Within 189

33. Mandawuy Yunupiŋu, "Yothu Yindi," *Race and Class* 35 no. 4 (1994): 114–120; Corn and Gumbula, "Rom and the Academy Repositioned," 188; Aaron Corn, "Sound Exchanges," *The World of Music* 51 no. 3 (2011): 30.
34. Corn and Gumbula, "Rom and the Academy," 187–189; Corn, "Sound Exchanges," 29–31; Aaron Corn, "Agent of Bicultural Balance," *Journal of World Popular Music* 1 no. 1 (2014): 24–45.
35. Wantarri J. Patrick, "Milpirri," *Ngoonjook*, 33; Patrick, Holmes, and Box, *Ngurru-kurlu*, 25.
36. Tracks Dance Company, "Lajamanu Tracks Relationship" explains how this company's Co-Artistic Director, Tim Newth, began the process of collaborating with the Lajamanu community to create these banners in 1989.
37. Miles Holmes, *Evaluation Report* (Sydney: Beit Holmes, 2013).
38. Incite Arts, *Red Sand Culture* (Alice Springs: InCite Arts, 2014), accessed January 25, 2017, http://redsandculture.com.
39. Holmes, *Evaluation Report*, 8–9; Tracks 2014.
40. Peter Read, "Northern Territory," in *Contested Ground*, ed. Ann GcGrath (Sydney: Allen, 1995), 269–305.
41. Carmel O'Shannessy, "Light Warlpiri," *Australian Journal of Linguistics* 25 no. 1 (2005): 31–57.
42. Greg Dickson, "No Warlpiri, No School?," *Ngoonjook* 35 (2010): 101–102; Samantha Disbray, "Evaluating Bilingual Education in Warlpiri Schools," in *Language Description Informed by Theory*, ed. Rob Pensalfini, Myfany Turpin, and Diane Guillemin (Amsterdam: Benjamins, 2014), 25–46; Lajamanu School, *Annual Performance Report*, 6.
43. Australian Broadcasting Corporation, "Chronology."
44. Northern Territory Department of Education, *Learning Lessons* (Darwin: Northern Territory Department of Education, 1999), 117–140, accessed June 13, 2017, http://pandora.nla.gov.au/pan/77669/20071116-1155/www.deet.nt.gov.au/education/indigenous_education/previous_publications/docs/learning_lessons_review.pdf.
45. Australian Broadcasting Corporation, "Chronology."
46. Gosford, "Remote NT Education Crisis."
47. Australian Curriculum Studies Association, "2007 Innovative Curriculum Award Winners," (Canberra: Australian Curriculum Studies Association, 2017), accessed June 13, 2017, www.acsa.edu.au/pages/page137.asp.
48. United Nations, *Convention on the Rights of the Child* (Geneva: Office of the High Commissioner for Human Rights, 1990), accessed January 25, 2017, www.ohchr.org/EN/ProfessionalInterest/Pages/CRC.aspx.
49. Scrymgour, "Education Restructure Includes Greater Emphasis on English."
50. National Assessment Program, "NAPLAN," (Sydney: Australian Curriculum, Assessment and Reporting Authority, 2016), accessed January 25, 2017, www.nap.edu.au/naplan.
51. Dickson, "No Warlpiri," 98.
52. Parliament of Australia, *Our Land, Our Languages* (Canberra: House of Representatives Standing Committee on Aboriginal and Torres Strait Islander Affairs, 2012), accessed January 25, 2017, www.aph.gov.au/Parliamentary_Business/Committees/House_of_representatives_Committees?url=/atsia/languages2/report.htm.
53. Ministerial Council on Education, Employment, Training and Youth Affairs, *Melbourne Declaration on Educational Goals for Young Australians* (Melbourne: Ministerial Council on Education, Employment, Training and Youth Affairs, 2008), accessed January 25, 2017, www.curriculum.edu.au/verve/_resources/National_Declaration_on_the_Educational_Goals_for_Young_Australians.pdf.
54. Australian Curriculum, Assessment and Reporting Authority, "Cross-Curriculum Priorities," (Sydney: Australian Curriculum, Assessment and Reporting Authority, 2016), accessed January 25, 2017, www.acara.edu.au/curriculum/cross-curriculum-priorities.

# 190   *Aaron Corn with Wantarri Jampijinpa Patrick*

55. Daniel Hurst, "School Curriculum Review Panellist Kevin Donnelly Hits Back at Critics," *The Guardian*, January 15, 2014, accessed June 9, 2017, www.theguardian.com/world/2014/jan/14/school-curriculum-review-conservative-panellist-hits-back-at-critics.
56. Australian Government Department of Education, *Review of the Australian Curriculum* (Canberra: Australian Government Department of Education, 2014), accessed June 9, 2017, https://docs.education.gov.au/system/files/doc/other/review_of_the_national_curriculum_final_report.pdf.
57. Dickson, "No Warlpiri," 102–105, 110; Disbray, "Evaluating Bilingual Education."
58. Holmes, *Evaluation Report*, 14–21.
59. Lajamanu School, *Annual Performance Report*, 2–6.
60. Ibid, 3–4.
61. Lajamanu School, "Yitaki-mani [sic]—Cultural Day," (Menlo Park: Facebook, 2017), accessed June 13, 2017, www.facebook.com/events/426 252401073057/?acontext=%7B%22ref%22%3A%223%22%2C%22ref_newsfeed_story_type%22%3A%22regular%22%2C%22action_history%22%3A%22null%22%7D.
62. Dabashi, *Can Non-Europeans Think?*, 32.
63. Connell, *Southern Theory*.
64. Dabashi, *Can Non-Europeans Think?*, 5–6.

## Bibliography

ANU. "Indigenous Music and Media." Canberra: ANU, 2014. Accessed March 27, 2017. http://programsandcourses.anu.edu.au/2014/course/MUSI2213.

Australian Broadcasting Corporation. "Chronology." Sydney: Australian Broadcasting Corporation, 2009. Accessed June 11, 2017. www.abc.net.au/4corners/special_eds/20090914/language/chronology.htm.

Australian Curriculum, Assessment and Reporting Authority. "Cross-Curriculum Priorities." Sydney: Australian Curriculum, Assessment and Reporting Authority, 2016. Accessed January 25, 2017. www.acara.edu.au/curriculum/cross-curriculum-priorities.

———. "Lajamanu School, Lajamanu, NT." Sydney: Australian Curriculum, Assessment and Reporting Authority, 2017. Accessed May 29, 2017. www.myschool.edu.au/SchoolProfile/Index/113213/LajamanuSchool/50060/2016.

Australian Curriculum Studies Association. "2007 Innovative Curriculum Award Winners." Canberra: Australian Curriculum Studies Association, 2017. Accessed June 13, 2017. www.acsa.edu.au/pages/page137.asp.

Australian Government Department of Aboriginal Affairs. *Report on a Review of the Administration of the Working Definition of Aboriginal and Torres Strait Islanders*. Canberra: Commonwealth of Australia, 1981.

Australian Government Department of Education. *Review of the Australian Curriculum*. Canberra: Australian Government Department of Education, 2014. Accessed June 9, 2017. https://docs.education.gov.au/system/files/doc/other/review_of_the_national_curriculum_final_report.pdf.

Australian Institute of Aboriginal and Torres Strait Islander Studies. "Finding Aid, WILD_S05, Sound Recordings Collected by Stephen Wild, 1972." Canberra: Australian Institute of Aboriginal and Torres Strait Islander Studies, 2010. Accessed March 27, 2017. http://aiatsis.gov.au/sites/default/files/catalogue_resources/wild_s05_finding_aid.pdf.

Behrendt, Larissa, Steven Larkin, Robert Griew, and Patricia Kelly. *Review of Higher Education Access and Outcomes for Aboriginal and Torres Strait Islander People Final Report*. Canberra: Australian Government, 2012.

Belconnen Community Service. *Wintaru* [sic *Wirntaru*]. Canberra: Belconnen Community Service, 2013. Accessed January 25, 2017. http://new.bcsact.com.au/latest-news/wintaru-hear-the-elements-talk/.

Bell, Diane. *Daughters of the Dreaming*. Melbourne: McPhee, 1983.

Biddle, Jennifer. "When Writing Is Not Writing." *Australian Aboriginal Studies* 1996 no. 1 (1996): 21–33.

———. *Breasts, Bodies, Canvas*. Sydney: UNSW Press, 2007.

Buckskin, Peter. "Engaging Indigenous Students." In *Big Fish, Little Fish*, edited by Susan Groundwater-Smith and Nicole Mockler, 155–174. Melbourne: Cambridge University Press, 2015.

Bunda, Tracey, Lew Zipin, and Marie Brennan. "Negotiating University 'Equity' from Indigenous Standpoints." *International Journal of Inclusive Education* 16 no. 9 (2012): 941–957.

Charles Darwin University. "Yolŋu Studies." Darwin: Darwin Charles University, 2017. Accessed June 14, 2017. http://learnline.cdu.edu.au/yolngustudies/.

Christie, Michael. "Yolŋu Studies." *Gateways* 1 (2008): 31–47.

Connell, Raewyn. *Southern Theory*. Sydney: Allen, 2007.

Coombs, Herbert C. *Aboriginal Autonomy*. Cambridge: Cambridge University Press, 1995.

Corn, Aaron. "Sound Exchanges." *The World of Music* 51 no. 3 (2011): 19–48.

———. "Agent of Bicultural Balance." *Journal of World Popular Music* 1 no. 1 (2014): 24–45.

———. "Nations of Song." *Griffith Review* (2014). Accessed June 14, 2017. https://griffithreview.com/nations-of-song.

——— and Joseph N. Gumbula. "Rom and the Academy Repositioned." In *Boundary Writing*, edited by Lynette Russell, 170–197. Honolulu: University of Hawai'i Press, 2006.

——— and Wantarri J. Patrick. "Singing the Winds of Change." In *Collaborative Ethnomusicology*, edited by Katelyn Barney, 147–168. Melbourne: Lyrebird, 2014.

———. and Wantarri J. Partick. "Pulyaranyi." *UNESCO Observatory* 4 no. 2 (2015). Accessed January 25, 2017. http://education.unimelb.edu.au/__data/assets/pdf_file/0007/1391686/002_CORN_V2.pdf.

Curran, Georgia. "The 'Expanding Domain' of Warlpiri Initiation Ceremonies." In *Ethnography and the Production of Anthropological Knowledge*, edited by Yasmine Musharbash and Marcus Barber, 39–50. Canberra: ANU E Press, 2011.

Dickson, Greg. "No Warlpiri, No School?" *Ngoonjook* 35 (2010): 97–113.

Disbray, Samantha. "Evaluating Bilingual Education in Warlpiri Schools." In *Language Description Informed by Theory*, edited by Rob Pensalfini, Myfany Turpin, and Diane Guillemin, 25–46. Amsterdam: Benjamins, 2014.

Doi, Yukihiro. "Milpirri at Lajamanu as an Intercultural Locus of Warlpiri Discourses with Others." PhD thesis., ANU, 2015. Accessed March 27, 2017. https://openresearch-repository.anu.edu.au/handle/1885/101475.

Dussart, Françoise. *The Politics of Ritual in An Aboriginal Settlement: Kinship, Gender, and the Currency of Knowledge*. Washington: Smithsonian Institution Press, 2000.

Elkin, Adolphus P. "Australian and New Guinea Musical Records." *Oceania* 27 (1957): 313–319.

Ford, Payi Linda. *Aboriginal Knowledge Narratives and Country*. Brisbane: Post Pressed, 2010.

Gabrys, Kasia and Petronella Vaarzon-Morel. "Aboriginal Burning Issues in the Southern Tanami." In *Desert Fire*, edited by Glenn Edwards and Grant Allan, 79–186. Alice Springs: Desert Knowledge Cooperative Research Centre, 2009.

Ginsburg, Faye. "Indigenous Media." *Cultural Anthropology* 6 no. 1 (1991): 92–112.

Glowczewski, Barbara. *Yapa*. Paris: Baudoin, 1991.

192 *Aaron Corn with Wantarri Jampijinpa Patrick*

———. "Returning Indigenous Knowledge in Central Australia." In *The Power of Knowledge, the Resonance of Tradition*, edited by Graeme Ward and Adrian Muckle, 137–152. Canberra: AIATSIS, 2005.

Gosford, Bob. "Remote NT Education Crisis." *Crikey* (January 18, 2011). Accessed June 11, 2017. www.crikey.com.au/2011/01/18/remote-nt-education-crisis-lost-in-the-warlpiri-triangle/.

Hale, Ken. *An Elementary Warlpiri Dictionary* (rev. ed.). Alice Springs: IAD Press, 1995.

Hinkson, Melinda. "New Media Projects at Yuendumu." *Continuum* 16 no. 2 (2002): 201–220.

Hogarth, Melitta. "Speaking Back to the Deficit Discourse." *Australian Educational Researcher* 44 (2017): 21–34.

Holmes, Miles and Wantarri J. Patrick. "Law for Country." *Ecology and Society* 18 no. 3 (2013). Accessed March 27, 2017. www.ecologyandsociety.org/vol18/iss3/art19/.

Hurst, Daniel. "School Curriculum Review Panellist Kevin Donnelly Hits Back at Critics." *The Guardian*, January 15, 2014. Accessed June 9, 2017. www.theguardian.com/world/2014/jan/14/school-curriculum-review-conservative-panellist-hits-back-at-critics.

Incite Arts. *Red Sand Culture*. Alice Springs: InCite Arts, 2014. Accessed January 25, 2017. http://redsandculture.com.

*Jardiwarnpa*. Directed by Ned Lander. Sydney: Australian Film Finance Corporation, 1983. VHS.

Kral, Inge and Robert G. Schwab. *Learning Spaces*. Canberra: ANU E Press, 2012.

Lajamanu School. "Annual Performance Report to the School Community 2014." Lajamanu: Northern Territory Government Department of Education, 2015. Accessed May 29, 2017. https://web.ntschools.net/w/antgsr/Annual%20Reports/2014_ar_lajamcec.pdf.

———. "Yitaki-mani [sic]—Cultural Day." Menlo Park: Facebook, 2017. Accessed June 13, 2017. www.facebook.com/events/426252401073057/?acontext=%7B%22ref%22%3A%223%22%2C%22ref_newsfeed_story_type%22%3A%22regular%22%2C%22action_history%22%3A%22null%22%7D.

Laughren, Mary and Robert Hoogenraad. *A Learner's Guide to Warlpiri*. Alice Springs: IAD Press, 1996.

Ma Rhea, Zane, Peter J. Anderson, and Bernadette Atkinson. *Improving Teaching in Aboriginal and Torres Strait Islander Education*. Melbourne: Australian Institute for Teaching and School Leadership, 2012.

——— and Lynette Russell. "The Invisible Hand of Pedagogy in Australian Indigenous Studies and Indigenous Education." *Australian Journal of Indigenous Education* 41 no. 1 (2012): 18–25.

Michaels, Eric. *Aboriginal Invention of Television*. Canberra: Australian Institute of Aboriginal Studies, 1983.

*Milpirri*. Directed by Wantarri J. Patrick. Fryerstown: People Pictures, 2014. SBS On Demand Video. www.sbs.com.au/ondemand/video/344924739668/milpirri.

Ministerial Council on Education, Employment, Training and Youth Affairs. *Melbourne Declaration on Educational Goals for Young Australians*. Melbourne: Ministerial Council on Education, Employment, Training and Youth Affairs, 2008. Accessed January 25, 2017. www.curriculum.edu.au/verve/_resources/National_Declaration_on_the_Educational_Goals_for_Young_Australians.pdf.

Munn, Nancy. *Walbiri* [sic *Warlpiri*] *Iconography*. London: Ithaca, 1973.

Musharbash, Yasmin. *Yuendumu Everyday*. Canberra: Aboriginal Studies Press, 2008.

Nakata, Martin. "The Cultural Interface." *Australian Journal of Indigenous Education* 36(Supplementary) (2007): 7–14.

———, Victoria Nakata, Sarah Keech, and Reuben Bolt. "Decolonial Goals and Pedagogies for Indigenous Studies." *Decolonization* 1 no. 1 (2012): 120–140.

Nash, David. "An Etymological Note on Warlpiri Kurdungurlu." In *Languages of Kinship in Aboriginal Australia*, edited by Jeffrey Heath, Francesca Merlan, and Alan Rumsey, 141–159. Sydney: Oceania, 1982.

National Assessment Program. "NAPLAN." Sydney, Australian Curriculum, Assessment and Reporting Authority, 2016. Accessed January 25, 2017. www.nap.edu. au/naplan.

Nelson, Michael Jakamara. *Possum and Wallaby Dreaming.* Canberra: Parliament House, 1985.

*Ngurra-kurlu.* Directed by Wantarri J. Patrick. Yuendumu: PAW media, 2008. YouTube video. Accessed January 25, 2017. www.youtube.com/watch?v=iFZq7AduGrc.

Northern Territory Department of Education. *Learning Lessons.* Darwin: Northern Territory Department of Education, 1999. Accessed June 13, 2017. http:// pandora.nla.gov.au/pan/77669/20071116-1155/www.deet.nt.gov.au/education/ indigenous_education/previous_publications/docs/learning_lessons_review.pdf.

O'Shannessy, Carmel. "Light Warlpiri." *Australian Journal of Linguistics* 25 no. 1 (2005): 31–57.

Parliament of Australia. *Our Land, Our Languages.* Canberra: House of Representatives Standing Committee on Aboriginal and Torres Strait Islander Affairs, 2012. Accessed January 25, 2017. www.aph.gov.au/Parliamentary_Business/Committees/House_of_representatives_Committees?url=/atsia/languages2/report.htm.

Patrick, Wantarri J. "Milpirri." *Ngoonjook* 33 (2008): 53–60.

———, Miles Holmes, and Alan Box. *Ngurra-kurlu.* Alice Springs: Desert Knowledge Cooperative Research Centre, 2008. Accessed January 25, 2017. www.nintione.com.au/resource/DKCRC-Report-41-Ngurra-kurlu.pdf.

Peterson, Nicolas, Patrick McConvell, Steven Wild, and Rod Hagen, eds. *A Claim to Areas of Traditional Land by the Warlpiri and Kartangarurru-Kurinji.* Alice Springs: Central Land Council, 1978.

Pink, Olive. "Warlpiri Material, Anthropological and Linguistic, Miscellaneous Notes and Correspondence." Canberra: Australian Institute for Aboriginal and Torres Strait Islander Studies, 1932–48.

Poirier, Sylvie. *A World of Relationships.* Toronto: University of Toronto Press, 2005.

Read, Peter. "Northern Territory." In *Contested Ground*, edited by Ann McGrath, 269–305. Sydney: Allen, 1995.

Scrymgour, Marion. "Education Restructure Includes Greater Emphasis on English." Darwin, Northern Territory Government, 2008. Accessed January 25, 2017. http://newsroom.nt.gov.au/mediaRelease/4656.

Simpson, Jane. "Perceptions of Meteorology in Some Aboriginal Languages." In *Windows on Meteorology*, edited by Eric Webb, 20–28. Melbourne: CSIRO, 1997.

Stojanovski, Andrew. *Dog Ear Café.* Melbourne: Hybrid, 2010.

Sutton, Peter. *Country.* Canberra: Aboriginal History, 1995.

Swartz, Stephen M., comp. *Interactive Warlpiri—English Dictionary* (2nd ed.). Darwin: AuSIL, 2012. http://ausil.org/Dictionary/Warlpiri/lexicon/index.htm.

Tracks Dance Company. "Lajamanu Tracks Relationship." Darwin: Tracks Dance Company, 2015. Accessed January 25, 2017. www.tracksdance.com.au/ lajamanu-tracks-relationship.

———. "Milpirri 2012 (Pulyaranyi)." Darwin: Tracks Dance Company, 2015. Accessed January 25, 2017. http://tracksdance.com.au/milpirri-2012-pulyaranyi.

United Nations. *Convention on the Rights of the Child.* Geneva: Office of the High Commissioner for Human Rights, 1990. Accessed January 25, 2017. www.ohchr. org/EN/ProfessionalInterest/Pages/CRC.aspx.

Warlpiri-patu-kurlangu Jaru. *Submission to the House of Representatives Sanding Committee on Aboriginal and Torres Strait Islander Affairs National Inquiry into Language Learning in Indigenous Communities.* Yuendumu: Warlpiri-patu-kurlangu Jaru, 2011. Accessed June 13, 2017. www.aph.gov.au/Parliamentary_Business/Committees/House_of_Representatives_Committees?url=atsia/languages/subs/sub121.pdf.

Wild, Stephen A. "Recreating the Jukurrpa." In *Songs of Aboriginal Australia*, edited by Margaret Clunies Ross, Stephen A. Wild, and Tamsin Donaldson, 97–120. Sydney: Oceania, 1987.

*Wintaru* [sic *Wirntaru*]. Performed by Wantarri J. Patrick. Canberra: Belconnen Community Service, 2013. YouTube video. Accessed January 25, 2017. www.youtube.com/watch?v=QGWDnBIcZbc.

Yunupiŋu, Mandawuy. "Yothu Yindi." *Race and Class* 35 no. 4 (1994): 114–120.

# 10 Connecting Sami Education to the Land and Lived Experience

*Ylva Jannok Nutti*

## Introduction

> An older Sámi woman was lying in the hospital. Her family visited her, and everyone knew that her life would soon be over. Soon, a beloved mother and grandmother would no longer be among them. The family tried to avoid thinking about this, as they sat at her bedside and chatted about the weather, the calf marking which just occurred, and everyday events. One of the grandchildren, a twelve-year-old girl, had recently been at a youth camp where she had learned to yoik. The girl told her grandmother about this. The grandmother directly asked her, "Who taught you to yoik?" The girl gave the name of the person. The grandmother replied, "I learned yoik from his father." The family was surprised. They did not know that she could yoik. In the hospital bed, on her deathbed, a glimpse of an unknown part of an elderly woman's life was revealed to her family. Afterward, several questions were raised by the family, and they asked themselves: "Why did they not know that she could yoik? Did the grandmother even have a yoik by her own? How was it?" These questions were not answered, as the grandmother passed away soon after.
>
> (Jannok Nutti 2015)

The Sámi are an Indigenous people; they live in Sápmi, the northern region of Scandinavia in Norway, Sweden, and Finland and on the Kola Peninsula of Russia. Yoik is practiced throughout the Sámi region. Roung stated that yoiking is the song and poetry of the Sámi.[1] The yoik tradition looks different in different areas and is nowadays strongest in Finnmark County in Norway.[2] Stoor explained that yoik is a verbal art that includes song and spoken messages. The first Sámi writer Turi explained that yoik is a way of remembering another person; some remember the person with love, others with hate or grief.[3] There are also yoiks about the land and animals, such as wolves and reindeer. Stoor highlighted that yoiking also can include performance. The performative aspect of yoiking influences the yoiking, as the yoiker can change the style and the yoik depending on the listeners. For example, if a yoiker yoiks to a younger audience, he or she perhaps chooses yoiks and a style of yoiking the yoiker feels younger people

196 *Ylva Jannok Nutti*

like. Stoor recalled an event from the 1970s. During a drive, a man yoiked, laughed, and told stories to the other passengers during the whole journey. Afterward, Stoor understood that he had not only witnessed but also participated in a performance. This was during a period when yoiking was often considered sinful, as the church considered yoik witchcraft, and even today, many do not want anyone to yoik in the Church. In Skaltje,[4] Divggak Nutá Juhán stated that it was seldom that he as a child heard his father yoiking, as he stopped yoiking if he noticed that he was listening. They did not yoik for the children in that area where he lived in those days.[5] Nevertheless, Skaltje explained that the yoik supports Sámi self-esteem and identity and strengthens Sámi as a people. The negative view of Sámi religion, yoik, culture, and language was part of the authority's strategy for weakening Sáminess and Sámi identity. Skaltje observed that in some way this strategy was successful, but the resistance of the Sámi has been strong, and today, the yoik social force is alive. The yoik tradition is, as Roung earlier emphasized, still a significant part of Sámi cultural identity.

Yoiks can pass on a story about any aspect of the Sámi culture and life from one generation to another. Kuhmunen, for example, yoiked about the land.[6] He describes that he gets to take part in previous generations' life, generations that lived the same kind of life that he does. Yoiking includes storytelling and is about remembering. Skaltje gave an example: Around a fireplace, you suddenly can remember an older relative, and as you are sitting there, you just have to yoik the relative's yoik. The Sámi storytelling tradition is also strongly connected to certain places.[7] Once I was traveling with my daughter, and when we passed a special location, I told a story.[8] Afterward, my daughter asked, "Why do you not tell stories like this more often?" I could not answer directly; but after a while, I explained that I rarely think about all the stories that I heard as a child. Now, as we passed this particular place, the story just came to me. In an action research project, some teachers worked with the theme Sámi storytelling tradition with Sámi pupils in school.[9] After the theme, a father reported that when his daughter came home and told him about the school project, he, with this support, told many old stories to his children. For me, a specific location functions as a reminder. For the father, the work in school functioned as a trigger for telling stories, and through the stories, knowledge transfer from one generation to another was made possible. In my teaching in the Sámi teacher education program, I have tried to give space for storytelling and for students to exchange experiences. Similarly, Balto and Østmo used students' stories and experiences in teaching to enhance cultural sensitivity, and their method functioned as a means of examining teaching methods and teaching content.[10]

Sámi teacher education programs for early childhood, primary, and lower secondary school teachers are provided by the Sámi University of Applied Sciences. The Sámi University of Applied Sciences has provided these programs since it was established in 1994. The programs are taught in Sámi and are based on Sámi cultural practices, such as the storytelling and discussion described above. Many believe that Sámi is only one language, but it is several different Sámi languages. Today, the instruction in teacher preparation programs is conducted in north Sámi. If students speak another language, they are able to write their tasks and take language teaching courses in their Sámi language. This said, a significant number of Sámi no longer speak any of the varieties of the Sámi language. Pite Sámi, for example, is nearly extinct. Furthermore, not all Sámi have maintained connections to culture-based practices, as many live in cities outside the core Sámi area. This is complicated by the fact that Sámi culture is multifaceted; similar to all other cultures, everyone does not perform the same culture-based practices. Today, students who attend the programs speak Sámi, but the question is, when many Sámi neither speak any of the languages nor have links to Sámi culture-based practices, how should Sámi teacher education be designed and implemented so that it reflects all students' cultures and languages? What should be taught, and how should it be taught? Further, can this teacher education be useful for other students? In this chapter, I discuss how teacher education can be shaped in a way that is appropriate to Sámi culture-based methods of teaching and learning in the context of contemporary society. I explore this topic based on previous research about Sámi child-rearing practices and livelihood experiences.

## Sámi Child-Rearing Practices and Livelihood Experiences

In the historic self-sufficient Sámi society, important skills took into account the local environment by using nature as the source of livelihood, such as reindeer herding, fishing, hunting, and preparing food or clothes in order to survive.[11] These activities were season- and location-based, when and where the resources were available. Today, natural resources are still used as they have been historically. Many Sámi children were and still are raised in a close relationship to the land: they learn where the best fishing or berry-picking places are, and they learn to know the land where their families moved with reindeer herds. During livelihood activities, knowledge is passed on based on participation, i.e., experientially. The children participate in livelihood activities with family members and other society members.[12] In the book *Democracy and Education*, Dewey stated, "Society not only continues to exist by transmission, *by* communication, but it may fairly be said to exist *in* transmission, *in* communication."[13] Dewey also stated that people live in a community by virtue of the things they have in common; and communication is the way in which they come to possess things in common. Knowledge in Sámi society was passed on by involving children from a very young age in activities that were necessary for the common good of the family and the community.[14] A reindeer herder stated, "As a child you are always following your parents. You are with them and you see."[15]

198  *Ylva Jannok Nutti*

The goal of Sámi child-rearing was to contribute to children's autonomy, so they would learn and become independent and manage necessities, such as feeding themselves.[16] In the book *How We Think*, Dewey treated experimental logic and instrumental epistemology with reflective thinking.[17] Dewey described reflective thinking as a process in steps ending with multiple testing of hypotheses. The observed fact and its evidence have to be analyzed and controlled in relation to the problem that should be solved. For Sámi children in the historic self-sufficient Sámi society, the need to be able to feed themselves created a need for experience in specific areas, such as working in harmony with nature and becoming able to use the available resources as sources of livelihood. Children were brought up to manage and to handle situations by themselves. In this setting, finding the way from one location to another in the forest or on a mountain is an important skill to master.[18] To master that skill, children get to know the land through walking; they learn to see suitable walking paths in diverse terrain through experiences. When children are out walking, they are encouraged to be observant, to be aware of their surroundings, and to notice significant landmarks. The rivers and the wind are important features that help orient oneself in the environment. Children are taught to observe the rivers and the direction of the flow in the area. If the weather conditions get bad, the rivers can be used as a means of navigation. The wind is an important indicator of direction; if one feels the wind from another direction, then one has probably changed direction. In addition to noticing the features of the land, children are encouraged to walk in front, not behind, adults, and the skill and capacity to walk fast or a long way are praised.[19]

Children in reindeer-herding families need to become familiar with pastures, migratory routes, calving areas, and other places important for reindeer herds.[20] When a reindeer herder describes where the reindeer are grazing, the herder uses place names as a starting point for the description, and all significant places have names.[21] The names are connected to the use of the land and traditional livelihoods.[22] Many stories are connected to local places; through these stories, children and young people get to know the land.[23] Places where people have lived have their own yoiks, and yoik can carry memories from old days.[24] Through stories, children can take part in an earlier generation's way of life, a life similar to the life that they live.[25] A story can take into account earlier experiences about the place, and the experience of the place can thus be stored in a story. The stories can, for example, describe good or bad hunting or grazing areas, and there are also many stories about specific sites or terrains that are dangerous to pass. Often beginning with an accident that occurred on the site, a story can then contain a warning to make people more observant when they pass through the area.[26]

Reindeer herders' families have strong ties to the land, and Oskal emphasized that some sites are believed to possess protective spirits. A suitable way to camp safely where the reindeer herd was to ask for permission from the

Connecting Sami Education to the Land    199

spirits and the land to camp and to wish good health for the herd. Then, upon leaving, one would thank the pasture for the good care. These behaviors showed humility with the aim of getting along well with the environment. Children also collected the bones of the reindeer meat after eating, while at the same time wishing for future good "reindeer luck," the notion that the reindeer would survive over time and the herd prosper.[27]

This approach to children's upbringing is still central today; however, Sámi culture is multifaceted, and not all children perform the same culture-based practices or live the same type of lives. Sámi children attend educational institutions. Some children attend institutions that support their Sámi culture and language, and some attend institutions that do not.

## Sámi School History

The Sámi do not have, similar to other Indigenous peoples, a long history of organizing culture-based knowledge in formal educational institutions; education for Sámi children instead has played a central role in colonization.[28] Education for Sámi children was carried out according to the interests of the majority of society up until the middle of the twentieth century and was used as an instrument for assimilation and segregation purposes.[29] Education did not support the use of the Sámi language, and Sámi children were prevented from developing knowledge of their own culture.[30] In the book *"When I Was Eight Years Old I Left My Home and I Have Not Yet Come Back": Memories from the Sámi School Time*,[31] memories about a boarding school in the Swedish region of Sápmi are presented.[32] The book describes how the state and the Church tried to assimilate and colonize Sámi. In this chapter, I will not discuss the boarding school and the consequences of this school system; instead, I briefly present experiences from Sámi school research. Education for Sámi children differs between countries; however, the national states carried out assimilation through different national school systems in Sweden, Norway, and Finland. In the 1800s, the desire to create a strong national state arose in all Nordic countries.[33] In Norway, Norwegianization was practiced. The government of Norway founded a special fund to promote Norwegian language skills, and teachers who taught Norwegian to Sámi-speaking children received a higher salary.[34] Although the Norwegian language was supported, the most important aspect of the assimilation education, Christianity, was still taught in Sámi.[35] Then in areas that were completely Sámi speaking, Sámi could be used as the language for instruction.[36] Thereafter, when the Norwegianizing measures did not have the desired effect, the regulation became more stringent, and the use of Sámi was completely prohibited.[37] As an impact of the intensive Norwegianization, the Sámi language remained outside the school walls from the early 1900s to the late 1950s.[38] In the Education Act of 1959, a regulation concerning Sámi as a language of instruction was added, and since 1967, the primary level in schools has been taught in Sámi languages in

## 200  *Ylva Jannok Nutti*

Norway.[39] Similar assimilation occurred in Sweden and Finland. Although schools were instruments for assimilation, the Sámi school is an old idea. Hirvonen pointed out, "When studying Sámi history, we notice that, for ages, there have been people in the Sámi communities who have dreamed of a world where even minorities would have it better. A Sámi school has been one of the dreams."[40]

### Sámi School Research

Sámi syllabi in several subjects, including Sámi language and a syllabus that were to some extent adjusted to Sámi conditions (such as Christianity, English, environmental studies, social studies, music, Sámi handicrafts, and home economics), were introduced in 1987 in Norway, and since 1997, a Sámi curriculum has been applied.[41] Hirvonen and her research group investigated the first Sámi curriculum reform for the ten-year primary school in 1997.[42] In their evaluation, they examined whether and how the Sámi curriculum was realized. In the research, teachers claimed that Sámi children and young people learn best through practical work outside the school building through "an outdoor school." Key factors for Sámi culture-based learning approaches were pointed out to be freedom, independence, closeness to the outdoor environment, and storytelling. The Sámi curriculum intended to try to make visible knowledge of the local community: from the older generations, relatives, and local knowledge. Hirvonen and Keskitalo compared the Sámi school with a symphony.[43] They then posed the following questions: How is the reform realized? Is it a complete symphony? They meant that the realization of the Sámi curriculum was an incomplete symphony. The schools lacked cultural and linguistic skills to be able to realize the Sámi curriculum. To realize the intentions in the curriculum, teachers need additional training and practice; they need to learn new skills and ways of thinking; thus, a change in teacher education and training is important. Beyond the change in the school system in Sweden from boarding schools to Sámi schools, there is a need for adequate teaching aids and tests (if we choose to use tests in school) that aim to preserve and develop Sámi language and culture.[44] Hirvonen highlighted that we need measures to make the Sámi culture and language the starting point of all school activities; Sámi values and perspectives could then be part of everyday practices and school subjects. Keskitalo et al. further emphasized that the schedules, classroom environment, physical design, and role of teachers should be redefined in order to reduce the distance between the majority culture and Sámi culture and meet the intentions in the Sámi curriculum.[45] In Norway, this curriculum was replaced with another Sámi curriculum in 2006,[46] but no evaluation research has been conducted.

Based on Hirvonen's research, I carried out action research in the Sámi school in the Swedish region of Sápmi.[47] The teachers expressed views on Sámi culture-based learning approaches similar as those in Hirvonen's

# Connecting Sami Education to the Land   201

earlier research.[48] One teacher in the action research project justified culture-based teaching with the idea that the home would become part of the school. Another teacher expressed that culture-based teaching could give Sámi children the opportunity to learn based on their own language and their own culture but also give them the opportunity to participate in Sámi culture-based knowledge. However, the teachers felt that they had neither the knowledge nor the time to develop culture-based teaching, and they expressed doubts about it. One said, "Traditions are good, but do they help the pupils to become successful?" The teachers felt that they had to prepare and give pupils the best conditions to perform well on national tests and equip pupils for future schooling in national schools. This tension was also visible in a study of Sámi schools. In this study, the researchers stated that there is a need for knowledge regarding how national aims can be transformed into an Indigenous school context.[49] Since the establishment of the Sámi University of Applied Sciences, teachers and researchers have been working to establish Sámi higher education and research, to develop teacher education and school research, for example, in the process *Luohkkálanjas várrečohkkii*—from the classroom to the top of the mountain.[50] Based on these experiences, we need to develop and make sure that student teachers get the opportunity to participate in the process to transform Sámi culture into culture-based teaching.

In the next section, I explore this idea in connection with teacher education. I discuss two outdoor themes, the campfire and walking. The themes are two concrete examples of Sámi livelihood activities. The focus is teaching children during these activities. These themes are chosen because it is central to be able to navigate and make a fire in an outdoor classroom, and the themes are part of the teaching in teacher education at the Sámi University of Applied Sciences. The themes are discussed based on outdoor teaching examples, previous research experiences, and stories. As we are searching for a common teaching view, stories can constitute a common horizon of understanding and make it possible to discuss the philosophy of Sámi education.[51]

## *Árran*: Around the Campfire

Once, a group of student teachers and I, the teacher educator, went outside and made a fire. Before we went outside, we had discussed in class the concept "reindeer luck" with the suitable way to show humility and gratitude by asking for permission from the land and the spirits to camp on a site.[52] The students and I practiced this humble attitude and discussed possible practical implications for an educational institution: What can it mean for us as teachers if we, together with children, request permission and are grateful for visiting? When we arrived at our site, we put down our backpacks and built a fire. The fire offers rest; children often go to the campfire to rest and play during, for example, berry picking. In Sámi

202  *Ylva Jannok Nutti*

culture, it is important to be able to make a fire. Teachers at a Sámi school said that their pupils were responsible for making the fire.[53] Every time they went to their campsite, the pupils wanted to collect wood for the fire and make the fire as soon as they got there. Larsson-Lussi explained that we are happy when a fire is burning as a fire means warmth and light.[54] He stated that, when he was a child each family had their own campfire, and nobody would use another family's campfire. Collecting wood for the fire and making a new one can be a little problematic when out with an educational institution depending on where you are and the regulations in the area. When a colleague and I were out camping with a group of youth, we had to problematize the view of making a fire as we were in an area where we did not want to leave any new traces from our short visit.[55] Balto presented the story of a grandfather that illuminates the relationship between the environment and humankind.[56] The grandfather was nearing the end of his life and was teaching his grandson as they walked together on the land. The grandfather showed the meadows and told the story of how he was the one who had cleared this land in the wilderness, and how he then took down all of the fences that he had put up on the property. The grandson got very upset, but the grandfather explained that he did this because nobody in the family wanted to continue to cultivate or use the land. Therefore, he wanted the traces of humankind's labor to vanish. He said, "I only borrowed the land for as long as I needed it."[57]

I, among many other Sámi, was brought up with a similar story. My mother often tells the story when her mother removed all the traces from their old summer dwelling as they moved to another location. This cultural practice gives direction for living a sustainable way of life, and the environment is not seen as an object but more as a living source to respect and to be thankful toward.[58] Balto and Kuhmunen also stated, "Nowadays we seldom hear or listen to this ethical voice, a voice from our ancestors that is the opposite of materialism, amidst the greed and selfishness we participate in."[59] Therefore, as we were out with the youth, we wanted them to be aware of the ethical dimension of not leaving traces as we wanted to be respectful guests during our visit. These reflections were addressed and discussed with the student teachers as we were out on the land.

For practical reasons and in line with regulations, schools often bring wood with them, but it is still important to make children and students aware of what kind of wood we need to be able to light a fire. When my sister and I were children, we were responsible for collecting birch bark for kindling, and as we became older, we collected wood. My father did not allow us to take wood with us to the forest. As I got older, I understood why: He wanted us to practice the skill of lighting a fire in bad weather conditions without dry wood.

During the youth camp, elders were invited to participate, and the youth and the elders put up a *lávvogoahti* (a tent or tipi) and made a fire pit inside in the middle.[60] Over the fire, the youth cooked their own food on their barbecue sticks. Elli-Karin, an elder, showed how to make a barbecue stick and thereafter how to cook fish on the stick over the fire. Earlier, the youth and Elli-Karin had baked *gáhkku* (flat bread) which they ate as they waited for the fish to be ready. The youth thereafter ate their fish on plates of birch bark. Bread must be baked every day; otherwise, it is too hard. Elli-Karin showed how to roll the dough into fine round cakes. All baked their own *gáhkku*. We baked the bread over the open fire; we first baked one side of the bread in the pan over the fire, and then we baked the other side on one of the flat campfire stones. For many of the youth, this was a well-known chore they usually perform at home, or preschool, or school. While the bread was baking, experiences were shared. For Elli-Karin it was important that children were encouraged and given opportunities to be involved so that they can learn. She meant that it is important that children experience the forest because experiences such as picking berries and then tasting the berries you just picked brings one in greater harmony with the forest.[61] This can be part of giving children the opportunity to develop positive self-esteem, zest for life and joy, which Balto stressed is important. In the *lávvogoahti* around the fire, we, after eating, listened to stories from the elders' childhood.[62] They talked about the different rooms and the codes of conduct in the *lávvogoahti*. Everyone in the family had a special place, and moving around in the *lávvogoahti* was done with great caution.[63] No one was ever allowed to step over the campfire or over the kitchen area. These conduct rules were addressed and discussed with the youth as we sat there.

At the camp, the youth were given the task to search for signs of other fires, one of the most common archaeological traces of Sámi in use in pre-historic periods.[64] A fire pit is familiar for them. We also looked on some newly made campfires in the area, and several had modern traces, such as rubbish and so on. This is problematic since, in Sámi culture, nature is only on loan and should be left as it was found. The teachers in the Sámi school noticed that in addition to practical knowledge for lighting a fire, the pupils observed that there are different approaches in terms of where and how a fire should be made and left.[65] Their reflections included value consider-ations as it is important to show respect for natural resources, including for the fish the youth ate at the camp. Thus, they collected the fish bones and put them in the birch bark, brought them out, and covered them with moss and stones. It is a way to honor the animal, the fish or reindeer as Oskal pointed out.[66] Sámi children were taught to wish for reindeer luck while collecting the bones from the reindeer meal. A reindeer herder told us that his family carried the legs of the animal to a special place in the for-est.[67] This can also have practical implications, while also showing respect to other animals, as it is also a way to prevent dogs from ingesting sharp bones.[68] The students and I also practiced this humble attitude and dis-cussed possible practical implications for them afterward as teachers at an educational institution.

## 204  *Ylva Jannok Nutti*

## Walking Tour

A group of students in the teacher preparation program and I walked to a fire site, and on another occasion, we did a walking tour.[69] When we arrived at the site, we talked about what educators do to instruct children and pupils about the rules during a visit to the site. If one is not familiar with a place, one should not venture too far away from the fire. Small children are instructed that they should always see the fire or the adults. The educator, Elin Baer,[70] made the children pay attention to how she was dressed to be able to recognize and locate her in the big crowd when they visited a marketplace. She thus gave the children the responsibility to be aware of where she was, while also giving them the freedom to have their own experience at the market. Similarly, during the camp, the youth were not given rules that stopped them from walking around; instead, they received instructions about how to look after each other.[71] This is similar to the practice in reindeer herding when herders "hoot" to let the other reindeer herders know where they are.[72] At the camp, when we hooted to youth, they needed to respond by hooting back. There is a Sámi saying, "On the mountain you need to have eyes, in the forest you need to listen." The youth felt that they in this way got the freedom and opportunity to explore and discover the nearby surroundings. A girl said that it was fun to have this freedom, because they could be somewhat on their own as they were allowed to explore the nearest surroundings.[73]

The teachers at the Sámi school experienced that the pupils knew that being out in the forest does not mean that you should be noisy; there is an expectation that you should not shout or be destructive. Once the pupils met another class out in the forest and they said that the other class was really shouting, and they understood that we do not behave that way out of respect for the forest. The teachers said that they and the pupils would talk about how to behave in the woods, and not shout or hit and destroy trees and plants.[74]

Walking is an essential part of lived experience,[75] and we experience the environment tied to our sensory inputs of vision, hearing, touch, taste and smell.[76] If visibility is poor, reindeer herders take the wind direction into consideration, and a reindeer herder said that the wind is his compass.[77] Knowledge of the environment is embedded in locally situated practices, and the herders are used to being out in all kinds of weather conditions and are very familiar with the land, paying attention to various features: swamps, clearings, hills, different types of vegetation, clusters of trees, standing dead trees, big or peculiar shaped and positioned rocks, rivers, etc.[78] Remembering what one has seen in sequences serves a practical function as it is crucial to find one's way back. Children are also urged to look backward while walking so that they take notice of the formation of the landscape in the other direction. To become familiar, children need to learn the land through walking, and they are urged to be observant, to remember the sequence, and to pay attention to everything that can be an indication of where you are and in what direction you should continue. Moving from one place to another means remembering the way, and it is about creating your own memories and connections to the path based on your or someone else's previous movements. Teacher preparation classes, thus, emphasize the importance of being aware that wayfinding is an active process that demands active participants who encounter landmarks while walking. To be able to find the path, while walking, I need to experience the environment with the help of my eyes and ears, by the touch of my footwear on the ground and perhaps even by smelling. I need to see landmarks or to hear sounds, remember sequences of marks, and perhaps remember to change direction or make a turn. To be able to do that, I need to be present, and I need to experience myself in the surroundings. Wayfinding is about positioning myself in relation to my surroundings. Wayfinding is lived experiences that demands presence, high ability to take in the surroundings by my sensory inputs, and the skill to interpret the sensory inputs so that I know where I am and where I shall go next.

The teachers at the Sámi school used to walk past a natural spring during their hikes to a campsite in order to fetch water. They felt this was important for the children to understand the importance of fresh water, to learn the water cycle, and to understand the global need to protect water sources. The first several times, the teachers walked in front to show the way, but after several hikes, the pupils were encouraged to go in front. The teachers at the Sámi school initially felt a bit worried about letting the pupils go ahead of the teachers. In spite of their worries, the teachers let the pupils do this, and all became very good at helping each other find the way to the campsite.[79] Trying to take advantage of livelihood experiences such as reindeer herding functioned as starting points for discussions in class. Importantly, however, we cannot learn to walk and be comfortable in the forest or on the mountain by being inside in the classroom.

## Summary Remarks

How should Sámi teacher education be designed and implemented? What should be taught, and how should it be taught? In this chapter, I have—through description of the campfire and walking tour—provided examples of content in teacher education and tried to highlight how important it is that the teaching is shaped in a way that is appropriate to culture-based teaching methods and thereby becomes institutionalized in schools. Participation and students' place-based experiences at the campfire and along the walking path are centered. Through activities like these, being outdoors and experiencing oneself in the surroundings based on his or her own sensory inputs, children engage in communication with everything around them, including the natural world so central to Sámi life. As I noted, children are taught not only to look ahead of them while walking through the forest, but also

# 206  *Ylva Jannok Nutti*

behind them. This becomes a way of knowing, looking back for understanding, being aware of their surroundings to inform the totality of their path. In existential terms, this might be described as a nascent wide-awakeness, "an awareness of what it means to be in the world."[80] Their experiences also provide them a moral awakeness as they are taught to treat nature with respect and experience its rewards.

Being wide-awake in the world serves a central goal of Sámi child-rearing which is to contribute to children's autonomy, so they would learn and become independent and manage necessities as being able to navigate in the forest or at the mountain. This suits well with an experimental outdoor teaching approach as we cannot learn these things without being outdoors. Central cultural values include the need to be able to manage to use the available resources, to work in harmony with the natural surroundings. Important to take into teacher education is the ability to work in harmony with the land, and to implement teacher education that exists in transmission, communication expressed with help of Dewey's words. Being outdoors is a source of life, local identity, and experiences. Such experiences represent life by transmission, whereas other cultural aspects, such as the yoik, become explicitly life by communication. There interaction between people and nature, and the outdoor education highlight the ethical responsibility in the management of nature. And, through the symbiotic relationship between transmission and communication, such interaction becomes a way of knowing and being. As we are searching for a common teaching view, experiences like these must be part of an education that relies on a congruent theory of experience. In other words, "curriculum is an historically constructed narrative that produces and organizes student experiences in the context of social forms, such as language usage, organization of knowledge into high- and low-status categories, and the affirmation of particular kinds of teaching strategies."[81] For Sámi children such strategies must be participatory and experiential, lending themselves to the creating of stories that can not only constitute a common horizon of understanding but also contribute to their own stories, their autonomy, their yoiks.

## Notes

1. Israel Ruong, Samerna *i historien och nutiden*, 4 [The Sámi People In History and Present Time] (Stockholm, Sweden: Bonnier Fakta, 1982).
2. Kristen Stoor, *Juoiganmuitalusat—Jojkberättelser: En Studie av Jojkens Narrativa Egenskaper* [Yoiking Stories: A Study of the Yoik's Narrative Properties] (Umeå, Sweden: Samiska Studier, Umeå Universitet, 2007).
3. Johan Turi, *Muitalus Sámiid Birra*, 3 [The Story of the Sámi People], ed. Mikael Svonni (Karasjok, Norway: Cállid Lágádus, 2010).
4. Maj Lis Skaltje, *Luondu juoiggaha* [Nature Is Suddenly Singing Yoiks] (Kautokeino, Norway: DAT, 2005).
5. In Gällivare of the Swedish region of Sápmi.
6. Lars-Ante Kuhmunen, *Birrasis: (Cd)* (Karasjok, Norway: Iđut, 2005).

## Connecting Sami Education to the Land 207

7. Jens-Ivar Nergård, *Den levende erfaring: En studie i samisk kunnskapstradisjon* [The Living Experience: A Study of Sami Knowledge Tradition] (Oslo, Norway: Cappelen Akademisk Forlag, 2006).

8. Ylva Jannok Nutti, "En Betraktelse över Samisk Skolutveckling" [A Review of Sami School Development], in *"När jag var åtta år lämnade jag mitt hem och jag har ännu inte kommit tillbaka": Minnesbilder från samernas skoltid* [When I Was Eight Years Old, I Left My Home and I Have Not Yet Come Back: Memorials from Sámi School Time], ed. K. Huuva and E. Blind (Stockholm, Sweden: Verbum AB, 2015), 222–236.

9. Asta Balto and Gunilla Johansson, *"Gal dat oahppá go stuorrula": Hvordan styrke det samiske perspektivet i skolen? Et skoleinitiert forskningsprosjekt ved to skoler/førskolor/fritidshem i svensk Sápmi.* Arbetsrapport 17.09.07 (Kautokeino, Norway: Sámi allaskuvla, 2007).

10. Asta Mitkija Balto and Liv Østmo, "Multicultural Studies from a Sámi Perspective: Bridging Traditions and Challenges in an Indigenous Setting," *Issues in Educational Research, Special Issue in Intercultural and Critical Education* 22 no. 1 (2012): 1–17.

11. Mikkel Nils Sara, "Tradisjonell samisk kunnskap i grunnskolen" ["Traditional Sámi Knowledge in Primary School"], in *Samisk Skole i Plan og Praksis: Hvordan Møte Utfordringene i L97S? Evaluering av Reform 97* [Sámi School in Plan and Practice: How to Meet the Challenges of the Reform L-97S? Evaluation of Reform 97], ed. Valtteri Hirvonen (Kautokeino, Norway: Sámi University College, 2004), 114–130.

12. Ibid.

13. Dewey (1916), 5.

14. Anton Hoem, *Sosialisering: en teoretisk og empirisk modellutvikling* [Socialization: A Theoretical and Empirical Model] (Vallset, Norway: Oplandske Bokforlag DA, 2012).

15. Ylva Jannok Nutti, *Matematiskt Tankesätt inom den Samiska Kulturen Utifrån Samiska Slöjdares och Renskötares Berättelser* [Mathematical Thinking within the Sámi Culture on Basis of the Stories of Sámi Crafters and Reindeer Herders] (Luleå, Sweden: Luleå University of Technology, 2007), 62. Author's translation.

16. Asta Balto, *Samisk barneoppdragelse i endring* [Sámi Child Rearing in Change] (Oslo, Norway: Ad Notam Gyldendal AS, 1997).

17. Dewey (1910/1933).

18. Ylva Jannok Nutti, Mathematical thinking within the Sámi Culture on basis of the stories of Sámi Crafters and Reindeer Herders; Solveig Joks, "Boazodoalu Máhtut Aiggis Aigái. Etniid Doaibma Arbeviroláš Oahpaheamis Boazodoalus" [Reindeer Herding Knowledge from Year to Year: The Mothers' Function in Traditional Teaching within Reindeer Herding], *Dieđut*, Volume 3/2007 (Kautokeino, Norway: Sámi instituhtta, 2008).

19. Jannok Nutti (2007); Joks (2008).

20. Nils Oskal, "On Nature and Reindeer Luck," *Rangifer* 2–3 no. 20 (2000): 175–180.

21. Ibid.

22. Kaisa Rautio Helander, "Sámi Báikenamat 1700-Logu Eanamihtideamis— Arbevieruid ja Riekteipmárdusa Dutkanfáddán" [Sami Place Names in the 18th Century: Land Surveying as a Theme for Researching Traditions and Conceptions of Justice], *Sámi Dieđalaš Aigečála* 1–2 (2007): 138–160.

23. Vergard Nergård, *Slekt og rituelt slektskap i samiske samfunn – Innspill til en psykodynamisk forståelse av sosialisering* [Family and Ritual Relationships in Sámi Societies - Input to a Psychodynamic Understanding of Socialization]. (Oslo, Norway: Pedagogisk forskningsinstitutt, 2005).

24. Skaltje (2005).

208   Ylva Jannok Nutti

25. Kuhmunen (2005).
26. Nergård (2006).
27. Oskal (2000).
28. Jan Henry Keskitalo, *Education and Cultural Policies: Majority—Minority Relations: The Case of the Sami in Scandinavia. Dieut 1/94. Dieđut*, Volume 4/2008 (Kautokeino, Norway: Sámi Instituhtta, 1993); Rauna Kuokkanen, "Towards an 'Indigenous Paradigm' from a Sami Perspective," *Canadian Journal of Native Studies* 20 no. 2 (2000): 411–436.
29. Kenneth Hyltenstam, Christofer Stroud, and Mikael Svonni, "Språkbyte, språkbevarande, revitalisering. Samiskans ställning i svenska Sápmi" [Language change, language maintaining, revitalization. The Sami language situation in the Swedish part of Sápmi], in *Sveriges sju inhemska språk - ett minoritetsspråksperspektiv*, ed. Kenneth Hyltenstam. (Lund, Stockholm: Studentlitteratur, 2009).
30. Rauna Kuokkonen, "Towards an "Indigenous Paradigm" from a Sami Perspective," *The Canadian Journal of Native Studies* 20 no. 2 (2000): 411–436.
31. Kaisa Huuva and Ellacarin Blind, *"När jag var åtta år lämnade jag mitt hem och jag har ännu inte kommit tillbaka": minnesbilder från samernas skoltid* ["When I Was Eight Years Old, I Left My Home and I Have Not Yet Come Back": Memorials from Sámi School Time] (Stockholm, SE: Verbum AB, 2015).
32. For similar documentation of and research on Sámi school history in the Norwegian and Finnish regions of Sápmi, see *Sámi School History 1–6* (Lund, Boine, Johansen, and Rasmussen 2005–2013) and *Sámi School History in Finland* (Keskitalo, Lehtola, and Paksuniemi 2014).
33. Vuokko Hirvonen, *Sámi Culture and the School: Reflections by Sámi Teachers and the Realization of the Sámi School: An Evaluation Study of Reform 97* (Karasjok, Norway: Čálliid Lágádus, 2004).
34. Helge Dahl, Tromsø offentlige lærerskole *i* 150 år: 1826–1976 [Tromsø Public Teacher Education in 150 years, 1826–1976]. (Tromsø, Norway, 1957).
35. Ibid.
36. Hoëm (1976).
37. Dahl (1957).
38. Edel Hætta Eriksen, Norga vuođđoskuvla sámimánáide [Norway Primary School to Sámi children], *Dieđut* Vol. 2(1977).
39. Hirvonen (2004).
40. As early as the 1700s, it was documented that many priests and missionaries in the Sámi region realized that it was impossible to teach Sámi children only in the majority language of the country; this resulted in the publication of books in Sámi (Hirvonen 2004, 30).
41. Hirvonen (2004).
42. Ibid.
43. Vuokko Hirvonen and Jan Henry Keskitalo, "Samisk skole- en ufullendt symfoni?" [Sami school an imperfect symphony?] In *En likeverdig skole for alle? Om enhet og mangfold i grunnskolen* [An Equal School for All? About unity and diversity in elementary school], ed. Tor Ola Engen and Karl Jan Solstad. (Oslo: Norway, Universitetsforlaget, 2004), 200–219.
44. Jannok Nutti (2015).
45. Hirvonen (2004).
46. Udir (2007).
47. Ylva Jannok Nutti, *Ripsteg mot Spetskunskap i Samisk Matematik. Lärares Perspektiv på Transformeringsaktiviteter i Samisk Förskola och Sameskola* [Grouse Steps Towards Front Line Knowledge in Sámi Mathematics. Teachers' Perspective on Transformations Activities in Sámi Preschool and Sámi School] (Luleå, Sweden: Luleå University of Technology, 2010).
48. Hirvonen (2004).

## Connecting Sami Education to the Land 209

49. Asta Balto and Gunilla Johansson (2007); Balto, *Sámi oahpaheaddjit sirdet árbevirlaš kultuvrra boahttevašbuolvvaide: Dekoloniserema akšuvdnadutkamuš Ruota beale Sámis* [Sámi Teachers Passing on Traditional Knowledge to the Next Generation: Decolonialization through Action Research in the Swedish Part of Sápmi], Dieđut, Volume 4/2008 (Kautokeino, Norway: Sámi instituhtta, 2008); Johansson (2009). Parental involvement in the development of a culture based school curriculum, *Intercultural Education* 20 (4): 311–319.

50. This was discussed in a paper presented by Vuokko Hirvonen, Gunvor Guttorm, Elisabeth Utsi Gaup, and Ylva Jannok Nutti, at Wipce in Hawaii in 2014 (Hirvonen, Guttorm, Gaup, and Jannok Nutti, 2014). Hirvonen and Guttorm have worked there since the Sámi University of Applied Sciences was founded, Gaup worked there when this process was started, and I, Jannok Nutti, started to work at the institution long after this process was introduced.

51. Greta Gunn Bergstrom, *Tradisjonell Kunnskap og Samisk Modernitet: en Studie av Villkår for Tilegnelse av Tradisjonell Kunnskap i en Moderne Samisk Samfunnskontekst* [Traditional Knowledge and Sámi Modernity: A Study of Conditions for the Appropriation of Traditional Knowledge in the Context of the Modern Sámi Society] (Tromsø, Norway: University of Tromsø, 2011).

52. Oskal (2000).

53. Ylva Jannok Nutti, "Outdoor Days as a Pedagogical Tool," in *Crystals of School Children's Well-Being*, ed. Arto Ahonen, Eva Alerby, Ole Martin Johansen, Inna Ryzhkova, Eiri. Sohlman, and Heli. Villanen (Rovaniemi, Finland: University of Lapland, 2008), 199–208.

54. Yngve Ryd, *Eld: flammor och glöd – samisk eldkonst* [Fire: Flames ans Glos – Sámi Fireart] (Stockholm, Sweden: Nator och Kultur, 2005).

55. Ylva Jannok Nutti and Kajsa Kuoljok, *En Eldstad, Flera Berättelser: Unga Skapar Relationer till Tidigare Generationers Samiska platser* [A Fireplace, Several Stories: Youth Creates Relationships with Earlier Generations of Sami Places] (Jokkmokk, Sweden: Ájtte, Mountain and Sámi Museum, 2014).

56. Asta Mitkija Balto and Gudrun Kuhmunen, *Máhttáhit: re-educate them and us* (Karasjok, Norway: ČálliidLágádus AS, 2014).

57. Ibid., 60.

58. Ibid.

59. Balto and Kuhmunen, 62.

60. Jannok Nutti and Kuoljok (2014).

61. Jannok Nutti (2007).

62. Balto (2006).

63. Sigrid Drake, *Västerbottenslapparna under förra hälften av 1800-talet: etnografiska studier* [Västerbottenslapparna in the last half of the 19th century: ethnographic studies]. (Umeå, Sweden: Västerbottens museum, 1979/1918); Phebe Fjellström, *Samernas samhälle i tradition och nutid* [Lappish society in tradition and the present day]. (Stockholm, Sweden: Norstedt, 1985).

64. Jannok Nutti and Kuoljok (2014).

65. Jannok Nutti (2008).

66. Oskal (2000).

67. Jannok Nutti (2007).

68. Jannok Nutti and Kuoljok (2014).

69. Jannok Nutti (2017).

70. Asta Mitkijá Balto (2008).

71. Jannok Nutti and Kuoljok (2014).

72. Jannok Nutti (2007).

73. Jannok Nutti and Kuoljok (2014).

74. Jannok Nutti (2008).

210  *Ylva Jannok Nutti*

75. Tim Ingold, *Being Alive: Essays on Movement, Knowledge and Description* (London: Routledge, 2011).
76. Tim Ingold, *The Perception of the Environment: Essays on Livelihood, Dwelling and Skill* (London: Routledge, 2000).
77. Jannok Nutti (2007).
78. Nuccio Mazzullo and Tim Ingold, "Being Along: Place, Time and Movement among Sámi People," in *Mobility and Place: Enacting Northern European Peripheries*, ed. Jorgen Ole Bærneheldt and Brynhold Granås (Aldershot, UK: Ashgate Publishing, 2008), 27–37.
79. Jannok Nutti (2008).
80. Maxine Greene, *Releasing the Imagination: Essays on Education, the Arts, and Social Change* (San Francisco: Jossey-Bass, 1995), 35.
81. Peter McLaren, *Life in Schools*, 6th ed. (New York: Routledge, 2016), 128.

# 11 Ainu Puri

## Content and Praxis of an Indigenous Philosophy of a Northern People

*Jeff Gayman*

### Introduction

Philosopher of education Timothy Reagan, in the third edition to his *Non-Western Educational Traditions: Indigenous Approaches to Educational Thought and Practice*, lists the great traditions of East Asia, Japan and Korea as yet unexplored areas in his quest to examine the world's Indigenous educational traditions. After having lived in East Asia now for approximately three decades, I couldn't agree more with Reagan's sentiment. And yet, East Asia, including the People's Republic of China, Korea, Mongolia, Taiwan and Japan, simultaneously houses the traditions of a great diversity of Indigenous ethnic groups, which differ from the major religious traditions of these countries at the same time as they have been influenced by them to greater and lesser degrees. It is to one of these traditions, that of the Ainu Indigenous people of Japan and Russia, that this chapter focuses its attention.

The Ainu people of northern Japan and the surrounding islands believe that all material objects living or not, possess spirits which must be revered and treated with gratitude. To enter into the realm of Ainu spirituality is a journey into a world populated simultaneously by humans and deities in the form of fire, water, earth, animals, plants and animate objects, and of the many reciprocal relations deriving therefrom. The Ainu worldview culminates in a unique and humorous communication style, charming dances and songs, masterful artwork, sophisticated ceremonies, and one of the most extensive oral traditions in the world, all undergirded by values of respect, gratitude, moderation, earnestness and generosity. Education is a phenomenon of Ainu society embedded in everyday family and communal life in all of its manifestations, transmitted through acts of everyday livelihood, art and spiritual communion as practiced in the house, reinforced through the moral and didactic medium of Ainu oral literature, and fortified by periodic communal ceremonial events. I contend that these elements of Ainu *puri* (Ainu style of doing things) still remain vital to this day in the hearts, minds, and actions of Ainu adults and Elders, but stand in danger of being eradicated completely by the assimilative policies of colonization and the

## 212  *Jeff Gayman*

influences of urbanization and globalization. The Ainu society being portrayed here is one which currently exists at best in a piecemeal fashion. In the matter of addressing it, how the process of colonialism seriously undermined the conditions necessary for Ainu well-being cannot be emphasized enough.

This chapter sets out to examine this Ainu spirituality/philosophy by portraying it in the context of traditional Ainu society. The chapter begins by briefly outlining the history of colonialism in northern Japan. Next, characteristics of Ainu society critical for understanding how Ainu thought manifests in societal norms will be described, followed by a more detailed explanation of the belief (thought) systems behind the Ainu worldview which underlie the maxims of behavior in Ainu communities. Then, how children are raised according to the Ainu philosophy will be touched upon, followed by a consideration of the prospects for an Indigenous Ainu philosophy of education in contemporary Japan.

Indigenous philosophy is very much a product of the context in which it was developed. Since the issue of Indigenous futures cannot be separated from the matter of Indigenous policy self-determination, a position mandated by international law and grounded in moral and ethical frameworks of human rights, how the Ainu constitute an Indigenous people is a matter for initial examination. As to how Ainu educational philosophy manifests in praxis geared toward Ainu community development, which in turn is shaped by policy parameters, just who the Ainu people are and what they might concretely do as an Indigenous people given policy rights, is also an issue directly relevant to this chapter, and it is to a broad description of who the Ainu are that I will first direct my exposition. Here, let me first state that the definition of Indigenous to be used in this chapter is that put forth in this volume's introduction.

As the issue of relations with surrounding ethnic groups has major bearing on the issue of schooling for the Ainu to be addressed later in this paper, it should also be pointed out that the Ainu people have traditionally been very open to the inclusion of people of different ethnicities into their communities, the history of the adoption of babies abandoned by Wajin[1] settlers escaping Hokkaido to return to their homelands in the south being one phenomenon often relayed with pride by Ainu Elders. Additionally, it is said that any man who moved to an Ainu community and made his best efforts to adopt his ways to the traditions of that community would be welcomed as a full-fledged member of that community.[2]

While much of the sociological description found in the first half of this chapter refers to Ainu society of the past and in that sense is at best considerably removed from the reality of Ainu living in the contemporary world, it is offered to provide context in which to ground the discussion in the theme of this book, that of Indigenous educational philosophy. While I am aware of the dangers of having chosen to write in the ethnographic present, I hope that this will simultaneously be interpreted as recognition of the Ainu right

Ainu Puri: Content and Praxis 213

to freely choose to revitalize tradition from the past whenever and howsoever they might wish. In sum, in choosing to run the danger of fitting Ainu reality into pre-fabricated categories,[3] it is the author's sincere hope that the perspective made possible by so doing will open up the possibilities for discussion with a wider audience and thus serve as a springboard for a continuing and fruitful discussion on the issue of an Ainu Indigenous philosophy of education and of how that might articulate with the project of schooling.

## The Background to the Ideological Context Surrounding the Contemporary Ainu

The Ainu are the Indigenous people of the northernmost island of current Japan, Hokkaido, as well as the surrounding Kurile archipelago and the southern half of the island of Sakhalin, now both in Russian possession, as well as having formerly inhabited the northern part of the Japanese island of Honshu. They were originally a hunting-fishing-gathering society who practiced limited agriculture while engaging in extensive trade with their neighbors: the Wajin Japanese to the south and with the Russians, Chinese and other Northern peoples to the north. Their traditional territory extends 1400 kilometers from north to south, and 1600 from east to west. According to an official census in 1807,[4] the Ainu population was 26,256. According to a survey on Ainu living conditions by the Hokkaido Prefectural government[5] in 2013, this figure had not grown but rather decreased to 16,000, a point which indicates not only the unreliableness of census data, but also the fact that many contemporary Ainu are hiding their ethnic identity by passing as Wajin Japanese. Given normal reproductivity rates, it is assumed that the actual population would be significantly higher, and Ainu themselves indeed presume that the actual figure extends from three to ten times the 2013 Hokkaido Prefectural survey numbers.

Great change has been wrought upon Ainu society through the processes of being incorporated into the Japanese capitalist economy, and by assimilatory processes of colonization. While many Ainu have managed to maintain their traditional sensibilities despite extraordinary odds, the physical conditions of the Ainu world have been dramatically altered by disenfranchising property legislation and processes of national development.

During the Edo period (c. 1603–1868), traditional patterns of social organization and politics were unraveled by forced dislocation and merging of *kotan* (Ainu villages) which had formerly been independent from one another. After the start of the Meiji Era in 1868, designation of the lands of Hokkaido as terra nullius justified Meiji government appropriation of Ainu territories and their subsequent redistribution to settlers from mainland Japan. As a result of this, even the Ainu who had been fortunate enough to continue to reside in their traditional territories became guilty of "poaching" for fish and game, and "stealing" firewood or other materials necessary for their daily lives, and the Ainu traditional hunting-gathering

## 214  *Jeff Gayman*

lifestyle was decimated. In 1899, the implementation of the patrimonial and discriminatory Hokkaido Former Aborigines Protection Act capped these legal shackles by encouraging forced agrarianism amongst the Ainu.

Resulting cycles of poverty and associated discrimination have created conditions in which many Ainu choose to leave their hometowns for urban centers in search of a more materially fulfilling life, and of those few who remain in the countryside, only a limited number live in the one or two villages existing with a dense enough Ainu population to be considered remotely "traditional." In most other locations, where Ainu live at best in scattered clusters, current legislation has complicated the praxis of Ainu traditional culture by introducing systems of honorariums for "participation" in Ainu events, leading to a division between those who refuse to "practice culture for money" and those who don't, and to a confusion of all things educational as being part of the corrupted Cultural Promotion system. In this way, the context from which the original Ainu philosophy originated has changed in such a drastic way as to be almost unrecognizable. It is against these ideologies of national development, and capitalism which drive them, that the issue of Ainu educational philosophy and how it can be revitalized needs to be contextualized.

Meanwhile, the formatting of knowledge which lies at the basis of the standardized testing which drives contemporary educational processes, especially after the secondary school level, is another factor complicating the picture. Due to rapidly decreasing numbers of Ainu Elders versed in the Ainu language and cultural protocols, the process of learning the Ainu tradition through living culture bearers has become an increasingly difficult and complicated task. The question of how much to maintain and promote the Ainu tradition through such "living sources" and how much to do so through the study of historical written texts and analysis of oral literature is another pressing issue.

## Overview of Ainu Society

Ainu societal structures and practices require explanation because they are the vehicle through which the Ainu worldview manifests in everyday life. Due to varying physical environs and the influence of neighboring ethnic groups, the Ainu culture displays considerable regional variation in terms of housing, settlement patterns, livelihood, language and religion. For example, Kurile Ainu were basically sea nomads who lived in subterranean sod houses, while the Ainu of southern Hokkaido lived mainly settled lifestyles in thatched huts. Basing myself largely on research conducted by the Ainu Museum at Shiraoi, the Ainu society which I briefly describe below is that of the southern Hokkaido region, and in particular that of the Saru River drainage.

Until the start of the Meiji Era, Ainu lived in villages (*kotan*) on average consisting of 5–30 houses (*cise*), around which the *kotan* claimed sole

## Ainu Puri: Content and Praxis    215

rights to a set hunting hunting/fishing/gathering territory (*iwor*). Significant amounts of time were spent outdoors in these hunting, fishing and gathering activities, which can be quite perilous due to snowy or icy conditions, to transit on steep mountainsides, along waterways via boats, as well as due to the presence of dangerous animals such as bears, thus necessitating due caution.

In contemporary Ainu society, women are still responsible for cooking, gathering of plants, embroidery and childcare, while men take responsibility for hunting and fishing, ceremony and ritual, and the manufacture of tools used for such. "Hands that never rest" is a phrase used to describe how constant their work can be. When the author lived in the Ainu village of Nibutani for two years, one Elder from whom I learned much was fond of saying that a man is required to play dual roles of being a carpenter and a priest.[6]

Amidst such social configurations, women before the age of menopause are not allowed to hold any position of responsibility during prayer rituals and in this case have a lower status than those of men. However, they can still serve in deliberative groups responsible for major decisions regarding the *kotan*. In any case, relations between men and women in Ainu society are complementary rather than stratified and separate, as they often are interpreted to be in the West.

Social organization and political patterns deserve mention here because they are closely related to Ainu spiritual practices. Ainu follow a dual lineage system, with women tracing their lineage through the mother's side, and men tracing theirs to the father's side. Until the Meiji Era, housing arrangements were basically based upon the nuclear family, with sons moving out to live close by in separate houses upon marriage, and the youngest son remaining living the closest to his parents. Since men are responsible for prayer, which is the most crucial duty in protecting the household, and since Ainu follow a system of ancestor worship in which the unbroken descent of the male line is indispensable, in the past a widowed woman would sometimes "marry" into the household of her deceased husband until her children were old enough to live independently.

Lineage systems are significant symbolically in maintenance of pride in family history, spiritually in terms of specific ceremonies conducted only by one family, and in that they provide family crests (*itokpa*) for men, and patterns of weaving (in the chastity belt, *kut*) and embroidery for women which are handed down from generation to generation and used to be used to prevent the incidence of consanguineous marriage. Thus, until approximately a century ago in the upper reaches of the Saru River drainage, the political leader of the village was an elder member of a clan sharing the same *itokpa* and religious ceremonies.

Up until the start of the Meiji Era, while the Ainu had no police system, breaches of community sanction such as murder, adultery and theft, including trespassing onto another *kotan*'s *iwor* to obtain game, were dealt with

## 216  *Jeff Gayman*

quite severely by a court-like system wherein the trial conducted by two male representatives of the plaintiff and defendant was overseen by a number of elders who served as the jury. Trials, which were known as *caranke*, consisted of the two representatives facing one another and debating until one had thoroughly exhausted his argument, at which time his opponent won the case. Punishment could come in the form of payment of goods to the bereaved family (in the case of one *kotan*) or offended community (in the case of inter-*kotan* battles), a public thrashing or, in severe cases, banishment from the community, although in the latter case it was possible for an individual to be penitent by taking up residence in another *kotan* and doing his best to make amends by becoming a model citizen there. As far as the author can tell, considerable flexibility and largesse in terms of reaching reconciliation were made possible by this system of community courts centered around the *caranke* debate. This system also serves to foreground the crucial and continuing importance of oratory within Ainu society.

Until the Meiji Era, in the case that two clans occupied the same village, it is generally accepted that the more eloquent clan headsman would be the one who became the leader of the village. One gauge of qualification for leadership in such cases is known by the Ainu phrase *siretok, rametok, pawetok*, which roughly translates as possession of *siretok*, beauty (internal beauty or moral fiber, generosity); *rametok*, pluck, or courage; and pawetok (eloquence). As can be gleaned from the above description, mere eloquence alone was not sufficient to win *caranke* debates, and considerable odds could be at stake if a situation of war was imminent between two *kotan* or Ainu from two different regions which necessitated powers of discrimination and courageous foresight. In any case, all major decisions were conducted in tandem with the Elders of the village, and sometimes in consultation with a shaman.

Likewise, until the Meiji Era, *Kotan-kor-kur*, or village leaders, in addition to defending their constituencies, also bore the responsibility of accurately listening to and conveying news to their constituencies from the leaders of other villages. It should also be mentioned that until this day Elders who serve as officiants for large communal prayers, in other words, the ones who guide the ceremony and lead the prayers, also carry a heavy spiritual responsibility and are expected to be highly versed in the complex language and protocols of the ritual.

## The Ainu Worldview

Ainu elder Osuga Rueko[7] has stated that the primary ethics embodied in Ainu society are 1) reverence for the *kamuy* (Ainu gods), 2) respect for family and ancestors, particularly reflected in care for the elderly, 3) moderation (not harvesting more than necessary), 4) gratitude for the benefits which one has received, 5) offering help to those in need and, 6) not cheating or hurting others. In order to appreciate the core of this normative philosophy of

## Ainu Puri: Content and Praxis 217

the Ainu people, understanding of the structure of Ainu society delineated above must be comprehended in combination with a grasp of the basic Ainu worldview, which I explain here.

To begin with, the Ainu have a phrase, *urespa mosir*, which roughly translates as a world in which everything is mutually fostered by one another. In order to comprehend the philosophy behind this metaphysical concept, any discussion of Ainu spirituality must begin with an exploration of the Ainu relation to their *kamuy*, which can be understood broadly as gods, spirits or deities. In the Ainu belief, two worlds, the temporal, *Ainu mosir*, or the land of humans, and the metaphysical, *kamuy mosir*, or the land of the gods, exist simultaneously, and are understood to be populated by humans and things, and by gods and the spirits of ancestors, respectively.

Gods, which are cognate and basically have a human form when in *kamuy mosir*, move back and forth between the material and metaphysical world, providing the material elements necessary for the sustenance of human life by appearing in the human world in the form of animals, plants, natural phenomenon and so on. They might descend to the temporal world clothed in fur and meat, as the bear god, *kimun kamuy*, or in the shape of an Ainu traditional house, a boat or so on, depending upon the qualities of the particular god. All natural phenomenon over which human beings have no control, such as fire, wind and thunder, and all man-made objects without which the Ainu would be seriously in trouble, for instance houses, boats or items such as mortars and pestles, are thus considered to be gods, and thereby within the Ainu worldview must be treated with gratitude and reverence.

In other words, in this conception of the universe inhabited by gods, things and humans, humans and gods possess reciprocal duties and rights: gods have a duty to provide sustenance to humans and they have the right to receive tribute in the form of prayer and offerings; humans have the right to receive sustenance from the gods but they also have the duty to offer gratitude. The only talent humans are deemed to be endowed with is their ability to use language and to do ritual. Through this, man seeks to create harmony between humans, gods and things, and fulfills his duty in the scheme of things.

For example, when an animal or object's role on earth has finished they are "sent back" to *kamuy mosir* by the Ainu in what is known as a spirit-sending ceremony, accompanied by much praise and lavish offerings of sake, meat, dumplings, fruits and so on. At this time it is said that they assemble all of the other gods in *kamuy mosir* to relay how well-hosted they were by the humans and to convey what a wonderful time they had in *Ainu mosir*. They express their desire to return as quickly as possible to *Ainu mosir* and at the same time convince all the other gods to do so as well. Gods who have traveled to *Ainu mosir* many times thus accrue prestige in the world of the gods.

For this reason the Ainu perform prayer ceremonies regularly throughout the different seasons of the year, such as at the new year's, at the beginning

## 218  *Jeff Gayman*

of the harvest and so on. They also conduct them at times of celebration or grief, such as weddings and house-raisings or funerals, or at any other time when deemed necessary or appropriate, such as the onset of famine or the threat of an epidemic.[8]

Prayer ceremonies always involve the use of fire, as well as generally involving offering of a gift of alcohol, which is poured into the offertory vessel by someone other than the officiant, thus necessitating participation by more than one person. Although also held at the domestic level as well, their basic character is communal.

Prayer ceremonies held at the communal level are a vehicle for effecting more powerful influence upon the gods; the more participants the better, but upon the condition that the feelings and thoughts of each individual must also be pure. Interestingly, if community member's conduct has been good and yet prayers for beneficence are not met with witness-able changes in material circumstances, the Ainu have the right to argue with the gods to effect change. Effectiveness of prayer ceremonies can be gauged by witness-able changes in the environment, as well as by the appearance of *kamuy* in dreams.

Additionally, and equally significant for our explorations into Ainu normative philosophy, is the importance allotted to one's ancestors. Ancestors also play a vital role in the Ainu belief system, as the symbol of all prior good deeds done by one's family, and as residents of *kamuy mosir* who must be nourished by the physical offerings of food by their descendants in *Ainu mosir*. Thus, accompanying all major prayer ceremonies held throughout the year, the Ainu engage in *sinurappa* or *icarpa*, ancestral-remembrance ceremonies. During a *sinurappa*, the names of ones' ancestors five generations into the past are recited, food is broken and offered at a makeshift altar, and prayers given that it be delivered to all of the ancestors in the other world. This is thought to be the only way for someone who has passed into the spirit world to be able to obtain food, and for this reason the Ainu place critical importance on not allowing one's lineage to become broken, as well as in behaving in a manner befitting of being remembered by one's descendants.

In other words, in the Ainu belief, in order for one's name to be remembered five generations into the future, one must have lived a sufficiently appropriate and upright life by following Ainu customs and contributing to the community appropriately to the normative values of community and cooperation. Thus, in Ainu society, the ultimate compliment which can be paid to a person is for them to be referred to as *Ainu nenoan Ainu*, someone revered as a "human amongst humans."

In this way, the norms listed by Osuga-san of reverence for the *kamuy* (through ritual), respect for family and ancestors (again, via ritual), gratitude for the benefits which one has received (as gifts from the *kamuy*), and moderation (for example, avoidance of greedy harvesting of nature's bounty, which is a gift from the *kamuy*), can all be understood in terms of

*Ainu Puri: Content and Praxis*   219

the above-described Ainu epistemology. Human life is therefore basically guided by two simple (as one Ainu acquaintance put it, "rational") maxims of respect and modesty, which articulate in day-to-day life in various manifestations, as I will explore in more detail below.

In any event, a worldview such as the Ainus' is significant in that it accentuates the importance of a positive attitude, responsible engagement with one's environment and the circumstances of one's life, as well as belief in the power of words to change one's fate.

## Philosophical Norms within Ainu Society

Having overviewed the Ainu worldview and the general value parameters which it generates for action in Ainu society, in this section I turn to more specific norms by which these values are conveyed to future generations, a point crucial for any examination of education.

Teaching and learning within traditional Ainu society are embedded within the worldview of the *kamuy* described above as it manifests particularly in the life of the family at home, as well as in the experience and observation of communal activities and ceremonies within the Ainu *kotan*. As one Elder born in 1935[9] put it, "the space around the hearth was my classroom." At the same time, skills such as oratory, which are so important for men, as well as the complicated ritual language of Ainu ceremony, are imbibed through actual observation while participating in Ainu social life through events such as weddings, funerals, ground-breaking ceremonies and other periodic communal prayer functions.

Since the two realms of the household and the community are the main ones in which teaching and learning take place in traditional Ainu society, an examination of the particular axioms or norms which give shape to behavior there is in order. In order to contextualize this examination I will occasionally be utilizing the example of the *Iyomante* Bear-Spirit Sending Ceremony. This is because ceremonies in Ainu society represent the culmination of the many skills[10] honed at home, required by both men and women, at the same time as providing the opportunity to share thanks with gods, ancestors and neighbors communally. The Iyomante is the largest of all Spirit Sending Ceremonies, lasting for three days, and is often taken to be the quintessential manifestation of Ainu culture, as it combines reverence for Kimun-kamuy, the bear god, considered to be one of the most powerful spirits in the Ainu pantheon, with the Spirit-sending ceremony, a central Ainu ritual for returning the spirits of things which have fulfilled their duty in this world, to kamuy-mosir. Abbreviated Iyomante take place in the mountains by hunters, but in the three-day Iyomante a bear which has been raised by the local villagers with great care from the age of being a cub, is sacrificed.

First, common to both the realm of the hearth and that of the community gathering space is the value placed in Ainu society on the spoken word,

## 220   *Jeff Gayman*

which is the lifeblood of oratory but also forms the backbone of the Ainu oral literature, a vital element of home life. The Ainu maxim *siretok, rametok, pawetok*, which was introduced above as a gauge of qualification for leadership, indicates Ainu moral and aesthetic priorities evident in both the human relations aspect of community functions, as well as in the material culture which is ever present in community gatherings as well as in the everyday life of the household. *Pawetok* (eloquence) constitutes a verbalized conception of the Ainu priority on the value of the spoken word.

The Ainu have a saying that "Words are something that can energize people, and they are also something which can cut them down like a sword." In line with the gravity of this adage, as related above, *caranke*, or extended debate, was the central means by which legal and diplomatic processes were carried out within and between *kotan*, and thus oral prowess was an integral and important aspect in the maintenance of community integrity as well as autonomy.

Simultaneously, however, the Ainu oral tradition, often borne by women cultural bearers, formed a central part of education and entertainment, especially within the home. Granted that in some regions of Ainu country as much as half of the year was spent indoors snowed in by winter, the Ainu have one of the most extensive and sophisticated oral traditions in the world. *Ucaskuma*, or moral tales, tend to be told in prose, often ending with an admonition to the listener to uphold the moral of their story. *Yukar*, heroic tales, and *kamuy yukar*, mythic tales, on the other hand, often tend to be sung in a lyrical manner according to a melody unique to the reciter or to his family. They are accompanied by the beating of rhythm by a stick on the wooden frame of the fireplace, and tailored to the particular audience, who respond with rousing shouts at particularly exciting or dramatic climaxes in the story, thus multiplying the piece's entertainment value. *Kamuy yukar* involve personification of Ainu deities, in that they are usually recited as if being told in the first person by a particular deity. Their charming perspectives remind us of the Ainu's insightful perception into the natural world with which they are so intimate. Content is commonly reflective of keen observation of animal behavior, and thus also serves a didactic function.

To this day, recitals of these various types of Ainu oral literature often take place when people gather together for leisure, accentuating their social function. In this sense, the conclusion of *Iyomante* Bear Spirit-Sending Ceremonies with a recital for the departing bear spirit by a woman Elder of a *yukar*, which is cut off at the very climax of the story in order to arouse the bear god's desire to return to earth yet once more to hear the conclusion of the tale, has a strong social element. The ongoing priority being placed in contemporary Ainu society on the memory and recitation of oral literature thus can be witnessed in upcoming generations' intimacy with its entertainment value as engaged communication between reciter and listener, as well as perhaps also additionally with the prestige associated with being able to recite a yukar in premiere social events such as the *Iyomante*.

Second, the standard of *siretok*, or beauty. Another aspect of everyday life in Ainu society in which Ainu reverence for the natural world and the deities that it represents manifests is the elegance and sophistication of Ainu embroidery, carving, weaving and mat-making. Beauty continues to be a guiding priority within the Ainu culture, albeit perhaps at times somewhat removed from its original context. Designs carved into knife sheathes and embroidered onto the outer surface of clothing are believed to have the function of protecting their wearer from misdeed by evil spirits. On the other hand, carved and whittled *inaw* prayer sticks to be used in prayer ceremonies or installed into altars are customarily carved and whittled with the highest degree of precision and symmetry, befitting to the god whom they represent, while *ikupasuy* libation (prayer) sticks used to convey the participant's wishes to the gods during the Ainu prayer ceremonies similarly are carved with the greatest deal of care and affection.

Indeed, the mark of a grown man capable of participating in an Ainu *kamuynomi* is that he is capable of carving his own *inaw*, while the ability for a man to elaborately carve the sheathe of a *makiri* hunting knife, and for a woman to embroider hand coverings are the prerequisite for marriage, as the items are traditionally exchanged to one's partner during the marriage ceremony. Since Ainu men customarily carved their own hunting implements, skill in carving was seen as being indispensably linked to success in hunting. In this way, the norms of Ainu life, tightly interwoven into the holistic life philosophy of co-existence with the *kamuy*, simultaneously carry a highly practical function. "Even without a word for 'art',"[11] the Ainu people's aesthetic sense—as manifested in items which today are commonly seen en-masse during prayer ceremonies—is responsible for some of the most beautiful man-made objects created from natural materials that this author has ever seen.

If Ainu "art" is the medium by which Ainu devotion is expressed aesthetically, Ainu song and dance is the affective medium through which it is shared with the deities and with one's neighbors in communal prayer gatherings and weddings or other celebratory occasions, as well as being the "hook" which today draws many Ainu children and youth into Ainu cultural praxis. Song and dance were traditionally a means for Ainu to share their joy with the gods during celebratory occasions, such as the Iyomante Ceremony, and as such, in the present-day liveliness and exuberance are encouraged during practice sessions at Cultural Preservation Societies and elsewhere.

In any event, the importance of the community as unit of communion with the *kamuy* is reflected in social values as well. Moderation, modesty, caring and hard work are the virtues which see Ainu through hard times. On the other hand, gratitude and generosity are the hallmark of the Ainu communal ceremony, which also serves as a chance for participants to let loose and share their joy for life with abandon.

Opportunities for children to participate in such communal ceremonies have the educational function of exposing them to aesthetic, linguistic and

## 222   *Jeff Gayman*

cultural manifestations of Ainu knowledge and their associated values/norms, priming them affectively for participation in Ainu society. In general, Ainu children, who are seen as being "closer to god," are to this day treated with great care by Ainu adults. For example, it is not uncommon to witness elder children or neighbors taking care of an Ainu child at a community event, nor for a child to receive a meal at a neighbor's house. In this sense, Ainu education should very much be an experientially and community-oriented one. Whether these customs still continue in the home today is an issue which I will address in the section following the next.

### Teaching and Learning in Traditional Ainu Society

First, multiple Ainu children's games are designed to foster agility and endurance necessary for hunting and fishing. In the past, from the age of six or seven, Ainu children were also allowed to learn the basics of Ainu livelihood by helping out with everyday household chores. In regard to the topic of rites of passage, the Ainu Museum team claims that successful participation in community ritual, usually around one's mid-teens, was a rite of passage for young men to begin to engage in hunting and fishing activities, while for a woman being tattooed was the final rite of passage before becoming eligible to be married.

To venture an educated hypothesis, in line with the importance of orality and the oral tradition in Ainu culture and the Ainu dictum that, "That which is written down is forgotten," memory is probably the key element to Ainu teaching and learning. This predilection is encapsulated in the way that Ainu youth heading into the mountains are encouraged to memorize the location of all flora important to the local Ainu *kotan* so that they will be able to gather them immediately when need arises. Meanwhile, until the 1960s inside of the *cise*, women would similarly instill a sense into their daughters for Ainu patterns by tracing a design into the ashes of the hearth, which they would then erase and have their children recreate from memory. Finally, all important dictums for life in the Ainu *kotan*, societal protocols, as well as fascinating insights into the surrounding natural world, are conveyed through the medium of the Ainu oral literature, which one Elder[12] referred to as a class in "Ainu ethics."[13]

Ainu Elder Osuga Rueko[14] has thus relayed that Ainu children were exposed in their daily lives to chances to learn "a great many things," and that they were educated through the medium of the Ainu oral literature. She also claimed, without giving any specific examples, that Ainu children were taught "with ingenious methods," likening the teaching method of Ainu adults and grandparents to "expending half of one's entire energy (in teaching)." One Ainu elder has relayed the story of how his grandmother got him to ponder the importance of a person's name by giving him a piece of candy per day whenever he wrongly answered her riddle as to "the most important thing in the world." Another Elder's oft-quoted episode relays the enticement of the elder as an infant by his grandmother, who coaxed him with the words, "Please get some water for me now, and then when you grow old I shall repay you in kind." Alternatively, the beauty of the higher language of prayer and the dignity with which Ainu Elder prayer officiants direct their underlings to perform the requisite stages of the rituals, possess an enticing allure to youth which stimulates their desire to master these skills in hopes of someday taking the Elder's place. On the other hand, the pedagogical method of "teaching with the fist" exemplified in one middle-aged Ainu friend's admonition to "bring a helmet" along to a meeting with a former Ainu bear hunter, reflect the danger inherent in the Ainu's everyday environment which continues to effect an influence until this day.

For now, if I were to venture any normative statement regarding Ainu education, it would have to be one based on a notion of the engaged relationality in all of these cases between teacher and student. All pedagogical techniques share the common factor of intense engagement between pupil and teacher.

## Contemporary Considerations

Ainu spiritual belief hints to us the importance of relationality to our natural environment, of learning *from* nature, the role of genealogy as a record of history and source of sense of responsibility for one's posterity, and a confirmation of community values in events such as ceremony and in the care and raising of children. Traditional Ainu teaching methods allowed for children and youth to absorb these values via inculcation through oral literature, as well as via experiential learning of the skills necessary for life and citizenship during everyday life within the home and the community. Teaching was something which was carried out with intense engagement. In terms of education, I believe that these values and methods, to a large degree, are still plausible ones amongst many Ainu individuals and communities.

Yet despite the above rich legacy of community values, how the Ainu philosophy might be merged with the modern project of schooling is an issue which the dampening and fragmenting experiences of colonialism have served to obscure and to make ambivalent. To give one illustration, I once inquired of a well-respected Ainu woman Elder about Ainu methods of child-raising, only to be told that, "I'd say that would depend on the family; different strokes for different folks."

Whether the contemporary reality of Ainu society is one in which neo-liberal trends of fragmentation of society and erosion of traditional values have proceeded to the degree that methods of Ainu child-raising/education are no longer mutually visible in the community (a potent possibility), or whether they have always been implicit, as the Elder's offhand utterance seems to suggest, is something which only the Ainu themselves can say. Yet one thing which can be said with certainty is that policy support which

## 224   Jeff Gayman

might allow for a communal exploration within Ainu society upon this issue is yet not seen to be forthcoming.

When it comes to the question of the application of the philosophy to the phenomena of present-day education, I feel it necessary to draw the line with caveats about the danger of outsider interpretation/appropriation, the nature of contemporary schooling in Japan, and the general status of Ainu knowledge and ethnic identity in Hokkaido and in Japan. Particularly, if one is to distinguish between Ainu philosophy and Ainu educational philosophy, much to the chagrin of many Ainu people, as a result of lack of proper knowledge of Ainu history and due to popular fad, the former receives multifarious attention whereas the latter receives none. The phenomenon of contemporary schooling in Japan, on the other hand is a process which is very much driven by materialist values and a reductionist, compartmentalizing perspective of knowledge, as well as narratives of the superiority of Wajin culture which do not mesh well with Ainu identity nor encourage their communitarian values and methods of education.

Inheriting the tenets of post-colonial theory, which emphasizes the self-determination of Indigenous peoples as well as a valuation of all aspects of their cultures, languages and knowledge systems, indigenous educators from throughout the world have advocated a "Philosophy of Indigenous Education." Such a philosophy encompasses the Indigenous worldview, covers all stages of life of the individual from birth to death, recognizes the Indigenous right to self-determination in all matters pertaining to the development and growth of Indigenous cultures and societies, contributes to such growth on all fronts—economic, social, legal and political—is anti-racist in nature, and fundamentally recognizes and celebrates Indigenous culture, religion and society as Indigenous people choose to perceive and to practice them.[15]

In the Japanese case, on the contrary, Ainu policy in general still remains largely in the hands of Wajin specialists, scholars and bureaucrats, who refuse to admit to Japan's colonialist past. Indeed, they encourage the legacy of such by refusing to allow Ainu collective rights to be recognized on any front, including that of education. In this way, great change on policy fronts remains to be seen in order for a holistic application of one Indigenous philosophy of education, that of the Ainu people, to be realized in a comprehensive manner.

In this sense, in analyzing issues of potential application to education of Ainu philosophy, context is everything. For many Ainu people, the very project of examining the applicability of Ainu philosophies to the contemporary institution of schooling could be considered a wrong and painful one since their society and culture have been wrought by processes of colonization.[16] After all, schools have historically functioned as agents of colonization and assimilation.

At the very least, introducing elements of the Ainu philosophy piecemeal into the current mainstream curriculum mandated by the Japanese Course

## Ainu Puri: Content and Praxis   225

of Study in a diversionary fashion will not suffice. To isolate Ainu philosophy from the context in which it originated is tantamount to the appropriation which has been conducted against Indigenous peoples all throughout the history of colonization. Only if contextualized in a framework of Ainu empowerment can it rightfully be addressed. Then the true value of this grand East Asian Indigenous tradition may finally be recognized.

An important realization in the Ainu case is that there exists a multitude of attitudes and identities, as well as a degree of embrace of each, amongst the various age generations, and between various regions of Hokkaido, not to mention the rest of Japan or Russia. Recent changes in societal attitudes toward "Otherness," brought about at least in part, ironically, by the implementation of the 1997 Ainu Cultural Promotion Act, have made it easier to come out and live "as an Ainu." Some of the "traditionalists" who "refuse to practice culture for money" have joined forces with Ainu college students and curator-trainees to create virtual online communities for speaking and learning the Ainu language and for sharing Ainu history and culture with one another. Fitful attempts at teaching children the Ainu language are also being made. On the other hand, one young man in Biratori has chosen to prioritize the Ainu philosophy in his own way by becoming self-employed as a professional deer hunter. It is they who are likely to be the driving force behind deliberations regarding the future of the "Ainu philosophy."

## Notes

1. Mainstream ethnic Japanese.
2. Incidentally, I must make it clear from the outset that I am not Ainu, nor can I claim to any high degree to be a representative of the Ainu. I took on the writing of this chapter fully aware that time constrictions would probably forbid me from gaining extensive comment from Ainu research collaborators on my draft prior to submission. While the observations here are grounded in thirteen years of fieldwork, life, and work with the Ainu people centered on the theme of commencing an official Ainu Indigenous educational program, and while I have made every effort to cite information other than that gathered through ethnographic field methods, the conclusions offered here must be taken as mine, and all mistakes in content those of the author and the author alone.
3. cf Smith, 1996. Linda Tuhiwai Smith, *Decolonizing Methodologies* (London: Zed Books, Ltd, 1999).
4. Brett Walker, "Foreign Contagions, Ainu Medical Culture and Conquest." in *Ainu: Spirit of a Northern People*, ed. William Fitzhugh and Chisato Dubreuil (Washington, DC: Arctic Studies Center, National Museum of Natural History, Smithsonian Institution in Association with University of Washington Press, 1999), 106.
5. Hokkaido Government, Department of Environment and Lifestyle, Administrative Division, Ainu Affairs Office, *To Understand the Ainu*, trans. Foundation for Research and Promotion of Ainu Culture (Hokkaido, Japan: Author, 2000), (Revs. 2001).
6. For lack of any other expressions, he used the Japanese terms obousan, a Buddhist priest responsible for conducting funerals and ancestral-remembrance ceremonies, and guji, Shinto priest responsible for conducting ground-breaking

# 226 *Jeff Gayman*

and roof-raising ceremonies and weddings, even though the underlying beliefs and protocols of these three traditions historically had nothing to do with one another.

7. Rueko Osuga, *Yukara ni Motoduku Ainu no Kokoro* (The Heart of the Ainu as Seen in Yukar [Ainu Oral Literature]). Talk given at Sapporo Jyu Gakkou Yu (Sapporo Freedom School), 25 June 2013.
8. Recently, Ainu ceremonies have also been conducted to initiate major international conferences and gatherings held in Hokkaido or in Japan.
9. A quote from Ukaji Shizue of Urakawa on the radio. Source currently unlocalizable.
10. It is said that preparation for a Bear-Spirit Sending Ceremony begins in earnest two weeks prior.
11. Phrase borrowed from Fitzhugh and Dubreuil, Ainu, p. 286.
12. Yamamichi Yasuko of Nibutani, personal communication.
13. Similarly, drawing of patterns into the hearth has been referred to as "training for the eyes," and recitation of the oral tradition as "training for the ears."
14. Osuga, *The Heart of the Ainu.*
15. World Indigenous Peoples Conference on Education (WIPCE) (1993). The Coolangatta Statement on Indigenous Rights in Education. Coolangatta, New South Wales, Australia: Author.
16. Amidst remaining prejudices and concomitant general reluctance to openly broadcast one's Ainu identity, many Ainu cultural bearers seem to have stopped short of even considering the possibilities. Others ignore the option of schooling full stop in favor of personal efforts via unofficial group praxis.

## Bibliography

Ainu Minzoku Hakubutsukan, eds. *Ainu Bunka no Kiso Chisiki* (Fundamentals of the Ainu Culture). Tokyo: Soufukan, 1993.

Fitzhugh, William and Chisato Dubreuil. *Ainu: Spirit of a Northern People.* Washington, DC: Arctic Studies Center, National Museum of Natural History, Smithsonian Institution in Association with University of Washington Press, 1999.

Fujimura, Hisakazu. *Ainu, Kamigami to Issho ni Ikiru Hitobito* (Ainu, People Who Live Together with the Spirits). Tokyo: Fukusei Shoten, 1985.

Gayman, Jeffry. "Toward Cultural Congruency and Self-Determination in Ainu Education." MA thesis, University of Alaska, Fairbanks, 2005.

———. "The Ainu." In *Native Nations: The Survival of Fourth World Peoples*, edited by Sharlotte Neely, 55–72. Vancouver: J. Charlton Publishing, 2014.

Hokkaido Government, Department of Environment and Lifestyle, Administrative Division, Ainu Affairs Office. *To Understand the Ainu.* Translated by Foundation for Research and Promotion of Ainu Culture. Hokkaido, Japan: Author, 2000. (Revs. 2001).

Kayano, Shigeru. "Ainu Ethnic and Linguistic Revival." In *Indigenous Minorities and Education: Australian and Japanese Perspectives of Their Indigenous Peoples, the Ainu, Aborigines and Torres Strait Islanders*, edited by Noel Loos and Takeshi Osanai, 360–367. Tokyo: Sanyusha, 1993.

Keira, Masanori. "Ainu no Kokoro (The Soul of the Ainu)." Accessed December 2, 2005. www13.plala.or.jp/yayyukar/sikiainu.html.

———. *Kita no Saijiki: Ainu no Sekai e* (A Northern Floral Tale: Into the World of the Ainu). Tokyo: Commons, 2008.

Keira, Tomoko. *Ainu no Shiki: Fuchi no Tutaeru Kokoro* (Four Seasons of the Ainu: The Heart That Fuchi Conveyed). Tokyo: Ashiya Shoten, 2003.

Osuga, Rueko. *Yukara ni Motoduku Ainu no Kokoro* (The Heart of the Ainu as Seen in Yukar [Ainu Oral Literature]). Talk Given at Sapporo Jyu Gakkou Yu (Sapporo Freedom School), 25 June 2013.

Peng, Fred C. and Peter Geiser. *The Ainu: The Past in the Present*. Hiroshima, Japan: Bunka Hyoron, 1977.

Reagan, Timothy. *Non-Western Educational Traditions: Indigenous Approaches to Educational Thought and Practice* (3rd ed.). New Jersey and London: Lawrence Erlbaum Associates, 2005.

Sannyo-Aino, Toyooka. "The Future of Humankind and the Creation of a Third Philosophy." In *Indigenous Minorities and Education: Australian and Japanese Perspectives of Their Indigenous Peoples, the Ainu, Aborigines and Torres Strait Islanders*, edited by Noel Loos and Takeshi Osanai, 250–260. Tokyo: Sanyusha, 1993.

Smith, Linda Tuhiwai. *Decolonizing Methodologies*. London: Zed Books, Ltd., 1999.

Walker, Brett. "Foreign Contagions, Ainu Medical Culture and Conquest." In *Ainu: Spirit of a Northern People*, edited by William Fitzhugh and Chisato Dubreuil, 102–108. Washington, DC: Arctic Studies Center, National Museum of Natural History, Smithsonian Institution in Association with University of Washington Press, 1999.

World Indigenous Peoples Conference on Education (WIPCE). *The Coolangatta Statement on Indigenous Rights in Education*. Coolangatta, New South Wales, Australia: Author, 1993.

Yamamoto, Tasuke. "Ainu Minzoku no Shite Kyoiku" ("Ainu People's Education for Children"). In *Kyoiku no Naka no Ainu Minzoku: Sono Genjyo to Kyoiku Jissen* (The Ainu People in Education: Present Circumstances and Praxis), edited by Inoue Atsushi, 72–75. Tokyo: Ayumi Shuppan, 1981.

# 12 Everyday Hope
## Indigenous Aims of Education in Settler-Colonial Societies

*Joanna Kidman, Adreanne Ormond, and Liana MacDonald*

What should be the aims of education for indigenous students in settler societies? In the wake of nineteenth-century British colonial invasion and occupation, indigenous philosophies of education around the world were interrupted or publicly silenced as imperial schooling systems were overlaid across existing native practice. British colonial authorities placed indigenous children at the centre of the 'civilizing mission'—[1]establishing an educational order aimed at creating a new kind of citizen; one who would adopt British ways of life, uphold British imperial values and 'pass muster' in anglo-settler society.[2] Indigenous children continue to be a focus of state education policy in many former British colonies today but while reference is frequently made to the importance of including indigenous ways of being and knowing in the classroom, often little is done to put this into practice meaningfully.[3] Throughout the twentieth and early twenty-first centuries, however, indigenous education movements in Canada, New Zealand, Australia and the Unites States have reasserted, or indeed, reinvented native epistemologies and ontologies within and beyond the colonial educational encounter.

In this chapter we turn our attention to the aims of education in the Antipodean South and explore what it means to be a native citizen in a settler-colonial environment of ongoing cultural and ethnic tension. We begin by placing the colonizer at the centre of our analysis to explain the contested nature of educational philosophies in settler-colonial states. Focusing firstly on nineteenth-century New Zealand, we look at how the highly racialized political environment of the colonial period shaped the aims of the state-run Native schooling system and the ways that Victorian ideas about racial hierarchies contributed to this. Then, drawing on Charles Mills's ideas about the Racial Contract,[4] we explore how these beliefs continue to influence state educational philosophies for indigenous children. In the second part of the chapter, we examine contemporary Māori responses to the imperial legacy and interrogate the ethical possibilities of indigenous everyday hope, a transgressive *docta spes* that provides native children both with a counter-response to settler-colonial educational aims and a strategic framework for mobilizing indigenous ways of knowing and being. Ernst Bloch writes of the *docta spes* as a form of educated or informed hope which provides a

*Everyday Hope: Indigenous Education Aims*  229

concrete 'methodology' for people to act collectively in the interests of their own becoming. This concept resonates with many contemporary Māori educational initiatives, and we draw on it here to distinguish between political expressions of hope geared towards liberation and more generic expressions of optimism.[5]

## The Treaty of Waitangi

One of the distinguishing features of colonization in New Zealand was that colonial authorities, on behalf of the British monarch, entered into a Treaty with Māori leaders that laid out the terms of the future relationship between Māori and the Crown.[6] This agreement, known as the Treaty of Waitangi, was signed in 1840. It gave Māori and their descendants the same legal rights and protections as British subjects. As well, Māori were promised collective rights to live as Māori and to retain full and exclusive chieftainship over their lands, villages, properties and treasured parts of their culture and ways of life. In signing the Treaty, Māori believed they were entering into a sacred partnership with the Crown to create a nation-state together. The problem was that two versions of the Treaty existed, one in English and the other in Māori, and they did not match up. Almost before the ink was dry, the Crown reneged on promises it had made, initiating an aggressive quest for land and power that led to an extended period of violent conflict in the colony.

Within the racial polity that emerged in New Zealand, the notion of contract (or Treaty) was seen by colonial authorities as a decisive signifier of civilized and civic peoples. At first glance, the Treaty was an apparent recognition that formal agreements could be made with the indigenous inhabitants.[7] However, central to the concept of contract is the notion of consent and in settler-colonial societies, ideas about consent can be slippery[8]—sometimes little more than a legal or moral fiction used to legitimize colonization.[9] In New Zealand, the contested nature of consent is evidenced not only in ongoing Crown breaches of the Treaty of Waitangi but also in the ways that the social contract between Māori and Pākehā [peoples of European descent or settler heritage] is enacted in state education environments, as we discuss in the section below.

## Settler-Colonial Aims of Education in New Zealand

Education played a critical role in the British colonial enterprise.[10] In nineteenth-century New Zealand, a rapidly expanding rural sector provided food and raw materials for export to the 'mother land'.[11] Alongside the Empire-centric curriculum, schooling in the colony was heavily focused on educating future agricultural, manual and domestic workers.[12] But from its inception, Victorian notions about the role of racial hierarchies in defining various degrees and levels of humanity underpinned the philosophies and aims of the state education system.[13] As a form of ideological conditioning, a primary purpose of schooling was to instil British values in the young and connect successive generations of children to the imperial project.[14] Indeed, a central tenet of colonial education was to forge a sense of belonging to the putative nation-state as well as foster a strong identification with the distant 'mother country.'[15] This was a "spiritual creed of empire";[16] an ethos of imperial glory that nurtured and maintained patriotic links and associations with Britain. Implicit in these ideas was the concept of a unified and unifying Englishness that could be passed through colonial education systems to the children of the British Empire, including to an extent, its native citizens.[17] While this was a fundamental premise of colonial schooling in British territories around the globe and one that was deeply enmeshed with imperial beliefs about British moral and racial superiority over native populations, in New Zealand, it was also implicated in late imperial era rule over Māori peoples.[18]

A system of state-run Native elementary schools was introduced in New Zealand in 1867 during an especially turbulent period. Relationships between colonial authorities and Māori had been increasingly volatile in the preceding years as the New Zealand Wars raged across the North Island.[19] These Wars involved a series of violent armed conflicts between the colonial government, sometimes supported by British Imperial troops, and Māori tribes. Conflict began after British promises made in the Treaty of Waitangi that Māori would retain undisturbed possession of their lands and ways of life had largely been broken. In the years following the signing of the Treaty, Māori communities around the country defended themselves and their lands against wave upon wave of colonial invasion. James Belich writes that these conflicts were not, as some have suggested, "storms in a teacup or gentlemanly bouts of fisticuffs, but bitter bloody struggles, as important to New Zealand as were the Civil Wars to England and the United States."[20] In this respect, the New Zealand Wars were not simply about an unjust colonial land grab, they also were a battle over who would define the systems of power in a divided and heavily racialized nation-state in the future.

Patrick Wolfe argues that invasion "is a structure not an event"[21] and this was certainly the case in New Zealand. The military might that was brought to bear on small tribal communities led to large swathes of Māori land being placed under colonial control by the mid-1860s. Four years prior to the establishment of the Native School system, the colonial government sensing victory over North Island Māori, passed the 1863 New Zealand Settlements Act which allowed land to be confiscated from Māori tribes that had fought against the Crown. This Act, along with others that came later, led to widespread dispossession of Māori people from their tribal lands, much of which were later sold off to meet the demands of a massive influx of settlers who were arriving in search a new life in the colony. By the time the Native School system was introduced, the settler population outnumbered Māori,[22] many of whom were by then landless and living in penury.

The timing of the establishment of the Native Schools system was significant. Heavy fighting was still taking place in various districts, but by

*Everyday Hope: Indigenous Education Aims*   231

1867, less overtly aggressive forms of colonial rule were beginning to find favour and schooling was at the heart of this thinking.[23] Native uprisings in India and elsewhere in the middle and latter decades of the nineteenth century had shown the limits of coercive or armed rule over indigenous groups.[24] In response, many colonial governments began to look towards a "more hegemonic assertion of colonial power."[25] Education administrators in New Zealand considered that a state-run system of schooling for Māori children would be an efficient means of securing British dominance through the assimilation of its youngest native inhabitants.[26] But this view was tempered by an awareness, based on witnessing staunch resistance to colonial invasion during the Wars, that Māori would not quietly submit to the assimilative values in the school curriculum and education policy. Hugh Carleton, an Auckland School inspector and Member of Parliament, suggested that rather than force the issue of state schooling, Māori should take the initiative in requesting for schools to be built in their districts,

> If we hunt them into education as we have hunted them into selling their lands, a spirit of resistance will naturally be engendered. . . . Make education part of the Runanga [Māori tribal councils]; give the direction of it to themselves. Let them feel it is their own work.[27]

To this end, consultation with Māori communities was built into aspects of the schooling system but the reins of curriculum control lay firmly with the Department of Native Affairs and later with the Department of Education. Many Māori communities were, in fact, eager for Native Schools to be established in their districts and were closely involved with the school committees that were set up in each region to oversee the day-to-day management of the schools.[28] While the official aims of native schooling were directed towards an assimilationist agenda, Māori had their own plans for the education of their children. Literacy, in particular, was a high priority and some families insisted on English-medium instruction.[29] There was a sense of urgency in several Māori communities about gaining this knowledge. This was a period when Crown agents had behaved duplicitously in many of their land dealings with Māori and these transactions had been conducted in written English. As James Belich notes, "[l]iteracy in Māori alone gave Pākehā a monopoly over what Māori could read."[30] This monopoly had not always been used honestly or in good faith by government representatives and many Māori had lost land as a consequence of their dealings with them.

Accordingly, the aims of education for Māori children were frequently a point of heated debate between educational authorities and members of Māori communities who had their own ideas about the kind of social contract they wanted, but there was also intermittent agreement about what was taught. Increasing children's fluency in written and spoken English was a priority for colonial education authorities of the era but their reasons were very different from Māori. The English language was considered to be a key

232  *Joanna Kidman et al.*

attribute of a 'civilised' people and from the outset this was their primary focus. The debates that took place about this matter were telling. Henry Taylor, one of the first Native School inspectors,[31] was a strong advocate for schooling conducted in the English language, arguing that the Māori language, "is another obstacle in the way of civilization. So long as it exists there is a barrier to the free, unrestrained intercourse which ought to exist between the races," he said.[32] This view was heartily endorsed by others in the colonial service, including school inspector and Member of Parliament, Hugh Carlton, who considered that the time had come to either civilize Māori or exterminate them.[33] During a Parliamentary debate, he argued, "civilization cannot be advanced beyond a very short stage through means of the aboriginal tongue. The Maori tongue is sufficed for the requirements of a barbarous race, but apparently would serve for little more."[34] These ideas were widely held by colonial education administrators and were the main drivers of curriculum policy for the Native Schools.

The move to eradicate the Māori language had devastating long-term repercussions, including widespread language loss, over time.[35] McCarty argues that it is through language that "we come to know, represent, name and act upon the world."[36] If language is the lens through which we perceive our humanity, then the loss of indigenous languages or the threat to their survival strikes directly at the heart of indigenous ways of being and knowing. The colonial administration in New Zealand never fully held the whip-hand of power in the Native Schools. Māori always found ways of subverting the narratives of conquest that lay at the centre of the education project but these policies, nevertheless, had far-reaching consequences. In order to understand how these ideas gave rise to later indigenous resistance, we need a framework for explaining settler-colonial power relations, as is discussed in the next section.

## The Settler Contract

How might we understand the principles that guided the architects of the Native School system in New Zealand? Charles Mills offers a way of thinking about this. In his work, *The Racial Contract*,[37] Mills argues that the political, epistemological and social accords that form the social contract are underwritten by a more insidious set of agreements that benefit and privilege "whites" as a group in relation to "non-whites" as a group.[38] Accordingly, the classic social contract tradition, which posits a hypothetical agreement among "free and equal individuals in a well-defined initial state,"[39] is rewritten in settler societies as,

> that set of formal or informal agreements or meta-agreements [. . .] between the members of one subset of humans, [. . .] designated as "white," and co-extensive [. . .] with the class of full humans, to categorize the remaining subset of humans as "non-white and of a different

# Everyday Hope: Indigenous Education Aims  233

and inferior moral status, subpersons, so that they have a subordinate civil standing in the white or white-ruled polities.[40]

The designation of one group as being fully human and the other group as subpersons fitted neatly around nineteenth-century explanations of human nature as a progression from a state of nature towards a state of civilization. Jean-Jacques Rousseau, for example, had earlier drawn a series of distinctions between those in a state of nature and those in civil society. He argued that in the state of nature, 'man' acts instinctively or by impulse whereas in the civil state, he is led by justice and reason.[41] At the same time, Rousseau pointed to the corruptive influence of society[42] and consequently the need to protect those in a state of nature—such as children—from its excesses so they may in time become exemplary citizens able to live in the civic state whilst yet retaining elements of 'naturalness'. In the context of colonial rule, this kind of thinking held sway. Indigenous peoples across the British Empire were positioned as beings in a state of nature and in need of guidance, protection and help to take their place as citizens in civic society, but as Mills contends, this also provided a tidy philosophical justification for colonial domination,

> [transformed] abstract raceless "men" from denizens of the state of nature into social creatures who are politically obligated to a neutral state, becomes the founding of a *racial polity*, whether white settler states (where pre-existing populations already are or can be made sparse) or what are sometimes called "sojourner colonies," the establishment of a white presence and colonial rule over existing societies (which are somewhat more populous or whose inhabitants are more resistant to being made sparse).[43]

Mills argues that a fundamental premise of the racial polity is white denial that previous societies existed[44] and this is where the demarcation between states of nature and civil society become critical to the establishment of a racialized social order. In line with this, Carole Pateman contends that in the nineteenth-century colonial world, constructions of nature—the wilderness and wild woods—as empty, uncultivated, deserted, unpeopled or owned by no one was at the heart of a new kind of political configuration.[45] Within these untamed, pre-modern landscapes, she argues, indigenous groups were depicted as living without a discernible form of sovereign government; a state of nature, as opposed to civil beings operating within a structured polity based on universally agreed rules, norms and mores. The establishment of settler-colonial societies in distant lands was therefore justified on the basis of settler denial that previous societies (or societies with systems of governance recognized by the imperial metropolis) were in existence prior to colonization and this lies at the heart of educational thinking in the late imperial era. As Pateman argues, the "modern state can have no competing sovereignties within its borders."[46] Native

234   *Joanna Kidman et al.*

peoples were not considered adequately advanced to produce a nation-state framework of their own, and were therefore "forcibly incorporated into new state jurisdictions."[47] This is ultimately what happened in New Zealand. The Treaty of Waitangi did not provide Māori people with the egalitarian partnership they envisaged and in the years following the signing of this agreement, the Crown quashed any possibility of a genuine association between coequals.

These ideas were reflected in the Native Schools in subtle ways. For example, official stories about the founding of nations frequently omit or sanitize acts of imperial violence or military force against indigenous peoples. Over time these silences can harden into denial over what took place in the past and this has a significant impact on settler-indigenous relations in the present.[48] Charles Mills has delved into the repression of uncomfortable or difficult memories in these contexts, naming them as a form of white ignorance. In a society structured by domination, he argues,

> with one group suppressing precisely what another wishes to commemorate there will be both official and counter-memory, with conflicting judgments about what is important in the past and what is unimportant, what happened and does matter, what happened and does not matter, and what did not happen at all.[49]

The ways that different groups remember and forget the difficult or violent histories that sit beneath official 'birth of the nation' stories also influence what is taught in schools. This has been described as a form of "cognitive imperialism"[50]—a rewriting and reorganizing of colonial violence whereby acts of brutality and invasion are transformed into patriotic tales of settler and pioneer heroism which then seep into the curricula and pedagogical practice of education. Accordingly, the ideological basis of these education systems rests on an 'imagined community' whereby the Settler Contract is ever present but rarely if ever formally acknowledged.[51]

These refusals to acknowledge or remember the violent past underpin an important aspect of education policy and practice referred to as an epistemological "sub-contract."[52] This sub-contract facilitates and maintains cultural and historical amnesia with regard to the curriculum (what is taught in schools), pedagogy (how things are taught) and education policy (the framework for deciding what is taught and how it is delivered). Support for this view comes from Anna Marie Smith who argues that, "most whites collude in hoarding sociopolitical resources and educational opportunities for themselves, while disavowing their concerted efforts and subscribing to a wide range of self-serving myths pertaining to the cultural inferiority of the so-called black "underclass.""[53] The epistemological sub-contract then, buttresses notions of white superiority in schooling environments, albeit in covert ways and this resonates with the New Zealand education environment where the nation's difficult colonial past history and its ongoing consequences are rarely taught or mentioned.[54]

*Everyday Hope: Indigenous Education Aims*  235

The Settler Contract and the related epistemological sub-contracts of New Zealand education differ in some respects from other former British colonies. New Zealand was colonized relatively late in the imperial era at a time when interventionist notions of empire and universalist conceptualizations of culture were gradually being supplanted by a focus on 'cultural difference.' Colonial administrators in New Zealand were divided about whether assimilation would be an effective means of bringing Māori under control. From the outset there were some who argued that threading aspects of indigenous ways of life and culture into state systems of native education would be more productive than attempting to eliminate cultural differences altogether. This was a more hegemonic exercise of power that did not demand eradicating or assimilating indigenous groups but rather, as Mantena argues, "native social and political forms would [. . .] be patronized as they became inserted into the institutional dynamics of imperial power."[55] By the early twentieth century, this approach was the primary means through which the Settler Contract was enacted through the Native schooling system. Thus, in settler-colonial societies, education for indigenous children has often been a zero-sum game and in New Zealand it has been a trade-off between giving Māori communities selective access to educational decision-making as citizens of the nation-state at the same time as denying their claims for justice as troublesome, combative or a threat to peaceful race relations. In the next sections we explore the Māori response to the Settler Contract in education and the creation of indigenous epistemological spaces that have emerged over the past forty years.

## A Legacy of Hope

In the face of settler-colonial denial, historical amnesia and epistemological ignorance the task of indigenous educators has been to create new forms of social contract that directly engage with the past and clear the way for a more hopeful future. In these contexts, hope can be a powerful humanizing force. Indeed, Paulo Freire, suggests that it is an "ontological need"[56] and one that is intimately connected with the "dream of humanization"[57] especially for peoples with a history of violent dispossession from land, culture, language and ways of life. Making critical links with the past within the education domain allows indigenous peoples to situate themselves temporally as agentic and connected beings in a dynamic present and this can happen in a variety of ways. As an example, we recount below, the story of a particularly brutal episode in New Zealand's past that has come to stand as a beacon of hope for many Māori today—this is the story of the Battle at Ōrākau.

### *The Battle at Ōrākau: Ka whawhai tonu mātou. Ake! Ake! Ake!*[58]

Throughout the 1850s and 1860s, Māori tribes in the Waikato district of New Zealand experienced a lengthy period of prosperity, peacefulness and stability. At a time when violent conflicts were taking place around the

236   *Joanna Kidman et al.*

country between other Māori tribes and the Crown, Waikato Māori had established a flourishing trading economy that brought significant wealth to the government coffers.[59] But the colonial government of the era could not accommodate an extensive system of Māori tribal governance over a region so rich in natural resources and were impatient with Māori refusals to sell land to the Crown. In the winter of 1863, British Imperial troops mounted a full-scale invasion of the district. The government was well-prepared for this offensive and had brought in troops from England; at one point, more British Imperial troops were stationed in the area than anywhere else in the British Empire outside of India.[60]

The campaign waged against the Waikato tribes was brutal and there were significant casualties on both sides. It ended ten months later in April 1864 at a Māori settlement called Ōrākau. Here, after months of heavy fighting, Māori tribes from around the North Island gathered to defend themselves against the invading forces. Throughout the months of invasion, they had been heavily outnumbered and this time, without access to food or fresh water and depleted in numbers, they faced certain defeat. This was to be the decisive battle in the Waikato war and a significant turning point in Māori-Crown relations in the colony. On the morning of April 2, following a day of heavy combat, the British troops were close to victory. The British Lieutenant-General, Duncan Cameron, instructed that Māori be called upon to surrender. In the preceding months, however, when British troops had laid siege to other settlements, non-combatants, including women, children and the elderly had been killed, as were others who tried to surrender. Consequently, Māori leaders on the battlefield at Ōrākau that day had little faith that the British would act honourably if they capitulated. When called upon to do so, the reply came back, "Ka whawhai tonu mātou. Ake! Ake! Ake!" ["We shall fight on forever and ever!"] The final chaotic hours of the battle at Ōrākau included scenes of terror and great cruelty as Māori men and women on foot were hunted down and shot or bayoneted by armed cavalry.[61] By the afternoon of that day, in a haze of bullets and bloodshed, the ten-month war on the Waikato was over.

Imperial victory in the Waikato paved the way for settler and European dominance in the years to come and the Crown regularly acted in breach of the Treaty of Waitangi, refusing to consult on matters concerning Māori peoples and their lands. This has been described as a "relentless"[62] settler hegemony that ultimately drove Māori to the far edges of colonial society where many ended up in destitution. Yet for many Māori today, this is also a story of courage, endurance and hope. The refusal to surrender at Ōrākau is widely interpreted as a call to later generations of Māori to carry on the fight for justice and the words spoken on the battlefield that terrible day have become a catch-cry for Māori in their dealings with the Crown.[63] Nowadays, the words are treated both as a prophecy and a call to action; frequently appearing as a catchphrase on placards in Māori protests or chanted during demonstrations.[64] As Linda Tuhiwai Smith writes,

*Everyday Hope: Indigenous Education Aims*   237

A nineteenth-century prophecy by a Māori leader predicted that the struggle of Māori people against colonialism would go on forever and therefore the need to resist will be without end. This may appear to be a message without hope, but it has become an exhortation to Māori people that our survival, our humanity, our world-views and language, our imagination and spirit, our very place in the world depends on our capacity to act for ourselves, to speak for ourselves, to engage in the world and the actions of our colonizers, to face them head on. Māori struggles for social justice in New Zealand are messy, noisy, simultaneously celebratory and demoralizing, hopeful and desperate.[65]

Indigenous educators have always found creative ways of 'speaking back' to the forces that exclude and marginalize them and many actively challenge prevailing ideas about citizenship and the nation. In settler-colonial societies, like New Zealand, indigenous hope is often forged in times of struggle. As such, it has become embedded in the web of social relations that coalesce around refusals of the Settler Contract. In Māori terms, this is an assertion of indigenous solidarity and personhood but also resistance. Thus, hope becomes an affective 'capital' and a form of political and cultural agency.[66] This is the *docta spes* in action—an educated and reflective form of hope that is less an act of being than a future-focused process of becoming.[67] Kanien'kehaka scholar and educator, Taiaiake Alfred, writes that indigenous processes of becoming require the activation of "radical imagination"[68]— a re-envisaging of existence that recognizes and acknowledges, "the fact of a meaningful prior Indigenous presence, and taking action to support struggles not only of social and economic justice, but political justice for Indigenous nations as well."[69] In education contexts, however, hope and the radical imagination must also be grounded in educational practice and aligned with indigenous political struggle, as is discussed below.

### Breaking the Settler Contract: Hope and Indigenous Education in New Zealand

Throughout the 1960s and 1970s Māori protest against the government gathered momentum as anger mounted about the cumulative effects of tribal land loss and the difficult economic and living conditions that many Māori were experiencing in consequence.[70] Out of this political struggle, new forms of resistance to the Settler Contract emerged which led many Māori to build radical political agendas in relation to education, health, broadcasting, housing, justice and economics. A large number of these engagements are shaped by Kaupapa Māori[71]—an intellectual movement emerging in the 1980s[72] that draws heavily on critical theory and which is closely linked to Māori protest movements. A central aim shared by Kaupapa Māori advocates is to create epistemological and intellectual spaces that combine an analysis of the structural conditions of colonization with political mobilization.[73] As a

238 *Joanna Kidman et al.*

form of indigenous praxis, it closely follows Paulo Freire's conscientizing programme of critical dialogue and direct action.[74] In line with this, political acts geared towards social change are informed by the debates and analyses that take place around broader themes of social and cultural injustice. Graham Hingangaroa Smith argues that,

> Kaupapa Māori strategies question the right of Pākehā to dominate and exclude Māori preferred interests in education, and assert the validity of Māori knowledge, language, custom and practice, and its right to continue to flourish in the land of its origin, as the tangata whenua (Indigenous) culture.[75]

Education is central to these challenges to the status quo. Throughout the 1980s, Māori began to establish their own schooling programmes beginning with early childhood centres dedicated to offering Māori-medium[76] education to babies and toddlers. These facilities, known as Kōhanga Reo [Language Nests], endeavour to keep Māori language and traditions alive by immersing very young children in Māori culture at the earliest stages of their lives. Nation-wide systems of Māori-medium elementary and secondary schooling based on Māori cultural traditions, knowledge, philosophies and cultural practices have since been established and in 1981, the first Māori tribal university was opened and others have followed since.[77] These initatives are closely aligned with the Māori communities they serve and Māori families, sometimes several generations of family members, have high levels of involvement in the daily lives of these schools. The state is now involved in funding these initiatives and while this makes it possible to sustain these learning environments over time, relationships with state education authorities are often unpredictable. One of the risks, of course, is that the Settler Contract will find its way into these arrangements. Thus, there is a constant tension between enacting the principles of transformative education for Māori children and being co-opted by state agendas.[78]

Despite these challenges, many Māori view these educational ventures as expressions of hope—an "oppositional utopianism"[79] that blends indigenous political aspirations with grassroots pedagogical practice in the everyday lives of Māori children. In many respects, this is a 'mundane' or everyday type of utopian thinking but one that carries with it the potential to generate new social and cultural practices and arrangements.[80] Here, the *docta spes* acts in tandem with the radical imagination to provide Māori with avenues for envisaging different kinds of society and forms of political agency beyond the Settler Contract. These are not abstract utopias but rather dreams forged in the heat of battle or during times of political regression. With this in mind, what then should be the aims of indigenous education in settler-colonial societies? We have argued here that one of the primary motivations is hope. Everyday hope in the face of struggle and dispossession. Hope that speaks back to the Settler Contract. Hope that connects

# Everyday Hope: Indigenous Education Aims  239

indigenous children with their histories and their future. Hope that opens up the imagination. The struggle goes on. Ka whawhai tonu mātou. Ake! Ake! Ake!

## Notes

1. Judith A. Simon and Linda Tuhiwai Smith, *A Civilising Mission? Perceptions and Representations of the New Zealand Native Schools System* (Auckland, NZ: Auckland University Press, 2001).
2. Timothy H. Parsons, *Race, Resistance, and the Boy Scout Movement in British Colonial Africa* (Athens, OH: Ohio University Press, 2004).
3. Aimee Carillo Rowe and Eve Tuck, "Settler Colonialism and Cultural Studies: Ongoing Settlement, Cultural Production and Resistance," *Cultural Studies <—> Critical Methodologies* 17, no. 1 (2017): 3–13.
4. Carole Pateman and Charles Mills, eds., *Contract and Domination* (Cambridge and Malden: Polity Press, 2016).
5. Ernst Bloch, *The Principle of Hope* (Cambridge, MA: MIT Press, 1995).
6. New Zealand is a constitutional democracy but as a member of the Commonwealth the Head of State is the British Monarch (represented by a Governor-General). The New Zealand government or state is therefore commonly referred to as 'the Crown.'
7. Nan Seuffert, "Contract, Consent and Imperialism in New Zealand's Founding Narrative," *Law and History* 2 (2015): 1–32.
8. Ibid., 3.
9. Ibid., 31.
10. John Willinsky, *Learning to Divide the World: Education at Empire's End* (Minneapolis and London: University of Minnesota Press, 1998), 3.
11. Gareth Shaw and Paul Hudson, "Edge of Empire: Transnationalism and Identity in Wellington, New Zealand, ca. 1860–ca. 1920," *Landscape Research* 27 no. 1 (2002): 51–66.
12. John Barrington, *Separate but Equal? Māori Schools and the Crown 1867–1969* (Wellington, NZ: Victoria University Press, 2008).
13. Brendan Hokowhitu, "'Physical Beings': Stereotypes, Sport and the 'Physical Education' of New Zealand Māori," *Culture, Sport, Society* 6 nos. 2–3 (2003): 192–218.
14. M. Daphne Kutzer, *Empire's Children: Empire and Imperialism in Classic British Children's Books* (New York and London: Garland Publishing, 2000).
15. Helen May, "Nineteenth Century Early Childhood Institutions in Aotearoa New Zealand: Legacies of Enlightenment and Colonisation," *Journal of Pedagogy* 6 no. 2 (2015): 21–39.
16. Katie Pickles, "A Link in 'the Great Chain of Empire Friendship': The Victoria League in New Zealand," *Journal of Imperial and Commonwealth History* 33 no. 1 (2005): 29.
17. Michelle J. Smith, *Empire in British Girls' Literature and Culture: Imperial Girls, 1880–1915* (Basingstoke: Palgrave Macmillan, 2011), 10.
18. Allison McNaught, "English Curriculum against the Peace," *Peace Review* 9 no. 2 (1997): 287.
19. The New Zealand Wars is a term coined by historians in the 1980s to describe this series of conflicts between the government and Māori between 1845 and 1872.
20. James Belich, *The Victoria Interpretation of Racial Conflict: The Māori, the British, and the New Zealand Wars* (Montreal and Kingston: McGill-Queen University Press, 1989), 15.

240 *Joanna Kidman et al.*

21. Patrick Wolfe, "Settler Colonialism and the Elimination of the Native," *Journal of Genocide Research* 8 no. 4 (2006): 388.
22. Ian Pool, *Colonization and Development in New Zealand between 1769 and 1900: The Seeds of Rangiatea* (Switzerland: Springer International, 2015), 204.
23. Joanna Kidman, "Shifting Margins, Shifting Centres: Development Paradigms in Māori Education," *International Journal of Development Education and Global Learning* 2 no. 1 (2009): 5–18.
24. Mahmood Mamdani, *Define and Rule: Native as Political Identity* (Cambridge: Harvard University Press, 2012), 6.
25. Mahmood Mamdani, "Historicizing Power and Responses to Power: Indirect Rule and Its Reform," *Social Research* 66 no. 3 (1999): 862.
26. See, Joanna Kidman, "Māori Young People, Nationhood and Land," in *Geographies of Children and Young People: Space, Place and Environment*, ed. Tracey Skelton (Singapore: Springer, 2016): 28–45; and Larry Prochner, Helen May, and Baljit Kaur, "'The Blessings of Civilisation': Nineteenth Century Missionary Infant Schools for Young Native Children in Three Colonial Settings—India, Canada and New Zealand 1820s–1840s," *Paedagogica Historica* 45 nos. 1–2 (2009): 83–102.
27. John Barrington, *Separate But Equal? Māori Schools and the Crown 1867–1969*, 19–20.
28. Ibid., 73–89.
29. Ibid., 111–112.
30. James Belich made this point in the "Foreword" to Judith A. Simon and Linda Tuhiwai Smith, *A Civilising Mission? Perceptions and Representations of the New Zealand Native Schools System* (Auckland, NZ: Auckland University Press, 2001), ix.
31. The Native School Inspectors were government officials who had considerable authority. They were sent out to the regions twice a year to examine how the curriculum was taught in the Native School, identify problems, recommend improvements and report back to the Department of Education.
32. John Barrington, *Separate but Equal?*, 19.
33. Ibid., 20.
34. Ibid.
35. Rachael Ka'aai-Mahuta, "The Impact of Colonisation on Te Reo Māori: A Critical Review of the State Education System," *Te Kaharoa* 4 (2011): 196.
36. Teresa L. McCarty, "Revitalising Indigenous Language in Homogenising Times," *Comparative Education* 39 no. 2 (2003): 148.
37. Charles W. Mills, *The Racial Contract* (Ithaca, NY: Cornell University Press, 1999).
38. Ibid., 13.
39. Wolfgang Kersting, "The Classic Social Contract Tradition," in *Handbook of the Philosophical Foundations of Business Ethics*, ed. Christophe Luetge (Dordrecht and New York: Springer, 2013), 605.
40. Mills, *The Racial Contract*, 11.
41. See, Christopher Bertram, *Routledge Philosophy Guidebook to Rousseau and The Social Contract* (London and New York: Routledge, 2004), 82.
42. John Petrovic and Kellie Rolstad, "Educating for Autonomy: Reading Rousseau and Freire toward a Philosophy of Unschooling," *Policy Futures in Education*, 0 no.0 (2016): 1–17.
43. Mills, *The Racial Contract*, 12.
44. Ibid., 13.
45. Carole Pateman, "The Settler Contract," in *Contract and Domination*, ed. Carole Pateman and Charles W. Mills (Cambridge and Malden: Polity Press, 2016),

Everyday Hope: Indigenous Education Aims    241

35–78. Following Pateman's example, we refer hereafter to the 'Settler contract' in relation to the New Zealand context.

46. Ibid., 39.

47. Ibid.

48. For an example of denial in the New Zealand context, see, Vincent O'Malley and Joanna Kidman, "Settler Colonial History, Commemoration and White Backlash: Remembering the New Zealand Wars," *Settler Colonial Studies* (2017): 1–16, accessed March 27, 2017, doi:10.1080/2201473X.2017.1279831.

49. Charles Mills, "White Ignorance," in *Race and Epistemologies of Ignorance*, ed. Shannon Sullivan and Nancy Tuana (Albany: State University of New York Press, 2007): 29.

50. Marie Battiste and James (Sa'ke'j) Youngblood Henderson, *Protecting Indigenous Knowledge and Heritage: A Global Challenge* (Saskatoon: Purich Publishing, 2008). See chapter 5, "Decolonizing Cognitive Imperialism in Education."

51. Michael W. Apple, "Can Critical Pedagogies Interrupt Rightist Policies?" *Educational Theory* 50 no. 2 (2000): 242.

52. Zeus Leonardo, "Contracting Race: Writing, Racism, and Education," *Critical Studies in Education* 56 (2015): 93.

53. Anna Marie Smith, "The Racial Contract, Educational Equity, and Emancipatory Ideological Critique," *Politics, Groups, and Identities* 3 no. 3 (2015): 504.

54. Mark Sheehan, "Little Is Taught or Learned in Schools: Debates Over the Place of History in the New Zealand School Curriculum," in *History Wars and the Classroom: Global Perspectives*, ed. Tony Taylor and Robert Guyver (Charlotte, NC: Information Age Publishing, 2011), 107–124.

55. Karuna Mantena, *Alibis of Empire: Henry Maine and the Ends of Liberal Imperialism* (Princeton, NJ: Princeton University Press, 2010), 2.

56. Paulo Freire, *Pedagogy of Hope* (London: Bloomsbury Academic, 2015), 2.

57. Ibid., 89.

58. This phrase translates as, "We shall fight on forever and ever!"

59. Vincent O'Malley, "'The Great War for NZ Broke Out Less Than 50 Km from Queen St': Vincent O'Malley on the Waikato War and the Making of Auckland," *The Spinoff*, December 6, 2016b, accessed January 19, 2017, http://thespinoff.co.nz/society/06-12-2016/the-great-war-for-nz-broke-out-less-than-50-km-from-queen-st-vincent-omalley-on-the-waikato-war-and-the-making-of-auckland.

60. Vincent O'Malley, "What a Nation Chooses to Remember and Forget: The War for New Zealand's History," *The Guardian*, October 18, 2016c, accessed January 19, 2017, www.theguardian.com/commentisfree/2016/oct/18/what-a-nation-chooses-to-remember-and-forget-the-war-for-new-zealands-history.

61. Vincent O'Malley, *The Great War for New Zealand: Waikato 1800–2000* (Wellington, NZ: Bridget Williams Books, 2016a), 326.

62. Ibid., 601.

63. For a discussion on the use of this phrase in contemporary Māori activist thinking, see Ranginui Walker, *Ka Whawhai Tonu Mātou: Struggle without End* (Auckland, NZ: Penguin Books, 1990).

64. See Aroha Harris, *Hīkoi: Forty Years of Māori Protest* (Wellington, NZ: Huia Publishers, 2004), Chapter 4.

65. Smith, *Qualitative Inquiry—Past, Present, and Future: A Critical Reader*, 349.

66. Joanne Bryant and Jeanne Ellard, "Hope as a Form of Agency in the Future Thinking of Disenfranchised Young People," *Journal of Youth Studies* 18 no. 4 (2015).

67. Athanasios Marvakis, "The Utopian Surplus in Human Agency: Using Ernst Bloch's Philosophy for Psychology," in *Citizen City: Between Constructing*

## 242   *Joanna Kidman et al.*

*Agent and Constructed Agency*, ed. Vasi Van Deventer, Martin Terre Blanche, Eduard Fourie, and Puleng Segalo (Ontario: Captus Press, 2007).

68. Ibid.
69. Ibid.
70. See Danielle Celermajer and Joanna Kidman, "Embedding the Apology in the Nation's Identity," *The Journal of the Polynesian Society* 121 no. 3 (2012): 219–242.
71  "Kaupapa Māori" means Māori principles, philosophies, practices and values. Here, the term refers to a political and social movement that promotes these ideas.
72. Leonie Pihama, Fiona Cram, and Sheila Walker, "Creating Methodological Space: A Literature Review of Kaupapa Māori Research," *Canadian Journal of Native Education* 26 no. 1 (2002): 31.
73. See Graham Smith, "Interview: Kaupapa Māori: The Dangers of Domestication," *New Zealand Journal of Educational Studies* 47 no. 2 (2012): 10–20.
74. Freirean praxis involving "reflection and action directed at the structures to be transformed" is a highly influential concept in Kaupapa Māori thinking. See Paulo Freire, *Pedagogy of the Oppressed* (New York: Continuum, 2002), 126.
75. Graham Smith, "The Development of Kaupapa Māori: Theory and Praxis" (PhD thesis., Auckland, New Zealand: University of Auckland, 1997), 273.
76  'Māori-medium' refers to education conducted in the Māori language.
77. Kimai Tocker, "The Origins of Kura Kaupapa Māori," *New Zealand Journal of Educational Studies* 50 (2015): 23.
78. See Graham Smith, "Interview: Kaupapa Māori: The Dangers of Domestication."
79. Henry A. Giroux, "Youth, Higher Education, and the Crisis of Public Time: Educated Hope and the Possibility of a Democratic Future," *Social Identities* 9 no. 2 (2003): 158.
80. See Ruth Levitas, *Utopia as Method: The Imaginary Reconstituion of Society* (New York: Palgrave Macmillan, 2014), xiii.

## Bibliography

Alfred, Taiaiake. "What Is Radical Imagination? Indigenous Struggles in Canada." *Affinities: A Journal of Radical Theory, Culture, and Action* 4 no. 2 (2010): 5–8.

Apple, Michael W. "Can Critical Pedagogies Interrupt Rightist Policies?" *Educational Theory* 50 no. 2 (2000): 229–254.

Barrington, John. *Separate but Equal? Māori Schools and the Crown 1867–1969.* Wellington, NZ: Victoria University Press, 2008.

Battiste, Marie and James (Sa'ke'j) Youngblood Henderson. *Protecting Indigenous Knowledge and Heritage: A Global Challenge.* Saskatoon: Purich Publishing, 2008.

Belich, James. *The Victoria Interpretation of Racial Conflict: The Māori, the British, and the New Zealand Wars.* Montreal and Kingston: McGill-Queen University Press, 1989.

Bertram, Christopher. *Routledge Philosophy Guidebook to Rousseau and the Social Contract.* London and New York: Routledge, 2004.

Bloch, Ernst. *The Principle of Hope.* Cambridge, MA: MIT Press, 1995.

Bryant, Joanne and Jeanne Ellard. "Hope as a Form of Agency in the Future Thinking of Disenfranchised Young People." *Journal of Youth Studies* 18 no. 4 (2015): 485–499.

Celermajer, Danielle and Joanna Kidman. "Embedding the Apology in the Nation's Identity." *The Journal of the Polynesian Society* 121 no. 3 (2012): 219–242.

Freire, Paulo. *Pedagogy of the Oppressed.* New York: Continuum, 2002.

## Everyday Hope: Indigenous Education Aims   243

———. *Pedagogy of Hope*. London: Bloomsbury Academic, 2015.

Giroux, Henry A. "Youth, Higher Education, and the Crisis of Public Time: Educated Hope and the Possibility of a Democratic Future." *Social Identities* 9 no. 2 (2003): 141–168.

Harris, Aroha. *Hīkoi: Forty Years of Māori Protest*. Wellington, NZ: Huia Publishers, 2004.

Hokowhitu, Brendan. "'Physical Beings': Stereotypes, Sport and the 'Physical Education' of New Zealand Māori." *Culture, Sport, Society* 6 nos. 2–3 (2003): 192–218.

Ka'aai-Mahuta, Rachael. "The Impact of Colonisation on Te Reo Māori: A Critical Review of the State Education System." *Te Kaharoa* 4 (2011): 195–225.

Kersting, Wolfgang. "The Classic Social Contract Tradition." In *Handbook of the Philosophical Foundations of Business Ethics*, edited by Christophe Luetge, 605–629. Dordrecht and New York: Springer, 2013.

Kidman, Joanna. "Shifting Margins, Shifting Centres: Development Paradigms in Māori Education." *International Journal of Development Education and Global Learning* 2 no. 1 (2009): 5–18.

———. "Māori Young People, Nationhood and Land." In *Geographies of Children and Young People: Space, Place and Environment*, Volume 3, edited by Tracey Skelton, 27–45. Singapore: Springer, 2016.

Kutzer, M. Daphne. *Empire's Children: Empire and Imperialism in Classic British Children's Books*. New York and London: Garland Publishing, 2000.

Leonardo, Zeus. "Contracting Race: Writing, Racism, and Education." *Critical Studies in Education* 56 (2015): 86–98.

Levitas, Ruth. *Utopia as Method: The Imaginary Reconstituion of Society*. New York: Palgrave Macmillan, 2014.

Mamdani, Mahmood. "Historicizing Power and Responses to Power: Indirect Rule and Its Reform." *Social Research* 66 no. 3 (1999): 859–886.

———. *Define and Rule: Native as Political Identity*. Cambridge: Harvard University Press, 2012.

Mantena, Karuna. *Alibis of Empire: Henry Maine and the Ends of Liberal Imperialism*. Princeton, NJ: Princeton University Press, 2010.

Marvakis, Athanasios. "The Utopian Surplus in Human Agency: Using Ernst Bloch's Philosophy for Psychology." In *Citizen City: Between Constructing Agent and Constructed Agency*, edited by Vasi Van Deventer, Martin Terre Blanche, Eduard Fourie, and Puleng Segalo, 278–288. Ontario: Captus Press, 2007.

May, Helen. "Nineteenth Century Early Childhood Institutions in Aotearoa New Zealand: Legacies of Enlightenment and Colonisation." *Journal of Pedagogy* 6 no. 2 (2015): 21–39.

McCarty, Teresa L. "Revitalising Indigenous Language in Homogenising Times." *Comparative Education* 39 no. 2 (2003): 147–163.

McNaught, Allison. "English Curriculum against the Peace." *Peace Review* 9 no. 2 (1997): 287–292.

Mills, Charles. *The Racial Contract*. Ithaca, NY: Cornell University Press. 1999.

———. "White Ignorance." In *Race and Epistemologies of Ignorance*, edited by Shannon Sullivan and Nancy Tuana, 11–38. Albany: State University of New York Press, 2007.

O'Malley, Vincent. *The Great War for New Zealand: Waikato 1800–2000*. Wellington, NZ: Bridget Williams Books, 2016a.

———. "The Great War for NZ Broke Out Less Than 50 Km from Queen St': Vincent O'Malley on the Waikato War and the Making of Auckland." *The Spinoff*, December 6, 2016b. Accessed January 19, 2017. http://thespinoff.co.nz/society/06-12-2016/the-great-war-for-nz-broke-out-less-than-50-km-from-queen-st-vincent-omalley-on-the-waikato-war-and-the-making-of-auckland/.

———. "What a Nation Chooses to Remember and Forget: The War for New Zealand's History." *The Guardian*, October 18, 2016c. Accessed January 19, 2017. www.theguardian.com/commentisfree/2016/oct/18/what-a-nation-chooses-to-remember-and-forget-the-war-for-new-zealands-history.

——— and Joanna Kidman. "Settler Colonial History, Commemoration and White Backlash: Remembering the New Zealand Wars." *Settler Colonial Studies* (2017): 1–16. doi:10.1080/2201473X.2017.1279831.

Parsons, Timothy H. *Race, Resistance, and the Boy Scout Movement in British Colonial Africa*. Athens, OH: Ohio University Press, 2004.

Pateman, Carole. "The Settler Contract." In *Contract and Domination*, edited by Carole Pateman and Charles W. Mills, 35–78. Cambridge and Malden: Polity Press, 2016.

——— and Charles Mills, eds. *Contract and Domination*. Cambridge and Malden: Polity Press, 2016.

Petrovic, John E. and Kellie Rolstad. "Educating for Autonomy: Reading Rousseau and Freire toward a Philosophy of Unschooling." *Policy Futures in Education* 0 no. 0 (2016): 1–17. doi:10.1177/1478210316681204.

Pickles, Katie. "A Link in 'the Great Chain of Empire Friendship': The Victoria League in New Zealand." *Journal of Imperial and Commonwealth History* 33 no. 1 (2005): 29–50.

Pihama, Leonie. "Kaupapa Māori Theory: Transforming Theory in Aotearoa." *He Pukenga Korero: A Journal of Māori Studies* 9 no. 2 (2010): 5–14.

———, Fiona Cram, and Sheila Walker. "Creating Methodological Space: A Literature Review of Kaupapa Māori Research." *Canadian Journal of Native Education* 26 no. 1 (2002): 30–43.

Pool, Ian. *Colonization and Development in New Zealand between 1769 and 1900: The Seeds of Rangiatea*. Switzerland: Springer International, 2015.

Prochner, Larry, Helen May, and Baljit Kaur. "'The Blessings of Civilisation': Nineteenth-Century Missionary Infant Schools for Young Native Children in Three Colonial Settings—India, Canada and New Zealand 1820s—1840s." *Paedagogica Historica* 45 nos. 1–2 (2009): 83–102.

Rowe, Aimee Carillo and Eve Tuck. "Settler Colonialism and Cultural Studies: Ongoing Settlement, Cultural Production and Resistance." *Cultural Studies Critical Methodologies* 17, 1 (2017): 3–13.

Seuffert, Nan. "Contract, Consent and Imperialism in New Zealand's Founding Narrative." *Law and History* 2 (2015): 1–32.

Shaw, Gareth and Paul Hudson. "Edge of Empire: Transnationalism and Identity in Wellington, New Zealand, ca. 1860–ca. 1920." *Landscape Research* 27 no. 1 (2002): 51–66.

Sheehan, Mark. "'Little Is Taught or Learned in Schools': Debates Over the Place of History in the New Zealand School Curriculum." In *History Wars and the Classroom: Global Perspectives*, edited by Tony Taylor and Robert Guyver, 107–124. Charlotte, NC: Information Age Publishing, 2011.

Simon, Judith A. and Linda Tuhiwai Smith. *A Civilising Mission? Perceptions and Representations of the New Zealand Native Schools System*. Auckland, NZ: Auckland University Press, 2001.

Smith, Anna Marie. "The Racial Contract, Educational Equity, and Emancipatory Ideological Critique." *Politics, Groups, and Identities* 3 no. 3 (2015): 504–523.

Smith, Graham. "The Development of Kaupapa Māori: Theory and Praxis." PhD thesis., Auckland, New Zealand: University of Auckland, 1997.

———. "Interview: Kaupapa Māori: The Dangers of Domestication." *New Zealand Journal of Educational Studies* 47 no. 2 (2012): 10–20.

Smith, Linda. "Choosing the Margins: The Role of Research in Indigenous Struggles for Social Justice." In *Qualitative Inquiry—Past, Present, and Future: A Critical Reader*, edited by Norman K. Denzin and Michael D. Giardina, 349–371. Walnut Creek, CA: Left Coast Press, 2015.

Smith, Michelle J. *Empire in British Girls' Literature and Culture: Imperial Girls, 1880–1915*. Basingstoke: Palgrave Macmillan, 2011.

Tocker, Kimai. "The Origins of Kura Kaupapa Māori." *New Zealand Journal of Educational Studies* 50 (2015): 23–38.

Walker, Ranginui. *Ka Whawhai Tonu Mātou: Struggle without End*. Auckland, NZ: Penguin Books, 1990.

Willinsky, John. *Learning to Divide the World: Education at Empire's End*. Minneapolis and London: University of Minnesota Press, 1998.

Wolfe, Patrick. "Settler Colonialism and the Elimination of the Native." *Journal of Genocide Research* 8 no. 4 (2006): 387–409.

# Part 3
# Coda

# 13 Comparative Reflections on Philosophies of Indigenous Education around the World

*John E. Petrovic and Roxanne M. Mitchell*

## Understanding Indigeneity as Both a Frame and Identity

One of the questions relevant to philosophizing about indigenous education that we raised at the outset was: Who can and cannot rightly be referred to as "indigenous" and why? The chapters in the first half of this volume dealt with, either explicitly or implicitly, this question, complicating it in a variety of ways. Of course, a number of different organizations have sought to shed some light on how to characterize indigeneity and who is or is not indigenous. While not offering an official definition of indigeneity, the United Nations lists a number of taken for granted assumptions about what makes a people "indigenous." Accordingly, for example, indigenous peoples practice unique traditions and retain distinct social, cultural, economic, and political characteristics.

Commonly, discussions of indigeneity refer to a geographic area—ancestral lands—inhabited by peoples holding these distinct characteristics. [It is important to point out here, that while geography becomes a criterion for being identified as indigenous, it is also epistemically important to *being* indigenous, and such ways of knowing are crucial to any philosophy of indigenous education. Landry (*this volume*),[1] for example, points out the interesting epistemic orientations from place or time: the former being that of indigenous peoples and the latter of European immigrants.] On the one hand, momentarily setting aside Reagan's (*this volume*) interesting argument, indigeneity does strike of something self-evident identified in terms like "first peoples," "first nations," or "native peoples." On the other hand, in many cases, the survival of these peoples and their ways depends upon being recognized as such by dominant powers. Indeed, it is an unfortunate device of history that a group is often said to be indigenous only upon the condition of colonization, i.e., of having been somewhere before someone else arrived. As Sarivaara et al. note, "Often indigenous peoples are referred to as the disadvantaged descendants of the people that inhabited a territory prior to colonization or the formation of the existing state."[2] Thus, for Le Grange (*this volume*), indigeneity is always already a project of decolonization—requiring self-determination, including rights to land—and Indigenous peoples are those who share the experience of colonialism.

250    *John E. Petrovic and Roxanne M. Mitchell*

Given this, self-identification of the community is prerequisite to determining indigeneity. This also holds at the individual level, whereupon the individual then would need to be recognized by the community. In some ways, indigenous peoples must consider themselves separate from the dominant group, its norms, values, customs, and structures. Historically, of course, self-identification has been insufficient as dominant groups (sometimes with the overt or tacit consent of the indigenous group) have imposed a blood quantum criterion. These are political determinations that can vary quite widely depending on sociopolitical context. In the U.S., for example, one is considered native Hawaiian upon demonstrating 50 percent Hawaiian blood; whereas, in New Zealand, one can be Maori by merely having one Maori ancestor, regardless of how far back.[3] Because of the history of denying indigenous rights or the application of quite restrictive definitions of indigeneity, as in the case of Hawaii, the International Labor Organization advocates an unlimited right to self-identification for indigenous peoples.[4] But, as Jeff Corntassel points out, while strict definitional standards might exclude some legitimate groups, self-definition may encourage non-indigenous groups to seek the rights and protections proffered by various organizations.[5]

This objection may be applicable to Sun et al.'s (*this volume*) suggestion that "Chinese" might be read as indigenous. Indeed, the term indigenous is generally not applicable to dominant groups since by most definitions indigeneity consists of self-identification which distinguishes a group from the dominant society. Thus, on the one hand, it may be particularly problematic to identify Chinese as indigenous in China, especially given the want of dominant Chinese society to gloss over or even deny the existence of indigenous communities within China. In fact, the International Work Group for Indigenous Affairs notes that while China recognizes fifty-five ethnic groups within its borders, the Chinese government does not recognize the term "indigenous peoples." Further, self-identification is not recognized. For example, the Mosuo and Chuanqing peoples self-identify as ethnic minorities but are not recognized as such.

On the other hand, if indigeneity is about "a resistance to all forms of colonisation, including globalization," as Le Grange suggests, it would seem to provide an argument for at least *examining* the Chinese case through a lens of indigeneity in the way that Sun et al. do. This is not to suggest that the Chinese should be *identified* as an indigenous community. Nonetheless, thinking through globalization and the various forms of Western imperialism that globalization has exacerbated—including, in this case, Western philosophies and approaches to school leadership—induces fruitful reflection of the need for culturally relevant and philosophically grounded approaches to education. As Sun et al. point out, "modernization has also promoted the detachment from tradition, and resulted in the loss of foundational philosophies in education." Perhaps revealing this to the Chinese writ large might stir recognition of the need to recognize and engage with the numerous indigenous communities present in China.

*Comparative Reflections on Philosophies of Indigenous Education*  251

To the extent that the claim that the effects of colonization are not dissimilar from the effects that hegemonic globalization might hold, such reconsideration is even more justified in the case of the Deaf-world. As Reagan points out, "[Deaf people] live surrounded by hearing people, and are educated in and served by institutions designed, managed and staffed by hearing people." Thus, what is held as normative in such conditions reflects the dominant group to the detriment of the subordinate group. This follows a fairly classic definition of oppression. Is this similar enough to the effects of colonization to satisfy that particular criterion of indigenous? Taken alongside the other "strong parallels between Sign Language Peoples and First Nation Peoples," it seems that a strong case can be made for examining the Deaf Community as indigenous, even as Reagan recognizes some complications here such as the geographic criterion.

However, while a single criterion might be prerequisite (e.g., self-identification), no single criterion can or should be a final or absolute arbiter of "indigeneity." Thus, even as the Deaf Community cannot claim a geographic homeland, Reagan is compelling in his case that it can claim a culture distinct from the dominant group and a wish to retain a distinct identity.[6] In this case, this distinct identity is accentuated by the presence of a language different from the dominant group.[7] Language and identity are intimately intertwined. Indeed, language takes on epistemic proportion to the extent that it can shape how and what we know. Bilingualism, for example, can open up a bifurcated epistemological space such that one can know differently in two languages.[8] Again, language cannot be a sole arbiter. This would certainly be too restrictive and unjust, especially to communities who, through oppressive colonizing processes, have lost their traditional languages. Nevertheless, language must certainly be considered when it adds to a community's self-identification.

In the end, the question of who is indigenous can take a technical turn, identifying very specific criteria and matching those to some community's claim. This, of course, is the sociopolitical construction of indigeneity required by the modern nation-state to deny or accept a group's "legitimacy." However, taking indigeneity as a conceptual or philosophical frame from which to analyze and address/redress colonization, hegemony, and globalization is not a technical project and perhaps, therefore, more generative.

## Indigenous Education: One for All and All for One?

Setting up "indigeneity" as not just an identity but also as a conceptual frame, also sets up and, perhaps, informs the question of for whom an indigenous education should be intended. This requires defining, while problematizing, what that might mean. In the introduction to this volume, we made a distinction between philosophy of indigenous education and indigenous philosophy of education. We noted that the former is more a sort of metaphilosophy, concerning the boundaries and types of questions relevant to philosophizing about indigenous education. The latter focuses on the onto-epistemologies, customs, traditions, worldviews—among other characteristics—of an indigenous community in order to inform how educational policies and pedagogies might be reformed to become more relevant to the community as well as forces for cultural survival and even decolonization. In some cases, the two approaches merge, contemplating, for example, whether a given indigenous philosophy of education might be a philosophy of education writ large. In some ways, this is the approach that Lesley Le Grange takes. Given that Ubuntu is about becoming more fully human through deeper relationships with others as well as having an environmental ethics at its core, it seems that Ubuntu should be considered vital to the survival of humanity, education toward that survival being of utmost importance. As Le Grange tells it, Ubuntu can inform a radical rethinking of mainstream education. Similarly, Sun et al. note from Confucianism that "one becomes fully human through continuous interaction with other human beings."

Also, in arguing against what they refer to as Western theory imperialism, Sun et al. reflect on how theories of transformational leadership, differently embedded culturally and philosophically, might inform each other. Landry takes up an objection to orthodox Eurocentric philosophy and draws a similar conclusion. If there is "Western theory imperialism," Landry suggests, first, there is similarly a Western hegemony over the practice of philosophy in terms of what counts as philosophy. He argues, for example, that "Indigeneity may be manifest in literature or storytelling, or discussion of ethnoscience and sustaining the natural environment, yet not presented as formal philosophical essay or treaties." It is likely, he intimates, that such goes unrecognized as philosophy. Second, missing or ignoring the indigenous oral tradition as philosophy feeds into discounting indigenous knowledge and ways of knowing, ultimately excluded from the curriculum. In these ways, what these authors are raising is a notion of subjugated knowledge. Knowledge becomes subjugated through dominant knowledge validation procedures, about what counts as science, or philosophy, or even evidence.[9]

Given this, Landry, as others in this section, asks that we re-imagine or make "an attempt to look anew to see relevance in long present yet unacknowledged philosophies." To the extent that such a re-imagining should inform traditional public schools, Landry, too, suggests philosophy of indigenous education is broadly required: "what is needed is an indigenization of American education for the benefit of all children's education."

So, on the one hand, some of the chapters here present an argument for a philosophy of indigenous education for all students, presenting certain seemingly universal values toward humanness. On the other hand, Reagan's chapter on the Deaf community raises quite a different concern: Inclusion frequently does not represent the least restrictive environment. In other words, while being included in "mainstream" classrooms, deaf students are

*Comparative Reflections on Philosophies of Indigenous Education* 253

subjected to the curriculum, control, and worldview of the hearing world. One of the purposes of claiming indigeneity is to be able not only to maintain one's cultural traditions and worldviews but also to engage in their continuity and evolution. As Reagan notes, "People at deaf schools help pass on deaf folklore and folklife . . . from one generation to the next. Deaf parents of deaf children often send their children to residential schools so that they may participate in the Deaf community and culture." For the same reasons, to what extent must or should indigenous students (as more traditionally identified) also be separated in this way?

Certainly, traditional education should be reformed in light of indigenous ways of knowing. What indigenous communities seek, and thus why definitions become so important, is self-determination to some degree. This must also apply to "their" schools. So while indigenous philosophies can help to reconceptualize "mainstream" education, does that then mean that indigenous students should be limited to that reconceptualization to the extent that the presence of members of the dominant group inevitably affects the breadth and depth of indigenous curricular concerns? Pondering whether or not the deaf community should follow the political route of the indigenous (i.e., by claiming their indigeneity), leads to the question of whether the indigenous should follow the educational lead of the deaf community in terms of the control of their own educational experience. In other words, it is one thing to suggest an indigenous philosophy of education for indigenous students; it is a different calling with different challenges to suggest a philosophy of indigenous education for all students. As Landry points out in example, "critical awareness of such [Mayan and Aztec] highly developed civilizations is not taught in most schools in Meso-America or the United States." But, should a philosophy of indigenous education just be about curricular inclusion of such topics and themes? Does indigenous education not then just become what John Garvey, in reference to multicultural education, referred to as "managed care"?[10]

Apropos to this is the recent case of the Mexican-American Studies program in Tucson, Arizona (U.S.). The Mexican-American studies program decentered the philosophical approach away from the typical Anglocentric U.S. curriculum for a more Mexican-centric approach that drew heavily on the values of Mexican indigenous communities, even as the traditional liberal arts curriculum remained in place. For example, at the beginning of class, students would recite (bilingually) the Mayan poem, In Lak'ech:

> *Tú eres mi otro yo.*
> You are my other me.
> *Si te hago daño a ti,*
> If I do harm to you,
> *Me hago daño a mi mismo.*
> I do harm to myself.
> *Si te amo y respeto,*

254  *John E. Petrovic and Roxanne M. Mitchell*

> If I love and respect you,
> *Me amo y respeto yo.*
> I love and respect myself.

This certainly echoes the Ubuntu ideal of becoming more fully human. And, toward that same end, a number of Anglo students participated in the Mexican American Studies program. This is an important aspect if we take "any form of knowledge [as having] a commitment to critical consciousness forged through people's actions and dialogical relations with other human beings."[11] So, teachers in this program sought to control their curriculum toward indigenous and culturally relevant ends, while simultaneously making it universally available to all students. In this way, "mainstream" students were brought into the indigenous philosophy as opposed to the indigenous philosophy being brought to the mainstream students—such that it would inevitably become marginal to the "real" curriculum or, worse, fetishized as an interesting "Mexican thing" (i.e., becoming a form of managed care). In other words, instead of it just being a subject add-on, indigenous education must rest on a thorough-going, indigenous philosophical foundation. It must be holistic, capturing not only indigenous themes but ways of knowing and learning—issues brought more to the fore in the second half of the volume. Unfortunately, because Mexican-Americans in the U.S. lack legal status as indigenous, the ruling elite passed legislation to shut the program down as "seditious."

As Reagan observes, "Institutions designed to educate d/Deaf children and young adults have largely been founded and managed *by* hearing people *for* the deaf. Important decisions about policy, teaching methods, curricula, and so on have been controlled by hearing people." It is equally the case, then, that institutions designed to educate *indigenous* children and young adults have largely been founded and managed *by* the dominant group *for* the subordinated group. Important decisions about policy, teaching methods, curricula, and even the legality of these things have been controlled by the dominant group.

But, still, what must self-determination vis-à-vis education require? One school of thought, as intimated, is that an indigenous education requires submersion in indigenous ways of knowing, content, language (if still spoken), and experiences. But Davids and Waghid (*this volume*) ask us to step back a bit from such a thorough-going approach. For them, recall, "education ought not to be about that which is traditional, and hence already known and familiar." To the extent that preservation or reclamation of indigenous ways overrides a concern for individuation, indigenous education may be problematic. This sets up a false dichotomy between indigenous and Western forms of knowledge, which are always already in relation. Thus, a philosophy of indigenous education would respect the purposes of both socialization (into the particularities of the indigenous community) and individuation, the ability to reflect on those particularities.

*Comparative Reflections on Philosophies of Indigenous Education* 255

This is an education simultaneously toward group recognition and autonomy. On the one hand, socialization promotes recognition which, we think, should be understood as, say, Charles Taylor conceptualizes it. For Taylor, recognition begins with the presumption that cultures and different ways of knowing have equal worth.[12] Of course, this is more a matter of looking outward at other cultures while practicing epistemic humility. But, we think it is an important extension of recognition to note that, for indigenous communities working toward decolonization, the virtue of recognition must be actively applied to their own cultures while also recognizing other cultures. Again, according to Davids and Waghid, this must include the dominant culture, especially to the extent that it is already part of one's identity as a matter of history. Reflecting on the particularities not only of one's own community but that of others is an aspect of autonomy: the capacity for reasoned deliberation among competing conceptions of the good life (autonomy as described by Amy Gutmann, for example).[13] In some ways, what we are wrestling with here is a form of liberal-communitarianism. On the one hand, individuals become who they are as members of a community. On the other hand, the community cannot be so fixed or authoritarian so as to create an unjust situation. Sexist or racist community standards, for example, should be challenged, especially by members of the community. Toward meeting this dual purpose, Will Kymlicka notes that "national minorities" (synonymous to indigenous communities) must be provided external protections (i.e., some amount of self-determination and protection from the dominant culture) while rejecting internal restrictions (i.e., the ability of members to question the values, standards, practices, etc. of their community).[14]

Davids and Waghid, however, broaden the onto-epistemological subjectivity of indigeneity. It is not just that people become who they are as members of some particular community. It is that people become who they are as members of a particular community that is/has been always already in relation with other communities. For them, then, "indigenous education involves practicing socialization and individuation in relation to traditions, cultural histories, and scientific knowledge of various communities."

## Indigenous Philosophy of Education in Practice

While the first set of papers sought to grapple with the questions of what is a philosophy of indigenous education, who do we define as indigenous, and for whom is an indigenous education intended, the second group of papers deals more directly with what an indigenous philosophy of education might look like in practice. In the various cultural contexts represented in these chapters, are there principles that undergird educational methods and interventions that can be useful in establishing an indigenous philosophy and approach to education? If so what are some key components of such a philosophy and what might this look like? The interventions reported in

256   *John E. Petrovic and Roxanne M. Mitchell*

these papers are specific to the regions and settings in which they occur; however, we believe that underlying each of these methodologies are principles that can be useful in developing an indigenous philosophy of education that is multicultural. With this aim in mind we have identified six underlying themes or principles that seem to cut across these cases, namely; the principles of trust, sovereignty, survivance, community partnership, culturally relevant pedagogy, and cultural sustainability. In addition, this collection of papers also deals with the challenges faced by those who have embarked on efforts to create and design specific indigenous approaches to education, as well as their triumphs. Like these general principles that may be useful in defining an educational approach to indigenous education the challenges are also common to these communities and their efforts to bring about transformation and reform and are worthy of discussion. Yet their stories of triumph and courage in addressing these obstacles and challenges are what gives us hope that indeed it is possible to conquer these odds and bring about genuine transformation.

## Trust and the Importance of Trust Repair

Laying the groundwork for this discussion, in the context of schools in the United States in Washington and Montana, Hopkins (*this volume*) describes a policy environment where indigenous communities are being invited to the table under the guise of what is being described as *inclusive conversations*, for the purpose of shared decision making. His paper points out that it is impossible for genuine conversations to take place without reconciliation and reparation because of a lack of trust between the indigenous communities and mainstream educators, due to the legacy and lasting effects of colonization. Hopkins argues that indigenous communities and mainstream educators are not on equal footing and cannot come to the table until wrongs are admitted to, reparations made, and the right to sovereignty asserted, nor can trust be repaired without addressing these unspoken wrongs.

In fact, interventions by mainstream educators (often unilateral interventions) are most often perceived as suspect and as clandestine efforts to continue to foster the assimilationist and integrationist tactics of the colonizers. A prime example of how this distrust has been perpetuated in other contexts was given by Kidman et al. (*this volume*), regarding how the British settlers wrote up two different contracts supposedly aimed at supporting indigenous education with the Maori people in New Zealand, one in English and one in Maori, each with different terms and agreements. Indeed each paper spoke about disingenuous policies that indicated support for indigenous education but lacked the financial backing and the infrastructure needed to be carried out successfully.

Given the propensity of distrust of mainstream society that exists in all indigenous communities due to the violence and injustice that has been perpetrated against them, not only by past abuse but also by continued forms of oppression, it is impossible to craft meaningful and lasting solutions to the problems facing indigenous communities without addressing the reasons for this distrust. We would agree that in order for mainstream societies and indigenous communities to have genuine conversations that are capable of fostering successful educational interventions for indigenous communities, trust repair is essential. At minimum trust repair must begin with an acknowledgement of wrong doing, a willingness to make amends for the injustices that have occurred, and a commitment to addressing the ongoing political, social, and economic infrastructure that continues to support discrimination and oppression of indigenous peoples.[15] But trust repair is not a one-way street as Hopkins pointed out. While the onus is on the offending party, indigenous communities have to agree to be present at the table in order to assert their sovereign rights, assure that their voice is heard, and foster what Hopkins calls "decolonizing conversations." As he stated "these local alliances are important . . . because they lay the foundation for broader social and political changes." Tschannen-Moran argues that trust is an essential ingredient in the work of schools.[16] Trust is grounded in relationships between administrators, teachers, students, parents, the local community, and the larger geopolitical community. It can be described as both a lubricant and glue, facilitating the work of schools and holding relationships together. In the case where trust has been broken, the first step towards transformation and systematic change must be to make a commitment to repair broken trust and to work to foster trusting relationships moving forward.

## Sovereignty and the Importance of Self-Determination

The issue of sovereignty and the right of indigenous people to be actively involved in determining their course is central to the notion of an indigenous philosophy of education. Hopkins describes sovereignty as "the right of Indigenous peoples to determine and decide for themselves the direction of their own present and future circumstances." As previously noted, for too long colonialist societies have feigned support of indigenous education and inclusive policies but in fact have been guilty of perpetuating assimilationist pedagogies. This fundamental right to sovereignty and self-determination is supported by The United Nations declaration on the rights of indigenous peoples which states "Indigenous peoples have the right to self-determination. By virtue of that right they freely determine their political status and freely pursue their economic, social, and cultural development. "[17] As put forth by Kidman et al. the very survival of indigenous peoples is tied to their ability to act and speak for themselves and to confront their oppressors directly. And, as Gayman (*this volume*) points out, an indigenous philosophy of education "recognizes the Indigenous right to self-determination in all matters pertaining to the development and growth of Indigenous cultures and societies."

# 258 *John E. Petrovic and Roxanne M. Mitchell*

Not only must indigenous communities be granted the sovereignty to determine the aims, creation and perpetuation of educational endeavors, but also they must be trusted that they have the knowledge and skills to do so. As Corn (*this volume*) states in reference to Wanta's *Ngurra-kurlu* approach among the Warlpiri people in Australia,

> we can learn to trust that Indigenous educators know how to select and adapt traditional pedagogies to engage local youths in the processes of their own learning, that these approaches can complement the attempts of schools to equip Indigenous students for work and further study, and that they can also be applied to the broader intercultural contexts to facilitate learning opportunities that can hold intrinsic value and beneficial outcomes for all while simultaneously working to ensure the continuing survival of Indigenous ways of being and knowing.

Furthermore, acknowledging the sovereignty of Indigenous peoples means also accepting their right to confront the aggression and oppression that has decimated and continues to impact their communities without judging them as dissidents.

## Survivance: Resistance & Determination to Survive

Closely akin to the notion of sovereignty is the concept of survivance. This term first popularized by Gerald Vizenor and, applied to study of Native Americans, denotes both overt struggle and resistance against the oppressive forces of colonization and unified efforts to survive.[18] Hopkins put it this way "survivance means the continual realization by Indigenous peoples to assert their sovereign right to remain Indigenous, as the original inhabitants of this land and of these places." This bears a striking resemblance to the catch-cry generated at the Battle at Oraku, described by Kidman et al. where Maori tribesmen who were being decimated by the British army refused to surrender even though they knew that death and defeat was certain. Their response given to the British army in the final hours of the battle, "Ka whwhai tonu matou. Ake! Ake! Ake! (We shall fight on forever and ever)", has become a mantra of hope for the Maori people down through the ages. We concur that efforts to implement an indigenous philosophy of education require Indigenous communities and proponents of the rights of Indigenous peoples to actively oppose and resist continued structural efforts to impose oppressive colonialist agendas in policies and practices that would perpetuate the use of schools as agents of colonization, oppression, and assimilation. It is this resistance itself that gives hope and as Kidman et al. put it "indigenous hope is often forged in times of struggle." Such struggles, as Hüttner and Guilherme assert, have given indigenous communities tools to protect their traditions and knowledge, tools we suggest that include active resistance and the determination to survive.

## Comparative Reflections on Philosophies of Indigenous Education 259

## Community Partnership: Moving Beyond the Borders of the School

Jeff Gayman describes an Indigenous educational reform among the Ainu people of Northern Japan that is centered within the community and bolstered by the inclusion of their core values and beliefs. In this paper he situates this educational intervention largely outside of the traditional classroom. We found this to be a consistent theme in these papers and we would argue for a broader conceptualization of education that goes beyond the limits and compartmentalization of the classroom and the school building and that incorporates the knowledge, experiences, and practices that occur in the natural setting, incorporating the ways in which children in these communities have been traditionally taught such as around the hearth, at the feet of the elders, and in the city square. This idea was reiterated by Ylva Nutti (*this volume*) and her example of the Sami people of Northern Scandinavia. Hüttner and Guilherme (*this volume*) described this as "untamed education," vis-a-vis the Kokama people of Brazil, an education that happens within and without the boundaries of the school. They stated, "students learn through their imperfections to seek a balanced connection to their parents, their families, the village and the whole, and this means that everything is more malleable and fluid." This goes far beyond traditional perceptions of parent involvement to include the importance of the entire community in the education of the children. Given this conceptualization, even the school calendar is subject to the needs of the community. As Hüttner and Guilherme suggested, the calendar could be modified to allow children to help with the agrarian needs of the community and in hunting, farming, and fishing communities if the school was short on food the students and teachers could go fishing and harvesting. While these suggestions are context specific, the ideas behind them are not. This is a much more fluid conceptualization of schooling that allows for greater integration between the school and the community and fully embraces the lifestyle, beliefs, and values of the community.

## Culturally Relevant Pedagogy: Bringing the Community Within

Re-envisioning where schooling takes place and incorporating the community into the educational process goes hand in hand with notions of culturally relevant pedagogy. Culturally relevant pedagogy is a theoretical perspective that "not only addresses student achievement but also helps students to accept and affirm their cultural identity while developing critical perspectives that challenge inequities that schools perpetuate."[19] Within this approach is the objective to teach (1) respect of cultural values and (2) to assist students in critiquing oppressive structures. This aligns well with the principle of survivance in that not only are indigenous community members

260　*John E. Petrovic and Roxanne M. Mitchell*

charged with actively opposing and resisting oppressive structures but students are also empowered to become agents of change. Ladson Billings argues that the way teachers teach has a profound impact on how students learn. Culturally relevant pedagogy draws on students' cultural experiences and their cultural capital as a way to foster academic success. We see this in Corn's example of how Wanta's philosophy of indigenous education served to empower both pre-service teachers via seminars and field experiences and empowered students via their exposure to their culture, traditions, and rituals, by their participation in the Milpirri Festival.

In addition, this approach is well suited for indigenous communities because it is in direct opposition to deficit views of these communities that see indigenous children as incapable and their communities as undesirable. Culturally relevant pedagogy fosters high expectations for students. According to Tyrone Howard, it can help teachers identify pedagogical strategies that take into account students' cultural and social realities and help them make use of cultural characteristics as assets in their learning.[20] Moreover, it requires teachers to critically reflect on their own cultural biases and behaviors. Howard points out that critical reflection can help teachers build a culturally relevant pedagogy that:

(1) Will help teachers address the complexity of race, ethnicity and culture
(2) Will lead to a recognition that reflection is a lifelong process
(3) Will promote a realization that teaching is not a neutral act, it is highly politicized
(4) Will help teachers recognize and avoid deficit views and reductive notions of the children they teach.
(5) Will help teachers become more explicit about what they reflect on

Culturally relevant teachers hold students to high standards, believe that their students can achieve, and press to assist struggling students overcome obstacles. Ware views the inclusion of the students' culture into the classroom as an essential component to their academic success.[21] Gayman illustrated the importance of relationships between children and elders in the indigenous communities and between teachers and students in the school among the Ainu children. This type of close and caring relationship between teachers and students based on culturally relevant pedagogy may be just what is needed to stem the tide of indigenous students dropping out of school.

## Cultural Sustainability: Embracing Language, Ceremony, Tradition, and Ritual

Cultural sustainability has to do with the survival of indigenous people, their languages, ceremonies, traditions and rituals despite the decimation that they experienced at the hands of colonialists. In many cases indigenous people were

*Comparative Reflections on Philosophies of Indigenous Education* 261

massacred by white settlers, relocated, or forced into hiding. They were prevented from publically using their languages or engaging in their ceremonies, rituals, and traditions. This has resulted in language loss and a generation of students who are less familiar with their heritage. Furthermore, integrationist legislation aimed at assimilating indigenous populations into mainstream culture reinforced this loss of cultural heritage. Policies that refused to allow bilingual education further contributed to the language loss and dying out of many indigenous languages. Many of the chapters in the second section of this volume alluded to problems associated with cultural sustainability. The Ainu Puri of Northern Japan, the Sami people of Northern Scandinavia, the Maori people of New Zealand, the Warlpiri people of Australia, and the Kokama people of Brazil are all examples of this.

In each chapter, the authors carved out examples of courageous interventions that were aimed at restoring cultural pride and familiarizing young children with their heritage via the use of storytelling, music, dancing, ceremonies, and rituals. Kidman et al. referred to these attempts to keep the language and traditions alive by immersing young children in their Maori cultural heritage as "oppositional utopianism." They described this as a blending of indigenous political efforts with grassroots pedagogical practices aimed at preserving their cultural identity. Corn asserted that by exposing children to Warlpiri knowledge, it helped them to identify their place in the world. He argued that Wanta's Milpirri Festival "encouraged them to actively hunt for knowledge on their own initiative, and admitted them to greater levels of knowing and responsibility in reward for educational aptitude and attainment." Gayman emphasized the importance of oratory and storytelling among the Ainu Puri and cited one elder as stating "that which is written down is forgotten." Hüttner and Guilherme referred to this as "untamed education." We concur with these authors regarding the centrality and importance of traditional values, rituals, ceremonies, and language to an indigenous philosophy of education and to the sustainability of indigenous cultures. Irrespective of the context, incorporating the values and traditions of the indigenous community into the educational arena serves to reinforce identity, clarify motivation, fortify resolve to learn, and ensure the survival of Indigenous ways of being and knowing. This is not only useful for indigenous students but, connecting back to the overlap between philosophy of indigenous education and indigenous philosophy of education, as Corn suggested indigenous knowledge "holds intrinsic value for everyone, irrespective of heritage."

## Challenges and Triumphs: Overcoming the Odds

Understanding the challenges associated with implementing an indigenous philosophy of education is a discussion that is necessary if systems are to be put in place that will be effective and sustainable. But the challenges, as we saw from the issues raised in the first section of this volume, are even prior to implementation. Before we can consider what such philosophies look like in practice, we must consider to whom they should apply and why. This is the meta-philosophizing required by the philosophy of indigenous education. In the first section of this final chapter, we pointed out the many philosophical challenges in this regard. One repeated theme, for example, was that all students need an indigenous education, as a way to challenge their conceptions of the world, as a way to gain the capacity for rational deliberation among competing conceptions. Indeed, this was the defining characteristic of indigenous education for Davids and Waghid, especially for indigenous students who must engage with both their worlds in interrelationship. However, Hopkins reminds us that indigenous students may internalize the racist conceptions of themselves reflected back at them by the dominant group. This is the effect, in Charles Taylor's terms, of *mis*recognition. Mustn't indigenous students, then, be provided an indigenous philosophical space of their own to occupy in and out of schools and mightn't individuation, to the extent that it requires questioning those vary values which have been under constant scrutiny historically, undermine that? That said, isn't autonomy important and aren't indigenous students who they are because of the interrelationship with dominant ways of knowing? In the end, these should not be either/or propositions and therefore require careful reflection to inform implementation.

The challenges of implementation faced in each of the settings highlighted in the second section of this volume are also considerable. They begin with fundamental problems associated with the failure of mainstream society to admit to the colonial past and the sanitizing of violence and devastation that occurred and continues to occur due to structural and institutional barriers that prevent indigenous communities from realizing their hopes and dreams or, as Hopkins put it, "to assert their status as sovereign nations in an effort to revitalize their cultures and languages within both public and tribal schools." Kidman et al. refer to this refusal to remember the violent past as *historical amnesia* which also leads to unwillingness to admit how the curriculum and pedagogy in indigenous schools have been influenced by racist and oppressive educational policies. Additionally, because of this historical amnesia, schools are often viewed as agents of assimilationist and integrationist policies. Policies that prevent children from learning about their culture and systematically marginalize the opportunities for bilingual education are still prevalent in many areas.

Even in situations where legislation seems to favor an indigenous philosophy of education, there are often problems with funding and infrastructure to support these schools. In the case of the Sami educational system, Nutti tells us that teachers were ill-prepared to offer culturally relevant pedagogy and teachers were not able to speak the native languages of the students. In fact teachers questioned the viability of using culturally based pedagogies. In the case of the Kokama people in Brazil, Hüttner and Guilherme inform us that there are 178 different languages, further complicating efforts to

## Comparative Reflections on Philosophies of Indigenous Education 263

have teachers who are prepared to teach in the national and native language of the students, and that 65% of teachers have only a secondary education, and 12% have only an elementary education. Add to this the problems of lack of adequate school facilities, lack of infrastructure to support internet use, lack of textbooks (and in some cases no textbooks in the students' native language), and lack of resources to support professional development for teachers and we can see that the challenges facing these schools are substantial.

Amidst all of these challenges these authors leave us with a ray of hope. Kidman et al. speak to the determination of the Maori people of New Zealand, in light of their ancestral history in the Battle at Orakau, to fight on forever and ever until social change and transformation is realized. Or the case of Wanta in Australia's Warlpiri community who has developed his own transformational model of indigenous education, and is working both to immerse pre-service teachers in experiences that will prepare them to become culturally relevant educators as well as helping children to understand their own intellectual and cultural traditions as a strategy for cultural survival, by participation in the Milpirri Festival. To tackle the problems of lack of textbooks and curriculum, Hüttner and Guilherme report that teachers and students have taken on the task to develop original textbooks and other educational materials in the Alto Rio Negro area of the Amazon region. These interventions though bounded by specific contexts offer hope, triumph over adversity, and examples of indigenous people at the forefront of paving a way towards indigenous philosophies of education.

## Notes

1. In this concluding chapter, to remind the reader, we parenthetically identify authors of chapters in this volume at their first mention, but not subsequently. External references will be cited per usual.
2. Erika Sarivaara, Kaarina Maatta, and Satu Uusiautti, "Who Is Indigenous? Definitions of Indigeneity," *European Scientific Journal, Special Edition* 1 (2013): 369.
3. Ibid.
4. Jeff J. Corntassel, "Who Is Indigenous? Peoplehood and Ethnonationalist Approaches to Rearticulating Indigenous Identity," *Nationalism and Ethnic Politics* 9 (2003): 75–100.
5. Ibid. On the latter point, Corntassel relates the case of Dutch descendants seeking indigenous status in South Africa.
6. This latter criterion is included, for example, among four essential requirements of indigeneity by Benedict Kingsbury. See Benedict Kingsbury, "Indigenous Peoples in International Law: A Constructivist Approach to the Asian Controversy," *American Journal of International Law* 92 (1998): 414–457.
7. This criterion is included in the World Bank's definition of indigenous (See, Corntassel, op cit, Who is indigenous).
8. John E. Petrovic, *A Post-Liberal Approach to Language Policy in Education* (Bristol, UK: Multilingual Matters, 2015).

9. See for example, Patricia H. Collins, *Black Feminist thought* (New York: Routledge, 2000). In their chapter in this volume, Davids and Waghid refer in the same vein to "colonized knowledge."
10. John Garvey, "My Problem with Multicultural Education," In *Race Traitors*, ed. Noel Ignatiev and John Garvey (New York: Routledge, 1996). For Garvey, multiculturalism as managed care is a way to placate the minority while simultaneously setting a boundary of how far and deep multiculturalism might go such that it functions to maintain the status quo (i.e., placate the dominant group).
11. Davids and Waghid, this volume.
12. Charles Taylor, *Multiculturalism and the Politics of Recognition* (Princeton: Princeton University Press, 1992).
13. Amy Gutmann, *Democratic Education* (Princeton: Princeton University Press, 1987).
14. Will Kymlicka, *Multicultural Citizenship* (Oxford: Oxford University Press, 1995).
15. Roy J. Lewicki, Daniel J. McAllister, and Robert J. Bies, "Trust and Distrust: New Relationships and Realities," *Academy of Management Review* 23 (1998): 438–458.
16. Megan Tschannen-Moran, *Trust Matters: Leadership for Successful Schools* (San Francisco: Josey-Bass, 2014).
17. The United Nations Declaration on the Rights of Indigenous People, www.un.org/esa/socdev/unpfii/documents/DRIPS_en.pdf.
18. Gerald Vizenor, *Manifest Manners: Narratives on Postindian Survivance* (University of Nebraska Press, Lincoln, 2009).
19. Gloria Ladson Billings, "But That's Just Good Teaching! The Case for Culturally Relevant Pedagogy," *Theory into Practice* 34 (1995): 159–165.
20. Tyrone Howard, "Culturally Relevant Pedagogy: Ingredients for Critical Teacher Reflection," *Theory into Practice* 42 (2003): 195–202.
21. Franita Ware, "Warm Demander Pedagogy: Culturally Responsive Teaching That Supports a Culture of Achievement for African American Students," *Urban Education* 41 (2006): 427–456.

# Contributors

**Xuejun Chen** is a Professor and an Associate Dean of the College of Education Science at Nanjing Normal University (NNU) in China. He is also an associate of the Taos Institute, a member of the National Expert Committee for Case-Based Instruction in Academic Degree Programs in higher learning, and the secretary of the Jiangsu Professional Committee for Educational Administration in China. He is passionate and devoted to research and teaching about principalship. His areas of interest include school improvement, leadership succession, leader development, and the roles of educational leaders in changing environments. His work can be found in refereed journals, books, and book chapters. Some of these have been reprinted by the top journals in Chinese social science. His dissertation won the Excellent Doctoral Dissertation Award granted by the Degree Center of Jiangsu Province in China in 2009. He was selected as an excellent backbone young scholar by NNU in 2013.

**Aaron Corn** is an ethnomusicologist with a background in music, curatorial studies, and Indigenous studies. He is Director of both the Centre for Aboriginal Studies in Music (CASM) and the National Centre for Aboriginal Language and Music Studies (NCALMS) at the University of Adelaide. He collaborates closely in research of mutual interest with Australian Indigenous colleagues, and serves as Co-Director of the National Recording Project for Indigenous Performance in Australia (NRPIPA). His work with Indigenous musicians, festivals, and collections engages with intellectual traditions that remain fundamental to Indigenous cultural survival in Australia and inform contemporary Australian Indigenous engagements across cultures. He has produced numerous tours and concerts of Australian Indigenous performance traditions for major venues and festivals in Australia and internationally, and his work with Australian Indigenous colleagues and stakeholder communities to identify and access their collected cultural heritage has contributed to engendering new approaches to curatorial policies and practices among memory institutions around the world. He is the immediate Past National President of the Musicological Society of Australia and has served on the Australian Research Council (ARC) College of Experts.

## 266 *Contributors*

**Nuraan Davids** is an Associate Professor of Philosophy of Education. Her research interests include democratic citizenship education, Islamic education, and leadership and management inquiry. She is an Associate Editor of the *South African Journal of Higher Education*, and an Editorial Board Member of *Ethics and Education*. Her list of international books includes *Women, cosmopolitanism, and Islamic education: On the virtues of education and belonging* (2013, New York & London: Peter Lang Publishing); *Citizenship education and violence in schools: On disrupted potentialities and becoming* (with Y. Waghid, 2013, Rotterdam/Boston/Taipei: Sense Publishers); *Ethical dimensions of Muslim education* (with Y. Waghid, 2016, New York & London: Palgrave MacMilllan); *Educational leadership-in-becoming: On the potential of leadership in action* (with Y. Waghid, 2106, New York & London: Routledge); *Philosophy and education as action: Implications for Teacher Education* (with Y. Waghid, 2017, Lanham, MD (US): Rowan & Littlefield – Lexington Series); *Tolerance and Dissent within Education: On Cultivating Debate and Understanding* (with Y. Waghid, 2017, New York & London: Palgrave MacMillan).

**Jeff Gayman** is an Associate Professor in the Multicultural Education Studies Division, Hokkaido University Research Faculty of International Media and Communication (RFIMC)/Graduate School of Education. He is of German, Irish and English ancestry. He did his Master's work in the MA Program in Cross-Cultural Studies at the University of Alaska, Fairbanks, and completed a PhD in Educational Anthropology from Kyushu University. Originally from the state of Alaska, Jeff has been living, teaching and researching in Japan for more than 25 years, 13 of those working with Japan's Indigenous people, the Ainu, and two spent living in the Ainu village of Nibutani in Southern Hokkaido. Since being hired at Hokkaido University, he has been engaged in efforts to establish a collaborative research/educational platform between the RFIMC/School of Education and local Ainu communities. He has also been involved in information dissemination activities about the housing and repatriation on the Hokkaido University campus of Ainu ancestral remains. His research interests are Indigenous self-determination and voice in education, and intercultural education for improvement of understanding of/support for Indigenous peoples.

**Alexandre Guilherme** is an Adjunct Professor in the School of Humanities, Department of Education, Pontificia Universidade Catolica do Rio Grande do Sul, PUCRS, Brazil. He is the Coordinator of the Research Group on Education and Violence, conducting research into education as a form of violence and normalization of the individual, as well as into the types of violence that are present in education. He has published extensively on the topic of dialogical education as a tool for reconciliation between communities in conflict. He has also published material in the fields of philosophy and theology in connection to Spinoza, Fichte, and Schelling, and has translated a number of works by Leonardo Boff. He is the author of *Buber and Education: Dialogue as Conflict Resolution* and of *Philosophy, Dialogue and Education: Nine Modern European Philosophers*. He is currently preparing a monograph on the work of Ilan Gur-Ze'ev, the important Israeli philosopher of education and a major figure in critical pedagogy.

**John P. Hopkins** (Dakota/Lakota) holds a PhD in the Social and Cultural Foundations of Education from the University of Washington and an M.A in Philosophy from Marquette University. His academic interests include the philosophy of education, philosophical hermeneutics, multicultural education and theory, and Indigenous philosophy and education. Dr. Hopkins' research examines current efforts to reform Indigenous education in the Unites States. Specifically, he considers how decolonization strategies can inform these reform efforts in ways that promote curricular and instructional strategies to better recognize tribal sovereignty and support Native students in mainstream classrooms. Dr. Hopkins serves as the Associate Dean of Students and Director of Service & Diversity at Saint Martin's University in Lacey, Washington, and teaches courses in Communication Studies, Sociology, and Social Justice Education. He is also a member of the Crow Creek Sioux Tribe in South Dakota.

**Edison Hüttner** is an Adjunct Professor in the School of Humanities, Departments of Education and Theology, Pontificia Universidade Catolica do Rio Grande do Sul, PUCRS, Brazil, where he is the Director of the Research Centre in Afro-Brazilian and Indigenous Culture. In 2005 he organised the 1st International Indigenous Peoples Forum in Porto Alegre, Brazil. In 2001, he worked with the Kocama Indians and helped them build their Cultural Center in the Amazon, which became a focus for the community. He took part in a number of multidisciplinary actions focusing on indigenous groups in the Amazon region of Brazil; these actions focused largely, on healthcare involving various groups in Ji-Paraná and Upper Xingu, such as the Arara and the Gaviões. This work was recognized as important by the World Health Organization. He organized and published, in partnership with the Darcy Riberio Foundation, *Séculos Indígenas no Brasil: Catálogos de Imagens*, as well as various dictionaries on the Guarani-Portuguese languages.

**Ylva Jannok Nutti** is an Associate Professor at Sámi Allaskuvla/Sámi University of Applied Sciences in Guovdageaidnu/ Kautokeino, Norway. Dr. Jannok Nutti has been conducting several action research and school development projects with focus on transforming education on the basis of Sámi traditional knowledge and cultural-based learning perspectives.

268  *Contributors*

Her dissertation focused on how to transform mathematics teaching for Sámi children and pupils on the basis of Sámi traditional knowledge. Traditional knowledge and the outdoor environment remain the common factors in her continued research. Indigenous peoples have strong ties to the land and places. Recently she completed the action research project "Engaging the voices of Sámi children: Sustaining traditional knowledge through kindergarten, school and community knowledge transfer." She has published a number of journal articles and chapters in edited volumes. Her most recent book chapter, "Along Paths of Movements: Sámi children and Early Childhood Student Teachers Wayfarers," appeared in *The SAGE Handbook of Outdoor Play and Learning* (2017).

**Joanna Kidman** is Māori and has tribal affiliations with Ngāti Maniapoto and Ngāti Raukawa. She works in the field of indigenous youth sociology at Victoria University of Wellington in New Zealand where she is the Director of Te Kura Māori in the Faculty of Education. Her research centres on the politics of indigeneity, Māori youth, and settler-colonial nationhood. Over the past twenty-five years, Joanna has worked with Māori research partners and community-based tribal groups in different parts of New Zealand. She has also partnered with indigenous communities in Taiwan and the USA to establish indigenous knowledge systems in schools with large numbers of native students.

**Paul L. Landry** is an Assistant Professor of Education in the College of Education at Heritage University in Central Washington [USA], which primarily serves first generation Latinx and Native American students. He completed his PhD at The University of Alabama in Instructional Leadership, Social and Cultural Foundations, and his Master's degree in Curriculum and Instruction. A McNair Scholar, he also received the Whisenton award for highest achievement as African American Doctoral Candidate from The University of Alabama. Paul also earned a prior JD degree from Boston University, and has experience representing public school districts and teaching education laws and regulation. His research interests involve social justice in education policy and improving culturally responsive pedagogy through teacher education. His focus is on critical pedagogy in local multicultural classrooms and more broadly on critical engagement with intersections of education philosophy, policy and practices in an intercultural and global society. He is an Associate Editor for a peer-reviewed intercultural education journal, and has presented research papers and keynote addresses at professional conferences in the US, Europe, Mexico, and South America regarding the implications of education policies on ethnic and linguistic minority children in public schools.

## Contributors 269

**Lesley Le Grange** is Distinguished Professor in the Faculty of Education at Stellenbosch University, South Africa. He teaches and researches in the fields of environmental education, research methodology, science education, curriculum studies, higher education studies and assessment. He has 200 publications to his credit and serves on editorial boards of eight peer-reviewed journals. He has delivered more than 150 academic presentations (many as invited speaker) and is a recipient of several academic awards and prizes. He is a member of the Accreditation Committee of the Council on Higher Education in South Africa and Vice-President of the International Association of the Advancement of Curriculum Studies (IAACS). Lesley is a Fellow of the Royal Society of Biology (UK) and a rated social scientist in South Africa. His current research interests are: critically 'analyzing' sustainability and its relationship to education; developing *Ubuntu* as an environmental ethic and exploring its implications for education; exploring conceptual connections between *Ubuntu* and (post)human discourses; and exploring ways in which Indigenous and Western knowledge could be performed together.

**Liana MacDonald** is of Ngāti Kuia, Rangitāne and Ngāti Koata descent. She has ten years' experience working as a secondary school English teacher across a range of educational contexts in New Zealand. She is now in the final stages of her PhD, in which she investigates institutional silencing and racism through the lived experiences of Māori secondary school English teachers. Liana's research interests include indigenous studies and studies of whiteness and racism. She is also currently working on a research project investigating Maori youth and their hopes and fears about the future.

**Adreanne Ormond** is Māori and has tribal affiliations with Rongomāwahine, Ngāti Kahungunu and Ngāti Tūwharetoa. She has grown up on her ancestral land in the community of Te Māhia Peninsula, and this provides the background for her interest in social injustice and indigenous Māori youth-centred research. She is currently working at Victoria University of Wellington in New Zealand where she is a Senior Lecturer in the Faculty of Education. Adreanne is committed to supporting transformation within the indigenous Māori community and, along with her academic research, is involved in developing outreach programs that support her tribal communities and the development of her students.

**Steven Wantarri Jampijinpa Patrick Pawu-Kurlpurlurnu**, also known as Wanta, is a Warlpiri law-holder, artist and scholar from Lajamanu in the remote Tanami Desert in Australia's Northern Territory. He is an experienced educator, and his long-term collaboration with Tracks Dance Company, most recently as Creative Director of the Milpirri Festival at

Lajamanu, has reinvigorated the teaching of Warlpiri law and ceremonial traditions amid contemporary intercultural contexts. He has worked as an Assistant Teacher at Lajamanu School and served on the Lajamanu School Council and, in 2007, received an Innovative Curriculum Award from the Australian Curriculum Studies Association for his innovative educational approaches. Wanta worked as a Research Associate on the Australian Research Council (ARC) Linkage Project, "Warlpiri Songlines", led by anthropologist Nicolas in 2005–07, and later became the first Warlpiri investigator to lead an ARC project of any kind through his 2012–14 Discovery Indigenous project on "Early Collections of Warlpiri Cultural Heritage". While working on this latter project as the recipient of an ARC Discovery Indigenous Award at the Australian National University in Canberra, he collaborated in research and curriculum development with ethnomusicologist Aaron Corn.

**Timothy Reagan,** the Dean of the College of Education and Human Development at the University of Maine, has held senior faculty and administrative positions at a number of universities, including the University of Connecticut, the University of the Witwatersrand, Central Connecticut State University, Roger Williams University, Gallaudet University, and Nazarbayev University in Astana, Kazakhstan. His primary areas of research are applied and educational linguistics, education policy, and comparative education. Professor Reagan is the author of a dozen books and more than 150 journal articles and book chapters, and his work has appeared in such international journals as *Arts and Humanities in Higher Education, Critical Inquiry in Language Studies, Educational Foundations, Educational Policy, Educational Theory, Foreign Language Annals, Harvard Educational Review, International Journal of Intercultural Relations, Language Policy, Language Problems and Language Planning, Multicultural Education, Sign Language Studies,* and *Semiotica.* He is currently the Editor-in-Chief of *Language Problems and Language Planning.*

**Jing Ping Sun** is an Assistant Professor in the Department of Educational Leadership, Policy and Technology Studies at the College of Education, University of Alabama. She obtained her PhD at the Ontario Institute for Studies in Education, University of Toronto. Her research is about leadership models, leadership for student learning, policy evaluation and improvement, and research synthesis. Prior to joining the faculty at the University of Alabama, she worked at the Ontario Ministry of Education in Canada. Her experience at the provincial level was mainly with large-scale development of school and district leaders and policy evaluation. Her work can be found in well-known refereed journals, including *Educational Administration Quarterly,* book chapters, and a more recent book on how school leadership influences student learning through the Four

Paths, coedited with Dr. Leithwood and Dr. Katina Pollock. Dr. Sun has won awards for her research and promotes dialogue on leadership studies between countries.

**Yusef Waghid** is Distinguished Professor of Philosophy of Education and has produced seminal works in the areas of democratic citizenship education, African philosophy of education, and educational ethics.

**Xinping Zhang** is a Professor in Educational Administration at Nanjing Normal University (NNU). He is also the Director of the Institute for Educational Leadership and Management at NNU, the Vice-Chair of the China National Association for Educational Administration and the National Association of Education Effectiveness, an associate of the Taos Institute (U.S.) and the President of Taos China, and the Chief Expert overseeing Chinese National 985, large-scale research projects in educational administration. His research is mainly about educational leadership and administration. He is on the editorial boards of several major journals, including the *Journal of Primary and Secondary Schools Administration*, the *Journal of Primary and Secondary Management*, and *Teaching and Management*. He has published 160 articles in refereed journals, dozens of chapters, and 15 books, including the influential *On the Paradigms in Educational Organization and Administration*. He has obtained and directed several national grant studies, including ones on school standards and excellence.

# Index

Ainu: epistemology 219; oral literature 211; oral tradition 220; people 10, 211; philosophy 214, 225; society 211–215, 218
analytic philosophy 2
Anglocentrism 9, 185
anthropocene 7, 41, 43
Aristotle 2

Braidotti, R. 41–42, 48–49, 52
Brazilian Indian Foundation 9

Cesaire, A. 49
civilisatory paradigm of education 9
colonialism/coloniality 134–136
Confucianism 111–112, 118
crisis of humanism 7
culturally based pedagogies 262
Cultural Promotion 214
cultural sovereignty 27
cultural sustainability 260

deaf epistemology 86, 91
decolonization 249
decolonizing conversation 9, 130–131, 136, 142, 144
Deleuze, G. 45
Deloria, V. 23, 25, 28
Descartes, R. 42
Dewey, J. 30, 197–198, 206

enlightenment humanism 7
epistemology 2, 4, 86, 91, 228
ethnoepistemology 85
Eurocentrism 184

Fanon, F. 49
Foucault, M. 44, 49
Freire, P. 3

Guanxi 113–115

Humanism 42–44, 48, 52, 54
Hunhu 4

inclusion 130, 132
inclusive conversation 8, 143, 256
inclusive education 87
indigeneity 2, 5, 7, 8, 17–19, 22, 27–29, 61, 63, 73, 75–76, 249–251, 253, 255
indigenization 31
indigenous 2, 4, 8, 10, 18, 21, 40–41, 61, 63, 65, 84–85, 106–107, 129, 131–133, 139–140, 145, 149–150, 170–172, 195, 211, 224, 228, 233, 249, 253–254, 258, 260–261; communities 256; education 1, 5–6, 8, 106, 129, 144, 149, 160, 162, 228, 237–238, 249, 252, 255, 262; education philosophies 185, 212; educational reform 259; epistemologies 168; hope 237; philosophy 221, 224, 253; philosophy of education 4, 252–253; praxis 238; sovereignty 27; worldview 185

Kant, E. 43
Khoisan people 2
Kokama people 9, 154–156, 158–160

Locke, J. 3

Maori: communities 235; ethos of land and place 10; language 232, 238; people 10, 228, 230–231, 236–237, 258
metaphilosophy 3

## Index    273

Navajo people 6
*Nicomachean Ethics* 2

onto-epistemologies 252
ontology 1, 228

panhumanity 48, 51
philosophical traditions: analytical 1–2; metaphysical 1; normative 1–3
philosophy and education 1
philosophy of education 1, 3
philosophy of indigenous education 3, 4, 185
Plato's *Republic* 3

Sami: education 10; educational system 262; people 9–10, 195, 200–204
Settler Contract 234–235
survivance 138

transformational leadership 8

Ubuntu 4, 7, 40–41, 45–46, 50–53, 252, 254
Ukama 46–47
United Nations (UNESCO) 4
untamed education 9

Warlpiri: community 263; epistemology 185; people 9, 168–176, 179, 181, 183–184

xenophobia 48, 54
Xhosa people 67–69

Yakama Nation 7, 25–28, 30

Zulu people 69